WOMEN AND SLAVERY

VOLUME TWO

The Modern Atlantic

D1519738

WOMEN AND SLAVERY

VOLUME ONE

Africa, the Indian Ocean World,
and the Medieval North Atlantic

VOLUME TWO

The Modern Atlantic

*Edited by Gwyn Campbell,
Suzanne Miers, and Joseph C. Miller*

The editors wish to acknowledge the support of the Institute for American Universities, Avignon, and the Office de Tourisme, Courthézon, in organizing the conference "Women and Slavery" at which most of the papers appearing in these volumes were first presented; the discussants and participants at that conference; and especially Marianne Ackerman for creating an atmosphere that nurtured discussion and cemented friendships.

WOMEN AND SLAVERY

VOLUME TWO

The Modern Atlantic

Edited by

Gwyn Campbell

Suzanne Miers

Joseph C. Miller

OHIO UNIVERSITY PRESS

ATHENS

Ohio University Press, Athens, Ohio 45701
www.ohio.edu/oupress
© 2008 by Ohio University Press

16 15 14 13 12 11 10 09 08   5 4 3 2 1

Published separately: *Women and Slavery*, vol. 1, Africa, the Indian Ocean World, and the Medieval North Atlantic

Earlier versions of six chapters in this volume—those on the Caribbean by Henrice Altink, Laurence Brown and Tara Inniss, Myriam Cottias, and Bernard Moitt, as well as those by Laura F. Edwards and Richard Follett on the United States—appeared in the special issue of *Slavery & Abolition* on "Women in Western Systems of Slavery" (volume 26, no. 2, 2005). The introduction published here was revised from the introduction by Gwyn Campbell, Suzanne Miers, and Joseph C. Miller to the papers presented in that journal. The editors and Ohio University Press gratefully acknowledge the courtesy of Gad Heuman, editor, and Taylor and Francis, publishers of *Slavery & Abolition*.

Library of Congress Cataloging-in-Publication Data

Women and slavery / edited by Gwyn Campbell, Suzanne Miers, Joseph C. Miller.
  p. cm.
Includes index.
ISBN-13: 978-0-8214-1725-6 (hc : v. 2 : alk. paper)
ISBN-10: 0-8214-1725-8 (hc : v. 2 : alk. paper)
ISBN-13: 978-0-8214-1726-3 (pbk. : v. 2 : alk. paper)
ISBN-10: 0-8214-1726-6 (pbk. : v. 2 : alk. paper)
[etc.]
  1. Women slaves—History. 2. Slavery—History. I. Campbell, Gwyn, 1952– II. Miers, Suzanne. III. Miller, Joseph Calder.
HT861.W66 2007
306.3'6208209—dc22

2007018274

CONTENTS

A TRIBUTE TO SUZANNE MIERS

Martin A. Klein and Richard Roberts

It says a great deal about Suzanne Miers that she edited many of the chapters in this book, all of which originated as papers presented at a conference organized to honor her. This book was to be a Festschrift—but Suzanne seems to gain full satisfaction from working closely with contributors in refining their ideas and professes no desire to rest on her laurels and collect honors. At the conference that led to this book, whose subject she had suggested, she seemed almost embarrassed by the praise she received, presumably seeing herself as a modest trooper in the academic trenches.

Suzanne Miers is an American who has spent most of her life else-where. She was born in 1922 in Luebo, in the Democratic Republic of the Congo, where her father was a mining engineer. She spent most of her childhood in Belgium and England. She received a BA from the University of London in 1944 and an MA in 1949. She taught briefly at Bedford College for Women but, like many academic women of her generation, put any professional aspirations on hold to marry and have two children. When she followed her husband, Brigadier R. C. H. Miers, to Singapore, she taught for three years at the Singapore branch of the University of Malaya (1955–58). She returned to the academic world after the untimely death of her husband in 1962. In 1969 she received a PhD from the University of London. That dissertation, published in 1975 as *Britain and the Ending of the Slave Trade*,[1] opened up the subject of slavery and the slave trade as a theme in international relations and contributed to the upsurge of interest in African and comparative slavery. She has contributed significantly to that body of literature ever since, writing both about slavery in distant places and about the way governments have struggled with the often embarrassing question of human servitude. Only in the years when she was completing her dissertation did Sue return full-time to the United States, teaching several years at the University of Wisconsin and then spending sixteen years at Ohio University before retiring in 1992.

Important as Sue's scholarship has been, her most important contribution to the field of African history has been as a coeditor of four volumes on slavery, in two of which we collaborated with her. The most seminal was the first, *Slavery in Africa: Historical and Anthropological Perspectives* (1977), which she edited with Igor Kopytoff. Along with Claude Meillassoux's *L'esclavage en Afrique précoloniale* (1975), it launched what has since been one of the most important themes in historical research on Africa. Particularly important was the provocative eighty-page introduction, which advanced a powerful argument about the dynamics of incorporating slaves into African lineage systems. Not all specialists accepted Miers and Kopytoff's emphasis on integration, but whatever one's position on that point, it stimulated debate not only in African history studies, but more generally in slave studies, and made the understanding of slavery a central question for historians of Africa.

Her second collaboration was with Richard Roberts on *The End of Slavery in Africa* (1988). Central to this volume was the debate about whether the end of slavery in Africa was a smooth, virtually frictionless process or whether it ushered in a set of profound social, cultural, and economic changes. Sue was particularly interested, however, in the condition of women and child slaves. The model of African slavery as a mechanism of incorporating outsiders was primarily drawn from virilocal, patrilineal marriage patterns, where wives were married into their husband's lineages. Thus, the model of slavery in Miers and Kopytoff was taken to a large degree from female experiences. In editing *The End of Slavery*, Sue demanded that contributors address the specific situation of women and children slaves. She insisted that women and children had distinct vulnerabilities and that applying the gender-unspecific term *slave* or *freedman* obscured the significant differences between men, women, and children as they faced the choices posed by the ambiguous end of slavery. Sue Miers's interest in the gender-specific vulnerability of women in slavery, their agency in their escape from bondage, and her interest in comparative slavery led to her editing, with Maria Jaschok, *Women and Chinese Patriarchy: Submission, Servitude, and Escape.* Her own contribution to that volume was a study of a Chinese woman who had been sold in Hong Kong as a *mui ts'ai*, a servant girl. Sue's consistent concern with women slaves connects her early work to this current collection.

During the 1990s she and Martin Klein, together and separately, organized a series of panels on modern slavery at meetings of the African Studies Association. The central problem those panels addressed was why slavery or slavelike conditions had persisted so long in Africa. Whereas *The End of Slavery* had principally examined the moment of emancipation, the new studies explored why emancipation took so long and why it followed such uneven courses in different parts of Africa. A selection of those papers appeared as *Slavery and Colonial Rule in Africa* (1999). Her own contribution to this volume was an essay on "Slavery and the Slave Trade as International Issues, 1890–1919."

Sue's work as a scholar was never a purely academic concern. It is very hard for those of us who study slavery to forget that slaves were human beings, but many historians of slavery see modern forms of slavery as different from traditional forms. In Sue's case, however, recognition of the commonalities of experience among those coerced to labor for others led to an involvement in modern forms of slavery. In 1980 she attended a meeting of the United Nations Working Group on Slavery. She describes in the preface of her most recent book, *Slavery in the Twentieth Century: The Evolution of a Global Problem* (2003), the "disheartening experience" of bored experts and officials going through the paces in a ritual that was like throwing a bone to some of the nongovernmental organizations trying to raise questions about modern forms. It was a ritual encumbered by the era's rhetoric of confrontation, East-West around the Cold War and North-South between the developed and developing worlds. For much of this meeting, Sue was the only spectator in the room. She was deeply disturbed and left Geneva determined to write on the politics of antislavery, but in the years since the meeting, the situation changed. A number of NGOs were successful in raising issues of forced labor, forced prostitution, debt bondage, child labor, and other abuses, and the Group of Experts was transformed into the Working Group on Contemporary Forms of Slavery. Sue Miers was often in the gallery, but also active in groups like Anti-Slavery International,[2] which were raising questions about modern forms of servitude and kept pressure on international bodies to act against both slavery and the continued trafficking in people. She was also a trustee of Anti-Slavery International and regularly attended meetings of its management board in London. The result was a series of articles, some historical, some descriptive, that provided scholarly substance to political struggles that are still going on. The end product of much of this research was her magnum opus, *Slavery in the Twentieth Century*, which traces the decline of formal slavery, a process that ended only in 1970, and the growing struggle to deal with more modern forms of coerced labor.

The two of us have sometimes disagreed with Sue Miers, starting with the introduction to Miers and Kopytoff's *Slavery in Africa*. But that has not really affected our relations with Sue. She is a gentle warrior, and a determined one, recognizing that debate and disagreement are the essence of academic life and demanding only that disagreement be polite. She has been a superb collaborator, well organized and with a network of connections. She always knew who was doing what and could be asked to do an article to fill some need. A generous person herself, she could usually get contributors to follow through on their commitments with only the gentlest hectoring. She is a meticulous and careful editor, open to discussion, easy to work with, but often very persistent. She keeps her eye on the goal and works hard to achieve it. And she gets results. It is hard to say no to a woman who is both gentle and firm. Both of us have been informed by her research, enriched by our collaboration with her, and enlivened by her friendship.

NOTES

1. For publication details of works by Suzanne Miers, see the chronological list of published works that follows.

2. Anti-Slavery International is the world's oldest antislavery organization, having been founded originally as the British and Foreign Anti-Slavery Society in 1839. We thank Michael Dottridge for filling us in on Sue Miers's work with Anti-Slavery International.

THE PUBLISHED WORKS OF SUZANNE MIERS ON SLAVERY

Britain and the Ending of the Slave Trade. New York: Africana, 1975.

and Igor Kopytoff, eds. *Slavery in Africa: Historical and Anthropological Perspectives*. Madison: University of Wisconsin Press, 1977.

and Richard [L.] Roberts, eds. *The End of Slavery in Africa*. Madison: University of Wisconsin Press, 1988.

"Humanitarianism at Berlin: Myth or Reality." In *Bismarck, Europe and Africa: The Berlin Africa Conference 1884–1885 and the Onset of Partition*, edited by S. Forster, W. J. Mommsen, R. Robinson, 333–45. London: Oxford University Press, 1988.

and Michael Crowder. "The Politics of Slavery in Bechuanaland: Power Struggles and the Plight of the Basarwa in the Bamangwato Reserve 1926–1940." In *The End of Slavery in Africa*, edited by Suzanne Miers and Richard Roberts, 172–200. Madison: University of Wisconsin Press, 1988.

"Britain and the Suppression of Slavery in Ethiopia" In *Proceedings of the Eighth International Conference of Ethiopian Studies*, edited by Taddese Beyene, 2:253–66. Addis Ababa: Institute of Ethiopian Studies, 1989.

"Diplomacy versus Humanitarianism: British and Consular Manumission in Hijaz 1921–1936." *Slavery and Abolition* 10, no. 3 (1989): 102–28.

Maria Jaschok and Suzanne Miers, eds. *Women and Chinese Patriarchy: Submission, Servitude, and Escape*. Hong Kong: Hong Kong University Press, 1994.

"Mui Tsai through the Eyes of the Victim: Janet Lim's Story of Bondage and Escape." In *Women and Chinese Patriarchy: Submission, Servitude, and Escape*, edited by

Maria Jaschok and Suzanne Miers, 108–21. Hong Kong: Hong Kong University Press, 1994.

"Contemporary Forms of Slavery (review essay: [Anti-Slavery International], Sutton, *Slavery in Brazil*; Anderson, *Britain's Secret Slaves*; Sattaur, *Child Labour in Nepal*; Smith, *Ethnic Groups in Burma*)." *Slavery and Abolition* 17, no. 3 (1996): 238–46.

"Britain and the Suppression of Slavery in Ethiopia." *Slavery and Abolition* 18, no. 3 (1997): 257–88.

"Slavery and the Slave Trade as International Issues, 1890–1939." *Slavery and Abolition* 19, no. 2 (1998): 16–37.

and Martin Klein. Introduction to "Slavery and Colonial Rule in Africa." *Slavery and Abolition* 19, no. 2 (1998): 1–15.

and Martin Klein, eds. "Slavery and Colonial Rule in Africa." *Slavery and Abolition* 19, no. 2 (1998), special issue. Also published as *Slavery and Colonial Rule in Africa*. London; Portland OR: Frank Cass, 1999.

"Contemporary Forms of Slavery." *Canadian Journal of African Studies/Revue canadienne d'études africaines* 34, no. 3 (2000): 714–47.

"Slavery to Freedom in sub-Saharan Africa: Expectations and Reality." *Slavery and Abolition* 21, no. 2 (2000): 237–64.

"Slavery: A Question of Definition." In "The Structure of Slavery in Indian Ocean Africa and Asia," edited by Gwyn Campbell, special issue of *Slavery and Abolition* 24, no. 2 (2003): 1–16. Also as "Slavery: A Question of Definition," in *The Structure of Slavery in Indian Ocean Africa and Asia*, edited by Gwyn Campbell, 1–16. London; Portland, OR: Frank Cass, 2004.

"Mue Tsaï à travers les yeux d'une victime: Histoire de l'asservissement et de l'évasion de Janet Lim." *Cahiers des anneaux de la mémoire*, no. 5 (2003): 15–32. Extract translated from *Women and Chinese Patriarchy: Submission, Servitude, and Escape*, edited by Maria Jaschok and Suzanne Miers. Hong Kong: Hong Kong University Press, 1994.

Slavery in the Twentieth Century: The Evolution of a Global Pattern. Walnut Creek, CA: Altamira, 2003.

"Slave Rebellion and Resistance in the Aden Protectorate in the Mid-Twentieth Century." *Slavery and Abolition* 25, no. 2 (2004): 80–89.

"Slavery and the Slave Trade in Saudi Arabia and the Arab States on the Persian Gulf, 1921–63." In *Abolition and Its Aftermath in Indian Ocean Africa and Asia*, edited by Gwyn Campbell, 120–36. London; Portland, OR: Frank Cass, 2005.

PREFACE

The papers in this volume on women and slavery fall entirely within the relatively—but only relatively—coherent single context of the commercial economy and modern culture of the Americas, from Brazil to Barbados and Baton Rouge. Compared to the diversity of cultural and historical settings for the studies of slavery and women in the first of these two volumes, the relative coherence of the Americas presents an opportunity to explore nuances of the quite distinctive general context of modernity that all these chapters share. But this coherence also brings a risk, since it includes all the clichés to which we have ascribed the obscurity of slaves of either sex in Africa as well as women as slaves in modern plantation contexts in Africa and the Indian Ocean world. It is the commercialized world of slaves, men or women, as property, slavery defined and institutionalized by civic laws and simultaneously reviled by a humanistic ethic, but with its victims also subjected to racialized exclusion.

The "Introduction" following considers selected aspects of the academic field of slavery studies, with overtones referring to women's studies and to issues of conceptualizing gender, citing contributions to the volume as they are relevant. This preface presents the papers and the organization of the volume, citing the aspects of the fields to which they are meant to contribute—women, gender, and slavery, and secondarily also the quintessentially American problem of race—as they happen to have turned up. The editors hope that we have arranged our authors' contributions in combinations that tap the potential of focusing on female experiences and strategies of surviving enslavement to think in new and productive ways about slavery, about slavers' sexualizing (but not gendering) of the women they held as slaves, about the subsequent gendering of the women emancipated (as distinct from those manumitted, under slavery), and about the memories of racialized women and their children. We hope that this book thus usefully combines the three customary—but usually separated—theoretical perspectives of enslavement, gendered exclusions of women, and racialization of Africans and their (recognized) descendants.

Historiographies and cultural studies turned from the homogeneities of high modernity in the 1960s and 1970s to attempt to understand the multiple dimensions of human difference that national and other related ideologies of equality had obscured. Race, then slavery, followed soon after by women, and eventually by gender revealed distinctions in positions in modern civil society. Efforts to comprehend these differences formerly denied drew first on political economy and then extended through language, culture, and subjectivity into the current so-called postmodern, or historicized, tone of the early twenty-first-century humanistic academic disciplines. The four streams of inquiry relevant to this volume each developed within rich political and theoretical contexts of their own, though each relatively separate from the others. Conceptualizations of difference have also abandoned the initial singular framework of a presumed "structure"—social or economic or political—to identify infinitely multiple perspectives among those living even in the same times and places. Cultures, as they say, are constructed; perceived or claimed "structures" are ideologies. Hence in this volume we try to combine experientially and historically the three familiar theorized axes of inequality—or better, differentiation, since we are concerned to show how mere differences became deviance—as enslaved women and their owners and descendants lived them out in different times and places in the historical processes of creating modern slaveries in the Americas.

Institutionalized enslavement, racialized societies, and civic gender paralleled one another as metaphors for or legal/ideological means of creating and enforcing inequalities against the modernist premise of radical equality, particularly in the civic realms of nation-states in the modern Americas. Earlier the locus of community recognition and support, explored in the companion volume on the early North Atlantic, Africa, and the Indian Ocean region, had lain in households, large and small, linked through patronage and clientage. In the Americas these private and personal relationships receded into the background of the vast canvas of modernity, in which commercial relations among strangers, anonymous markets, and imagined communities like nations left individuals at the mercy of abstract categories and impersonal laws that defined and structured them—including, but not limited to, those defining and institutionalizing slavery. Laws distinguishing persons according to their personal characteristics became outrageous. Treatment by others in terms of such distinguishing personal attributes as "color" or "sex" or personal

favoritism violated the reigning impersonal—and in extreme cases dehu-
manized—standings before The Law.

In this respect, slavery, race, and gender carried strong overtones of "exploitation" as well as wasting the potential of a universal humanity. In-
tellectuals contemplating such "dehumanization" with alarm tended to
meld the three quite different strategies of exclusion into a single politically charged concept of unjust inequality. This strong moral sense of
wrong has oriented much of the academic work in these three fields toward exploring the overlaps of slavery with gender and race when applied to women defined as "black," or at least as "women of color," and
subject to mostly male masters who took advantage of their legal invul-
nerability as owners of human "property" to abuse these women, particularly sexually. The women thus portrayed almost exclusively as victims
are, to that degree, left capable of acting mostly by resisting the oppression that defines them. Predictably, the parallelism in this moralizing approach to slavery, race, and gender along the dimension of oppression—
though often politically appealing—has not analytically distinguished
these three historically differing ideologies of exclusion.

Our focus on the distinctively female experiences of the women enslaved in the Americas and the eventual engendering of the emancipated also enables us to avoid the conventional effort to explain differences among the several national experiences of slavery in the Americas
according to the cultural backgrounds of the enslavers. Iberian Catholic
contexts have customarily been depicted as more open to slaves' (implicitly) civic presence, or "moral personality," as Frank Tannenbaum fa-
mously phrased his initial 1948 formulation of this enduring contrast,[1] at
least for men. Subsequent studies, however, demonstrated extremes of
personal brutality in Portuguese and Spanish America enabled by slavery
comparable to the worst depictions of slavery in the Protestant English
Americas, as well as much lower—routinely negative—rates of reproduction. This national-culture explanation of alleged differences in "slavery
as an institution" not only reified modern national identities but also ahis-
torically projected these recent national identities back in time to as early
as the thirteenth century.

All of this debate around cultural contrasts imputed to masters took
place largely in terms of the conventional stereotype of the slave as male,
but the differences at issue implicitly rested more on female slaves than
most of the proponents of the approach recognized.[2] The prominence of
the women enslaved as concubines in New World Iberian colonies, and

the visibility of children recognized by white masters (and fathers) as "mulattoes" or other finely graded but fraught categories of "*castas*," were—contradictorily enough—used to contrast permeable Iberian racial categories to the rigid matrilineal heritability of slavery and the dichotomized racial divisions of the United States. The absolutism of the mutually exclusive civic categories of freedom and slavery (and the correspondingly polarized commercial metaphor of owner and owned) again was congruent with the black/white racial dichotomy of North America and also with the bipolar categories of gender derived from the elemental and emotionally charged metaphors of sex. Against this tight framework of hemispheric homogeneity, north and south, presumed on the basis of the very peculiar experiences in North America, the highly varied experiences of enslavement and slaving elsewhere in the Americas, as well as diverse constructions of race and gender, seemed anomalous rather than readily understandable in terms of their always unique particular historical circumstances.

To test the analytical strength of focusing on women's experiences of slavery ranging over nearly two centuries and across several parts of the Americas, we have organized the papers in this volume in five sections. The first takes up the distinguishingly female physical ability to conceive and bear children under the sexually undifferentiated and extremely depleting demands of slave labor in the canebrakes of the circum-Caribbean basin. The following section considers selected strategies available to enslaved women in specific circumstances ranging from the Africa-born in eighteenth-century Rio de Janeiro to (presumably) locally born women in antebellum North Carolina. We then move on, in the third section, to the legacies of enslavement for women in French and British islands in the Caribbean who freed themselves through personal strategies of manumission and eventually also dealt with the ambivalent consequences of categorical government emancipation. The fourth section takes up the charged ideological sexualization of women enslaved in Jamaica and then considers the dilemmas of enslaved and racialized motherhood in the United States as enslaved women's sons and daughters there memorialized them in fiction.

The final section offers contrasting overviews of women and slavery. The first assesses the failures of scholars of slavery to include the numerous women enslaved in instances they have studied; it also theorizes the "productive" aspects of enslavement as a way of bringing women into the picture as "laborers" along with the men enslaved. The other explores the dynamics of slaving as a series of historicized strategies to argue that the aspects of enslavement distinctive to slave women anywhere in the world, including the Americas, however hard they may also have worked, derived from their uniquely female abilities to bear children.

With respect to the female physiology of pregnancy and childbirth, the effective premise of seeing women slaves distinctively as mothers, Kenneth Morgan and Richard Follett both consult wide ranges of recent technical medical and nutritional literature to explore the implications of historical evidence for what they see as the severely depleting physical stresses of work in the canebrakes of eighteenth-century Jamaica and nineteenth-century Louisiana. Morgan assesses the extent of maternal morbidity and mortality in eighteenth-century Jamaica, as well as lost fetuses and infant mortality attributable to the exhausting labor discipline under West Indian conditions of enslavement. At the time, purchasing replacements from Africa seemed cheaper than raising children born in the islands. In the absence of detailed statistics, other than the gross evidence of resident populations of slaves who died faster than they could reproduce, Morgan sums up the likely cumulative inhibition of fecundity among pregnant women and deaths of new mothers and infants from diseases, filthy surroundings, poor nutrition, and lack of care, as masters, medical professionals, and other observers reported them.

Physical depletion and calculated managerial neglect, combined with ignorance of modern medical and nutritional science, Morgan finds more than sufficient to account for low natality and high infant mortality in Jamaica. On this basis, he challenges other scholars' attribution of the low rates of reproduction in the islands to a kind of feminist reproductive resistance to masters' presumed interest in slave infants. The supposed refusal of enslaved women to enrich their owners by bearing their human assets would have been congruent with a hypothesized maternal reluctance to expose potential children to the hardships of enslavement that they had suffered on sugar plantations in Jamaica.

Whether or not some enslaved women deliberately avoided conceiving or carrying fetuses to term, and for whatever reasons, such political strategies would have been, Morgan concludes, insignificant compared to the sheer physical deprivations of sugar slavery in contributing to the negative gross rates of reproduction on Jamaica. The doubts that he raises about the efficacy of reproductive resistance are not inconsistent with this volume's general accent on the value that men found in owning women whose children they had no paternal obligation to recognize or support.

Follett brings direct and detailed statistical evidence from nineteenth-century Louisiana sugar estates to bear on the nutritional insufficiencies corresponding to those that Morgan reports from Jamaica. Plantation records of births among the women enslaved in Louisiana in the 1830s show expectably low natality correlated with the physical exertions and nutritionally depleted female bodies subject to the discipline of cultivating sugar there. However, conceptions rose strongly at the particularly intense, and presumably most depleting, harvest phase of the annual cycle of seasons, sicknesses, and sugar-making. These conceptions, he argues, indicate intensified sexual activity and increased success in conception during the most demanding and depleting weeks of cutting and boiling the cane, when enslaved women might be expected to have been too fatigued to begin successful pregnancies.

To account for female fecundity (and frequency of sexual intercourse) sufficient to raise birthrates at the time observed, Follett emphasizes the caloric burst provided by "sirop" or molasses, the cheap by-product of boiling the cane juice down to refinable sugar, that masters fed to their slaves in the season of harvesting and boiling. Follett's research thus explores the implications of annual seasonal labor cycles for the uniquely female day-to-day private—even intimate—experience of reproduction for women who had no choice but to work. Women's reproductive rhythms thus correlated with the similarly irregular, nutrition-based "agonistic" outbursts of festival and rebellion that have been attributed to male slaves throughout the West Indies.[3]

The next set of three chapters turns to "women's initiatives under slavery" in less agonized physical circumstances. Mariza de Carvalho Soares has revealed the slaves' intricate interweavings of their backgrounds in Africa with their present lives in Brazil, based on close analysis of a petition sent to the Portuguese crown involving gendered conflict within a slave Catholic "brotherhood" in eighteenth-century Rio de Janeiro. She shows how women and men alike seamlessly integrated lineage politics in Africa with Portuguese Catholic sacraments on the other shore of the Atlantic. They also integrated the "baroque" past of Catholic sodalities with the emerging Enlightened framework of public law in later eighteenth-century Brazil. The holistic sense of multilayered lives that her rich research evokes from the petition implicitly questions the theorized dichotomies between Africa and America on which most approaches to Africans' lives in slavery depend.

Barbara Krauthamer similarly elucidates how enslaved African women in the Carolina Low Country drew on backgrounds in Africa to create

opportunities for themselves in the Americas. Some, at least, moved easily among the Native American communities, mostly "Creek," inland from
the English rice plantations along the Atlantic coast. Her evidence of
African women interacting with Native Americans represents an under-
appreciated general experience of the enslaved African immigrants—
men as well as women—in all parts of the Americas. Krauthamer explains
the ease of African women's interactions with Native Americans in
terms of parallels between the kinship idiom of community in Africa and
the same highly flexible strategies of defining and maintaining communities in the woodlands of southeastern North America. Readers might
refer to the companion volume in this set for further consideration of
both Soares's and Krauthamer's understandings of community, kinship,
women, and slavery in Africa.

The relevance of lives in Africa to the strategies of the women in both
Rio de Janeiro and Low-Country Carolina, though in differing ways,
highlights the importance of timing to understanding slavery and women
in the Americas. Africa in the minds of these women's children had
faded to stories their parents told, and the insecurities of growing up in
slavery had become primary. Laura Edwards's chapter may be assumed to
pick up the strategies of the American-born women who had survived
this experience in the antebellum United States and had learned how to
exploit its intricate interdependencies. By then, whatever the civil exclusions of public law, many women had complicated personal and family networks of their own, as well as ways of manipulating their owners
and their families.

Edwards uses the famed 1829–30 *State v. Mann* decision in a North
Carolina appellate court to accent these contrasts between abstract law
and community standing. John Mann, who had assaulted a slave woman,
Lydia, had been convicted by his local peers, but the North Carolina
Supreme Court reversed this decision by using the instance to create the
abstract, categorical law, irrespective of persons, that was becoming the
hallmark of modern nations. Federal law in the United States was then,
as she shows, undergoing its own formative process of the institutionaliza-
tion of the modern slavery of the 1840s and 1850s. She contrasts the
intimate circumstances in the small community in which the case originated with conversion of the issue, upon appeal, to one of the legal land-
marks along the road of nationalizing slavery to create an ultimately ir-
reconcilable sectional struggle. Edwards also teases out the skills of other
women slaves who, though excluded by their enslavement from the
growing national law of the United States, played powerfully on their

domestic circumstances for their personal advantage, and even to damage the standing of their male owners.

The broader implication for the general argument in this book and its companion volume emphasizes, once again, the inclusiveness of the large domestic household and the small village community, of the sorts prevailing in much of Africa and the Indian Ocean world, and the irrelevance of gender as a mode of exclusion. Gender would emerge, under the ideology of domesticity, in tandem with the impersonal categorical law of the later nineteenth century; so also would race, as distinct from the personal characteristics or backgrounds that remained prominent in less civically integrated American nations, like Brazil.

With new national governments empowered by the middle of the nineteenth century to intrude on the domestic privacy of households, emancipation by governmental fiat soon followed. Potential citizens, slaves rendered so by their co-residence, would no longer be sequestered from the public sphere as personal property under rights of ownership so absolute that—at least according to *State v. Mann*—a person whom one held in slavery could not claim a civic right to life or limb. For the women emancipated from enslavement, in British West Indian colonies in the 1830s, in the French islands in the Caribbean in the late 1840s and 1850s, and in the United States eventually in the 1860s, governmental authority as comprehensive as this new categorical and comprehensive law presented obstacles as well as opportunities. The last two sets of chapters in this book consider the strategies of the women thus enabled to rebuild lives as legally empowered citizens, and particularly around families they controlled and sustained, since they seldom, if ever, had access to commercially valuable land or other independent means of support. Modern government thus ended property interests in people but protected every other form of private wealth, and so it was to the laws of persons that freed women turned.

Bernard Moitt frames the background to French emancipation in the Antilles in 1848 by considering the uses that female slaves there made of a series of earlier legal provisions for personal manumission through self-purchase, or *rachat*. Self-manumitted women, or women who bought themselves, in Martinique, Guadeloupe, and Guiane appropriated new governmental subsidies under older laws even as the end of slavery loomed in the 1830s and 1840s. The laws and court records of the period reveal only a tiny minority of enslaved women (but more females than males) who managed even then to buy their own freedom and sometimes also that of their children, presumably as often as they were able, but less often that of their children's fathers, whoever they may have been.

The advanced years of the owners from whom these women bought themselves and their owners' frequent opposition to the enslaved women's efforts suggest the great determination and considerable time that these slave women must have devoted to their savvy exploitation of French law. Since these women aimed their strategies at manumitting their children as well as at saving themselves, they may well have exploited their relationships as women with men who owned them rather than engaging in the more ideological and political "resistance" that men, lacking such relationships, favored. Historians have, we think too often, extended this generic implicitly male confrontational sort of slave resistance to women slaves without carefully searching for the distinctive options open to them, even under slavery, as females.

Laurence Brown and Tara Inniss examine how slave families in Barbados, headed mostly by women, negotiated their "transition to freedom" during the period of highly dependent "apprenticeship" through which the people emancipated in the British West Indies passed in the 1830s. The positive rate of reproduction distinctive (in the Caribbean context) to this island's maturing slave population allowed the former masters, intent on denying significant autonomy to their former slaves, to exploit the former slave women's concern for the welfare of their children. Planters effectively starved the young families whom the emancipation law had forced them to free by converting former slave provision grounds to canebrakes. To blame their victims for the resulting starvation and mortality they cited moral deficiencies attributed to ex-slave parents, particularly mothers.

Freedom in the Antilles subjected the former women slaves, as Myriam Cottias shows, to similarly intense defamation as incompetent mothers. Emancipation there was caught up in the rush to define Republican civil society by excluding all women through gendered domesticity and responsibility for the family as nursery of future contributing citizens, raised by stay-at-home moms. This engendering civic domesticity of women accompanied the elevation of male citizens' rights to the sublime heights of the modern national republic everywhere in the Americas—as well as in Europe—and depended on male earning opportunities sufficient to support wives and children as dependents.

In fact, women slaves—and later emancipated female citizens of the French Republic—were widely active in the public commercial sphere in the smaller islands in the French Antilles. They consequently regarded the prospect of civil marriage—and accompanying civic exclusion—available to French citizens with reserve. These three chapters, through the experiences of slave, manumitted, and emancipated women, implicitly reveal how gendered exclusion of women from public spaces was integral to the process of creating modern civic nations. Modern nations created and funded the privileges of citizens by excluding women no less than colonies had enriched and ennobled the few by impoverishing the many, as slaves.

The owners and lawmakers engaged in the ideological struggles detailed in the preceding section fantasized contradictory intimate images of the women they enslaved and then freed and gendered as concubines and companions. Barbadian masters and officials, like their counterparts in the French Antilles, attributed racialized inherent deficiencies to former slave women as mothers. In doing so they drew on antecedent images of a half century earlier that had arisen in anticipation of slavery's approaching moment of reckoning. British abolitionists had made much of slavery's threat to the integrity of a slave family, invoking early formulations of the domesticated wife and mother of the later nineteenth century no less idealized than the Republican family in France. In the French Antilles, ex-slaves' failures to sign on to Republican expectations of the civically responsible patriarchal family were once again attributed to moral deficiencies of racialized African women and their descendants, reducing black female sexuality to sheer wantonness. They wished.

The following two chapters use literary readings to focus on the fantasies that the contradictions and anxieties of enslavement generated about slave women, first in the minds of English proslavery propagandists and Jamaican masters in the late eighteenth and early nineteenth centuries, and then in the hearts of the children of the generation of women freed in the United States in 1863 as they grew to productive literary maturity at the end of the century. As antislavery rhetoric in Britain swelled in the second half of the eighteenth century, British abolitionists condemned the sexual abuses of women that slavery enabled. Henrice Altink evokes "Jezebel," the suspect Jamaican seductress of dusky hue that the slavers favored to blame their female victims. This proslavery response arose mostly from afar, in Britain. At the same time, in Jamaica masters created a counterimage of the virtuous "housekeeper," a slave or freed woman living with the master of the house in a stable and devoted relationship, even as the acknowledged mother of his recognized children. Slavery thus exposed women to complex and contradictory displacements of male anxieties over the numerous threats—financial failure, slave revolt, and others—that loomed in the West Indies as slavery neared its end, as well as to sexual abuse and other physical brutalities.

In the United States at the end of the nineteenth century, as Felipe Smith shows, the first generation of African American writers to grow to literary maturity in the wake of emancipation repeatedly deployed images of the shame-bearing dark maternal ancestor to decry the divisiveness of racialized slavery, sometimes then reclaiming her spirit through inversion as the goddess of ancient Africa. The shamefulness of the Mother of visible African descent was a trope peculiar to English North America in its Jim Crow era, where a "one-drop rule" of attributed racial identity, referred to obliquely as the "condition of the mother," condemned anyone who acknowledged such ancestry, no matter how pale or "white" in appearance, to social ostracism and public humiliation.

In literary analyses of the novels of Pauline Hopkins and Charles Chesnutt, Smith shows how these writers developed the trope of the dark maternal ancestor to reveal the personal losses of loved ones through categorically defined and socially imposed racial standing of the sort pioneered in *State v. Mann* in 1830. Race separated families and loved ones in the postbellum generation just as the interstate slave trade had separated more than a million enslaved sons, husbands, and daughters from wives and mothers through sales to the antebellum cotton frontier in the Deep South. The maternal ancestor who could forever after come back to haunt her children was one legacy of these separations. The mystery created by loss of loved ones in Africa and subsequent arbitrary sales in the Americas today remains a spectre floating in the pasts of modern African Americans.

The two concluding essays offer broad theoretical and historical contexts for women's experiences of slavery in the modern Americas. Claire Robertson and Marsha Robinson define slavery rigorously as an institution of labor exploitation and then consider the ways in which the literature on slavery has, and more often has not, taken women into account in these terms. They review a wide range of recent writings to argue that a mistakenly narrow definition of labor as commercially productive—tobacco and rice fields, mines, canebrakes—has all but excluded women from explicit attention in this literature. They expand the concept of labor to include social reproduction in a sense much broader than the exertions of childbirth and also domestic services—including sexual ones—distinctive to women. Their commercialized definition of slavery as unremunerated labor applies more directly to the modern Americas, covered in this volume, than to the parts of the world presented in its companion.

My own essay problematizes this labor/production definition of slavery institutionalized as law and ideology uniquely in modern times, definingly in selected parts of the Americas. It bears very limited relevance to Africa, the Indian Ocean region, or to earlier eras in Europe. To highlight the distinctiveness of the modern Americas in terms of both slavery and opportunities denied women, enslaved and free, I sketch modern American slaveries as a historical series of ever more commercial, public, and eventually governmental reactions to their distinctively male demography and to their enormous scale. As more and more heavy-handed means of managing enslaved men, American slaveries—I argue—deviated unviably from age-old slaving practices centered on women and children, dispersed among numerous, often large domestic households in small and assimilable numbers.

My introduction to the first of these two volumes develops these arguments further, discussing women introduced into such domestic contexts by slaving from the early northern Atlantic to nineteenth-century Dutch farms in the Transvaal, from Muslim households from western Africa to Africa's Indian Ocean coast, and beyond. Slave women in these generally polygynous households created distinctive jealousies, and they turned these sensitive rivalries to their personal advantages. These female politics of the polygynous household contrasted radically with their helpless exclusion from the Christian monogamous households ubiquitous in the Americas, other than among Krauthamer's native Creek. The single legitimate wife banished all other women, particularly slaves, as Jezebel-like concubines. Monogamy, combined with slave descent through the mother, precluded the enslaved woman's children from competing with the legitimate heirs to the master's estate. The ambiguities created after slavery, when race came to serve the same excluding function, were the subject of Smith's authors in the preceding section.

The editors have tried to orient the chapters in both volumes toward detecting the experiences of enslavement distinctive to women, particularly as bearers of children whom they loved and protected and whom their masters often denied. We have not drawn primarily on the theoretical frameworks of institutionalized slavery, premised as they implicitly are on the slave as male. Nor have we projected feminist reactions to the post-slavery engendering of women to exclude them from positions of political or economic power back in time to the preceding era of enslavement. These, and studies of gender, we think, have sometimes been extended rhetorically, but inappropriately, into earlier, much more common practices of domestic patriarchy. Authors in this volume thus explore African options open to women on the other side of the Atlantic in the earlier eighteenth century and how they drew on them to find viable places for themselves in the Americas.

The succeeding sections of the book, on later decades, suggest that women born into slavery in the Americas by the late eighteenth century had only the constrained worlds of the plantations where they had been born available as options. These options prominently included their own children, and they artfully manipulated these small rural worlds, including people "free" by the doctrines of relatively remote public law. But national governments grew stronger, and the women and children they emancipated in the middle third of the nineteenth century were mostly American-born and expert at negotiating the new worlds of commercial economies and civic law, regardless of their nominal standing as slaves.

The fact that enslaved women raised any children at all on the hellish sugar plantations of Jamaica and Louisiana may also suggest their dedication to children, whom they repeatedly protected, in freedom as well as in slavery. Their masters defamed them as bad mothers and as destroyers of respectable (white) families, and framed laws around their biological reproductive powers, to claim their children as property and to exclude them from civic rights as well as from their owners' family inheritances. The repeated focus on reproduction perversely acknowledged enslaved women's greatest strength. Masters in the commercialized modern world of the Americas enslaved women primarily for their productive abilities and raped some to beat them into physically self-depleting submission, but the women enslaved may well have found their greatest triumphs, their means of self-realization, in the children they raised and the families they nurtured, in spite of it all.

As with all tragedy,[4] enslaved women's successes with these strategies gave their masters the means on which they seized to elicit productive, profit-earning "good" female behavior: the threat of depriving a mother of her children through sale.[5] In the classic Greek tragic dynamic, the heroic strong male had paid for his personal excess himself. Women's enslavement in the Americas displaced the tragedy by freeing modern owners from the consequences of their excesses through the legal power over others given them by institutionalized slavery. After slavery the impersonal modern civic state conveyed the same freedom from consequences to white males through the exclusionary ideologies of gender over all free women and of race over all persons of African descent.

—*Joseph C. Miller*

NOTES

1. Frank Tannenbaum, *Slave and Citizen: The Negro in the Americas* (New York: Knopf, 1947).

2. The exception was Carl N. Degler, *Neither Black nor White: Slavery and Race Relations in Brazil and the United States* (New York: Macmillan, 1971), which—though phrased structurally—implicitly focused on women as bearers of mulatto children and their rivalries with legitimate wives and recognized heirs.

3. Robert Dirks, "The Black Saturnalia and Relief Induced Agonism," in *The African Exchange: Toward a Biological History of the Black People*, ed. Kenneth F. Kiple (Durham, NC: Duke University Press, 1988), 167–94.

4. Patrick Manning, *Slavery and African Life* (New York: Cambridge University Press, 1990).

5. Walter Johnson, *Soul by Soul: Life inside the Antebellum Slave Market* (Cambridge, MA: Harvard University Press, 1999).

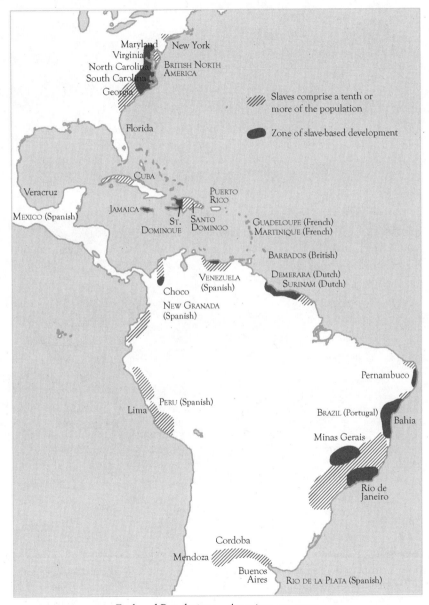

Maryland
Virginia
North Carolina
South Carolina
Georgia

New York

BRITISH NORTH
AMERICA

Florida

///// Slaves comprise a tenth or
more of the population

⬤ Zone of slave-based development

CUBA

Veracruz

MEXICO (Spanish)

JAMAICA

PUERTO
RICO

ST.   SANTO
DOMINGUE DOMINGO

GUADELOUPE (French)
MARTINIQUE (French)

BARBADOS (British)

Choco

VENEZUELA
(Spanish)

NEW GRANADA
(Spanish)

DEMERARA (Dutch)
SURINAM (Dutch)

Pernambuco

BRAZIL (Portugal)   Bahia

PERU (Spanish)

Lima

Minas Gerais

Rio de
Janeiro

Cordoba

Mendoza

Buenos
Aires   RIO DE LA PLATA (Spanish)

Enslaved Populations—Americas, ca. 1770.

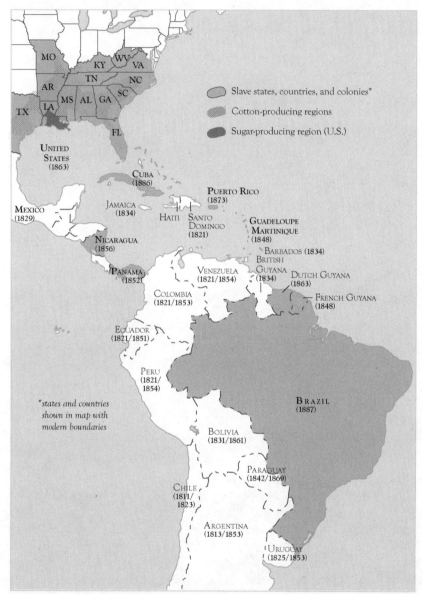

MO
KY WV VA
TN NC
AR
MS AL GA SC
TX LA
FL

UNITED
STATES
(1863)

○ Slave states, countries, and colonies*

▨ Cotton-producing regions

● Sugar-producing region (U.S.)

CUBA
(1886)

PUERTO RICO
(1873)

JAMAICA
(1834)

HAITI SANTO
DOMINGO
(1821)

GUADELOUPE
MARTINIQUE
(1848)

MEXICO
(1829)

NICARAGUA
(1856)

BARBADOS (1834)
BRITISH
GUYANA
(1834)

DUTCH GUYANA
(1863)

PANAMA
(1852)

VENEZUELA
(1821/1854)

FRENCH GUYANA
(1848)

COLOMBIA
(1821/1853)

ECUADOR
(1821/1851)

PERU
(1821/
1854)

BRAZIL
(1887)

*states and countries
shown in map with
modern boundaries

BOLIVIA
(1831/1861)

PARAGUAY
(1842/1869)

CHILE
(1811/
1823)

ARGENTINA
(1813/1853)

URUGUAY
(1825/1853)

Slave States, Colonies, and Countries—Americas, ca. 1840. Dates in parentheses are
those of emancipation, sometimes in steps extending over several decades. *Source:* Stanley
L. Engerman, Richard Sutch, and Gavin Wright, "Slavery," for *Historical Statistics of the
United States, Millennial Edition* (University of California Project on the Historical Statis-
tics of the United States, Center for Social and Economic Policy, University of California,
Riverside, March 2003), http://www.economics.ucr.edu/papers/papers03/03-12.pdf, viewed
September 8, 2007.

INTRODUCTION

STRATEGIES OF WOMEN AND CONSTRAINTS OF ENSLAVEMENT IN THE MODERN AMERICAS

GWYN CAMPBELL, SUZANNE MIERS, AND JOSEPH C. MILLER

Slavery studies have until recently focused overwhelmingly on male slaves. This relative neglect of women, and in particular the lack of analytically gendered consideration of their prominent presence among the enslaved, reflects in part the emphasis of scholars on the recent, and best-known, Atlantic system of slavery, in which some twelve million slaves, predominantly and most prominently males, were shipped to the mines and plantations of the Americas. Non-Western systems of slavery, in which the gender ratio was probably the inverse, as many of the studies in the companion volume to this one contemplate,[1] have until recently received scant scholarly attention.

However, the literature on women slaves in certain regions of the globe has grown rapidly over the last decade. A preceding version of this introduction[2] compared females in Western slave systems in a wide variety of geographical settings ranging from the plantations of the Americas to the Dutch Cape in southern Africa, the South African Republic, and British Mauritius. While male slaves outnumbered female slaves on the commercial plantations characteristic of most of these areas, women accounted for greater proportions of the people enslaved there than is customarily acknowledged. The literature has largely analyzed the slave owner–slave relationship in terms of the dominance of the legally empowered "insider" over vulnerable "outsiders" deprived of even basic human rights, and of owner violence and resulting slave resentment and sometimes revolt—with consequent brutal owner suppression and slave suffering.

I

Historians have concentrated on the contradictions inherent in the experiences of the women trapped in these vicious circumstances as mothers and on the dire effects of compulsory labor on themselves and on their children. In this volume Claire Robertson and Marsha Robinson "re-model slavery as if women mattered" to extend the concept from the conventional image of bondswomen in cotton fields and in the canebrakes of sugar plantations in the Caribbean to emphasize enslaved women's economic values as workers and to include their physical presence in every other way, including forced sex as work. Kenneth Morgan details the physiology of suppressed fertility, inhibited natality, and infant mortality on plantations in Jamaica, and Richard Follett demonstrates the biological stresses of the harsh labor discipline imposed on the slave women who cultivated sugar on the plantations of nineteenth-century Louisiana by correlating abnormal annual cycles of natality with the peak labor demands of the fall cutting and processing of the cane. Sugar slavery's distortion of biological rhythms implies that sugar planters, at least in the highly competitive circumstances of growing cane in the Americas, valued women more for the work they performed than for the additional children they might have borne under less strenuous labor.

Other studies in the present volume contribute to recent efforts to demystify the white male (i.e., owners') intense images of the women they owned, particularly in the English Americas. These traditional views of slave mistresses and mothers have—not entirely without contradiction—categorized slave women there as belonging to one of two broad types, the scheming "jezebel" or the nurturing "mammy."[3] Elsewhere in the Americas, particularly in Brazil but also in French Martinique, as Myriam Cottias emphasizes, owners and public officials, regarding themselves as custodians of the welfare of women, slave or free, gendered them as dependents within large patriarchal households. They customarily (albeit discreetly) included women other than legitimate wives, thereby rendering their presence less intensely emotional than for the English and North Americans.

Discarding American stereotypes of enslaved females as passive victims brings forward the issue of their agency, their priorities, their strategies. While discussion of the agency of slaves has traditionally focused on male slaves and their resistance, notably on relatively infrequent incidents of violent revolt, recent literature—including the studies offered here—has explored the subtler ways in which women have cannily assessed and expertly exploited even situations as theoretically oppressive as enslavement to create dynamic spaces of their own.

PROCESSES OF ENSLAVEMENT

Violence and coercion have been considered hallmarks of enslavement: since the eighteenth century, individual liberty became one of the most cherished human rights, particularly in parts of the Americas, and no one is assumed to surrender personal autonomy except under compulsion. Brute violence had been a widely employed strategy of slaving throughout the histories of every continent in the world, intensely so in Africa in the recent centuries in which that continent served as a source of the women and men enslaved in the Americas. Victors in war commonly enslaved the wives and daughters of the men they vanquished on fields of battle. Armed gangs of thugs also kidnapped innocent victims, sometimes from within their own or neighboring societies. Not all kidnap victims, often girls and women, or war captives, including men, were enslaved, as the abductors/ captors often kept and enslaved only those whom they could not ransom.[4]

The complex politics of female enslavement in the Americas revolved primarily around Native American women as the initial brutal confrontations between invading Spanish *conquistadores* and English settlers in North America settled into the routinized violence of ongoing trade and the politics of seizing or retaining land all along the settler-native frontier, from the St. Lawrence south to Tierra del Fuego.[5] In this volume, Barbara Krauthamer reveals the ways in which enslaved African women in the Carolina Low Country in the eighteenth century exploited these conflicts to escape the owners of the English rice plantations of the region. The Africans who replaced the escapees along the Atlantic coasts of both continents of the New World continued to suffer capture by violent means, though also in decreasing proportions as commercial relations with Europeans in Africa stabilized as the eighteenth century wore on, and as commercial debts, deceit, and corrupted legal systems supplemented wars in generating captives.

Thus, considering enslavement in a global, rather than "Atlantic" or American, historical context indicates that many people—often females—entered slavery through nonviolent means, notably because of family indebtedness or impoverishment. Joseph Miller's essay in this volume emphasizes the growing presence of merchants among the militarists who seized women by sheer violence from ancient times; indeed, debt was possibly the commonest cause of enslavement everywhere. Also, fathers, uncles, and other representatives of fundamentally patriarchal communities tended to try to lessen the problems of feeding the people for whom they were responsible by disposing of the girls and women who bore children in numbers they could not support; natural catastrophes, such as famine, often triggered this defensive strategy of selling girls to save other relatives.[6] Others sought to escape hunger or abuse by offering themselves to patrons voluntarily, accepting at least initially slavelike conditions of dependency and isolation to survive, although the contributors to this volume do not directly consider such circumstances or motivations. However, the majority of those enslaved for indebtedness or because of a natural catastrophe were probably women and children. Violence was indispensable only in the capture and enslavement of adult males, notably Africans destined for the Atlantic trade.

CONDITIONS OF SLAVERY FOR WOMEN

Although male slaves in the Americas suffered because of their slave status, as well as the racism and often the individual perverse cruelty of their owners, it has been contended that black slave women there suffered additionally because they were female.[7] In the modern commercial societies of the Americas, all slaves were legally chattels with no control over their working conditions, the product of their labors, the conditions in which they lived, or—for women—their sexual and domestic partners and their children. Both sexes, but particularly women, lived in constant fear of having their partners and their children sold away from them. Women were more vulnerable than men both to sexual abuse at the hands of their predominantly male owners and to separation from their children, for whom they had primary responsibility, particularly where positive rates of reproduction generated nuclear and extended slave families.

In slavery literature, "race" is traditionally described in terms of skin color—the contrast between the "European" slave-owning white and the black "African" chattel. The eventually almost comprehensive overlap of civic condition—slavery—and personal origin—Africa—in the English-speaking parts of the Americas has left the two very indistinctly differentiated, thus prompting this reference to "race" in an essay otherwise devoted to (women and) slavery. Racial division and this logical confusion were most evident in the Caribbean and American South, where large groups of black slaves lived and labored segregated from predominantly white owners. Speculatively, had only men been imported and enslaved, they could not have reproduced, and they would not have generated the same anxieties in English colonies that fecund "jezebels" and maternal "mammies" excited. Their very presence was disconcerting to owners determined to minimize their social and cultural existence. This racializing "white" reaction to these black Americans living amongst them but marginalized by enslavement may thus be said to be owing directly to the enslaved women present and their reproductive capacities.

Elsewhere in the world, patriarchal households had smoothly and discreetly absorbed the majorities of girls and women enslaved. There the universal patriarchal subordination of all females and their children needed no supplementary exclusion by arbitrarily "racialized" (and increasingly only ancestral) origin. Cottias's essay probes the conflicts that the 1848 French emancipation of slaves in Martinique, incidentally including women, created between the public inclusiveness of republican citizenship and inherited ideals of female domesticity and corresponding exclusion from public affairs. Felipe Smith explores the distinctively North American dilemma of the utter and tragic falsity of dichotomized "race" as it blurred the biologically integrated descent of the citizenry of the post–Civil War United States, white as well as black, as movingly portrayed in the literary production of the daughters of the generation of slave women freed there in 1863.

But concepts of race varied over time and region throughout the Americas, according to fluctuations in the numbers, backgrounds, and identities of slaves and other servile groups, and "free" people. Ira Berlin's recent surveys of North American colonial slavery emphasize the diversity of the personal backgrounds of the sailors, hustlers, dockworkers, and others who clustered together in the taverns of seventeenth-century port cities.[8] In this volume Laura Edwards demonstrates how, in local communities in the American South as late as the antebellum era, personal standing and respectability conflicted with growing abstract legal categorization as "black" or "white," as well as "slave" or "free."[9] Dichotomized and politicized "race," as well as slavery, she suggests, developed out of the necessity to define participatory "citizens" on a still-only-emergent level of "national" integration. The intensity of this process in the still-only-formatively united States, her study suggests, explains the uniquely polarized definition of "race" there and the sensitivity of the "condition of the mother"—as Smith puts it—in determining which children born there belonged and which, as slaves, did not. Beyond owners' economic interests in the value of the children born, which were also intense but which do not figure prominently in the novels Smith examines, the still-fragile (and eminently, and increasingly, false) identity of "Americans" as white, and dominantly of English descent, was at stake—in spite of the long-standing intimate relations that Edwards describes in the 1840s for the grandmothers of these writers of the 1890s.

"Color" might have been used earlier and elsewhere to describe individuals, among many other references to various personal attributes and accomplishments, but it did not operate as a blanket political mechanism of exclusion or even of individual condemnation. "Color," as distinct from politicized and categorical "race," operated in this relatively incidental way in all earlier and less tensely nationalizing contexts, even elsewhere in the Americas. Attempts by Winthrop Jordan[10] and others to derive North American slavery from Elizabethan English color symbolism founder on their failure to recognize this distinction between personal attribute and political categorization. The early literature highlighted the greatly varied relations between race and slavery throughout the Americas in spite of the uniform enslavement of Africans but failed to take account of the influence of varying female abilities to reproduce. As Miller's survey of the dynamics of the changes under way suggests, Brazil's apparent openness to the "mulatto" (in modern racialized terms[11]) children of the women brought there in slavery may have derived from the ability of slave owners there to replenish labor forces with new African males, in contrast to the dependence of North American planters on the reproduction of their enslaved women. Of course, Brazil also lacked the small, intimate households of male owner, (recognized) wife, and legitimate children that excluded the unrecognized "black" children of the master from the family estate. Further, well into the twentieth century Brazilian society had a less-developed civic sphere from which to exclude the humble by means of racial categorization. Thus the differing presences and positions of African women and their North American- or Brazilian- or Caribbean-born daughters and their varying conditions as slaves were prominent among the factors determining modern variations of "race" throughout the hemisphere.

In the Hispanic colonies, the women taken there in slavery arrived earlier in the seventeenth century, were relatively less numerous,[12] and were taken more often into the large households of merchants, ecclesiastics, and officials. The preponderance of males among the Africans and the intimacy of the domestic and urban environments in which they lived together quickly moved the children born to African women, as well as by other women to African men, into the familiar range there of *castas*, varying legally recognized combinations of personal descent from Africans, Native Americans, Spaniards, Romani ("gypsies"), and others; these were categories of persons, not politicized racial categories.[13] With independence in the Spanish mainland colonies in the early nineteenth century, egalitarian republican ideals overcame the relatively minor political significance of descent and the small numbers of the enslaved to end slavery.

In the British and French Caribbean, similarly smaller numbers of women, and the tendency that Kenneth Morgan documents here to work the women enslaved to infertility or even death, similarly diminished sensitivities like those in North America to the "race" of the children that the favored few among the women enslaved bore to their masters. The fathers of these locally born children, described as "colored" but not entirely excluded civically, were usually not their owners, who were mostly absentees settling into comfortable and respectable family life in the English countryside. Rather, the white fathers were hired managers, overseers, and other English men of lesser stature in a society that revered personal connections and patronage as much or more than categorical civic standing. Only with the simultaneous—and not merely coincidentally so—abolition of slavery and democratization of political participation in the 1830s did "color" become politically sensitized, and thus racialized. But in these English colonies, "color" coincided also with "local" (that is, island-born and hence "colonial" in the context of increasingly troubled relations with the metropole), with class (mainly middle-class artisans and merchants), and with culture (relatively Anglicized).

With emancipation and the threatened meaningful enfranchisement of the more recently arrived Africans, the "colored" children of slave women contributed to increasingly racialized local civic orders—in differing ways on different islands—by referring to "color" to distinguish themselves from the impoverished freed people, and siding with their fathers rather than with their mothers. In this volume, Henrice Altink delineates the centrality of enslaved women to these intricately gendered processes of racialization. Cottias and Bernard Moitt show how their specific presence played out in the French islands. Moitt emphasizes that women in the French Antilles who managed to purchase themselves used their freedom to purchase their children, rather than freeing them by acknowledging that their fathers were French. That is, they asserted their identities as reproducers. Their financial neglect of the unacknowledged fathers may implicitly confirm their children's paternal origin among French males, thus citizens of the Republic in no need whatsoever of being bought out of slavery.

"Race" in all its subtle and thoroughly historical variants may thus be both distinguished from the "condition of the mother" as a slave and then related to slavery by emphasizing the presence of women among the

enslaved. The key variable lies in slave women's ability, or failure, to reproduce American-born children. The economic value of the children
was, of course, important, and Robertson and Robinson emphasize this element of the calculus as the "labor" component of the worth of women's
work as slaves. But their enslavement obviated the need to politicize
"race" as a means of controlling their offspring, as suggested by the relatively open acceptance of Afro-Brazilians and the pre-emancipation tol-
eration of "colored" communities in the French Antilles (in French, *gens
de couleur*) and the British West Indies. The more women who were present among the slaves and reproducing, the greater their economic value
and the greater the sensitivity of the societies in which they lived to the
families they raised—all of which intensified the tensions by including
proportions of girls and women half again as large—at least—as the Atlantic trade delivered African women to American shores. North America was the extreme case.

FEMALE AGENCY AS SLAVES

Ungendered slaves, implicitly male, are often portrayed as having only
three options when subjected to the violence and abuses characteristic of
slave-owning societies: submission, flight, or revolt—all of them implicitly masculine strategies. However, in reality the work and lives of women
as slaves varied considerably more widely than did those of males, as did
their reactions to the differing kinds of exploitation that women and men
suffered. Whereas male slaves in Western systems of slavery were valued
predominantly for their physical strength, and from the mid-seventeenth
century were employed mostly as unskilled manual labor, for the slave
owner female slaves represented assets of greater flexibility and thus more
potential uses—including reproduction.

   In large-scale, particularly deeply indebted economic sectors, women
were forced into the same types of heavy labor as men. The conventional
Atlantic model of slavery is constructed around "plantations"—classically Caribbean sugar, but also rice and tobacco in colonial North America, later cotton in the United States, and also coffee (and also often-
neglected cotton) in Brazil—in which women worked unrelentingly
alongside men. Thus on the Caribbean sugar plantations, as Laurence
Brown and Tara Inniss as well as Morgan detail, adult men and women
comprised the "first" and "second" gangs assigned to hard labor in the
canebrakes.[14] However, this system was far from universal, even in the
Americas, and it was significantly differentiated for women and men. In

eighteenth-century Rio de Janeiro, as Mariza de Carvalho Soares suggests, as well as elsewhere in Brazil as proposed by Miller, slaves, male and female, were employed in a wide variety of tasks, often sexually differentiated, some of which involved considerable lack of constraint and the opportunity for self-enrichment. Women in towns in Brazil and the Caribbean were especially evident in petty trading.[15] Even in parts of the United States not ordinarily portrayed as open to female initiative, as Edwards shows for largely rural counties in the antebellum South, bondswomen subtly and artfully manipulated the personal connections they had built, even in slavery, beyond the domains of their owners.

Unlike men, female slaves were also valued for their reproductive capacities, for their nurturing abilities as uniquely female wet-nurses and maternally experienced nannies, for their more arbitrarily gendered domestic house skills, and for sexual services that only they—as physically women—could provide for white males. The emotionality of the political debates swirling around the acceptable Jamaican "housekeeper," potentially virtuous (in spite of her "race")—as distinct from the more probably guilt-induced image of the scheming "jezebel"—that Altink traces reveals the extent to which a relationship originating in purely physical terms between some slave women and lonely masters, unencumbered by competing wives, could result in fondness, even respect, on both sides. This greater variety of often intimate positions available to women slaves in turn presented them with a potentially wider range of strategies than the violent few at the disposal of enslaved males. Sex is a powerful tool, emotionally as well as physically.

Scholars have conventionally focused on revolt as the ungendered slave reaction to exploitation. This emphasis on violence has heightened the not fully merited attention given to male slaves, who comprised by far the largest number of those who planned or executed rebellions, and who formed large majorities in maroon communities in the Americas. There are cases of women voluntarily joining such "rebels," and Krauthamer analyzes in subtle detail the strategies of enslaved women in the South Carolina Low Country escaping to the Native American Creek towns inland from the eighteenth-century southern seaboard that served as the equivalents to maroon refuges in the Caribbean or in Brazil. Recent work on the allegedly "African" so-called maroon *quilombo* of Palmares in northeastern Brazil (modern Alagoas) has turned up archaeological evidence—mostly pots, made by women—of a strong Native American presence, presumably and quite reasonably therefore women, given the sexual demography of flight.[16]

African women in these settlements were relatively scarce, since female slaves characteristically refrained from fleeing, often to remain on plantations or in households with their children. The overwhelming majorities of men in maroon communities therefore sometimes resorted to stealing the women they desired, for sexual services and for companionship. However, as Robertson and Robinson remind us, the heavy labor demanded of women in these encampments was also very likely a consideration in limiting their interest in fleeing to them to escape slavery. In addition, maroon bands sought sanctuary in remote and generally inhospitable areas, where the harsh realities of life in forest locations deliberately chosen for difficulty of access and therefore in terrain that was difficult to cultivate may well have acted as a further disincentive to female flight there. The fieldwork to which they would there be compelled to dedicate themselves could hardly have seemed more attractive than the work they performed on English or Portuguese or French plantations. Krauthamer, in this volume, explores these contradictory considerations in terms of women who fled Carolina rice fields to the Creeks.

The male maroons were thus left to raid the plantations for food and supplies in order to survive. Few established a viably independent existence. Women tended to move more slowly than men and were thus recaptured more easily. Also, slave owners possibly exercised greater degrees of surveillance over female slaves, notably in situations where a pronounced sexual division of slave labor concentrated women within and around the masters' households. Thirdly, women with commitments to children and other enslaved kin or friends seldom considered flight or revolt a preferred option; in this volume Cottias and Krauthamer accent this consideration of enslaved women as reproducers.[17]

Nuanced analyses of slavery recognize that neither revolt nor flight was the sole or even necessarily the most effective response to slavery. Some forms of female slave resistance that took advantage of the specific attributes of women—thus converting potential vulnerabilities to strengths—are beginning to feature in the literature. In this volume, Edwards notes the ability of female slaves in the American South to manipulate rumors about white slave owners in order to damage their reputations in white society and also to undermine an owner's prosperity by humiliating themselves to diminish their value as human assets.[18]

Another form of female resistance that some Caribbeanist scholars have seen as widespread and often costly to their owners was bondswomen's alleged refusal to bear children. However, as both Morgan and Follett emphasize in this volume, the reasons for the generally low rate of slave reproduction in the West Indies were multiple and included a lethal range of physiological effects of overwork and undernourishment.[19] The physical and emotional stresses of slave life, the unsanitary conditions imposed on the slaves, and lethal tropical and subtropical disease environments where sugar grew profitably all depressed fertility and raised rates of infant mortality. Where a flourishing and well-financed trade in new Africans made replacements abundant and cheap, chiefly in the eighteenth-century Caribbean and in colonial Brazil, slave owners had little incentive to invest in measures that might promote natality. However, the rates of female slave reproduction did not improve even when slave owners imported younger slaves (as in nineteenth-century Brazil) or improved living conditions and provided primitive health care for slaves (as in the era of "amelioration" in the early-nineteenth-century West Indies), or where some slave women enjoyed comparatively more comfortable—if not leisured—lifestyles (as in Rio de Janeiro), implying that factors other than physical hardship were at work, including measures adopted by slave women to reduce conceptions and to induce early abortions.[20]

In this volume, however, Morgan contextualizes this contention of political intent in the physiology of reproduction under the brutalities of Jamaican sugar slavery. He concludes that the sheer physical exhaustion of forced labor in the canebrakes might have enabled antinatalist strategies, since it reduced fertility to marginal levels susceptible even to crude abortive and other techniques. Even so, sheer physical depletion probably was a factor of greater demographic significance than the political strategies that women slaves might have developed out of their bodily capacities as females. Follett's analysis of the uniquely detailed records of natality on Louisiana sugar estates confirms this argument, since the evident consistency of seasonal variations in births there with both work routines and nutrition seems to overwhelm intentional political strategies that presumably would not have varied throughout the year. We would observe also that the intricate relations of "production" and "reproduction" suggested here represent a significant and historicizing advance in conceptualizing this trope in the literature on women and slavery, as Robertson and Robinson cite literature that dichotomizes the two as logically incompatible abstractions. Logically, they may contrast; but historically, they both are among the multiple factors present in any given time and place, and in correspondingly varying combinations.

Thus, Follett, Morgan, and other scholars question a simplistic attribution of political intent or of the sheer ability of women slaves to control their reproductive bodies as significant influences on natality in the dangerous disease environments and brutal work regimens of sugar slavery.[21] Enslaved women could have curtailed their own reproduction out of a desire to avoid lives of slavery for their children, but only to limited degrees. In more instances they may, as women subject to the particular female burdens of slavery, have wanted simply to avoid the physical and material costs of bearing children. Or, as Cottias, Brown and Inniss, Smith, and Miller demonstrate in varying ways, they may have more often strategized politically in personal terms, not as a collective and categorical statement against slavery, to optimize their individual opportunities within it. Sexual relations with masters worked, as Altink suggests, at least for some; however infrequent the opportunities for or low the chances of success might be, it was an alternative more promising to women, uniquely as women, than resigning themselves to the ungendered isolation and neglect, if not also violence, of labor in the fields.

Enslaved females developed other tactics to improve their conditions of living and work.[22] Chief among these were matrifocal networks of kin, forged on both blood and fictive lines, again utilizing their ability to reproduce to lessen the burdens of forced production. Slave kinship relied not on single male heads of co-resident nuclear families but rather on a woman or a number of women. To the extent that owners tended to retain women more than men, clearly because of their potential as reproducers or nurturers, as well as sexual objects, these networks were more stable than male-centered strategies, since men were more likely than women to be sold or to escape. These matrifocal networks provided vital social and emotional support to all slaves. They also pulled in "kin" to assist in a wide variety of self-help measures, from the cultivation of small garden plots to providing child care for young mothers separated from their offspring to toil in the fields. Female networks like these may also have tended to decent burials for their members, privately—unlike men's public use of the Catholic Lay Brotherhood of Santo Elesbão and Santa Efigênia in eighteenth-century Rio de Janeiro.[23] It has even been contended that the overall experience of slavery enabled black women to claim an authority in America that they had lacked in Africa, although Soares argues that slave women could draw on African precedent for female authority.[24]

Some of the early literature crudely ascribed matrifocality among slave families in the Americas to extensions of central African "matrilineality."[25] In fact, female-centered households and local networks of quasi "kin" had no significant precedents in Africa. Matrilineality lodged authority over children primarily in males, the children's uncles (mother's brothers, hence *matri*-lineal) rather than in their fathers. The particular hardships of Western slavery provided ample reason for the women living together to care for one another and one another's children, using the terms of extended kinship from their personal backgrounds—and, for later generations, from their ancestry—to characterize entirely new and creative responses to the otherwise isolating conditions in which they lived. In this volume, Brown and Inniss delineate the multiple dimensions of these women-centered families and networks in Barbados, as strategies of women. American slavery denied the formation of a conjugal estate, a prohibition for which there was no African precedent. Insofar as matrilineality displaced authority over children from their fathers by tracing descent exclusively through their mothers, it condemned them to slavery as property of their owners, and later to exclusion on racial grounds.

The separation of female and male domestic spheres may have been more significant than "lineality," matri- or patri-, for women's strategies of surviving slavery as mothers. Separate residences for men and women, even as sexual partners and as parents, made economic sense by deriving income from two different sources. Emotionally, it lessened the—again African—heritage of patriarchal authority within the family. Their children, thus by implication their capacities as reproducing females, again figure prominently in the strategies of women peculiar to the highly commercial slavery of plantations in the Americas.

The descent rule of Western slavery—that the children followed the condition of the mother—also divorced biological fathers, free and white as well as "black" and slave, from any responsibility for, and often—for the enslaved—access to, their offspring. The taboo forbidding recognition of children of masters' sexual exploitation of their slave women operated most strongly in English/British colonies. In Jamaica, and presumably most other islands of the Caribbean, the enslaved partners in conjugal relationships lived on different plantations and could not share in raising infants they might have, for reasons of sheer practicality. Sale of a slave, for financial purposes or as a punishment, or distribution of the estates of deceased owners, separated mothers from their children less often than it sent adolescent and adult males off on their own. The pro-natal "amelioration" procedures adopted late in the history of slavery in British colonies rewarded women as mothers but not men as fathers. Diverse experiences in Africa, most of them in fact strongly patrilineal as well as patriarchal, could not have significantly contributed to the matrifocal and female-centered networks that women trapped together in slavery in the Americas created for themselves.

They also made these "kinship" systems means of sustaining cultural resistance to their owners. Within such networks of kinship, women elaborated ritual and belief systems, adapting and integrating elements both from their homelands and from Europe—notably Christianity, Catholic in Brazil, as Soares's paper demonstrates in intricate and intriguing detail. These shared customs of their own they also expressed in food rituals, dress and adornment, religion and magic.[26] A well-known example is the female rise to prominence in the *candomblé* "circles" among slave and freed women in northeastern Brazil.[27]

Sometimes the slave-owning society intervened, as in the earlier centuries in colonial Brazil, termed "baroque" by Soares, when the monarch charged the Catholic Church with channeling slave efforts to transcend their condition into hierarchical, male-dominated black "brotherhoods." Nevertheless, slave women challenged even these enclaves of male power, as Soares shows in her remarkable history of Victoria "Coura," an ex-slave woman in eighteenth-century Rio de Janeiro.[28] Slave women, she shows, became ironically empowered within slavery and assertive within their families and communities, slave and freed, in ways that contrasted sharply with the conventionally accepted image of female submissiveness and obscurity in the larger slave-owning society.[29] Analysis of "slaves" simply as labor, proprietarial and dominated, cannot reveal the gendered struggles within slavery any more than it can reveal the sexual and reproductive strategies of enslaved women to survive within slavery— itself a female strategy of resisting, as women, the masculinized ideology of civic exclusion, hence invisibility. Miller suggests intricate and varying but very substantive distinctions along these lines between gender and slavery that enabled enslaved women in the Americas to play off their multiple standings in these plural spheres to their personal advantage, and to the prospective advantage of their children.

Where the slave-owning society intensified civic standing to modern levels of prominence, female slaves adopted strategies to participate also in the institutions articulating it. Recent literature has revealed the considerable extent to which slaves, including women, exploited the openness of the Spanish judicial institutions necessary to create and control colonies to press their claims against their masters.[30] Even in the nineteenth-century United States, as Edwards reveals, female slaves acted upon the widespread recognition within local white communities that slaves were simultaneously "property" and "people" deserving of respect for socially responsible behavior. Some even developed ways to influence the practice of local law in their own favor.[31]

Slave women's involvement in the slave-owning societies in which they lived, essentially a "fifth-column" strategy, has been caricatured—no doubt by way of denying the real power of the strategy—as the Southern plantation "mammy." This idealized maternal presence was devoted to her master's household, a woman characterized by "rectitude, meekness, loyalty, unselfishness, a profound and sincere faith, devotion to the point of sacrifice, and a love of the family and children."[32] All these were qualities of the free, white domestic "wife and mother" developed at the same time in the broader gendering of the culture of the nineteenth-century United States.

The ideal domestic slave was a woman who had prior experience of work within a slave-owning household and came with a recommendation from her former master. Altink explores the ambiguities of the Jamaican slave women euphemistically accepted within white society, even at its higher levels, as "housekeepers." They raised respectable children of their fathers, even though they were also slaves by virtue of their mother's status.[33] The female slave companion of the master—often derogated as "concubine," seldom dignified as "mistress"—was a ubiquitous figure in the plantation zones of colonial and imperial Brazil, romanticized in retrospect in Gilberto Freyre's famous sociology of cultural and sexual miscegenation, as Miller accents.[34]

Some historians have interpreted the quasi-familial bonds forged between slaves and the members of the slave-owning family as "mammy," and also "auntie," both diminutives of legitimate mothers and aunts,[35] as self-serving collaboration by enslaved women that ignored the greater political interests of slaves in general. Although they demonstrate a female slave agency designed to alleviate personal hardships and overcome the isolation of slavery by creating a pseudo-family life, positions within the relatively trusting bosom of the master's family offered these female slaves endless opportunities to divert and extend the provisions and protection they received to members of their immediate families, and beyond them throughout the less privileged cohorts of slaves.[36]

Slave women who became the sexual partners or concubines of white men trod more treacherous personal and ideological terrain. Among whites, these women fed the caricature of the sensuous young black "jezebel" who threatened to undermine the family-based moral values of slave-owning society, and with them the central position of the legitimate wife rendered respectable as "white."[37] Slave women in informal liaisons might empower themselves through manipulating the white male, in some cases to the point that they obtained their freedom and joined the slave-owning society themselves. Their freedom gave them opportunities to free their own children, and this pattern appeared frequently in the coastal cities of colonial Brazil, and also in Barbados as Brown and Inniss detail in this volume. The issue, as Altink shows, acquired enormous political sensitivity in early-nineteenth-century Jamaica, as the freed descendants of masters and their slaves threatened to assume local political power in the unsettled politics of the era of emancipation.[38] Edwards shows how one domestic slave, Violet, in an extended white South Carolina planter family, confronted the son of the master and his wife on the basis of the highly personal privileges that she had evidently enjoyed in the household of the father.[39]

In societies governed by modern commercialized and civic categorical legal systems, which Edwards insightfully delineates as a creation of the nineteenth-century Atlantic region, unlike those governed by the Islamic *Sharia* or other earlier and much more personalistic seventeenth-century and earlier eighteenth-century European systems (including those of England and France), carried to the early colonies in the Hispanic and Lusophone Americas, the children of a slave woman and slave owner were not routinely freed if legally acknowledged by their father. Among the most extraordinary of such "successes" in North America was that of Anna Madgigine Jai Kingsley, enslaved in 1806 in Senegal, who was taken to Florida, where she became the concubine of her owner, Zephaniah Kingsley Jr., to whom she eventually bore four children. Kingsley subsequently married Anna Madgigine Jai, and in 1812, the year after he emancipated her and their children, she bought a five-acre plantation and twelve slaves.[40] Such successful transitions from the civic exclusion of slavery to success in the public sphere of a slave society were essentially individual, benefiting the women concerned and the offspring fathered by her owner, leaving the premise of slavery intact. Edwards contrasts the personalism of local communities in the antebellum U.S. South, which could recognize such individuals, even in slavery, with the exclusions defined by national courts as they categorized all slaves as "property" totally subject to the most brutal manifestations of absolute ownership.[41]

Finally, the great sensitivity in modern Western cultures to the presence of female slaves, and again unlike Africa, Asia, and even Europe before the sixteenth century, also reflects the growing importance of the nuclear family as a property-owning entity in a commercial culture based in individualism. Bondswomen acquired their images as dangerously sexually alluring, if not also fecund, jezebels or as safely postmaternal "mammies" as they and their children, empowered by growing degrees of civic "freedom," became potential competitors for the interests of the legitimate wife and her family in the master's estate. Successive New World regimes thus adapted the ancient Roman rule assigning the civil status of the child according to the condition of the mother, free or slave, not only denying the reproductive potential of the "jezebel" but also definitively excluding the master's offspring of her fantasized sexuality from any inheritance, except by express, public, and potentially humiliating manumission or testament.

These "legitimist" politics were realized in degrees varying throughout the slave colonies of the Americas. British North America led the way, following the ability of English women to survive in mid-seventeenth-century Virginia. In Jamaica, as Altink shows, British-based planting families condemned practices that they could not prevent. Brazilians accepted and even retrospectively celebrated the cultural and human contributions made by their female slaves.[42]

MANUMISSION, OR SELF-PURCHASE

Of the bondswomen in the Americas who obtained manumissions, relatively few did so through becoming the concubines or acknowledged companions of free white men of slave-owning households. More numerous were the female slaves, from Brazil to the Caribbean, but not in the United States, who purchased their freedom by accumulating sufficient funds to do so, and sometimes that of their children as well. In French colonies, the move to self-manumission by *rachat* (redemption, a euphemism for "purchase") among slave women of mixed European and African heritages gained momentum in the face of the refusal of white slave owners to acknowledge the children of their sexual liaisons with slave women by freeing them. The creation of the ideologically humanist French Republic had evidently sensitized French slave owners in the Antilles to the same threats to "legitimist" wives and affines that limited legal—though not personal, to judge from Edwards's Carolina legal cases—recognition of slave mistresses in the United States. Moitt reveals a surprisingly large number of such women in early-nineteenth-century French Guiana, Martinique, and Guadeloupe who sought to purchase liberty for themselves and their children. The French state proved amenable to their strategy, even subsidizing slave women's self-redemption; slave owners, whose agreement they had to obtain, and who were considerably less dedicated to abstract human rights, were less accommodating. Female owners of slaves—themselves not enfranchised, and therefore perhaps more dependent for personal standing and material comfort on the other women even more excluded from the civic realm—proved even more hostile than male masters to permitting women slaves to buy their freedom.[43]

Before 1800, and for most slaves for a long time after that, manumission thus had little to do with civic "freedom." While slavery endured, free women did not possess the franchise, even in the most developed western civic regimes; in their private lives the patriarchal domestic household prevailed. In North America at least, as several works have recently emphasized, manumission ended slave women's pervading fears of separation from kith and kin, through sale.[44] It mattered relatively little to them that it rarely also brought the passport to the autonomy and dignity for which "freedom" came to stand in the minds of male ex-slaves in the later nineteenth-century United States. The bonds of familial affection and passionate love severed by racial separation was a tragic heritage of slavery, as explored by Smith. If the sentiments of women writers in the Jim Crow era there reflected attitudes they had absorbed from their enslaved mothers' generation, "freedom" meant family. Personal or civic "freedom" for most emancipated women remained curtailed by a white patriarchal society that envisaged them racially as inferior and wanton beings who should follow respectable white women in welcoming the protection of male authority through marriage and limiting their activities to the domestic and religious spheres.

Former bondswomen resisted such pressures. As Brown and Inniss point out with reference to Barbados, former slave women fought to translate "freedom" into a vision of "family life" inspired by the kinship networks, fictive or biological, forged in slavery.[45] Indeed, it was only through this struggle in the transition to "freedom" that the structure and dynamics of families created by slaves under slavery in the West Indies became visible, in contrast to the American South, where slaves officially reconstituted families dispersed by the antebellum trade in slaves though availing themselves of postemancipation legal opportunities. In both regions emancipation revealed the importance of extended family networks and non-co-residential male-female partnerships rather than two-parent nuclear slave households. These broad and flexible "clusters of households of maternal kin"[46] had become critically important for the survival of plantation slaves in the British West Indies, at least in the generation that came of age by the last days of slavery, nearly three decades after abolition of the trade.

In the "transition" from slavery to freedom—a kind of categorical reversal, a civic rebirth, as white abolitionists and former slave owners saw it—these female slave networks were to be replaced with nuclear patri-centric families, reinforced—and controlled—by legalized marriage and its accompanying paternalist image of the domesticity of all females. Thus in the French West Indies, abolition rendered freed slave women subordinate to men as legal "minors" and excluded them from the vote, one of the primary rights of their newly gained French citizenship. Such civic subordination came close, in some cases, to a transfer of ownership rights from former slave owner to husband. Certainly for the assertive abolitionist state, patriarchal control was a vital means to ensure that newly freed women conformed to conventional patriarchal and domestic institutions of domination rather than establish potentially socially and politically destabilizing alternatives based on maternal-centered house-holds and nonlegal sexual and marital unions.[47] Former slave women's re-sistance to state-sponsored patriarchy also fed the fear in white society that in "free" female society they might sow the seeds of what they con-sidered to have been the female licentiousness, increasingly racialized, characteristic of slavery.[48]

For planters and other owners of enslaved women, the patriarchal nu-clear family had been a means to form small work units that could be ma-nipulated to supply their labor cheaply to meet the financial require-ments of the plantation economy. When formerly slave parents in the British West Indies resisted government attempts to force their free chil-dren into "apprenticeship" on the plantations, planters reacted by de-priving the parents of access to basic resources previously used to support families, such as garden plots, accommodation, and medical care, in an attempt to force their children off their parents' homesteads as the hard-ships of drought and famine had once, in Africa, compelled parents to sacrifice their offspring to slave dealers in the hope of saving their lives.[49]

By examining women as slaves in the Americas, this volume illustrates the many and varied strategies through time and space that slave owners used to exploit them as females. Women carried enormous weight in the fantasies of power, sexual as well as economic and political, of male mas-ters from the United States south to the Caribbean and Brazil, driving them to harass sexually and to abuse physically and mentally the women abandoned by the state—though less so by the Catholic Church—to their "owners." Moreover, bondswomen were less likely than male slaves to revolt against such abuses, or to flee and thus abandon their families and painfully constructed female networks within their enslavement. How-ever, the more varied and remunerative occupations of enslaved women, compared to their male counterparts, presented them with greater options to survive, beyond sheer resistance, than the violence to which competitive free male brutality forced enslaved men to resort. These female strategies of survival, of dignified endurance of humiliation, of preserving self and progeny, ranged from the forming of matrifocal kinship systems to ingratiating themselves as domestic "mammies" and working their ways into their owner's households as concubines. Tragically, by the Roman and modern Western rule of inheritance of the slave condition through women, they thus also risked condemning their children to slavery and themselves to the further challenges, ardently pursued by their masters' legitimate wives, of having to purchase freedom for their children, often at prices greatly inflated by the intense emotionalism of these exchanges. Some also found ways to undermine the reputation of their owners through rumor mongering or influencing local legal judgments in favor of acknowledging their personal presence as women, beyond their civic status as slaves.

Female slaves achieved manumission in greater numbers than men before the general movement to abolish slavery, many through exploiting their positions as concubines or devoted domestics, not to mention as mothers—acknowledged or not—of their masters' children. Some freed female slaves readily adapted to the rules of "free" Western society, a few themselves even becoming owners of slaves; perhaps their racially shaky standing in civic society compelled them to compensate by controlling others rendered even more vulnerable than themselves, by enslavement.

Once legally freed, women did not acquire the same civic liberty as their male counterparts, to whom they were generally forced, through marriage, to submit. However, some—at least in Barbados—strove to resist this renewed exclusion by maintaining matrifocal networks akin to those that they had forged in slavery. One senses a similar strategy in the French Islands. In the United States, they seem to have chosen the nuclear domestic family as their strategy; or, perhaps, the legal circumstances in which emancipation left them made husbands the advantageous choice, if only the lesser of two necessary evils. Ironically, free white women, confined in patriarchal households without that option, focused on securing their children's access to their husbands' wealth, and presumably their own futures as matriarchs.

Future research on bondswomen in Western and non-Western systems of slavery will reveal still more about the strategies by which women in slavery throughout the Americas sought to protect themselves and their children.[50] As this introductory essay has suggested, it will also give more

information about the distinctive roles of women slaves in intimate relationships of all sorts—even in the burgeoning Western commercial culture—and about their advantages as women, despite the growing categorical exclusion of slaves in Western nation-states that grew out of
slavery, and the subsequent exclusion of both "blacks" and "women" from
direct civic participation. Women's voluntary associations—"white" and
"black," religious and secular—thrived in every register throughout the
hemisphere, while a few determined suffragettes took on the political
challenge directly. We hope that the studies in this volume start to
reimagine, to rephrase Robinson and Robertson's title, women in slavery
and in freedom in ways that overcome the invisibility imposed upon
them by these modern commercial and national ideological worlds.

NOTES

1. Gwyn Campbell, Suzanne Miers, and Joseph C. Miller, eds., *Women and Slavery*,
vol. 1, *Africa, the Indian Ocean World, and the Medieval North Atlantic* (Athens: Ohio
University Press, 2007), hereafter referred to as the companion volume in this set.

2. "Women in Western Systems of Slavery," *Slavery and Abolition* 26, no. 2
(2005), special issue, ed. Gwyn Campbell, Suzanne Miers, and Joseph C. Miller. For
the papers on Mauritius, Cape Town, and the South African Republic included
there as "Western" see the companion volume in this set.

3. Henrice Altink, "Deviant and Dangerous: Proslavery Representations of Jamaican Slave Women's Sexuality, ca. 1780–1834," in this volume, places these images at the center of her analysis.

4. See, e.g., Gwyn Campbell, *An Economic History of Imperial Madagascar,
1750–1895* (New York: Cambridge University Press, 2005), 42; "Indian Slaves in
South Africa" (http://www.anc.org.za/ancdocs/history/solidarity/indiasa3.html, ac-
cessed 11/03/05); Paul E. Lovejoy, "Internal Markets or an Atlantic-Sahara Divide?
How Women Fit into the Slave Trade of West Africa," in the companion volume in
this set.

5. Juliana Barr, "From Captives to Slaves: Commodifying Indian Women in the
Borderlands," *Journal of American History* 92, no. 1 (2005): 19–46; and Brett Rush-
forth, "'A Little Flesh We Offer You': The Origins of Indian Slavery in New France,"
William and Mary Quarterly 60, no. 4 (2003): 777–808, among others. To date these
studies are primarily confined to North America; the almost certainly comparably
gendered aspect of ongoing enslavement of, and trade with, the natives of Portuguese Brazil has received less extensive attention, with the exception of the famous *bandeirantes* of seventeenth-century São Paulo; John Manuel Monteiro, *Negros
da terra: Índios e bandeirantes nas origens de São Paulo* ([São Paulo]: Companhia das
Letras, 1994).

6. See Gwyn Campbell, "Slavery and Other Forms of Unfree Labour in the Indian
Ocean World," in "The Structure of Slavery in Indian Ocean Africa and Asia," ed.

Gwyn Campbell, special issue of *Slavery and Abolition* 24, no. 2 (2003); Joseph C. Miller, "The Significance of Drought, Disease, and Famine in the Agriculturally Marginal Zones of West-Central Africa," *Journal of African History* 23, no. 1 (1982): 17–61.

7. Deborah G. White, *Ar'n't I a Woman? Female Slaves in the Plantation South* (New York: Norton, 1985).

8. Ira Berlin, *Many Thousands Gone: The First Two Centuries of Slavery in North America* (Cambridge, MA: Harvard University Press, 1999); shorter version in the expanded coverage of *Generations of Captivity: A History of African-American Slaves* (Cambridge MA: Belknap Press, 2003).

9. Laura F. Edwards, "Enslaved Women and the Law: Paradoxes of Subordination in the Postrevolutionary Carolinas," in this volume.

10. Winthrop D. Jordan, *White Over Black: American Attitudes toward the Negro, 1550–1812* (Chapel Hill: University of North Carolina Press, 1968).

11. Carl N. Degler, *Neither Black nor White: Slavery and Race Relations in Brazil and the United States* (New York: Macmillan, 1971).

12. David Eltis, "The Volume and Structure of the Transatlantic Slave Trade: A Reassessment," *William and Mary Quarterly* 58, no. 1 (2001): 17–46.

13. Magali Carrera, *Imagining Identity in New Spain: Race, Lineage, and the Colonial Body in Portraiture and Casta Paintings* (Austin: University of Texas Press, 2003); Ilona Katzew, *Casta Painting: Images of Race in Eighteenth-Century México* (New Haven: Yale University Press, 2004).

14. Laurence Brown and Tara Inniss, "Slave Women, Family Strategies, and the Transition to Freedom in Barbados, 1834–1841," in this volume. The uniformity of low skill levels was less the case in mines, where African slave labor was often skilled.

15. See, e.g., Mariza de Carvalho Soares, "Can Women Guide or Govern Men? Gendering Politics among African Catholics in Colonial Brazil," in this volume.

16. Pedro Paulo A. Funari, "Maroon, Race and Gender: Palmares Material Culture and Social Relations in a Runaway Settlement," in *Historical Archaeology: Back from the Edge*, ed. Pedro Paulo A. Funari, Siân Jones, and Martin Hall (London: Routledge, 1999), 308–27.

17. See Jennifer L. Morgan, *Laboring Women: Reproduction and Gender in New World Slavery* (Philadelphia: University of Pennsylvania Press, 2004), for by far the most sophisticated development of this emphasis.

18. Edwards, "Enslaved Women."

19. Kenneth Morgan, "Slave Women and Reproduction in Jamaica, ca. 1776–1834," in this volume.

20. E.g., Barbara Bush, *Slave Women in Caribbean Society, 1650–1838* (London: James Currey, 1990), and "Hard Labor: Women, Childbirth, and Resistance in British Caribbean Slave Societies," in *More than Chattel: Black Women and Slavery in the Americas*, ed. David Barry Gaspar and Darlene Clark Hine (Bloomington: Indiana University Press, 1996), or Michael Craton, *Searching for the Invisible Man: Slaves and Plantation Life in Jamaica* (Cambridge, MA: Harvard University Press, 1978); Marietta Morrissey, "Women's Work, Family Formation, and Reproduction among Caribbean Slaves," in *Caribbean Slavery in the Atlantic World*, ed. Hilary McD. Beckles and Verene Shepherd (New York: Markus Wiener, 1999), 670–82.

21. Richard Follett, "Gloomy Melancholy: Sexual Reproduction among Louisiana Slave Women, 1840–60," in this volume; see also Morgan, "Slave Women and Reproduction."

22. See, e.g., Jenny Sharpe, *Ghosts of Slavery: A Literary Archaeology of Black Women's Lives* (Minneapolis: University of Minnesota Press, 2003).

23. Soares, "Can Women Guide or Govern Men?"

24. Sharpe, *Ghosts of Slavery*; see also Soares, "Can Women Guide or Govern Men?"

25. E.g., Herbert G. Gutman, *The Black Family in Slavery and Freedom, 1750–1925* (New York: Pantheon, 1976).

26. Soares, "Can Women Guide or Govern Men?" See also Wendy Wilson Fall, "Malagasy in Antebellum Maryland and Virginia: Discovering Oral Traditions and Re-visiting Written Histories," unpublished presentation, conference on "Slavery, Unfree Labour and Revolt in Asia and the Indian Ocean Region / L'esclavage, la main-d'oeuvre forcée et la révolte en Asie et dans les pays riverains de l'Océan indien" (Colloque international/ International Conference, Avignon, 4–6 October 2001).

27. Maria Inês Côrtes de Oliveira, "The Reconstruction of Ethnicity in Bahia: The Case of the Nagô in the Nineteenth Century," 158–80, and João José Reis, "Ethnic Politics among Africans in Nineteenth-Century Bahia," 240–64, both in *Trans-Atlantic Dimensions of Ethnicity in the African Diaspora*, ed. Paul E. Lovejoy and David V. Trotman (London: Continuum, 2003).

28. Soares, "Can Women Guide or Govern Men?"

29. White, *Ar'n't I a Woman*; Brown and Inniss, "Slave Women, Family Strategies."

30. Jane Landers, "African-American Women and Their Pursuit of Rights Through Eighteenth-Century Spanish Texts," in *Haunted Bodies: Gender and Southern Texts*, ed. Anne Goodwyn Jones and Susan V. Donaldson (Charlottesville: University Press of Virginia, 1997), 56–76; Kathryn Joy McKnight, "The Diabolical Pacts of Slavery: The Stories of Two Mulatto Slaves before the Inquisition in New Spain," *Revista de estudios hispánicos* 37, no. 4 (2003): 509–36.

31. Edwards, "Enslaved Women."

32. Bonneville (1900) quoted in Myriam Cottias, "Free but Minor: Slave Women, Citizenship, Respectability, and Social Antagonism in the French Antilles, 1830–90," in this volume.

33. Altink, "Deviant and Dangerous."

34. Gilberto Freyre, *Casa-grande e senzala* (Rio de Janeiro: Olympio, 1933); translated as *The Masters and the Slaves: A Study in the Development of Brazilian Civilization*, trans. Samuel Putnam (New York: Knopf, 1946).

35. See, e.g., Edwards, "Enslaved Women."

36. A point emphasized in the paper by Elizabeth Grzymala Jordan, "It All Comes Out in the Wash: Engendering Archaeological Interpretations of Slavery," in the companion volume in this set, with reference to *Engendering African American Archaeology: A Southern Perspective*, ed. Amy Young (Knoxville: University of Tennessee Press, 2004).

37. Sharpe, *Ghosts of Slavery*.

38. Altink, "Deviant and Dangerous."

39. Edwards, "Enslaved Women."

40. Daniel L. Schafer, *Anna Madgigine Jai Kingsley: African Princess, Florida Slave, Plantation Slaveowner* (Gainesville: University Press of Florida, 2003).

41. Edwards, "Enslaved Women."

42. But not, apparently, in the sugar parishes of Louisiana, where rapid rates of economic growth and the maturing Victorian morality of the nineteenth-century United States kept most women slaves in male-like positions as brute labor, with the antinatal consequences that Follett details in "Gloomy Melancholy." Morgan, "Slave Women and Reproduction," implicitly focuses on the field slaves and their strategies of natality rather than the jezebels and mammies.

43. Bernard Moitt, "Pricing Freedom in the French Caribbean: Women, Men, Children, and Redemption from Slavery in the 1840s," in this volume.

44. See, e.g., Joseph Miller, "Retention, Re-invention, and Remembering: Restoring Identities Through Enslavement in Africa and Under Slavery in Brazil," in *Enslaving Connections: Changing Cultures of Africa and Brazil during the Era of Slavery*, ed. José C. Curto and Paul E. Lovejoy (Amherst, NY: Prometheus/Humanity Books, 2003), 81–121.

45. Brown and Inniss, "Slave Women, Family Strategies."

46. Christine Barrow, "'Living in Sin': Church and Common-Law Union in Barbados," *Journal of Caribbean History* 29, no. 2 (1996): 249, quoted in Brown and Inniss, "Slave Women, Family Strategies"; see also Cottias, "Free but Minor."

47. Cottias, "Free but Minor."

48. White, *Ar'n't I a Woman*; Cottias, "Free but Minor."

49. Brown and Inniss, "Slave Women, Family Strategies."

50. *Children in Slavery*, ed. Gwyn Campbell, Suzanne Miers, and Joseph C. Miller (in preparation).

1

The Reproductive Biology
of Sugar Slavery

1

SLAVE WOMEN AND REPRODUCTION
IN JAMAICA, CA. 1776–1834

KENNETH MORGAN

The problem of creating a self-reproducing population of slaves after the British Atlantic slave trade ended in 1807 meant that the fecundity of slave women became central to the viability of plantation slavery in the British Caribbean. Such women were noticeably less fertile than their North American sisters. In the second half of the eighteenth century 40 to 50 percent of the slaves on Jamaican sugar estates were females, but gross reproduction rates did not reflect that relative parity between the sexes.[1] About half the female slave population in the British Caribbean in the mid-eighteenth century and as many as a third at the time of emancipation remained childless, compared with only 10 percent of slave women in the United States.[2] Before 1807 British Caribbean slave owners regarded buying slaves—rather than breeding them—as a necessary practice. Planters calculated the costs of purchasing adult and adolescent Africans as opposed to rearing children themselves and concluded that

This chapter is a slightly revised version of an article published in *History* 91, no. 302 (April 2006): 231–53. I thank Joseph C. Miller for excellent advice about the shape and content of the article and an anonymous reader for *History*, who suggested additional references. Leigh Morgan provided helpful comments on a draft version. The usual disclaimer applies. I am grateful to Lord Clarendon for permission to cite documents from the Clarendon Deposit at the Bodleian Library, Oxford, and to the other archives cited that facilitated my research. The Leverhulme Trust provided funds to support my attendance at the Fourth Avignon Conference on Slavery and Forced Labour, University of Avignon, October 2002, where this paper was originally presented.

they would not encourage their seasoned women slaves to breed "as thereby so much work is lost in their attendance upon their infants."[3]

The low priority they gave to breeding slaves before 1807 was acknowledged during the American War of Independence by the attorney to Hope Plantation, a Jamaican sugar estate, who wrote that a decrease of slaves was "the case with every Estate in the Island, at least with very few exceptions; I have never heard but of two, and both those lye in the interior parts of the country."[4] After 1807, with the legal end of the British slave trade, planters faced a necessity to keep up the stock of slaves by breeding.[5] Yet the policy was not successful, because the slave population declined in all save one of the British Caribbean islands in the years leading up to slave emancipation in 1834.[6]

Both the scattered data available before 1807 and the much fuller statistics from the post-1817 period show that the crisis of reproduction was all too apparent. Although no imperial censuses document this demographic problem before the abolition of the British slave trade, occasional lists for individual plantations, scattered population data for some Caribbean islands, and statistics on slave imports allow estimation of general trends in fertility and mortality. Full registration requirements for slaves after 1817 meant, however, that six triennial censuses of the entire British Caribbean slave population are available for the final two decades of slavery. Statistics gathered from these sources show the extent of the demographic problem. Jamaica imported 575,000 African captives in the eighteenth century, but, owing to extensive mortality, this increased the enslaved population of the island by only around 250,000. Of these Africans disembarked in Jamaica, at least 60 percent were male because planters generally purchased healthy adult "saltwater" males in preference to African women.[7] Between 1807, when these purchases ended, and 1834 the Jamaican slave population fell by 43,000, a decline of 12 percent. Continuing high mortality, especially among aging African slaves, contributed significantly to this fall. Although a small percentage of the decline is attributable to manumissions and runaways, solid demographic evidence leaves no doubt that breeding failed to maintain the population of slaves after imports had ended.[8]

Matthew Gregory ("Monk") Lewis, the novelist and absentee Jamaican proprietor, summarized the problem: when visiting his sugar estate in Westmoreland Parish in 1817, a property with 330 slaves and more women than men, he noted that "in spite of all indulgences and inducements, not more than twelve or thirteen children have been added annually to the list of births." He acknowledged, however, that he had lost track of several infants who were not counted as births. In March 1817 he complained that he had only 8 women out of 150 on the "breeding list."[9] Modern analysis of two Jamaican sugar estates and one livestock "pen" (i.e., cattle-raising estate) between 1817 and 1832 shows that creole slave women at the height of their fertility, ages twenty-five to twenty-nine, bore 112 babies per thousand woman-years, while African women bore only 64. During the same period the relatively small ratio of 32 births per thousand woman-years was recorded for younger creole slave women at ages fifteen through nineteen, the first quinquennium after menarche. The fertility rates for a series of other plantations in Jamaica from 1754 to 1832 ranged much higher, from 79 to 108 births per thousand woman-years at ages fifteen to forty-four. However, all these ratios are much lower than peak fertility in modern Jamaica, which yields 299 infants per thousand woman-years at ages twenty to twenty-four.[10]

Historians have pointed to several possible reasons for these poor reproductive rates among British West Indian slaves. One line of interpretation emphasizes the debilitating consequences of slavery: the poor nutritional state of slaves, heavy infant mortality, strenuous working demands imposed by sugar cultivation, and the brutality of the overseer's whip. Dietary deficiencies in protein and calcium, the high incidence of deaths among infants, the severity of the gang system on plantations, and the underlying discipline imposed by white estate personnel on slaves are other essential parts of this explanation. The exact relationships among these factors, however, are recognized as difficult to determine.[11] A second line of interpretation emphasizes the agency of slave women in resisting biological reproduction as a political statement against the system of slavery. This view focuses on strategies deployed to avoid pregnancy and acts undertaken to curtail pregnancies and unwanted births, such as abortion and infanticide. In this line of analysis, slave women assume the major role in determining the predisposition to pregnancy and the fates of babies over the nine-month gestational cycle and in the first weeks of life. The emphasis falls on the political resistance of slave women in refusing to enrich their owners by bearing children who would be their property.[12] A third type of interpretation also places emphasis on slave agency in reproduction but with no overt political emphasis. The main focus here is on culture: prolonged lactation practices, which lengthened intervals between pregnancies, and taboos against the resumption of intercourse for several months after giving birth. These cultural practices, it is argued, stemmed from the women's African backgrounds, brought to Jamaica via the transatlantic slave trade.[13]

Many cultural practices limiting fertility lack convincing evidence, given the intimate nature of the subject. Thus, for instance, very little is known about the extent of sexual intercourse among adult slaves or about the resumption of intercourse by slave women after delivering children. But it may be useful to review all the potential barriers to reproduction among British Caribbean slaves, not to distinguish their relative effects but rather to assess their cumulative consequences for reproduction, particularly in the context of sugar plantations, and secondarily in relation to the agency that female slaves may have exercised through their own reproductive strategies. This chapter attempts such an evaluation for Jamaica, the largest and most productive sugar island in the British West Indies. In particular, it focuses on the difficult material circumstances of slavery that biologically constrained reproductive rates among Jamaican female slaves, well beyond the extent to which slave women's cultural and political preferences may explain their low fertility.

The source material used in the analysis consists of contemporary observations by doctors and planters; evidence produced by modern demographic, economic, social, and cultural historians; and the findings of modern biologists and students of third world fertility. The contemporary evidence is mainly taken from the writings of white planters, doctors and estate attorneys that dominate the documentary record on slavery in British America. Slaves left virtually no direct testimony on the issues discussed in this essay. Consequently, the views of slave women in Jamaica cannot be presented. The planters often had a prejudiced view toward their slaves, based on their sense of racial superiority and their economic need to maintain their slave labor force.

The period discussed here, however, was one when slave productivity and amelioration of the conditions in which slaves lived were both emphasized. Planters needed to work slaves hard to keep up output levels on sugar plantations, the more so after the British slave trade ended in 1808 and problems ensued in breeding slaves from existing stock. But planters were also under pressure from abolitionists to ameliorate slave working and living conditions in order to justify the continued existence of slavery. This tension between productivity and its hardships and amelioration in the interest of reproduction emerges in the writings of planters and their representatives. Some evidence cited below was written by absentee owners who never visited Jamaica; their views were therefore circumscribed by common assumptions and prejudices about the personalities and behavior of slaves.

PRODUCTION AND REPRODUCTION

Slaves' reproduction was inevitably linked closely to their material and working lives. Harm to the fetus during pregnancy, which can result in miscarriage or stillbirth, is generally caused by the mother's nutrition, by mechanical injury, or by abnormal positions while at work.[14] Inadequate nutrition was the constant predisposing factor in the background of slave women's lives in Jamaica. Since severe maternal malnutrition is the leading cause of stillbirths in third world countries today, it is safe to take seriously numerous reports of the nutritional deprivations of slavery in Jamaica as limiting slave mothers' ability to bear surviving children through the same mechanisms and thus to similar degrees.

Slaves were fed on a diet of mainly grain, vegetables, and dried fish. On Jamaica they were required to cultivate their own provisions to feed themselves rather than being able to rely on masters' rations. Imported foodstuffs sometimes added to the slaves' diets, but shortages occurred when periods of war reduced imported dry provisions (wheat, flour, other grains) from North America, notably during the American War of Independence.[15] Despite these imported foods, malnutrition was common among the West Indian slave population. The slave diet was monotonous and deficient in thiamine, calcium, and vitamin A, though quantitative estimates of rations provided by masters are patchy.[16] Robert Dirks's data suggest that the average plantation food allowance amounted to 1,500 to 2,000 calories and approximately 45 grams of protein per day.[17] Under average conditions men require roughly 3,200 calories a day and women 2,300, metabolic rates for women being slower than for men. Under conditions of exceptionally heavy labor, both male and female workers need at least an additional 450 calories.[18] Thus female slaves in the British Caribbean, let alone pregnant slaves, received minimally adequate calories at best.

The imbalanced diet weakened women slaves more than men, since female physiology requires three times more iron, owing to menstruation. Protein and calcium requirements for pregnant and lactating women are also higher than for adult males; 30 to 50 percent more thiamine is required.[19] Slaves deficient in thiamine would have been unable to utilize riboflavin and niacin, which would have upset the metabolism of all the B vitamins.[20] Yet evidence suggests that the all-important protein rations given to slave families were mostly consumed by men. Traditionally in West Africa men had taken priority in helpings from the cooking pot. Similarly, in the Caribbean during the slavery era, men ate most of the available animal protein.[21]

Contemporary observers saw irregularities in the menstrual cycle as in-hibiting Caribbean slave women's reproduction. Although they did not pinpoint malnutrition as a cause of amenorrhea (abnormal cessation of the menstrual period), they sometimes related malnutrition to slave women's practice of geophagy—"dirt eating." James Thomson, a doctor who practiced medicine in Jamaica and the author of a book on the dis-eases of black people there, wrote in 1820 that "women who indulge [in dirt eating] soon lose their monthly period."[22] Dirt eating was general in British Caribbean slave society: slaves regularly ate cakes of baked clay (*aboo*) as a natural, if unconscious, response to nutritional deficiency. Women, in particular, ate the fine clays, which they could purchase eas-ily in markets.[23] The white elite derided the practice. "Such is the craving appetite for this abominable custom," a planter manual stated, "that few, either children or adults, can be broken of it, when once they begin to taste and swallow its insidious, slow poison."[24]

It is now known that dirt eating can be beneficial for people suffering from thiamine deficiency.[25] Modern medical findings do not support the notion that geophagy directly halts menstruation, but it is a response to deficiencies in iron. Moreover, amenorrhea is generally linked to malnu-trition. Not only does malnutrition disrupt the regular menstrual cycle, it can also delay the onset of menarche and hinder postpartum recovery, thereby limiting further pregnancies.[26] Although planters often com-plained of slave women's "obstruction of the menses," they had no aware-ness of its underlying nutritional causes. Edward Long, the well-known planter-historian of Jamaica, suggested "their using restringent baths, or washing themselves in cool water at improper periods" could have re-sulted in these "obstructions."[27] Such beliefs have now been relegated to the realm of old wives' tales.

The psychological bases for interruptions in the menstrual cycle are still not fully understood but may also have contributed. Studies carried out on survivors of concentration camps give some weight to the argu-ment that emotional stress can halt the menstrual cycle. And yet one should not push the comparison too far. Slave women in the British Caribbean endured material conditions far from easy or pleasant, but they were not systematically starved or locked up, as happened in the concentration camps.[28] That slave women routinely undertook highly demanding physical labor suggests that their bodies could withstand the arduous agricultural work of the slave regime—though very likely only at the expense of halting their menstrual cycles.

Excessive labor also contributed to low slave natality. Most women slaves on sugar plantations labored in the two main field gangs that undertook the heavy agricultural work. In the British West Indies, women out-numbered men in the "great gangs," which carried out the most strenu-ous tasks of cane holing, planting, and harvesting sugar, all under enor-mous pressures of time. In a sample of four Caribbean slave societies in the late eighteenth and early nineteenth centuries—Barbados, Martinique, Jamaica, Cuba—the women in the fields outnumbered men. The crude birth rate remained low in all these islands except Barbados, the one British West Indian slave society that had a majority of women from the early eighteenth century onward.[29] Between 1801 and 1831 on Meso-potamia, a sugar estate in Jamaica's Westmoreland Parish, the 130 slave women in their prime childbearing years (twenty to twenty-nine) spent 88 percent of their working time in these gangs, mostly the great gang.[30] The attorneys for the estate claimed in 1812 that these slaves were not badly treated or worked hard and that there were "no Negroes in the parish of Westmoreland more indulged, better fed or better clothed."[31] But even though the absentee owner of this estate encouraged humane treatment of his female slaves, they were chronically overworked and failed to achieve good reproductive rates.[32]

Cultivating sugar was more physically demanding than working any other plantation crop, and sugar cultivation and high slave mortality have been connected on nineteenth-century Louisiana sugar plantations as well as in their Caribbean counterparts. The same link between sugar and mortality can also be found in Spanish Cuba and Portuguese Brazil.[33] The long hours of standing up and the heavy lifting of sugar cultivation would have inhibited the ovarian function and procreative fitness of many slave women.[34] The early months of pregnancy are when women are most susceptible to miscarriage, yet female Jamaican slaves, pregnant or not, were subject to excessive stooping, carried heavy weights, and toiled under unceasing compulsion during the crop period. Pregnant women worked in the cane fields until six weeks before expected delivery.[35]

Planters were well aware of the risks they imposed on the pregnant women they owned. In the last decade of slavery in Jamaica, when ter-mination of imported replacements had turned attention to local natal-ity, they excused women field workers from the great gang once they made it known they were pregnant. Four weeks after delivery they were per-mitted to return to work in the "second gang," responsible for weeding and other lighter tasks, so long as they continued to breastfeed.[36] Despite their awareness, planters had earlier found it difficult, or were unwilling, to excuse pregnant women from severely demanding fieldwork. The links between overwork and the low rates of reproduction in British West In-dian slave populations are therefore evident.

Reproduction among West Indian slave women was higher among those assigned to domestic tasks rather than work in the fields. Edward Long, who owned plantations in Jamaica and lived there for a number of years, noted in 1774 that "those Negroes breed the best, whose labour is least, or easiest. Thus the domestic Negroes have more children, in proportion, than those on penns; and the latter, than those who are employed on sugar-plantations."[37] In addition, African slave women had poorer reproductive histories than locally born creoles. Data for Worthy Park Plantation, in St. Thomas-in-the-Vale Parish, show that by 1834 the creole birth rate had surpassed the death rate, indicating that slaves on that sugar estate were approaching natural reproductive increase.[38] In the seventy years before 1831 only 49 percent (19 of 39) of the African women with complete birth histories at the Mesopotamia sugar estate had recorded live births; they averaged 2.7 children each. On the same plantation 53 of the 97 creole slave women (55 percent) had babies; they averaged 3.7 children each.[39] Demographic evidence for women whose age groups had the highest fertility in the British Caribbean as a whole shows that creoles were everywhere almost half again as fertile as Africans.[40]

Severe physical punishment must have also been antagonistic to their fertility, particularly against the background of the grueling demands that sugar cultivation placed on women's bodies.[41] White overseers and black slave drivers showed little accommodation in disciplining pregnant women. Thomas Thistlewood, an overseer in Westmoreland Parish, though a notoriously extreme example, regularly flogged slaves of both sexes and hired out his pregnant women as field laborers at the full rate of pay until they were within two or three months of delivery.[42] By the turn of the nineteenth century it had become standard practice to lay pregnant women face-down over a hole dug in the ground to receive their bulging belly and then to flog them on the back.[43] Monk Lewis stated that "white overseers and bookkeepers . . . [kicked] black women in the belly from one end of Jamaica to the other."[44] Black drivers, who often administered floggings, were just as harsh to female slaves as to males. Until the growing attention to natality during the final years of slavery, Jamaica's laws gave no special relief from beating for women, whether they were pregnant or not.[45] Severe beatings could sometimes lead to a prolapsed uterus, which, apart from causing lower abdominal pain and sometimes urinary incontinence, could result in premature labor and therefore miscarriage. John Williamson, a doctor who practiced medicine in Jamaica between 1798 and 1812, recorded in 1817 that "prolapses of the uterus or womb . . . in consequence of harsh treatment, are very common in Jamaica."[46] Given this extensive testimony, it is unsurprising that numerous abolitionist critiques drew attention to the cruelty of flogging pregnant slaves.[47]

Numerous infectious diseases compounded the morbidity among slave women in Jamaica attributable to malnutrition. Many of these infections had devastating effects on pregnancies. Syphilis, yaws, and elephantiasis, complaints common in the Caribbean, all increased the likelihood of miscarriage or stillbirth. Epidemics of smallpox, measles, and scarlet fever frequently added to general mortality rates. Dysentery was a major killer of those weakened by overwork and malnourishment. Diarrheal disease was more than twice as likely to affect female field hands as female domestics. Slaves sometimes caught colds and fevers through toiling in the fields in wet clothes. They were rarely issued shoes or stockings and consequently were prone to cuts and bruises on their feet, which could turn into septic sores or gangrene. Lack of shoes allowed the entrance of chigoes into the body, causing elephantiasis, and assisted the entrance of hookworm, which further depleted slaves' nutritional status. The interaction of malnutrition and infection was far more serious than would be expected from the combined effect of the two working independently.[48] Of course, not all the above diseases or infections were confined to women of childbearing years; but pregnancy considerably heightened the severity of diseases and infections to which female slaves were susceptible.

If the poor nutrition among sugar slaves and the diseases it aggravated, strenuous work demands in the fields, and severe physical punishment thus all inhibited reproduction among slave women, most planters were loath to search too closely for causes that would reflect badly on the slave regime that they enforced. Hence plentiful writings blamed low fertility on the dress, customs, habitual ignorance, and sexual immorality of the slaves themselves. They applied the classic slave myth of animal-like sexual promiscuity to a stereotyped "black woman." Her alleged incapacity for self-regulation justified economic and sexual abuse in the name of responsible discipline. The nakedness in which masters left their female slaves also encouraged that inaccurate image of wanton lust. White sojourners in the Caribbean were unaccustomed to seeing women unclothed in public, and they equated their own lascivious reaction to exposure of the flesh of Afro-Caribbean women with lax sexual mores on the parts of the women they observed.[49]

But it was not just slave women's habits of dress, forced or not, that excited white racial prejudice; customs were also criticized. The Jamaican committee responsible for the overseeing of slaves reporting to the government's 1789 inquiry into the slave trade condemned what it presented as casual mating practices and polygyny among Jamaican slave women.[50] The attorney of Mesopotamia plantation attributed the lack of pregnant slave women there to "their incontinency & their being so much addicted to polygamy which is scarcely possible to prevent."[51] The Unitarian minister Thomas Cooper, hired by absentee proprietor Robert Hibbert to convert the slaves on Georgia, his plantation in Hanover Parish, attributed the low birth rate on the estate to the morally degraded condition of the slaves and, in particular, to promiscuity, prostitution, and the spread of sexually transmitted diseases, though he also acknowledged hard work and severe punishment as additional contributing factors.[52] The Bristol absentee slave owner Richard Bright considered that "loose conduct" among the slave women on his Jamaican sugar estates had led to the frequency of miscarriages and stillbirths there. He implied that promiscuity and disease were common and that recent problems in sustaining live births were the result of "disease which had become inveterate in the Constitution and therefore can only be referred to as lamentable instances of the effects of early moral depravity."[53]

In fact, sexually transmitted diseases contributed to the prevailing low natality of slave women in Jamaica, if only to a limited extent. Syphilis in the last six months of pregnancy harms the fetus and usually results in stillbirth. Contemporaries singled out venereal disease as an affliction of pregnant slave women. Simon Taylor, the wealthiest Jamaican sugar tycoon of the eighteenth century, complained in 1789 that venereal disease was rife at his Golden Grove plantation and blamed these attacks on the lax mores of black women.[54] John Wedderburn, a planter who had lived in Jamaica for more than a quarter of a century, made the same point to a committee of the House of Commons in March 1790. Noting that Jamaican slave women did not breed as well as working women in Britain, he attributed the cause of their low natality to "promiscuous intercourse between the sexes" that "often occasions venereal complaints, which frequently destroy the constitution."[55] Thomson pointed to the "early and unbound indulgence in venereal pleasure [as] a common cause of sterility. The parts are left in so morbid a state as to be unfit for impregnation; the uterine and vaginal vessels are distended, and a perpetual discharge, or flux albus, is the consequence."[56]

In spite of these slights to slave women's morality, observers in fact noted low incidences of venereal disease among British Caribbean slave populations, and the West Indian variant of syphilis—often nonvenereal—

was less contagious than the strain found in Europe. Dr. Thomas Dancer, a trained physician who practiced in Jamaica at the end of the eighteenth century, considered that venereal disease found in the Caribbean was a relatively mild form of the pathogen and difficult to detect.[57] Only 0.5 percent of a sample of 2,394 slaves living on the Jamaican estates of William Beckford and John Tharp were reported as infected with venereal disease.[58] However, evaluating the validity of these contemporary comments is difficult because the strain of venereal disease is usually not mentioned, and therefore the specific effects it might have had on pregnant slave women cannot be pinpointed.

These attributions of the alleged promiscuity of slave women to their racial character and African backgrounds were, of course, inaccurate. Olaudah Equiano, the famous black writer and abolitionist of the late eighteenth century, wrote of women in his African homeland that he did not "remember to have ever heard of an instance of incontinence amongst them before marriage."[59] Promiscuity, where it existed, was sexual exploitation of black women by white overseers, managers, and other plantation personnel, who had sex with the black women whom they could subject to their demands.[60] Since the nuclear family was rather a precarious institution among slaves in Jamaica, male and female slaves often found cohabitation difficult, and some stable and exclusive intimate relationships involved travel from one estate to another for slaves allowed to do so. Such mobility could easily be mistaken by whites for promiscuity. When the truncated households and infrequency of mating—owing to limited movements between estates of the partners in stable relationships—are added to the white male pursuit and sexual violation of female slaves, the consequences for reproducing slave children were serious.[61]

One modern historical hypothesis to explain the poorer reproductive record of West Indian slaves compared with their North American counterparts argues that these fertility differentials can be explained, at least in part, "by the differences in the period of child spacing," and that "the latter were partially determined by lactation practices." African women in the British Caribbean appear to have nursed their children for two years, sometimes up to three or four years, whereas North American slave women breastfed their infants no longer than a year. Longer lactation, it is argued, would have served as a natural means of contraception, either through the physiological suppression of fertility in the mother by producing breast milk or through the social impact of constant nurturing of infants and consequent unavailability to men. Lactation periods of two, three, or four years have been interpreted as carryovers from traditions in West African societies.[62]

How well does this argument fit the evidence? Certainly, planters were concerned over the lengthy lactation of their female slaves. In 1811 Dr. David Collins, author of a well-known handbook on the management of slaves, wrote that "Negroes are universally fond of suckling their children for a long time. If you permit them, they will extend it to the third year."[63] The merchant and planter William Shand, who had interests in various Jamaican properties, reported in 1832 that "long weaning . . . is very much against their breeding."[64] The evidence for the postabolition nineteenth-century British Caribbean suggests that breastfeeding periods varied considerably but that the average nursing cycle lasted less than in earlier, prenatalist, periods—about eighteen months.[65] After the end of slavery the Jamaican population increased largely due to an excess of births over deaths.[66] One can hypothesize that this increase in reproduction and reduction in lactation periods occurred because free black women received better nutrition and endured less demanding work schedules than when most of them had been tied to the punishing work regimes of sugar.

Malnutrition increases amenorrhea to three to four years in societies where nursing and late weaning are common.[67] The contraceptive benefit of lactation may last no longer than a year in relatively well fed and medically sound populations,[68] but this modern finding would scarcely have applied to eighteenth-century Jamaica. Malnourished mothers there extended lactation because they found it difficult to secure reliable sources of other food for their infants. The evidence suggests that Caribbean slave rations contained little protein or fat, and that could have disrupted several reproductive functions of slave women, including a delayed age of menarche, irregular ovulation, and early menopause.[69] The precarious health of women slaves, aggravated by pregnancy, the rigors of childbirth, lengthy lactation, and early return to fieldwork, left many female slaves in a constant state of nutritional deprivation. Thomson noted that the practice of keeping the child on the breast "until, in their own phraseology, the child can bring its mother a calabash full of water" results in "numbers [of mothers] which never recover. . . . They fall into a consumption or emaciated state, in which they linger for a few years."[70]

Postpartum taboos against a mother's resumption of intercourse during the period of nursing young children are well attested for numerous societies around the premodern world. Such taboos protect the health of both mother and child. In Africa the period of abstinence was often two years.[71] Thus Thomas Winterbottom recorded that, on a visit to Sierra Leone in 1803, a strong prohibition against intercourse during lactation was believed to protect the child from sickness.[72] This means of extending birth spacing appears to have survived in the Afro-Jamaican population. It was particularly effective in preventing the dangers of pregnancy under slavery soon after a mother gave birth. Africans probably practiced extended birth spacing more than creoles. Certainly, at Mesopotamia estate the creole women extended their birth intervals to lesser degrees and had greater fertility than the African women.[73] It is likely that birth-spacing differentials among African and creole slave women in Jamaica were as much the result of avoiding postpartum intercourse as the result of prolonged lactation.

African women used certain herbs and infusions for contraceptive purposes. In addition, plants such as okra and aloe were transported to the Caribbean, where they were used as abortifacients.[74] Contemporaries—particularly planters—condemned slave women for widespread practices of self-abortion as well as for promiscuity. Dr. John Quier, an experienced doctor based at Worthy Park for fifty-five years, highlighted abortions, which he felt were "rather frequent amongst them" as the cause of their "lack of breeding."[75] Several other contemporary observers agreed with his diagnosis. The planter-historian Bryan Edwards, a prominent representative of the West India interest, told the Jamaican Council and the Jamaican Assembly that slave women in Jamaica "hold chastity in so little estimation, that barrenness and frequent abortions, the usual effects of a promiscuous intercourse, are very generally prevalent among them."[76] Thomson wrote that "many young females . . . whenever they find themselves pregnant, endeavour to procure abortion, by every means in their power, in which they are too often assisted by the knowery of others."[77] The others unidentified here may have been the obeahmen, or alleged practitioners of African remedies, sometimes accused of helping slave women in pursuing this choice.[78]

Henry Goulbourn, an absentee Jamaican plantation owner, was informed by his manager that the poor levels of fertility on his sugar estate resulted partly from the ability of pregnant slaves to procure abortions.[79] In the 1820s Joseph Foster Barham II, absentee owner of Mesopotamia, blamed his slave women for their low rate of reproduction and threatened to put any who had abortions or miscarriages into a special jobbing gang, which would be hired out to perform arduous manual labor. In 1825 he sent two slave women who delivered stillborn children to the workhouse as a punishment; after they returned to fieldwork the following year, one was listed as being "ill disposed" and the other as "evil disposed."[80] Dr. Collins also mentioned the use of drugs and physical violence to the fetus as methods of effecting abortion and considered that slave women took these measures when their pregnancies became burdensome.[81] A modern sociologist has cited these contemporary views to suggest that abortion was widely practiced in Jamaica.[82]

However, despite the use of such means of limiting fertility, it is doubtful that slave women had significant control over their bodies to combat the overpowering effects of disease, malnutrition, and brutal overwork. No testimony from the women themselves either supports or denies their white masters' widespread accusations with regard to abortion. Possibly revealingly, Monk Lewis made no mention of the practice of abortion on his Jamaican estate. Lewis was particularly interested in the reproduction of his slaves, and it is unlikely that practices damaging to the fertility he wanted to promote would have escaped his notice.[83] European doctors tended to attribute the high incidence of abortion to diseases contracted during pregnancy. During the influenza epidemic in Jamaica in 1802, Williamson noted that "in pregnant women the disease often brought on abortion, and many died. . . . [I]n females, thus circumstanced, it was on every occasion extremely dangerous."[84]

Some modern historians have nonetheless claimed that British West Indian slave women practiced deliberate abortion as a desperate act of resistance against their woeful condition of perpetual chattel slavery. For the same political reason the high rate of infant mortality in the British Caribbean might have included deaths from maternal infanticide. Slave women would thus deliberately have asserted control over their reproductive capacities, both in obtaining or inducing self-abortion and, in particular, in allowing children they could not prevent being born to die to frustrate the planters' desire to breed slave children.[85] However, it is likely that spontaneous miscarriage (before twenty-eight weeks of pregnancy) and stillbirths (after twenty-eight weeks), rather than calculated abortions, were responsible for high rates of fetal loss. Indeed, what were alleged as self-induced abortions might equally have been spontaneous miscarriages: on plantations it would have been difficult to distinguish these two causes of prematurely terminated pregnancy. On the other hand, botched self-abortions may well have been recorded or regarded as miscarriages, and spontaneous miscarriage was so common that it must have enabled abortion to be concealed.[86] Thistlewood laconically recorded many "miscarriages" in his diaries as if they were a common and expected feature of life in Jamaica.[87] Such mortality was sometimes referred to as endogenous death—that is, the result of a mal-formed fetus.[88]

A handful of contemporary sources suggest that black female slaves fought to maintain their roles as mothers despite the trauma and rigors of slavery. They fought against separation from their children and defended their rights to suckle them. It was not uncommon for slave women to adopt other slaves' children in addition to coping with their own.[89] Female slaves without children lived in lonely, dispiriting circumstances. Slaves on plantations lived largely isolated lives, cut off from the normal social rela-tions of free society. Slave women knew that the birth of a child would lead to an uncertain existence for a slave infant in a context where planters and other white personnel controlled people as chattel property, eventually di-vided and bequested to an owner's heirs. Moreover, slave children would lose their mother's culture in living with slaves from many different African backgrounds; those from cultures that emphasized circumcision as a mark of responsible adulthood would remain uncircumcised. They would speak English rather than their mother's tongue. In these ways the bodies of mothers and infants were commodified.[90] And yet to give birth to a child was probably the main way in which a female slave could achieve fulfillment. Moreover, African-born slaves had come from soci-eties where fertility was regarded as women's greatest gift. Children were regarded as the life force through which men and women achieved inte-gration into the universe. People from such a background viewed kinship structures as essential parts of inheritance and succession, which accorded a high status to fertility and opprobrium to barrenness.[91] For these vari-ous reasons, the impulse to care for a child among Jamaican slave women, despite living in an unpropitious location for parenting, was very strong.

In view of slave women's evident dedication to their children, how often would they have aborted their sole prospect for respect as women? It seems unlikely that the practice would have been as common as their owners believed. Any woman who attempted self-abortion, especially younger ones who might not have fully understood the techniques or risks, was very likely to end up with hemorrhaging, septicemia, and likely death. It is far more plausible that the prevalence of miscarriage and still-birth under Jamaican slavery was related to the intensity of the labor regime imposed on slave women during the sugar harvest.[92] The evidence cannot be determinative either with regard to infanticide as a cause of death, since infanticide was nearly always a mother's solitary act of des-peration. It was extremely difficult to determine whether a dead baby was stillborn or premature or whether a relatively healthy child had died at the hands of the mother. Jamaican courts regarded infanticide as more difficult to prove than any other offense brought before them.[93]

Underregistration of births may exaggerate the bleak pictures of fertility as calculated from births reported. Significant variation limited the accuracy of the birth registries; a few masters noted children born dead, but most recorded slave births only after the child had survived at least a week, thus concurring—or at least coinciding—with Africa-derived delays among their slaves in embracing hopes for an infant's survival. In itself this hesitation appears to reflect high infant mortality among slaves.[94] Most infant deaths occurred soon after birth. Around 80 percent of infant deaths in the eighteenth-century Caribbean occurred in the first two weeks of life; in the nineteenth century, the proportion was 50 percent.[95] The health of babies depended crucially on the nutritional intake and bodily strength of their mothers. Given the prevalence of physical brutality, malnutrition, and disease, and the fact that most infants died soon after birth, it is clear that their deaths resulted from prenatal deprivation rather than from postnatal circumstances leading to deaths among infants born healthy.[96] Postnatal tetanus, however, was also a major killer of slave babies. In 1788 Long estimated that this infection, often incurred from severing the umbilical cord with unclean instruments, destroyed about one-third of the young children on his Jamaican plantation.[97] Another contemporary writer attributed the spread of tetanus to the midwives' practice not to change the infant's clothes for the first nine days.[98] Tetanus probably accounted for around 20 percent of total slave mortality in the British Caribbean.[99]

Data from three sugar estates indicate that many pregnancies either never reached term or resulted in births of fatally weak infants. At Mesopotamia between 1762 and 1831 around half the recorded pregnancies resulted in miscarriages, stillbirths, or the death of infants within a few days after birth.[100] Impressionistic reporting for Amity Hall plantation, in Vere Parish, suggests that half the pregnancies on this sugar estate also ended in miscarriage.[101] Rose Price's information on births and miscarriages on Worthy Park in May 1795 provides uniquely precise, if limited, information on the extent of miscarriage. He owned 240 female slaves at the time, of whom 72.5 percent had reached menopause. Some 37.1 percent of these women had given birth 352 times in all, but live births had totaled only 275. These numbers indicate one miscarriage for every 4.6 live births, or around 18 percent.[102]

The slim evidence available on maternal mortality in childbirth suggests that mothers did not commonly die during childbirth or shortly after delivery. The records for Mesopotamia show that three mothers out of seventy-two (just over 4 percent) died in childbirth.[103] Golden Grove sugar estate, in St. Thomas-in-the-East Parish, had similarly low incidences of female death in and after childbirth: only four out of fifty-two slave women (under 8 percent) who died there between 1817 and 1832 are known to have given birth within three years before their deaths.[104]

Contemporary writings offered contradictory accounts of the difficulties that slave women, seen as "blacks," suffered during childbirth. The veteran planter, Long, exposing his familiarity with racial theories of the Enlightenment that romanticized "noble savages" by likening them to "natural" creatures, wrote that "their women are delivered with little or no labour; they have therefore no more occasion for midwives, than the female oran-outang, or any other wild animal. A woman brings forth her child in a quarter of an hour, goes the same day to the sea, and washes herself." Yet he also wrote that "childbirth is not so easy here as in Africa."[105] In fact, the most frequent cases of maternal mortality in third world countries today are caused by postpartum hemorrhage. The risk of severe bleeding is greatly increased when the woman is suffering from anemia and also when she has had multiple births; maternal death rates are five times higher in anemic than in nonanemic women.[106] Labor for poorly nourished women can be prolonged by as much as five hours, with attendant risks for already weakened mother and baby. Malnourishment also heightens the risk of obstructed labor. In severe cases, when a woman lacks a good blood supply and her uterus fails to contract properly, the risks of a difficult birth increase. Weak contractions and lengthy labor would cause fetal distress and tire the mother, so that stillbirth would be a significant risk.[107]

Jamaica's plantocracy, for all its racial prejudices, obstetric ignorance, and denials of the lethal effects of overwork and malnourishment, was vaguely aware of the dangers of childbirth in unsanitary conditions. Concerned with the need to boost the natural increase in the slave population, once slave imports came under abolitionist pressures in the 1780s, planters promoted pro-natalist policies long before an official government policy of "amelioration" came into effect in the mid-1820s. In 1789 the Jamaican Assembly offered overseers a bounty of one pound for each slave child born under their authority who survived until its first birthday. The Assembly increased the amount to three pounds in 1792. Yet it did not specify that overseers should provide sanitary birthing facilities. In 1792 the Jamaican Assembly also exempted any slave woman who had six children alive from field labor and relieved her owner of any taxes otherwise owing upon her.[108] This legislation recognized that reproduction among Jamaican slave women derived as much from successful delivery and caring for a child during its first year of life as from difficulty conceiving.

A battle between masters and slaves over the respective benefits of home delivery and lying-in rooms raged from the late eighteenth century through to slave emancipation in 1834. A contemporary set of rules and instructions for overseers on plantations, dated 1 January 1810, encouraged pregnant slave women to enter a lying-in house, attended by a midwife. The midwife was to receive ten shillings if the child was living at the end of the month. The mother was to be furnished with a calico or linen frock for herself and likewise for her infant. Overseers were charged to treat slave mothers with tenderness and to provide them with every comfort.[109] Williamson reported in 1817 on the "considerable difficulty experienced, to persuade female negroes that on approach of labour pains they would be better accommodated, in every respect, by removing from their own houses to the lying-in rooms." If these birthing facilities, evidently provided by planters, were connected directly to the slave hospital, or "hothouse," the women raised the "greatest objection."[110] And with evident reason, since male and female slaves were seldom separated in the hothouse, and slaves with communicable diseases were treated immediately alongside women giving birth. In the 1790s ordinances were enacted for the provision of suitable lying-in wards, and some planters erected structures separate from the slave hospital for this purpose.[111] Despite the increased availability of lying-in rooms, women continued throughout the period of slavery to give birth in their own huts.

Other slave women featured prominently in the care of new mothers and their infants. Planters commonly designated infirm and elderly women as hospital and children's nurses. On John Tharp's estates in Jamaica in 1805 seven women, who ranged between the ages of thirty and sixty, were listed as midwives, only one of whom was described as being physically able or healthy.[112] On the other hand, planters complained widely of inadequacies they attributed to these women. Long, among others, blamed the "unskilfulness and absurd management of the Negro midwives" for much of the maternal and infant death.[113] Some modern observers have seen the practice of charging older women or young women in poor health with the responsibility for attending new mothers as an inadequate way of dealing with their health needs.[114] That these women were often elderly, however, does not necessarily mean that they lacked ability; they were in fact likely to have gained effective experience

in midwifery. That they were sometimes infirm, or weakened by the rigors of their labors, does not imply that they were uncaring or incompetent. Slave nurses were often considerate and patient despite their age or
state of health.[115] Since European obstetric knowledge offered little assistance at the time, the care of European doctors cannot have alleviated
the dangers for women. The psychological support provided by slave
midwives must have been a comfort for their patients, even if it did not
save their newborns' or their own lives.

Among the many causes of low reproduction among Jamaican slave
women, the material circumstances of overwork, dietary deficiencies, and
physical punishment certainly provided a lethal cocktail. Planters during
the early nineteenth century attempted to alleviate the workload for
pregnant women shortly before and after childbirth, but these provisions
left the hardships of sugar slavery unrelieved during the early months of
pregnancy when the dangers of miscarriage are greatest. By the time
Britain abolished its slave trade in 1808, any improvements in Jamaican
slaves' diets were probably mitigated by increased demands on their work
routines as planters sought to maximize the productivity of the labor forces
they already owned. It was not until the mid-1820s, when the Jamaican
Assembly, in spite of its early manifest concern with overseer brutality,
partially adopted the government's policy of amelioration, that natality
was officially encouraged.[116]

The harsh material circumstances and brutal treatment of slave
women in Jamaica are clearly enough established to account fully for the
limited biological reproduction in the island's slave population—or
throughout most of the British Caribbean. It is unnecessary to turn to social and cultural factors deriving from Africa to explain low rates of reproduction under Jamaican slavery. Planters' accusations of promiscuity
were based on evident prejudice and consequent misreadings of slave
couples they had prevented from living in the same households, whether
on the same or sometimes on different estates. Irregularities in the menstrual cycle, notably those attributable to psychological stress, though
difficult to document, may be presumed. Extended lactation and taboos
against postpartum intercourse may have contributed to wide child spacing, but they may equally have represented desperate measures to protect
malnourished infants and themselves under the deprivations of slavery.
Stillbirths and miscarriages occurred frequently, but malnutrition and
mistreatment are much more likely as causes than self-abortion or infanticide. Venereal disease—which planters often linked to immorality and

the low fertility they attributed to it—in fact had a low incidence and a relatively mild pathology in the Caribbean. Planter attempts to improve delivery conditions for slave mothers with lying-in rooms seem infrequent and ineffective, but midwives may well have been more caring than planters realized.

Whether self-abortion, abstinence, or infanticide were political strategies against enslavement pursued by slave women in Jamaica cannot be verified from surviving evidence. Even if some slave women abused themselves for such reasons, their strategies are unlikely to have contributed significantly to the observable low rates of natality and reproduction from many other causes. So many documented material and epidemiological factors contributed to the low reproductive performance of Jamaican slave women that self-induced abortion or abstinence are unlikely to have contributed significantly. Thus, until knowledge improves about the ways in which Jamaican slave women controlled their own fertility, it remains tendentious to suggest that they opposed breeding as a form of political resistance to the injustices of their enslavement, as some historians have suggested.[117] One historian has written unequivocally about the "resolve among slave women not to bring children into a world of harsh labour."[118] Another has dubbed the supposed refusal of Jamaican slave women to reproduce a "gynecological revolt."[119] Another has speculated, more cautiously, that "many [slave] women may have taken steps to avoid conception" and that slave motherhood was restricted by "the potential impulse women may have felt to interrupt . . . obscene calculations" made by planters in treating slave mothers as commodities.[120] Less cautious statements can also be found: slave women, realizing the planters' need after 1807 to reproduce the slave population, "sought to free their previously enchained wombs, refusing to bear children who would, themselves, be enslaved."[121] Low rates of reproduction are not evidence for slave women's own agency, political or not.

It is less difficult to accept that slave women might have limited their reproduction to lessen the burdens of slavery on themselves through limited mating practices with their partners. Yet it is no less likely that most slave women sought to confirm themselves as females in a brutally ungendered regime of labor and discipline through their unique ability to reproduce. The choices available to slave women are especially pertinent when one considers the implications of planters' or overseers' rapes of black women. In such circumstances, such women had the option of either cherishing the resulting child either as a bridge to white society through the "free colored" status recognized in Jamaica or terminating the pregnancy out of resentment, disgust, and hatred. The sexual act could therefore serve as a strategic opportunity for betterment for their off-spring or represent a hated intrusion into Jamaican slave women's selves. Pregnancy was thus both a severe physical vulnerability under the duress of Jamaican slavery and a potential strategy of personal affirmations of several sorts.

Without direct testimony of any sort on the matter from the women themselves, both arguments remain difficult to evaluate conclusively. What is clear, however, is that the primary reproductive challenges for slaves in Jamaica stemmed from the dietary inadequacies and hard labor of slavery, which compounded epidemiological and whatever social, cul-tural, and political factors may have motivated female slaves in Jamaica concerning their own reproductive capabilities. No one—not European medical doctors, not prejudiced planters, and certainly not enslaved women—had enough control over reproductive biology to overcome the lethal effects of slavery itself.

NOTES

1. David Beck Ryden, "Producing a Peculiar Commodity: Jamaican Sugar Pro-duction, Slave Life, and Planter Profits on the Eve of Abolition, 1750–1807" (PhD diss., University of Minnesota, 1999), 31.

2. J. R. Ward, *British West Indian Slavery: The Process of Amelioration, 1750–1834* (Oxford: Oxford University Press, 1988), 179.

3. William Beckford, *Remarks upon the Situation of the Negroes in Jamaica* (Lon-don: printed for T. and J. Egerton, 1788), 24–25.

4. Henry E. Huntington Library, San Marino, California, Edward East to Anna Eliza, Duchess of Chandos, 23 September 1778, Stowe Collection, Brydges Corre-spondence, STB box 25: Jamaican estates. A similar phrase appears in National Li-brary of Jamaica, Kingston, Edward East to Roger Hope Elletson, 23 September 1778, Robert Hope Elletson letterbook (1773–80).

5. Gilbert Mathison, *Notices Respecting Jamaica in 1808–1809–1810* (London: printed for J. Stockdale, 1811), 12.

6. B. W. Higman, *Slave Populations of the British Caribbean, 1807–1834* (Balti-more: Johns Hopkins University Press, 1984), 74–75. The exception was Barbados, which experienced an absolute increase in its slave population between 1807 and 1834.

7. Richard B. Sheridan, "The Slave Trade to Jamaica, 1702–1808," in *Trade, Government and Society: Caribbean History, 1700–1920*, ed. B. W. Higman (Kingston: Heinemann, 1983), 3.

8. Higman, *Slave Populations of the British Caribbean*, 417–18.

9. Matthew Gregory Lewis, *Journal of a West India Proprietor, 1815–17*, ed. Mona Wilson (London: G. Routledge and Sons, 1929), 268, 314–15, 321; Kenneth F.

Kiple, *The Caribbean Slave: A Biological History* (Cambridge: Cambridge University Press, 1984), 133. Lewis's sugar estate had more women than the norm in Jamaica. There must be some doubt about how accurately Lewis estimated these figures. If one-sixth of the 330 were reproductive females, then 13 infants out of 55 gives about 25 percent surviving births per year. If infant mortality is estimated at 50 percent, these women were giving birth every other year. This would yield about 50 pregnancies, 25 births, and 13 surviving children. If one assumes, taking the second calculation, that one-third of the 150 women on the "breeding list" were of reproductive age and had births every other year and pregnancies twice that again, on an annual basis 8 out of 50 at a given moment would produce 16 pregnancies in a year, which seems low compared with the figure just derived. My thanks to Joseph C. Miller for help with this note.

10. B. W. Higman, *Slave Population and Economy in Jamaica, 1807–1834* (Cambridge: Cambridge University Press, 1976), 154; B. W. Higman, *Montpelier, Jamaica: A Plantation Community in Slavery and Freedom, 1739–1912* (Kingston: Press, University of the West Indies, 1998), 39; Ward, *British West Indian Slavery*, 138–39.

11. Higman, *Slave Populations of the British Caribbean*, 347–78; Ward, *British West Indian Slavery*, 167–84.

12. Barbara Bush, *Slave Women in Caribbean Society, 1650–1838* (London: James Currey, 1990), 137, 139–42, 147–49; Stella Dadzie, "Searching for the Invisible Woman: Slavery and Resistance in Jamaica," *Race and Class* 32 (1990): 21–38; and studies by Orlando Patterson, Selwyn H. H. Carrington, Jennifer L. Morgan, and Verene A. Shepherd, cited in nn. 117–21, below. Note that Patterson provides no contemporary evidence to support his argument about slaves' refusal to reproduce.

13. Herbert S. Klein and Stanley L. Engerman, "Fertility Differentials between Slaves in the United States and the British West Indies: A Note on Lactation Practices and Their Possible Implications," *William and Mary Quarterly*, 3rd series, 35 (1978): 357–74; Jerome S. Handler and Robert S. Corruccini, "Weaning among West Indian Slaves: Historical and Bioanthropological Evidence from Barbados," *William and Mary Quarterly*, 3rd series, 43 (1986): 111–17.

14. Cicely D. Williams, Naomi Baumslag, and Derrick B. Jelliffe, *Mother and Child Health* (London: Oxford University Press, 1984), 61; D. B. Jelliffe, *Child Nutrition in Developing Countries: A Handbook for Fieldworkers* (Washington, DC: U.S. Office of the War on Hunger, 1969), 14.

15. Richard B. Sheridan, "The Crisis of Slave Subsistence in the British West Indies during and after the American Revolution," *William and Mary Quarterly*, 3rd series, 33 (1976): 615–41.

16. Ward, *British West Indian Slavery*, 284–85; Higman, *Slave Populations of the British Caribbean*, 205, 212, 217, 237.

17. Robert Dirks, "Resource Fluctuations and Competitive Transformation in West Indian Slave Societies," in *Extinction and Survival in Human Populations*, ed. Charles D. Laughlin and Ivan A. Brady (New York: Columbia University Press, 1978), 146.

18. Lucius Nicholls, *Tropical Nutrition and Dietetics*, 4th ed. (London: Baillière, Tindell and Cox, 1961), 310.

19. Williams, Baumslag, and Jelliffe, *Mother and Child Health,* 70, 77.

20. Kiple, *Caribbean Slave,* 80–85.

21. Ibid., 81.

22. James Thomson, *A Treatise on the Diseases of Negroes as they occur in the island of Jamaica with Observations on the Country Remedies* (Jamaica, 1820), 45.

23. Robert Dirks, *The Black Saturnalia: Conflict and Its Ritual Expression on British West Indian Slave Plantations* (Gainesville: University Press of Florida, 1987), 87.

24. Thomas Roughley, *The Jamaica Planter's Guide; or, A System for Planting and Managing a Sugar Estate, or Other Plantations in That Island, and throughout the British West Indies in General* (London, 1823), 118.

25. Higman, *Slave Populations of the British Caribbean,* 295–97.

26. Williams, Baumslag, and Jelliffe, *Mother and Child Health,* 47, 67.

27. Edward Long, *A History of Jamaica,* 3 vols. (London, 1774), 2:436.

28. The link between concentration camps and slave plantations has been suggested by Bush, *Slave Women,* 137–39, and, more circumspectly, by Michael Craton, *Searching for the Invisible Man: Slaves and Plantation Life in Jamaica* (Cambridge, MA: Harvard University Press, 1978), 97–98, 410n20.

29. Marietta Morrissey, "Women's Work, Family Formation, and Reproduction among Caribbean Slaves," in *Caribbean Slave Society and Economy: A Student Reader,* ed. Hilary Beckles and Verene Shepherd (London: James Currey, 1991), 283.

30. Richard S. Dunn, "Sugar Production and Slave Women in Jamaica," in *Cultivation and Culture: Labor and the Shaping of Slave Life in the Americas,* ed. Ira Berlin and Philip D. Morgan (Charlottesville: University Press of Virginia, 1993), 62.

31. James Colquhoun Grant and J. R. Webb to Joseph Foster Barham, 19 October 1812, Barham Papers, Bodleian Library, Oxford, Clarendon MSS, Dep. C.358.

32. Richard B. Sheridan, *Doctors and Slaves: A Medical and Demographic History of Slavery in the British West Indies, 1680–1834* (Cambridge: Cambridge University Press, 1985), 233–34; Richard S. Dunn, "A Tale of Two Plantations: Slave Life at Mesopotamia in Jamaica and Mount Airy in Virginia, 1799 to 1828," *William and Mary Quarterly,* 3rd series, 34 (1977): 59–64.

33. Michael Tadman, "The Demographic Cost of Sugar: Debates on Slave Societies and Natural Increase in the Americas," *American Historical Review* 105 (2000): 1534–75; Russell R. Menard and Stuart B. Schwartz, "Was There a Plantation Demographic Regime in the Americas?" in *The Peopling of the Americas,* 4 vols. (Proceedings, Vera Cruz, 1992) (Liège, Belgium: International Union for the Scientific Study of Population, 1992), 1:51–66.

34. Lyliane Rosetta, "Female Reproductive Dysfunction and Intense Physical Training," *Oxford Review of Reproductive Biology* 15 (1993): 113–41.

35. Barbara Bush, "Towards Emancipation: Women and Coercive Labour Regimes in the British West Indian Colonies, 1790–1838," *Slavery and Abolition* 5 (1984): 225–26.

36. Higman, *Slave Populations of the British Caribbean,* 206–7.

37. Long, *History of Jamaica,* 2:437. Long's mention of "penns" referred to cattle-raising estates, often in the western part of the island, where men managed the animals and the women present had less arduous duties.

38. Craton, *Invisible Man*, 97.

39. Dunn, "Sugar Production," 66.

40. Higman, *Slave Populations of the British Caribbean*, 398.

41. Rhoda E. Reddock, "Women and Slavery in the Caribbean: A Feminist Perspective," *Latin American Perspectives* 12 (1985): 67–68.

42. Ward, *British West Indian Slavery*, 156.

43. Sheila Lambert, ed., *House of Commons Sessional Papers of the Eighteenth Century*, 145 vols. (Wilmington, DE: Scholarly Resources, 1975), 82: 77, 20.

44. Quoted in Barbara Bush, "Hard Labor: Women, Childbirth, and Resistance in British Caribbean Slave Societies," in *More than Chattel: Black Women and Slavery in the Americas*, ed. David Barry Gaspar and Darlene Clark Hine (Bloomington: Indiana University Press, 1996), 197.

45. Ibid.

46. John Williamson, *Medical and Miscellaneous Observations Relative to the West India Islands*, 2 vols. (Edinburgh: Smellie, 1817), 2:205; Sheridan, *Doctors and Slaves*, 36.

47. Henrice Altink, "'An Outrage on All Decency': Abolitionist Reactions to Flogging Jamaican Slave Women, 1780–1834," *Slavery and Abolition* 23 (2002): 113.

48. Higman, *Slave Populations of the British Caribbean*, 312; Kiple, *Caribbean Slave*, 89–103; D. B. Jelliffe, "Interactions between Nutrition and Infection," in *Child Health in the Tropics: A Practical Handbook for Medical and Para-medical Personnel*, ed. Jelliffe, 3rd ed. (London: Edward Arnold, 1968), 265. *Elephantiasis* usually refers to lymphatic filiariasis, which is caused not by chigoes but by nematodes whose vectors are generally mosquitoes.

49. Bush, *Slave Women*, 12, 14.

50. Bush, "Hard Labor," 202.

51. J. R. Webb to Joseph Foster Barham, 16 June 1809, Bodleian Library, Clarendon MSS, Dep. C.358, Barham Papers.

52. Thomas Cooper, *Facts illustrative of the Condition of the Negro Slaves in Jamaica with Notes in an Appendix* (London: J. Hatchard, 1824), 10.

53. Richard Bright to Edward Smith, 27 October 1821, 4 May 1827, University of Melbourne Archives, Richard Bright letterbooks 7, 18, Bright family papers, boxes 27, 29.

54. Betty Wood and Roy Clayton, "Jamaica's Struggle for a Self-Perpetuating Slave Population: Demographic, Social and Religious Changes on Golden Grove Plantation, 1812–1832," *Journal of Caribbean Studies* 6 (1988): 290.

55. Lambert, *House of Commons*, 72:82.

56. Thomson, *Diseases of Negroes*, 111.

57. Thomas Dancer, MD, *The Medical Assistant; or, Jamaica Practice of Physic: Designed chiefly for the use of Families and Plantations* (Kingston: Alexander Aikman, 1801), 212–13.

58. Klein and Engerman, "Fertility Differentials," 366; Ryden, "Peculiar Commodity," 38.

59. *The Life of Olaudah Equiano, or Gustavus Vassa, the African*, ed. Paul Edwards (London: Longman, 1989), 8.

60. For an extreme example of a sexually active white overseer, see Trevor Burnard, "The Sexual Life of an Eighteenth-Century Jamaican Slave Overseer," in *Sex and Sexuality in Early America*, ed. Merril D. Smith (New York, 1998), 163–89; Burnard, *Mastery, Tyranny, and Desire: Thomas Thistlewood and His Slaves in the Anglo-Jamaican World* (Chapel Hill: University of North Carolina Press, 2004); Shepherd, "Gender and Representation," 706.

61. Ward, *British West Indian Slavery*, 182–83.

62. Klein and Engerman, "Fertility Differentials," 358, 368; Handler and Corrucini, "Weaning," 111–17; Lucille Mathurin, "The Arrivals of Black Women," *Jamaica Journal* 9 (1975): 4.

63. [David Collins], *Practical Rules for the Management and Medical treatment of Negro Slaves in the Sugar Colonies* (London: printed by J. Barfield for Vernor and Hood, 1803), 146.

64. Quoted in Higman, *Slave Populations of the British Caribbean*, 353. Shand's definition of "long weaning" was sixteen to eighteen months.

65. Ibid., 353–54.

66. George W. Roberts, *The Population of Jamaica* (Cambridge: Cambridge University Press, 1957), 42, 44.

67. Alan S. McNeily, P. W. Howie, and Anna Glasier, "Lactation and the Return of Ovulation," in *Natural Human Fertility: Social and Biological Determinants*, ed. Peter Diggory, Malcolm Potts, and Sue Teper, proceedings of the twenty-third annual symposium of the Eugenics Society, London, 1986 (London: Macmillan, in association with the society, 1988), 102–17.

68. Anrudh Jain, J. C. Hsu, Ronald Freedman, and M. C. Chang, "Demographic Aspects of Lactation and Postpartum Amenorrhea," *Demography* 7 (1970): 255–71. Other demographers consider that variations in the age of weaning, between ten and twenty months, can affect fertility considerably. See R. J. Lesthaege and H. J. Page, "The Post-partum Non-susceptible Period: Development and Application of Model Schedules," *Population Studies* 34 (1980): 143–69.

69. Kiple, *Caribbean Slave*, 76–119.

70. Thomson, *Diseases of Negroes*, 117.

71. Angus McLaren, *A History of Contraception: From Antiquity to the Present Day* (Oxford: Oxford University Press, 1990), 116–18; Bush, "Hard Labor," 202.

72. Thomas Winterbottom, *An Account of the Native Africans in the Neighbourhood of Sierra Leone*, 2 vols. (London, 1803), 2:218.

73. Dunn, "Sugar Production," 66; Dirks, *Black Saturnalia*, 111; Kiple, *Caribbean Slave*, 110.

74. Morgan, *Laboring Women*, 114.

75. Report of the Jamaica House of Assembly on the slave issue, 20 November 1788, PRO, CO 137/88, app. C.

76. Bryan Edwards, *A Speech delivered at a free Conference between the Honourable the Council and Assembly of Jamaica, held the 19th November, 1789, on the subject of Mr. Wilberforce's propositions in the House of Commons, concerning the slave-trade* (Kingston, 1789), 46. Similar remarks were made by the planters Gilbert Francklyn and George Wedderburn: see *Parliamentary Papers*, 1790–91, *Report from the Select*

Committee of the House of Commons on the Slave Trade, in Lambert, *House of Commons,* 71:88, 72:374.

77. Thomson, *Diseases of Negroes,* 111.

78. The best studies of obeahmen deal with their presence in Barbados, though they were also part of black society in Jamaica. See Jerome S. Handler, "Slave Medicine and Obeah in Barbados, circa 1650 to 1834," *New West Indian Guide/Nieuwe West-Indische Gids* 74 (2000): 57–90; Handler and Kenneth M. Bilby, "On the Early Use and Origin of the Term 'Obeah' in Barbados and the Anglophone Caribbean," *Slavery and Abolition* 22 (2001): 87–100.

79. Thomas Samson to Henry Goulburn, 1 April 1806, Surrey History Centre, Woking, Goulburn Collection, 304/J/1/10 (6).

80. Dunn, "Sugar Production," 56.

81. Collins, *Practical Rules,* 134.

82. Orlando Patterson, *Sociology of Slavery: An Analysis of the Origins, Development and Structure of Negro Slave Society in Jamaica* (London: MacGibbon and Kee, 1967), 106–7.

83. Ibid., 108.

84. Williamson, *Medical and Miscellaneous Observations,* 2:208.

85. Bush, *Slave Women,* 137–42, 147–49; Bush, "Hard Labor," 205–6, 209–10.

86. Dirks, *Black Saturnalia,* 105.

87. Douglas Hall, *In Miserable Slavery: Thomas Thistlewood in Jamaica, 1750–86* (London: Macmillan, 1989), 68, 125, 145, 186, 210, 240, 279, 286, 288–89.

88. Robert W. Fogel, *Without Consent or Contract: The Rise and Fall of American Slavery* (New York: Oxford University Press, 1989), 143.

89. Patterson, *Sociology of Slavery,* 169.

90. Morgan, *Laboring Women,* 108, 115, 121–22, 129, 200.

91. Mathurin, "Arrivals of Black Women," 5.

92. Dunn, "Sugar Production," 68.

93. Jonathan Dalby, *Crime and Punishment in Jamaica: A Quantitative Analysis of the Assize Court Records, 1756–1856* (Kingston: Social History Project, Dept. of History, University of the West Indies, 2000), 42–43.

94. Higman, *Slave Populations of the British Caribbean,* 26; Higman, *Slave Population and Economy,* 48–49.

95. Ward, *British West Indian Slavery,* 130.

96. For a more detailed discussion, see Kenneth Morgan, "The Struggle For Survival: Slave Infant Mortality in the British Caribbean," paper presented at the 5th Avignon conference on Slavery and Forced Labour, May 2004.

97. PRO, Pitt Papers, 30/8/155, 40, cited in Michael Craton, James Walvin, and David Wright, eds., *Slavery, Abolition and Emancipation: Black Slaves and the British Empire: A Thematic Documentary* (London: Longman, 1976), 102.

98. Mathison, *Notices Respecting Jamaica,* 29.

99. Sheridan, *Doctors and Slaves,* 209.

100. Dunn, "Sugar Production," 66.

101. Thomas Samson to Henry Goulburn, 28 April 1813, 11 August 1815, Surrey History Centre, Goulburn Collection, III/3H.

102. Craton, *Invisible Man*, 87.

103. Dunn, "Sugar Production," 66.

104. Wood and Clayton, "Jamaica's Struggle," 303.

105. Long, *History of Jamaica*, 2:380, 436.

106. Williams, Baumslag, and Jelliffe, *Mother and Child Health*, 61, 70.

107. Kiple, *Caribbean Slave*, 85, 91, 133.

108. PRO, CO 139/147, act no. 819.

109. Mathison, *Notices Respecting Jamaica*, 110–11.

110. Williamson, *Medical and Miscellaneous Observations*, 2:202, 205.

111. Sheridan, *Doctors and Slaves*, 273–76.

112. Ibid., 92–93.

113. Long, *History of Jamaica*, 2:436.

114. See, for example, Lucille Mathurin Mair, "A Historical Study of Women in Jamaica from 1655 to 1844" (PhD diss., University of the West Indies, 1974), 320.

115. Sheridan, *Doctors and Slaves*, 226.

116. Ward, *British West Indian Slavery*, 188; William A. Green, *British Slave Emancipation: The Sugar Colonies and the Great Experiment 1830–1865* (Oxford: Oxford University Press, 1976), 103, 105.

117. Patterson, *Sociology of Slavery*, 112. The same ideology has been claimed for the antebellum southern United States and is embedded in Toni Morrison's *Beloved*.

118. Selwyn H. H. Carrington, *The Sugar Industry and the Abolition of the Slave Trade, 1775–1810* (Gainesville: University Press of Florida, 2002), 197. A similar comment appears on p. 201.

119. Patterson, *Slavery and Social Death: A Comparative Study* (Cambridge, MA: Harvard University Press, 1982), 133. See also Dadzie, "Invisible Woman," 27.

120. Morgan, *Laboring Women*, 114, 200.

121. Shepherd, "'Petticoat Rebellion'? The Black Woman's Body and Voice in the Struggles for Freedom in Colonial Jamaica," in *In the Shadow of the Plantation: Caribbean History and Legacy*, ed. Alvin O. Thompson (Kingston: Ian Randle, 2002), 24.

2

GLOOMY MELANCHOLY

Sexual Reproduction among Louisiana Slave Women, 1840–60

RICHARD FOLLETT

Mincing few words on the evils of slavery in the sugar mills of Louisiana, George William Featherstonhaugh described the slaveholding plantocracy as "white men with liberty and equality in their mouths," driving African Americans "to perish, [there] where the duration for a sugar mill hand does not exceed seven years." The hellish nature of sugar work condemned those in the cane fields to "the lower circle in Dante's Hell of Horrors," where the slave—Francis Kemble Butler observed—seemed "to have reached the climax of infernal punishment." Ex-slave Frederick Douglass concurred, noting that Louisiana's grisly reputation as a "life of living death" instilled terror and trepidation within the African American community. Those unfortunate enough to be sold there "cried out with one voice as though the heavens and earth were coming together," former bondsman Jacob Stroyer remembered, for "Louisiana was considered by the slaves as a place of slaughter."[1]

Louisiana's reputation as that "old debble Lousy-Anna" haunted the slave community. Along the Mississippi, its tributaries, and bayous in

This chapter was originally presented at the Avignon Conference on Slavery and Forced Labour, "Women in Slavery—In Honour of Suzanne Miers," 16–18 October 2002. A much longer version was published as "Heat, Sex, and Sugar: Childbearing in the Slave Quarters," *Journal of Family History* 67, no. 4 (2003): 510–39. The *JFH* has kindly given permission to republish the article in this condensed and altered format. The author wishes to acknowledge the generous assistance of Joseph Miller in editing and amending this article.

southern portions of the state, enslaved African Americans toiled on industrial-scale plantations where cane farming and sugar production advanced at punishing rhythms. Located on the northern fringe of the Caribbean sugar producing belt, Louisiana's sporadically icy climate compelled planters to set the pace of cutting and processing the canes at a lethal pace, before the first killing frosts descended in November or December. Facing acute ecological risks and a volatile Gulf climate, planters ordered their harvest crews, including most of the women they owned, into the fields in mid-October or early November. For the following six to ten weeks, these agricultural factories operated around the clock as enslaved women and men worked feverishly to cut and crush the crop. Fourteen- and sixteen-hour shifts taxed physical reserves and contributed to grisly levels of mortality. Thomas Hamilton testified to the human wastage of the cane fields when he concluded that sugar cultivation "was only carried on at an appalling sacrifice of life." During the annual harvest or grinding season, Hamilton observed, "the fatigue is so great that nothing but the severest application of the lash can stimulate the human frame to endure it." Fully cognizant that planters impelled their slaves to work at a ferocious pace, Claude Robin added that the slaves awoke long before dawn and toiled late into the night before finally returning to their quarters. The exhausting discipline of the sugar world, Robin deduced, checked slave fertility and elicited atrocious rates of demographic decrease. "The gloomy melancholy of these unfortunate people," the Frenchman concluded, was entirely understandable, for on a plantation of twenty slaves, deaths surpassed live births by such a degree that within two decades the slave force had mostly perished.[2]

Louisiana slavery's morbid history was unique in the American South. In the tobacco and cotton districts, the slave population grew swiftly, but in the cane world, the decennial natural growth rate for the 1850s may have been as low as 6 or 7 percent, a figure only one-fourth the Southern mean and similar to that of the dwindling populations of the West Indies. And also like the Caribbean, Louisiana's appalling demographic record derived from the specific labor requirements of producing sugar, the dearth of women, and high rates of infant mortality. Those few bondswomen who had the misfortune of being sold to Louisiana's cane world experienced low fertility rates, gave birth to correspondingly few children, and suffered high maternal and infant mortality. Female slaves, in particular, suffered under the sugar barons' regime as heavy physical labor and inadequate nutrition, particularly a diet deficient in protein, led to abnormally low rates of conception, depressed libido, and provoked miscarriages.[3]

Recent scholarship has frequently underscored the agency of slave women, particularly in regard to their capacity to undermine the slaveholders' narrow definition of them as physical and reproductive labor. Despite the enormous burdens that enslavement imposed on them, such scholars argue, bondswomen challenged the misogynist assumptions that underpinned plantation slavery and practiced, historian Barbara Bush contends, "psychological contraception." By consciously avoiding pregnancy or through gynecological resistance, black women reclaimed their own bodies, frustrated the planters' pro-natalist policies, and in turn defied white male constructions of their sexuality. Whether swallowing abortifacients such as calomel and turpentine or chewing on natural contraceptives like cotton roots or okra, slave women wove contraception and miscarriages through the dark fabric of slave oppositional culture. Enslaved women who resisted the planters' untrammeled sexual aggression in these ways were undoubtedly lionized by fellow bondswomen as gritty survivors, but few of those in the sugar country were able to overcome the destructive ecological and nutritional factors of the sugar regime. Ultimately, the structural demands of Louisiana's slaveholding order defined the capacity of slave women to conceive and deliver their offspring. The marked seasonality of pregnancy and childbirth on the plantations stands as testimony to the distorting intensity of Louisiana sugar.[4]

The impact of labor processes on the fertility of slave women has long received scholarly attention. William Taylor reported to the British House of Commons in 1832 that the decrease in the slave population was "materially affected by the nature of the employment" on the Jamaican cane estates. While some scholars of the American South, notably Michael Tadman, have addressed the overall negative effect of sugar cultivation and Louisiana slaveholders' predilection for male workers on slave fertility (using live births as a proxy), this chapter examines the specific physiological mechanisms affecting the slave women subject to the harsh regimen of sugar. In the Louisiana cane districts, inadequate diet, excessive workloads, climate, and hormonal imbalances all seriously compromised fecundity (the biological capacity for reproduction).[5]

REPRODUCTIVE PHYSIOLOGY UNDER ASSAULT

As physiologists indicate, heavy physical work undermines reproductive fitness, specifically ovarian function, and thus limits success in procreation. Intensely fit female ballerinas, athletes, and military recruits frequently experience delayed menarche, irregular menstrual cycles, and amenorrhea (cessation of menstruation). Although farm labor hardly qualifies as vigorous athletic training, research conducted among rural Nepali women indicates that seasonal increases in heavy physical work also suppress progesterone levels and limit ovarian function. To assess reproductive readiness, physiologists commonly measure levels of progesterone. The ovary secretes this hormone in the two weeks after ovulation, and it is the subsequent decrease in production of progesterone that allows menstruation. Higher levels of progesterone during this "luteal phase" indicate that women have ovulated and are in a fertile state. During the Nepalese monsoon, when women labored on agricultural tasks for more than eight hours per day, they lost weight and their progesterone levels dropped, indicating a reduction in fecundity derived from the combination of extreme labor and related weight loss. Parallel studies on Polish agricultural workers underscore that physical exertion, even among well-fed women, reduces progesterone levels and suppresses ovarian function. While exercise-induced weight loss clearly reduced progesterone levels in Nepal among marginally nourished women, the Polish evidence strongly indicates that energy expenditure alone can induce seasonal troughs in the reproductive fitness of well-fed females.[6]

Although the antebellum sugar lords measured the physical strength of their human property by varying indices, they of course left no progesterone samples for consideration by historians. In their plantation registers, however, they recorded live births and thus provided the modern observer with a proxy to consider the ovarian function and rates of conception in the slave community that might have produced the infants born. By relying on these birth dates as the principal data, we can infer the seasonality of conceptions that had resulted in the recorded successful births, although this procedure cannot track the seasonality of miscarriages or abortions, be they spontaneous or induced by the bondswoman. Figure 2.1 summarizes recorded births by months and presents the estimated months of conception of 1,223 slave women on ten Louisiana sugar plantations. The data derive principally from the 1840s and 1850s, a period during which Louisiana's sugar industry rapidly industrialized, producing one of the most oppressive labor regimes in the slave states. Births include all infants reported as born on an estate (including those who would die as babies).

The solid line charting imputed conceptions precedes the index of recorded births by nine months. Its sharp rise in the harvest months of November and December indicates a surprising seasonal peak in reproductive success at the very time when labor proved most draining for

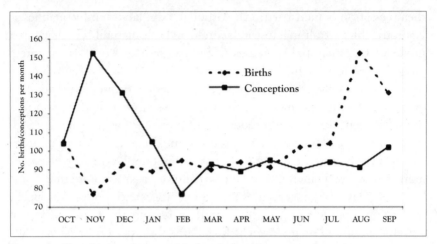

Figure 2.1. Slave birth and conception data for Louisiana sugar plantations.

men and women alike. The November spike in conceptions, for instance, contrasted sharply with the below-average numbers of conceptions for seven months across the year and numbers hovering at or just above the average for three additional months. This concentration of conceptions at the height of the exhausting season of sugar making defies explanation in terms of the known ability of physical exertion to suppress fertility. If the cited research on the deleterious impact of stressful physical work on ovarian function is pertinent, then November and December should exhibit the lowest indices of successful fertilization. The inverse, however, turns out to have been the case![7]

FOOD AND FECUNDITY IN THE CANE WORLD

In a parallel study of birth seasonality on the rice plantations of the Georgia and South Carolina Low Country, Cheryll Ann Cody concludes that one-third of the children born there (twice the average rate) were conceived from December to January. At first glance, this pattern matched that of Louisiana, but the marked seasonality in Low-Country conceptions mirrored the lull in labor demands on rice estates. During the winter months slaves enjoyed more leisure time, were less exposed to the risk of malaria, and accordingly enjoyed better health and had additional opportunities for family life.

The same winter decline in subtropical fevers held true in the Louisiana sugar country, but conceptions there did not show the same correlation with seasonal availability of free time and relief from heavy physical exertion. If they had, conceptions might have risen in the summer months during the lay-by period, when the sugar canes required minimal attention. Despite changing workloads, however, the lay-by hardly proved to be a period of peak reproductive success. By contrast, successful reproductive behavior peaked in the late autumn harvest months and then collapsed during the late winter and early spring periods. Slave women on the sugar estates accordingly experienced a bimodal annual variation in their reproductive lives; whether they had sexual intercourse frequently or not, bondswomen would surely have noted that birth dates tended to cluster and that many among them were at similar stages of pregnancy. To be sure, exogenous factors such as climate and disease shaped birth seasonality, but it is the relation between diet and workload that ultimately explains the seasonal peaks and troughs in slave births, at least in Louisiana.[8]

Life—including nutrition—on antebellum plantations marched to the burdensome beat of the agricultural calendar; as such, Louisiana slaves toiled incessantly to plant, cultivate, and harvest the canes before finally manufacturing sugar. It was a grueling labor cycle that peaked in the annual harvest but continued almost unchecked throughout the year. In the first instance, the danger of frost damage impelled planters to cut and process their matured canes at double-quick time. Second, the introduction of steam-powered sugar milling in the 1840s imposed a relentless tempo on harvest work as slaves labored at feverish speed to supply the powered mills with freshly cut canes. These two harvest-specific pressures conspired to form a punishing labor regime. To encourage the slaves to toil the long hours required in act in the planters' interest, slaveholders threatened their bondspeople with whips but also supplied them with multiple incentives. These inducements took the shape of cash payments, Christmas bonuses, enhanced leisure time at other points in the year, postharvest festivities, and above all food.

These concessions were, of course, self-serving. In return for a little cash or extra food, the slaveholders gained labor stability, and the extra rations doled out at harvest ensured that the slave crews began their shifts with full bellies and the energy to work long hours. Such incentives, however, lasted only as long as the harvest. Following a brief respite over Christmas, when the planter normally supplied the slaves with adequate food to celebrate at least one postharvest or vacation meal, the slaves returned to work to seed the canes and tend the shoots. Until mechanization, planting cane required prolonged backbreaking work that gave way to less burdensome labor only in the spring, when slaves hoed and chopped away weeds that grew among the sprouting canes. By the mid-summer lay-by, the cane shoots were robust enough to survive without constant attention. Labor, however, seldom slowed as planters redirected their work crews elsewhere; other crops were harvested, buildings and farm equipment needed maintenance, and the vast quantity of cordage required as fuel for the steam-powered sugar mills was cut from woods in the backswamps.[9]

The pace of work during the nine-month cultivation season never matched the intensity of the harvest, and slaveholders found a weekly ration of corn and pork sufficient to sustain their slaves' efforts. Slaves sometimes added to their miserly ration with food they cultivated on their garden plots or fished, trapped, or even purchased, but their diet was barely adequate for the workload. By contrast, during the harvest, they were provided with additional rations and molasses that in all probability matched or surpassed the energy requirements for sugar work, even during the grinding season. That energy and associated weight gain proved critical in shaping the slaves' annual reproductive calendar. The frequency with which slaves had sex during the harvest is impossible to quantify, but we can deduce that whatever the level of coital activity, it was sufficient to lead to a high number of successful births nine months later.

Slaves, almost assuredly, took the opportunity of the postharvest "holiday" to spend leisure time with their families, but the seasonal rise in August and September births is too great to ascribe to a single week of free time (almost always the Christmas week), although it unquestionably played a role in shaping the birth calendar on many estates. Rather, it was the enhanced caloric consumption during the harvest, combined with a set of additional environmental factors, that ultimately explains the seasonal peak in conceptions. Conversely, the withdrawal of the additional rations (without a commensurate decline in labor extracted) explains the dip in conceptions through the spring and summer. The experience of slave women in Louisiana's cane world appears to have been similar to the !Kung San of Botswana, a similarly rural and seminourished people, whose seasonal crest in births followed peak body weight by nine months, indicating that food availability directly enhanced reproductive fitness and that nutritional stress during other parts of the year impaired their capacity to bear children. The improved diet and associated weight gain during the harvest months similarly provided Louisiana bondswomen with adequate calories and body weight to conceive successfully. By contrast, at other times of the year, nutritional stress reduced the fecundity of Louisiana's slave women.[10]

BACKGROUND NUTRITIONAL DEFICITS

Although food supply varied from estate to estate, the slave diet during these routine parts of the agricultural year averaged 1 to 1.5 pecks of corn and 3.5 to 4 pounds of pork per week per hand (approximately 9 liters of corn and 1.4 kilograms of meat). This monotonous diet barely sufficed as raw caloric intake but woefully lacked nutritional balance. Although some slaves may have improved their own diet from their gardens, plantation records consistently indicate that they also frequently sold their produce for specie or supplies at the estate commissary. "Enterprising and intelligent" planters occasionally increased rations of pork, corn, molasses, yams, and other vegetables to ensure that field hands would "keep healthy and strong." As agricultural journalist Solon Robinson observed, these enhanced rations expressed raw self-interest. On his visit to Thomas Pugh's Madewood Plantation, Robinson informed his readers in the *American Agriculturist* that working hands drew weekly rations at the top of the general range—1.5 pecks of corn, 5.25 pounds of mess pork, and vegetables. Pugh's modest generosity, however, had a hollow ring, for the improved rations accompanied his introduction of a steam-powered mill that sharply upped the pace of labor in the cane fields. Toiling to supply the railroad that brought the freshly cut canes to the mill and the conveyor belts that whisked them into the sugarhouse, slaves at Madewood evidently needed every ounce of energy they could obtain to keep up with the incessant pace of modern sugar processing technology. Other slaves, however, proved less well nourished, receiving daily rations of only half a pound of pork, a quantity close to the standard slave allowance. Indeed, as one Louisiana physician noted, "the diet of Negroes on most plantations being mostly salt pork, corn bread, and molasses—rarely eating fresh meat and vegetables—a condition of the system is thus produced closely allied to scurvy."[11]

CALORIE DEPRIVATION AND ENERGY SUPPLY

By providing such limited food, estate mangers barely satisfied their slaves' caloric requirements for strenuous labor. The World Health Organization estimates that a male engaged in heavy work for eight hours burns 3,490 calories per day. The basic daily slave ration amounted to 4,056 calories and should have met or exceeded this standard. But Richard Sutch has calculated that an average adult male weighing 65 kilograms (143 pounds) who slept nine hours per day, who rested for an additional three hours, and who expended two hours in eating, dressing, and other light personal activity would have burned 1,200 calories without working at all. The remaining 2,856 calories in the standard slave ration would have been expended in labor at a rate of 4.8 calories per minute. By using the Christensen system of energy expenditure, Sutch maintains that slaves would have exceeded the caloric value of the standard ration by working only "lightly." Where planters ordered heavier work or longer hours on laborious tasks such as ridging, digging, plowing, and preparing the land for cultivation, they had to resort to compulsion to maintain prescribed work speeds, while their slaves experienced fatigue and weight loss as they depleted their energy stores.[12]

During the arduous cane-planting season, African Americans required approximately 3,500 to 4,000 calories to perform their field duties. To meet their total energy budgets, however, slaves needed to consume up to 5,000 calories per day. Although some slaves almost certainly obtained more than the basic ration, most African Americans consumed, at best, only the minimum food required for their work and, at worst, some 20 to 40 percent less than they required to maintain weight and energy. The fact that the vital and high-energy-consuming "prime field hands" in the sugar country were younger, slightly taller, and perhaps "sturdier" than slaves in other regions would have further exacerbated the inadequacies of the standard ration, especially for those in the final stages of adolescence.[13]

This dietary shortfall, when combined with the heavy physical exertion required of sugar work, proved particularly deleterious for slave women. Above all, it triggered weight loss and associated decline in fecundity. Research conducted among contemporary Lese women in rural Zaire complements the data from Nepal, Poland, and Botswana to suggest that ovarian function for marginally nourished females appears to be compromised by even modest loss of weight. Significantly for Louisiana slave women, modern research shows that ovarian dysfunction occurs most noticeably in the month following weight loss. The nutritional deprivation that female slaves experienced during the planting season further suppressed the rate of conceptions in February and March.[14]

Since the low rates of conception during the spring planting season reflect how physically taxing African Americans found their lives on Louisiana's sugar plantations, it appears anomalous that the harvest, with its even longer hours and much more physically punishing workload, should have produced the highest rates of conception. Workdays were much longer, and the work more intense, during October, November, and

Table 2.1. Daily work and calorie expenditure		
WORK EXPENDITURE	14-HOUR SHIFTS	16-HOUR SHIFTS
4.5 kcal/minute	4,500 kcal	4,900 kcal
5.45 kcal/minute	5,300 kcal	5,800 kcal
6.175 kcal/minute	5,900 kcal	6,500 kcal
6.9 kcal/minute	6,500 kcal	7,200 kcal

December than at other times of the year, as the bondspeople cut and processed the cane at breakneck speed in twelve- to sixteen-hour shifts. The slaves then expended enormous quantities of energy that far outstripped their caloric intake from their standard ration. Considering the number of hours, collective stress, and exhaustion of this work in the hot and sticky sugar mill, it appears realistic to assume that slaves expended between 5,000 and 6,500 calories per twenty-four hours for working, resting, and sleeping. Table 2.1 charts the potential energy expenditure for fourteen- and sixteen-hour shifts across a range of assumed rates of caloric expenditure, including associated sleeping and relaxing over the daily and nightly cycle.[15]

SIROP AND THE FUELING OF NORMAL MENSTRUAL CYCLES

Planters fueled the increased energy expenditure required for harvest work by increasing rations, as Thomas Pugh evidenced, and by distributing extra provisions of either molasses or "sirop" (molten sugar dissolved in water) to the cane workers. Those who worked in the sugarhouse, milling the canes and producing the granulated sugar, additionally received a plentiful supply of coffee and hot molasses as well. Doling out these sweet and sticky by-products of the production process cost the planters little and proved particularly appealing and energizing to the slaves. As Joseph Ingraham noted, the slaves "revive and become robust and healthy" upon consuming liquid sugar or molasses. The caloric high of the sugar harvest received signal attention as physicians urged that "it is only . . . at the rolling season when the operatives on sugar estates are observed to become fat and healthy." Explaining these "fattening qualities" of sugar, Dr. Samuel Cartwright recorded that they emerged most markedly among boiling house workers, who enjoyed ready access to the hot cane juice or sirop. Freshly milled liquid sugar (in its molten state, prior to final granulation), Cartwright maintained, proved rich in calories, while vapors inhaled from the sugar clarifiers possessed singular medicinal features that eased consumptive, catarrhal, bronchial, and dyspeptic infirmities. The most emaciated individuals, Cartwright propounded in the New Orleans–based *De Bow's Review*, would "soon recover their health and get fat" after an extended spell in the sugarhouse. Even the New York periodical *Plow* cited Cartwright's research, clarifying the palpable incongruity that slaves appeared "healthy" despite working eighteen hours per day on the harvest.[16]

Bondspeople who freely drank sirop or consumed semimolten molasses experienced marked increases in caloric intake, as carbohydrate-rich sugar provides considerable energy from relatively small doses. One gram of high-grade sugar provides 3.85 kilocalories of energy; consequently, slaves who consumed thirty grams (about one ounce—approximately the same amount of sugar as in one medium-size sixteen-ounce bottle of commercially available sports drink) of dissolved sugar most probably gained approximately 115 calories. Like today's athletes who guzzle sugar-rich drinks, African Americans on Louisiana's sugar plantations fueled their energy expenditures by consuming a carbohydrate-rich diet throughout the day. On the job those cumulative grams of sugar delivered a concentrated energy jolt that fueled muscle expenditure throughout the work shift. And by rotating slaves through a revolving system of shift work, planters assured that all hands gained frequent access to the molten sirop.[17]

While planters and contemporaries could not have calculated calories to workload, their concerns with production and profit focused their attention on sucrose's intensely energizing effect during the grinding season. Some slaveholders remained miserly in their weekly allowances, but most acted on their association of strength and productivity with diet. Sketching overseers' duties, the reform-minded Thomas Affleck warned that sickness often derived from negligent slave management, including inappropriate or poorly cooked food. Preventative maintenance required an ample and varied diet of "wholesome *well-cooked* food" supplied "at *regular hours*." Although the slaves' quarters never quite resembled a barrack complex, the factory compound on most Louisiana sugar estates included compact housing where the planter could maintain a watchful eye over his laborers' every move and every ration consumed.

Centralized canteen-style preparation of food further ensured that the planter could regiment the slaves' diet as workloads peaked, while additionally saving hours that could be reallocated to producing sugar. Albert

Patterson, who grew up in Plaquemines Parish, attested to centralized meal services in at least one instance when he recalled a cook who managed a large kitchen on the estate where he had grown up and prepared meals for the slaves while they worked. On other estates, planters consolidated cooking operations prior to the cane-crushing season, while others prepared for the impending drudgery of the harvest by directing the elderly and infirm to cook for the hands. Although these planters focused on the potential gain in field labor from centralizing food preparation, their time-thrifty management also ensured that the work gangs began each shift nutritionally prepared for its draining demands.[18]

Like most midcentury Americans, sugar masters did not understand that these provisions were inadequate in terms of the minerals and vitamins necessary for a nutritious diet, but by introducing sirop and molasses, they at least temporarily boosted the calories available. Beyond the immediate contribution of the sucrose-supplemented slave diet to production that concerned the planters, the increased calories also raised the bondspeople's fertility. We have seen that not only does malnutrition reduce female fecundity but also that starvation and poor diet delay menarche and that even a relatively small associated weight loss of 10 to 15 percent of normal weight (for height) prompts amenorrhea. Accordingly, Louisiana slaves who gulped sirop or consumed extra rations during the harvest season almost certainly attained their caloric requirements while additionally gaining "easily mobilized energy" indispensable for the maintenance of normal menstrual cycles. Given that seasonal changes in food supply correlate with reproductive success, it is highly probable that the slaveholder's dietary supplements provided the bondswomen with adequate calories and weight gain (relative to other parts of the year) to conceive successfully. By contrast, at other times of the year when the diet proved marginal, at best, and slave women very likely lost weight (despite lower workloads), nutritional stress reduced their fecundity to the low summer levels observed in figure one. The evidence thus leads to the overwhelming conclusion that inadequate food and poor nutrition, when combined with heavy labor duties, compromised fertility throughout the year and that harvest-season peaks in food supply overcame the even more intense workloads of those months to spur episodic reproductive success.[19]

Slaves toiling on Jamaica's cane estates would have easily understood the hunger of the enslaved population in Louisiana. As historian Kenneth Kiple indicates, malnutrition in the West Indian cane islands similarly suppressed growth rates throughout the region and in all probability led to abnormally high numbers of stillbirths. But Jamaican planters, like their Louisiana neighbors, also gave their slaves unrestricted access to cane juice during the grinding season and similarly prided themselves on the momentarily healthy and cheerful appearance of their bondspeople. Yet, as John Masterson Waddell observed, their smiles derived merely from full bellies. "Ere the season closed," the Presbyterian missionary continued, "they began to suffer, were fagged and sickly, from excessive toil and want of food." Waddell's concerns with nutritional deprivation rang true throughout the sugar-producing Caribbean, including Louisiana, where they combined with environmental factors, disease, and the intense workload to produce dismal records of low fertility, impaired fecundity, and erratic capacity to conceive.[20]

ENVIRONMENTAL AND EPIDEMIOLOGICAL CONSIDERATIONS

Although nutrition levels proved critical in shaping the slaves' procreative lives, seasonal oscillation in birth patterns was not unique to the slave experience in the premodern world. In fact, the nutritionally driven winter peak in slave conceptions actually reinforced the physiological tendency among tropical peoples toward reproductive seasonality. As many physiologists contend, environmental and nutritional factors commonly influence annual rhythms in human reproduction. Conspicuously, ambient temperature, the availability of food, daylight, and the prevalence of disease alter the neurological clock that calculates the optimal time of the year to become pregnant or deliver offspring. In the upper, cooler latitudes, this cycle ensures that the summer months tend to be the prime periods of reproductive activity, while in the warmer lower latitudes, conceptions peak in the winter.

Traces of these seasonal rhythms in conception and ovulation remain today but are significantly less pronounced than in the nineteenth century or before. In subtropical southern Louisiana, these environmental factors continued to affect birth seasonality until the widespread diffusion of air-conditioning in the 1960s. Not only did heat and humidity obviously suppress copulation rates during the sultry summer months, but the stifling local climate also led to suppressed production of ova, decreased testosterone levels, lowered sperm counts and reduced motility, and increased ratios of immature and defective sperm. Indeed, as little as a five-degree (F) increase in the mean August temperature prompts a decline of 10 percent in conceptions.[21]

While summer heat compromised both male and female fecundity, the marked cooling of temperature in late October and November through southern parts of Louisiana reinforced the tendency toward a midwinter crest in conceptions. In all probability, this drop in temperatures (13 percent from October to November) increased reproductive activity even among fatigued and heat-drained slaves who had just endured six months of muggy and oppressive night heat in rude wooden shacks. Around their dismal huts lolled pigs, poultry, and dogs, all adding their feces to the human waste and stagnant pools that surrounded the cabins. Within the cabins, the primary living, cooking, and sleeping environment, ambient temperatures probably far exceeded open-air maximums during the lengthy summer, while providing only modest refuge from January chills. When combined with oppressive heat and sapping humidity, these spartan facilities almost certainly limited reproductive activity during the summer.[22]

Disease further limited slaves' fecundity and fertility everywhere in the Caribbean and the American South. Few bondspeople, however, lived in epidemiological environments more challenging than those in the Louisiana sugar country. The hot and swampy cane fields proved perfect breeding grounds for disease and, above all, for the malaria-carrying mosquito. African Americans possessed limited inherited immunity from falciparum malaria, but parasitical mutations ensured that the large number of slaves imported to the sugar region from Virginia and Maryland faced unfamiliar and virulent strains. Cholera struck periodically with still greater morbidity and mortality, as did yellow fever. African Americans debilitated by these diseases succumbed easily to hookworm and other diarrhea-inducing infestations of parasites that multiplied in the stagnant pools in which slaves washed and from which they drew water to cook and drink. No part of the year was infection free, though May through September proved especially unhealthy as tropical diseases spread among exhausted adult laborers and the newborn.

All premodern humans adapted to these seasonal epidemiological dangers by conceiving during relatively narrow "breeding seasons." Often triggered by greater availability of food in the fall harvest season, lower temperatures after the heat of summer, or reduced risk of disease during cooler nights, these "seasons" reflect generations, indeed centuries, of spontaneously preferred late-summer delivery dates. The prevalence of summer infections in both West Africa and in the U.S. South in all probability enhanced the slaves' tendency toward winter conceptions and term deliveries when temperatures began to drop later in the year and when disease proved less threatening.[23]

MISCARRIAGE AND EARLY PREGNANCY LOSS

Naturally weakened by the sugar masters' regime, slave women quite possibly also experienced greater fetal loss than those residing in the cotton South. Measuring the effect of workplace exhaustion or nutritional stress on the frequency of miscarriages or spontaneous abortions proves extremely difficult, but it seems highly probable that the sugar masters' labor regime took its toll in miscarriages following the harvest and planting seasons. Most research on spontaneous abortions indicates that between 14 and 43 percent of all conceptions result in an early miscarriage that usually materializes as a late or heavy menstrual period. Even among contemporary healthy women who seek to become pregnant, 31 percent of all conceptions fail. How often this happened to a Louisiana slave woman remains her secret, but some tangential evidence suggests that bondswomen in the sugar country suffered in all likelihood from luteal phase progesterone deficiency (LPD).

Since heavy physical labor suppresses the secretion of progesterone and reduces fecundity, a number of related conditions might explain fetal loss among Louisiana slaves. Progesterone deficiency, for instance, ensures that the womb is unsupportive for the successful implantation and sustained growth of the fertilized egg and it furthermore triggers a series of physiological responses that harms the endometrial environment within the uterus and makes it less able to react to pregnancy-related hormones. Undernourishment and vitamin deficiency further compromise ovarian function and contribute significantly to the frequency of miscarriages. Given the seasonal demands of workloads throughout the year, Louisiana slave women, in all probability, experienced LPD and endured pregnancy loss throughout the year, although most particularly during the winter and spring months. Women who additionally contracted summer diseases or "fevers" were also more likely to miscarry, ensuring that miscarriage remained a persistent feature of life throughout the sugar country. Infection, for instance, harms the placenta and compromises its ability to transmit nutrients to the fetus. Malaria is especially culpable, although fever-inducing infections are recognized as a common cause of early miscarriage and late fetal wastage. The disastrous combination of maternal overwork and undernourishment left a grim birthright for those children that were born into slavery; maternal malnutrition compromises the child's immune system during fetal growth, stillbirths are more frequent, and overworked and underfed mothers deliver offspring at least two hundred grams lighter than those of less active mothers. Workplace fatigue, moreover, slows fetal growth and the perpetual stooping and stretching involved with farming sugar cane reduces blood supply to the placenta. Neither planters nor slaves, of course, recognized these unintentional side effects of sugar production, but the labor order wrought a frightening toll among those alive and those yet to be born.[24]

Elsewhere in the U.S. South, family life protected enough slaves from the savage excesses of their masters' drive for profits that slave populations grew. But along the swampy bayous of the lower Mississippi Valley, the prospects for slave reproduction and thus children were profoundly compromised by the intense demands of mechanized sugar production that slaveholders introduced in the antebellum years. Unquestionably, environmental factors shaped the slaves' natural proclivity toward winter conceptions. The more significant for the seasonal variation, however, was the momentary surge in calories relative to energy expenditure that free consumption of sirop gave them during the harvest. The anomalous peak in harvest-time conceptions derived from Louisiana's plantation elite satiating the slaves' energy budget during the harvest but failing to do so at other key points in the agricultural cycle. Slave women thus faced the cruellest imposition on their dignity of all, for the overwhelming power of the sugar regime left an enduring inheritance at almost every stage of conception, pregnancy, and childbearing. Whether from reduced ovulation, hormonal imbalances, weight loss, or sheer exhaustion, sugar production in Louisiana materially harmed the slave woman's body. The sugar regime thus bequeathed an appalling legacy of human suffering. Little wonder then, that the enslaved called it "old debble Lousy Anna."

NOTES

1. George William Featherstonhaugh, *Excursion through the Slave States*, 2 vols. (London: J. Murray, 1844), 1:120; Frances Anne Kemble, *Journal of a Residence on a Georgian Plantation in 1838–1839*, ed. John A. Scott (Athens: University of Georgia Press, 1984), 122; Frederick Douglass, *Life and Times of Frederick Douglass* (Hartford: Park, 1881), 173; Jacob Stroyer, *My Life in the South* (Salem, MA: Salem Observer Book and Job Print, 1885), 42–43.

2. John S. Kendall, "New Orleans' Peculiar Institution," *Louisiana Historical Quarterly* 23, no. 1 (1940): 1; Claude C. Robin, *Voyage to Louisiana, 1803–1805*, trans. Stuart O. Landry (New Orleans: Pelican, 1966), 240.

3. Michael Tadman, *Speculators and Slaves: Masters, Traders, and Slaves in the Old South* (Madison: University of Wisconsin Press, 1989), 68; Tadman, "The Demographic Cost of Sugar: Debates on Slave Societies and Natural Increase in the Americas," *American Historical Review* 105, no. 5 (2000): 1534, 1554; Robert W. Fogel, *Without Consent or Contract: The Rise and Fall of American Slavery* (New York: Norton, 1989), 123–26. On the Caribbean, see Barry W. Higman, *Slave Populations of the British Caribbean, 1807–1834* (Baltimore: Johns Hopkins University Press, 1984), 375; Higman, *Slave Population and Economy in Jamaica, 1807–1834* (Cambridge: Cambridge University Press, 1976), 124; Michael Craton, "Hobbesian or Panglossian? The Two Extremes of Slave Conditions in the British Caribbean, 1783 to 1834," *William and Mary Quarterly* 35, no. 2 (1978): 347; Richard B. Sheridan, *Doctors and Slaves: A Medical and Demographic History of Slavery in the British West Indies, 1680–1834* (Cambridge: Cambridge University Press, 1985), 225–28. On physical activity and reproduction, see David C. Cumming, Garry D. Wheeler, and Vicki J. Harber, "Physical Activity, Nutrition, and Reproduction," *Annals of the New York Academy of Sciences*, no. 709 (1994): 57–60.

4. On contraception, see Liese M. Perrin, "Resisting Reproduction: Reconsidering Slave Contraception in the Old South," *Journal of American Studies* 35 (2001): 255–74; Sharla M. Fett, *Working Cures: Healing, Health, and Power on Southern Slave Plantations* (Chapel Hill: University of North Carolina Press, 2002), 176–77; Barbara Bush, *Slave Women in Caribbean Society, 1650–1838* (Bloomington: Indiana University Press. 1990), 138. On women who rejected the planters' attempts to control their lives, see Brenda Stevenson, "Gender Conventions, Ideals, and Identity among Antebellum Virginia Slave Women," in *More than Chattel: Black Women and Slavery in the Americas*, ed. David Barry Gaspar and Darlene Clark Hine (Bloomington: Indiana University Press, 1996), 169–90; Barbara Bush, "'The Family Tree Is Not Cut': Women and Cultural Resistance in Slave Family Life in the British Caribbean," in *In Resistance: Studies in African, Caribbean, and Afro-American History*, ed. Gary Y. Okihiro (Amherst: University of Massachusetts Press, 1986), 119–22; Darlene Clark Hine, "Rape and the Inner Lives of Black Women: Thoughts on the Culture of Dissemblance," *Signs* 14 (1989): 912–20. While not underestimating the significance of resistance, Jennifer L. Morgan has recently cautioned historians to avoid romanticizing women who practiced birth control. Morgan, *Laboring Women: Reproduction and Gender in New World Slavery* (Philadelphia: University of Pennsylvania Press, 2004), 114.

5. Cheryll Ann Cody, "Cycles of Work and Childbearing: Seasonality in Women's Lives on Low Country Plantations," in Gaspar and Hine, *More than Chattel*, 61–78; Taylor, quoted in Sheridan, *Doctors and Slaves*, 242; Tadman, "Demographic Cost of Sugar," 1534–75. For other approaches to work and pregnancy, see John Campbell, "Work, Pregnancy, and Infant Mortality among Southern Slaves," *Journal of Interdisciplinary History* 14 (1984): 793–812; Marietta Morrissey, *Slave Women in the New World: Gender Stratification in the Caribbean* (Lawrence: University of Kansas Press, 1989), 119–43; Marie Jenkins Schwartz, *Born in Bondage: Growing Up Enslaved in the Antebellum South* (Cambridge, MA: Harvard University Press, 2000), ch. 1. On fertility and fecundity, see James W. Wood, "Maternal Nutrition and Reproduction:

Why Demographers and Physiologists Disagree about a Fundamental Relationship," *Annals of the New York Academy of Sciences*, no. 709 (1994): 109. This relationship is not to be confused with the fertility ratio—the ratio of children to women.

6. Lyliane Rosetta, "Female Reproductive Dysfunction and Intense Physical Training," *Oxford Review of Reproductive Biology* 15 (1993): 113–41; David C. Cumming, "The Effects of Exercise and Nutrition on the Menstrual Cycle," in *Biomedical and Demographic Determinants of Reproduction*, ed. Ronald Gray, with Henri Leridon and Alfred Spira (Oxford: Clarendon Press, 1993), 132–56; C. Panter Brick, D. S. Lostein, and T. Ellison, "Seasonality of Reproductive Function and Weight Loss in Rural Nepali Women," *Human Reproduction* 8 (1993): 684–90; G. Jasieńska and T. Ellison, "Physical Work Causes Suppression of Ovarian Function in Women," *Proceedings of the Royal Society of London* B 265 (1998): 1847–51.

7. Although gestation varies significantly due to premature and late deliveries, most obstetricians use the nine-month or 270-day rule as their best working average. See Campbell, "Work, Pregnancy," 798. Slave birth data are drawn from Vital Register, 1832–62, Samuel McCutchon and James McCutchon (and Family) Papers, Louisiana and Lower Mississippi Valley Collections, Hill Memorial Library, Louisiana State University, Baton Rouge (hereafter cited as LSU); "Register of Births among W. J. Palfrey's Negroes, commenced August 1843," Palfrey (William J.) and Family Papers, LSU; vol. 17., List of Negroes on Waterloo Plantation 1848, 1852, and Southdown Plantation, 1852, William J. Minor and Family Papers, LSU; "A Memorandum of the Births of Negro Children," Record Book, 1817–52, Kleinpeter (Joseph) and Family Papers, LSU; vol. 9, "List of Mothers, Births, and Deceased," DeClouet (Alexandre) Papers, LSU. Anonymous Planters Ledger, LSU; Aime (Valcour) Slave Records, Louisiana State Museum, New Orleans; White (Maunsell) Papers, Southern Historical Collection, Manuscripts Department, Library of the University of North Carolina at Chapel Hill.

8. Cody, "Life and Labor," 69.

9. On the nature of slavery in the antebellum sugar country, see Richard Follett, *The Sugar Masters: Planters and Slaves in Louisiana's Cane World, 1820–1860* (Baton Rouge: Louisiana State University Press, 2005); J. Carlyle Sitterson, *Sugar Country: The Cane Sugar Industry in the South, 1753–1950* (Lexington: University of Kentucky Press, 1953); John Rodrigue, *Reconstruction in the Cane Fields: From Slavery to Free Labor in Louisiana's Sugar Parishes, 1862–1880* (Baton Rouge: Louisiana State University Press, 2001), 9–32; Roderick A. McDonald, *The Economy and Material Culture of Slaves: Goods and Chattels on the Sugar Plantations of Jamaica and Louisiana History* (Baton Rouge: Louisiana State University Press, 1993).

10. L. A. Van der Walt, E. N. Wilmsen, and T. Jenkins, "Unusual Sex Hormone Patterns among Desert-Dwelling Hunter-Gatherers," *Journal of Clinical Endocrinology and Metabolism* 16 (1978): 658–63; Paul W. Leslie and Peggy H. Fry, "Extreme Seasonality of Births among Nomadic Turkana Pastoralists," *American Journal of Physical Anthropology* 79 (1989): 103–15.

11. Solon Robinson, "Agricultural Tour South and West, No. 4," *American Agriculturist* 8 (April 1849): 118; "Agricultural Tour South and West, No. 9," *American Agriculturist* 8 (September 1849): 283; "Agricultural Tour South and West, No. 10,"

American Agriculturist 9 (October 1849): 315; "Agricultural Tour South and West, No. 11," *American Agriculturist* 10 (November 1849): 337; V. Alton Moody, *Slavery on Louisiana Sugar Plantations* (1924; reprint, New York: AMS Press, 1976), 77; Frederick L. Olmsted, *A Journey in the Seaboard Slave States* (New York: G. P. Putnam's Sons, 1904), 343, 350, 363; J. Carlyle Sitterson, "The William J. Minor Plantations: A Study in Ante-Bellum Absentee Ownership," *Journal of Southern History* 9, no. 1 (1943): 66.

12. *Energy and Protein Requirements*, World Health Organization Technical Report Series, no. 724 (Geneva: WHO, 1985), 77; Richard Sutch, "The Care and Feeding of Slaves," in *Reckoning with Slavery: A Critical Study in the Quantitative History of American Negro Slavery*, ed. Paul A. David et al. (New York: Oxford University Press, 1976), 265–67; Kimberly A. Hammond and Jared Diamond, "Maximal Sustained Energy Budgets in Humans and Animals," *Nature* 386 (1997): 457. On the Christensen system, see J. V. G. A. Durnin and R. Passmore, *Energy, Work, and Leisure* (London: Heinemann Educational Books, 1967), esp. ch. 4. On adaptation to underfeeding, see J. S. Garrow, "Energy Balance and Weight Regulation," in *Human Nutrition and Dietetics*, ed. Garrow and W. P. T. James, 9th ed. (Edinburgh: Churchill Livingstone, 1993), 141–42.

13. Tadman, *Speculators*, 65; Richard H. Steckel, "A Peculiar Population: The Nutrition, Health, and Mortality of American Slaves from Childhood to Maturity," *Journal of Economic History* 46 (1986): 721–26.

14. On ovarian function, see Peter T. Ellison, Nadine R. Peacock, and Catherine Lager, "Ecology and Ovarian Function among the Lese Women of the Ituri Forest, Zaire," *American Journal of Physical Anthropology* 78 (1989): 519–26; Catherine Lager and Peter T. Ellison, "Effect of Moderate Weight Loss on Ovarian Function Assessed by Salivary Progesterone Measurements," *American Journal of Human Biology* 2 (1990): 303–12.

15. For fourteen-hour shifts, assume slaves slept for seven hours and rested for three additional hours (712.2 kcal); for sixteen-hour shifts, assume slaves slept for six hours and rested for two additional hours (562.8 kcal). These estimates most probably underrecord extrawork activities, as cane cutters probably expended 9.8 kcal/minute, gathering canes and loading them onto wagons required from 5.5 to 6.8 kcal/minute, while labor in the sugar mill probably varied from moderate to heavy in Christensen's energy classification. See Durnin and Passmore, *Energy, Work*, 31, 39, 72, 62, 75.

16. Olmsted, *Seaboard Slave States*, 317; Joseph H. Ingraham, *The Southwest by a Yankee*, 2 vols. (New York, 1835), 1:240; *De Bow's Review* 13 (December 1852): 598–99; *Plow* 1 (November 1852): 352.

17. Sidney W. Mintz, *Sweetness and Power: The Place of Sugar in Modern History* (London: Penguin, 1985), 191; Judith E. Brown, *The Science of Human Nutrition* (San Diego: Harcourt, Brace, Jovanovich, 1990), ch. 5.

18. Thomas Affleck, *The Sugar Plantation Record and Account Book. No. 2* (New Orleans: B. M. Norman, 1854); interview with Albert Patterson (22 May 1940), WPA Ex-Slave Narrative Papers, LSU; Frogmoor Plantation Diary 1857, Turnbull-Bowman-Lyons Family Papers, LSU; Oaklands Plantation Document 1859, McCutchon

(Samuel D.) Papers, LSU; "Rules and Regulations on Governing Southdown and Hollywood Plantations," vol. 34, Plantation Diary 1861–68, William J. Minor and Family Papers, LSU.

19. Rose E. Frisch and J. W. McArthur, "Menstrual Cycles: Fatness as a Determinant of Minimum Weight for Height Necessary for the Maintenance and Onset," *Science* 185 (1974): 949–51; Rose E. Frisch, "Body Fat, Puberty, and Fertility," *Biological Reviews* 59 (1984): 161–88; Michelle P. Warren, "Effects of Undernutrition on Reproductive Function in the Human," *Endocrine Reviews* 4 (1983): 363–77; Lager and Ellison, "Effect of Moderate Weight Loss," 303–12. On decreased energy intake and reproduction, see Rose E. Frisch, "Nutrition, Fatness and Fertility: The Effect of Food Intake on Reproductive Ability," in *Nutrition and Human Reproduction*, ed. W. Henry Mosley (New York: Plenum Press, 1978), 99. Also, see Zena Stein and Mervyn Susser, "Fertility, Fecundity, Famine: Food Rations in the Dutch Famine 1944/5 Have a Causal Relation to Fertility, and Probably to Fecundity," *Human Biology* 47 (1975): 131–54.

20. Kenneth F. Kiple, *The Caribbean Slave: A Biological History* (Cambridge: Cambridge University Press, 1984), 113–15; Reverend Hope Masterton Waddell, *Twenty-Nine Years in the West Indies and Central Africa: A Review of Missionary Work and Adventure* (1863; reprint, London: Frank Cass, 1970), quoted in Sheridan, *Doctors and Slaves*, 153. In offering sirop, planters mirrored the long-standing Caribbean precedent of offering grog or rum to stimulate workers in the sugarhouse. David Barry Gaspar, "Sugar Cultivation and Slave Life in Antigua before 1800," in *Cultivation and Culture: Labor and the Shaping of Slave Life in the Americas*, ed. Ira Berlin and Philip D. Morgan (Charlottesville: University Press of Virginia, 1993), 108. For comparisons with Tobago and Berbice birth seasonality, see B. W. Higman, *Slave Populations of the British Caribbean, 1807–1834* (Baltimore: Johns Hopkins University Press, 1984), 364, 686.

21. On environmental factors, see Till Roenneberg and Jürgen Aschoff, "Annual Rhythms of Human Reproduction: I. Biology, Sociology or Both?" *Journal of Biological Rhythms* 5 (1990): 195–216; Thomas A. Wehr, "Photoperiodism in Humans and Other Primates: Evidence and Implications," *Journal of Biological Rhythms* 16 (2001): 348–64; F. H. Bronson, "Seasonal Variation in Human Reproduction: Environmental Factors," *Quarterly Review of Biology* 70 (1995): 141–64; Brian K. Follett, "The Environment and Reproduction," in *Reproduction in Mammals*, book 4, *Reproductive Fitness*, ed. C. R. Austin and R. V. Short, 2nd ed. (Cambridge: Cambridge University Press, 1984), 103–32; F. Hoffmann and D. Kawiani, "Seasonal Variations in the Birth Rate and Conception Rate within the Last 200 Years," *Geburtshilfe und Frauenheilkunde* (Stuttgart) 36 (1976): 780–85; A. Lerchl, M. Simoni, and E. Nieschlag, "Changes in Seasonality of Birth Rates in Germany from 1951 to 1990," *Naturwissenschaften* 80 (1993): 516–18. On sperm levels, see David A. Lam and Jeffrey A. Miron, "Global Patterns of Seasonal Variation in Human Fertility," *Annals of the New York Academy of Sciences*, no. 709 (1994): 9–28; R. J. Levine, B. L. Bordson, R. M. Mathew, M. H. Brown, J. M. Stanley, and T. B. Starr, "Deterioration of Semen Quality during Summer in New Orleans," *Fertility and Sterility* 49 (1988): 900–907; R. J. Levine, "Male Factors Contributing to the Seasonality of Human Reproduction,"

Annals of the New York Academy of Sciences, no. 709 (1994): 29–45; Grace M. Centola and Shirley Eberly, "Seasonal Variations and Age-Related Changes in Human Sperm Count, Motility, Motion Parameters, Morphology, and White Blood Cell Concentration," *Fertility and Sterility* 72 (1999): 803–8. On U.S. reproductive seasonality, see D. A. Sevier, "Trend and Variation in the Seasonality of U.S. Fertility, 1947 to 1946," *Demography* 22 (1985): 89–99; Sevier, "Seasonality of Fertility: New Evidence," *Population and Environment* 10 (1989): 245–57. On temperature, see David A. Lam and Jeffrey A. Miron, "The Effect of Temperature on Human Fertility," *Demography* 33 (1996): 294; National Oceanic and Atmospheric Administration, *Monthly Normals of Temperature, Precipitation, and Heating and Cooling Degree Days 1951–80, Louisiana*, Climatography of the United States, no. 81 (Asheville, NC: National Climatic Center, 1982); Louisiana State University in New Orleans, *Statistical Abstract of Louisiana 1994* (New Orleans, 1994), 3–7.

22. Solon Robinson, *Solon Robinson, Pioneer and Agriculturist: Selected Writings*, ed. Herbert Anthony Kellar, 2 vols. (Indianapolis: Indiana Historical Bureau, 1936), 172, 180; William Howard Russell, *My Diary North and South*, ed. Eugene H. Berwanger (New York: Knopf, 1988), 176; John Michael Vlach, *Back of the Big House: The Architecture of Plantation Slavery* (Chapel Hill: University of North Carolina Press, 1993), 191.

23. On disease, see Kenneth F. Kiple and Virginia Himmelsteib King, *Another Dimension to the Black Diaspora: Diet, Disease, and Racism* (Cambridge: Cambridge University Press, 1981), 23, 50–58, 151; K. David Patterson, "Disease Environments of the Antebellum South," in *Science and Medicine in the Old South*, ed. Ronald L. Numbers and Todd L. Savitt (Baton Rouge: Louisiana State University Press, 1989), 152–65; Todd L. Savitt, *Medicine and Slavery: The Diseases and Health Care of Blacks in Antebellum Virginia* (Urbana: University of Illinois Press, 1978), 49–82. On breeding seasons, see J. Gyllenborg, N. E. Skakkebæk, N. C. Nielson, N. Keiding, and A. Giwercman, "Secular and Seasonal Changes in Semen Quality among Young Danish Men: A Statistical Analysis of Semen Samples from 1927 Donor Candidates during 1977–1995," *International Journal of Andrology* 22 (1999): 34.

24. Joe Leigh Simpson and Sandra Carson, "Biological Causes of Foetal Loss," in Gray, Leridon, and Spira, *Biomedical and Demographic Determinants*, 308; A. J. Wilcox et al., "Incidence of Early Loss of Pregnancy," *New England Journal of Medicine* 319 (1988): 189–94; J. Neela and L. Raman, "The Relationship between Maternal Nutritional Status and Spontaneous Abortion," *National Medical Journal of India* 10 (1997): 15–16; Michael A. DeLuca and Paul W. Leslie, "Variation in Risk of Pregnancy Loss," in *The Anthropology of Pregnancy Loss: Comparative Studies in Miscarriage, Stillbirth, and Neonatal Death*, ed. Rosanne Cecil (Oxford: Berg, 1996), 113–30; C. R. Weinberg et al., "Is There a Seasonal Pattern in Risk of Early Pregnancy Loss?" *Epidemiology* 5 (1994): 484–89; Donna D. Baird et al., "The Relationship between Reduced Fecundability and Subsequent Foetal Loss," in Gray, Leridon, and Spira, *Biomedical and Demographic Determinants*, 335; Maxine Weinstein and Marya Stark, "Behavioral and Biological Determinants of Fecundability," *Annals of the New York Academy of Sciences*, no. 709 (1994): 134. If the corpus luteum cannot secrete adequate progesterone to sustain the embryo until the placenta becomes self-

sustaining (approximately five weeks after conception), the pregnancy will fail. On maternal overwork, undernutrition, and infant survival, see N. Tafari, R. L. Naeye, and A. Gobezie, "Effects of Maternal Undernutrition and Heavy Physical Work during Pregnancy on Birth Weight," *British Journal of Obstetrics and Gynecology* 87 (1980): 222–26; Aaron Lechtig et al., "Evidence of Maternal Nutrition on Infant Mortality," in Mosley, *Nutrition and Human Reproduction,* 147–74; Sophie Moore et al., "Season of Birth Predicts Mortality in Rural Gambia," *Nature* 388 (1997): 434.

2

Women's Initiatives under Slavery

3

CAN WOMEN GUIDE AND GOVERN MEN?

Gendering Politics among African Catholics in Colonial Brazil

MARIZA DE CARVALHO SOARES

During the colonial period throughout the Americas, males had all the power. One infrequently considered issue is the gendered bias of male control of writing. It is thus important to keep in mind that the history of slavery relies on documents written, or in some other way produced, by men. Thus we may presume that these sources exhibit a male point of view, especially in the ways that they describe women.[1] Even taking account of this male approach, available data offer a plethora of information about female slaves and gender.[2] The struggle of the African slave woman I am writing about emerges from colonial documents like these in eighteenth-century Rio de Janeiro, in Brazil.

Her Christian name was Victoria. She probably disembarked from Africa, in slavery, in Rio de Janeiro and went to the gold-mining region in Minas Gerais around 1741. In 1742 she was baptized Victoria Coura.[3] Father Leão Sá recorded the sacrament and described her as a twenty-five-year-old woman, short, with no diseases or physical disabilities, and bearing on her face the marks of her country, the country of Coura (*terra de Coura*) in Mina Coast (*Costa da Mina*), West Africa.[4]

Research for this chapter was supported by the Ministério da Educação-CAPES, Brazil, and by the Harriet Tubman Resource Centre on the African Diaspora, York University, Toronto. A first draft was presented at the Tubman Centre. I am grateful to Ola Tunji Ojo and Paul Lovejoy, who have given me valuable suggestions. I am also grateful to Joseph Miller for his support while I was writing the present version. The chapter has emerged from ongoing research and is still under revision at many points.

At that time Coura slaves were already well known in the interior mountainous region of the mines, where they had begun arriving as early as the 1720s. Pierre Verger mentions the presence of *couranos* in the Portuguese fort at Ouidah on the Slave Coast of western Africa in 1743, while describing problems involving the fort's director, João Basílio.[5] One or two years before, Victoria could have been sent to Brazil from Ouidah, Jaquem, or another port along the coast. I argue that those people called couranos by the Portuguese came from very far inland.[6]

In that same period the Portuguese/Brazilian documentation mentions African slaves called *coura* (Koura?), *cobu* (Kabou, Kobu?), *chamba* (Chamba, Tchamba?), *maki* (Mahi), *sabaru* (Savalu), *agolin* (Agonli), *cabrerá* (Kabré?), *daça* (Dassa), and *iono* (Oyo).[7] These are eighteenth-century names related to places north of the principal slave-selling polity of the time, Dahomey.[8] These locations trace a slave route running directly south to the littoral from a well-defined region in the interior. South of those places, in the Mahi country, are Savalu and Dassa, the latter a Yoruba village. From there, crossing Dahomey or going around it, one could reach Ouidah or any other Atlantic port. In addition, consolidation of the Dahomey polity during these decades displaced the violence of conquest of the littoral in the 1720s north into the interior.

Different authors mention those places as sources of slaves at that time. Parrinder describes the Yoruba migration reaching Dassa and Savé, and from there, up to Bassila, the limit between Yoruba and the Kotokoli (or Cotocoli) languages. North of Bassila, close to the sources of the Mono River, he locates a village called Aledjo, a Yoruba term for stranger.[9] Robert Cornevin refers to Aledjo as Aledjo Koura—that is, "Koura foreigners," presumably eligible for capture and sale. According to him, when the Kotokoli came from Gourma they crossed Aledjo Koura in their way to Soudou, Koumandé, and Aledjo Kadara, in present-day Togo. He also mentions a route from Djougou to Savalu[10] and identifies Kabou as an important local slave market.[11] N. L. Gayibor shows Aledjo, Kabou, and Tchamba on a map tracing the routes of the kola trade during the nineteenth century: Aledjo Koura and Kabou are both along the route from Zaria to Salaga, and Tchamba is connected to that route.[12]

The most precise information about those groups and how they could have reached the coast come from Paul Lovejoy's book about the Hausa caravans of kola in the region. There he mentions the "Malais" on the coast in the early eighteenth century, arguing that "almost certainly

[they] were Wangara traders from the northern centres." Although he does not mention Koura or Kabou, he points to the slave trade in their region: "'Thiamba,' 'Chamba,' and 'Kotokoli' were shipped to the Americas as early as the 1750s. All came from the Dedaure region, which Muslims usually referred to as 'Kotokoli.' The use of the term indicated that Gonja, Dagbon, and perhaps Dahomey were raiding the area for slaves, but a trade centre could also have been located there."[13]

As these descriptions demonstrate, the problem is not confirming the presence of a slave trade route but rather the chronology of the trade between this remote hinterland and the coast. Robin Law, quoting Des Marchais, mentions Muslims trading in the littoral as early as 1704, but we don't know how important the route may have been at the time.[14] Based on Brazilian ecclesiastical documents, I argue this slave route was in regular use at least since the 1720s, perhaps earlier, and actually its use could have decreased later in the eighteenth century.

After the 1750s, Coura slaves were no longer arriving in Brazil, but many Coura were clearly very well settled in Minas Gerais and Rio de Janeiro. Victoria Coura was one of them, and for now it is enough to suggest that she may have come among those taken around 1741 from the vicinity of Aledjo Koura. Sometime after 1742 Victoria moved to Rio de Janeiro, where in 1755 she purchased her freedom for 180,000 réis. In 1759 she married Ignácio Gonçalves do Monte, known simply as Monte. Victoria's letter of manumission attested that she changed her name to Victoria Correa Campos, a name she evidently took from her first master, Domingos Correa Campos. In her husband's will she was called Victoria Correa da Conceição, invoking the name of the parish of Our Lady of Conception, where she had been baptized.[15] Monte was from Mahi, another of the countries neighboring Dahomey to the north.[16] He had arrived in Rio de Janeiro around 1741. The Mahi arrived in Brazil at least from the 1720s until the end of the eighteenth century.[17] He spent his years of slavery, and later his freedom until he died (in 1783), working in Rio de Janeiro as a barber. Victoria survived him and was declared by him in his will to be its executor and Monte's only heir.[18]

In Brazil, Mahi and Coura—presumably not unlike other Africans—made simultaneous use of both their African backgrounds and the new circumstances they faced under slavery in Brazil, organizing themselves around new identities that combined the African country (terra) they had come from and the Brazilian nation (nação) in which they were classified, as in all the Americas, as slaves (or former slaves). Nations often referred to the major transatlantic trade routes that had brought the enslaved to America.[19] Slaves from Bight of Benin used to have a strong and effective social identity as Mina in both Rio de Janeiro and Minas Gerais.[20] Referencing both (but not using either to subdivide the other), they refined such identities as "Mina-Mahi nation," "Mina-Coura nation," or just "Mahi nation" and "Coura nation." Thus, within these nations they drew on their differing countries of background in Africa to contest the internal politics inevitable in so large a collectivity.

Monte (Mahi) and Victoria (Coura) were among these Mina people living in Rio de Janeiro. Victoria and Monte would not be different from many other obscure slave couples in Brazil if they had not been who they were in African terms. Monte declared himself to be a grandchild of Victoria's father: "my wife is my consanguine relative in the third degree, being the daughter of my grandfather [Eseú] Agoa; well known as a king, he was among the heathen people from that coast in the kingdom of May, or Maqui."[21]

Though Victoria was Coura and Monte was Mahi, they had a father or grandfather in common. Such a relationship could have stemmed from a series of Mahi-Coura marriage exchanges extending over at least two generations, or they could also refer to a broader classificatory genealogical calculus characteristic of African systems of kinship. What is important here is that this claim pointed to exchanges of women, some possibly through slaving, between Mahi and Coura peoples in Africa, specified as earlier than the 1720s, the supposed date of Victoria's birth. Victoria's father, whom Monte called Agoa, had the same name (or title, or perhaps a name changed to a title) as the founder of the Mahi people remembered in the twentieth century, whom Robert Cornevin mentioned as Agoua-Guédé.[22] We do not know the exact relationship between Monte's grandfather and the later remembered Agoua-Guédé, but the name Agoa is obviously somehow related to his Mahi ancestry. Monte wrote his will in 1763—two decades before he passed away (1783)—at the very moment of his prime, one year after he was elected king of the Mahi in Rio de Janeiro (1762), having Victoria for his "queen."

Understanding the events of Victoria's life and career in Brazil demands some prior explanation of how people from the Mina coast played their roles in eighteenth-century Rio de Janeiro, where Mina was a minor but strong local identity amid a majority of Angola and other west-central African nations. However, Mina people were the majority of those who paid for their own letters of freedom[23] and the majority of those who wrote their own wills.[24]

BLACK BROTHERHOODS FOR MINA COAST PEOPLE IN RIO DE JANEIRO

Eighteenth-century Brazil was a hierarchical society, often called baroque, where the main goal of everyone, including slaves, was to reach upper positions within its elaborate systems of ranking.[25] Some Mina people quickly understood that enslavement did not necessarily last for long and was not the same for all the enslaved. They also realized that however they might climb social ladders by converting from heathen to Christian, assimilating from a *boçal* (new, unacculturated slave) to a Portuguese-speaking, perhaps Christian, ladino slave, or advancing in civil status from slave to freedman, they would remain in the lowest rank of society, which contained all those who had ever been a slave at any time in their lives.

Catholic lay brotherhoods in Brazil offered spaces for sociability to those who belonged to them, while simultaneously reinforcing the colonial hierarchical society. The number of brotherhoods to which one affiliated, the contributions one made to each of them, and the positions one attained in their hierarchies were public demonstrations of personal prestige and power. Africans slaves took advantage of being accepted in those brotherhoods and made them one of the most important colonial institutions where they could recover relational senses of themselves, which their enslavement in Africa had destroyed, and organize within slavery.[26]

Since at least the sixteenth century in Portugal, black people had dedicated themselves to Catholic saints and had elected kings and queens within brotherhoods consisting of slaves and former slaves.[27] In Rio de Janeiro the Black Brotherhood of the Rosary (Nossa Senhora do Rosário) dated at least from the seventeenth century. It allowed any black person to affiliate, but its governing council was composed exclusively of the majority Africans from Angola and Kongo, and by Brazil-born *crioulos*.[28] The increasing production of gold from the mines in Minas Gerais during the first decades of the eighteenth century brought enormous wealth to the city of Rio de Janeiro. Even slaves benefited from its opportunities, increasing the number and the pomp of their brotherhoods.

To afford membership in a brotherhood was also the best way to integrate oneself in a network that would guarantee mutual care and benefits for the living and prevent abandonment and dishonor of dying alone and unremembered. Masters who did not want to pay for the requisites of Catholic burials threw the bodies of many slaves who died in swamps or left them on beaches for the tide to wash away. Others were buried for free, with the necessary Catholic sacraments but without honor, in collective graves. Catholic burial had numerous and expensive rites that included the proper attire (at least a white sheet), payment for a priest to bless the cadaver, and two slaves to carry the body on their shoulders in a hammock to the church or cemetery, as well as masses and candles. If there were penance to be paid or belongings to be distributed, it was required to hire someone to draft a will.

Women were more successful than men in achieving respectable standing through decent burials. In a sample of registered burials between 1724 and 1736, of 499 black people interred in Rio de Janeiro, 251 were women, 248 men. Of the women, 44 (17.5 percent) were from the Mina coast people as were 35 (13.5 percent) of the men.[29] Considering that most slaves arriving through the slave trade were male, the slight preponderance of decent female burials must indicate women's superior opportunities of earning and saving money to pay for these interments. Note, however, that only a very small percentage of Africans, most of them freed, could afford Catholic burials. Further, those who achieved this small measure of respectability probably were among an elite in the black brotherhoods, perhaps overlapping with similarly elevated rankings in their African backgrounds.

The baroque Catholic Church, and particularly the associated lay brotherhoods, actively recruited new slaves. Victoria, at the time of her husband's death in 1783, was probably a very different person than she had been in 1742, when she first tasted the blessed salt of baptism. The brotherhoods created spaces for group organizations and even reinforced ethnic reelaboration with direct connections to the slaves' African pasts. But despite the congruences in tone between some African and Catholic hierarchies, such radical redefinition of self did not always happen, or did not happen always in the same way.

In Brazil slaves who came from around the Bight of Benin identified themselves by names of well-known kingdoms in the region, like Allada and Dahomey. They also identified themselves as coming from "countries" like Mahi and Coura. Unlike Allada and Dahomey, the two large and highly militarized polities, Mahi people were not centralized, and so they had no kings.[30] Dahomey, Oyo, and Mahi waged wars throughout the eighteenth century and later; but they also traded, allied, and intermarried with one another. Beyond sharing political traditions of origin, those neighbors' close ongoing relationships created strong links within a broadly shared social and cultural background. The people taken from the region to Rio de Janeiro drew on these shared backgrounds in their everyday lives under slavery, perhaps even overcoming initial strong animosities.

THE FEMALE PRESENCE WITHIN BROTHERHOODS

After Victoria's husband passed away in 1783, she became involved in a conflict within the black brotherhood of which she had been a member for more than twenty years. This dispute suggests intriguing outlines of the way in which multicultured Africans appropriated their African background to resolve conflicts generated by the more competitive differentiation of baroque Brazil.

The conflict involved Victoria and Francisco Alves de Souza, her deceased husband's Mahi successor as king, or regent, of the black Brotherhood of Santo Elesbão and Santa Efigênia.[31] Freed Africans in Rio had created the brotherhood in 1740. Unlike white brotherhoods—where women took part only as wives, daughters, or widows of male members—black brotherhoods, while also primarily male institutions, allowed women to participate directly, perhaps drawing on some African sense of gender complementarity. In the Brotherhood of Santo Elesbão women could affiliate, but an exclusionary regulation allowed them to elect their own council, with the same number of judges as the male council but without the privilege of electing the major judges of the brotherhood. For this limited participation female councillors were nonetheless required to pay the same membership and initiation fees as men.[32]

Since the founding of the Brotherhood of Saint Elesbão, its Mina members had organized a Mina congregation within it, thus distinguishing themselves from the members from Cape Verde, São Tomé Island, and Mozambique. Following the hoary Portuguese tradition for black brotherhoods, they elected kings and queens. In 1748 the Mina king was Pedro Costa, and his successor was Clemente Proença, both probably Dahomeans.[33] Victoria and Monte were both members of this Mina congregation when Monte came into strong conflict with Clemente Proença. In 1762 Monte broke away to create a separate Mahi congregation, with himself as king. Other subgroups from the Mina congregation joined him in this new grouping. The listed composition of the Mahi congregation thus offers a diagram of the Mahi country in Africa and the surrounding ethnopolitical landscape, including members from Agonli, Dassa, Za, and Savalu.[34] Despite Victoria's prominence within the Mahi congregation, her Coura background was never mentioned by Souza or Cordeiro.

From the membership lists and other information we have about the councils in other black brotherhoods, we know that high-status members normally occupied a series of different official positions over time.[35] Since both colonial society in Brazil and the Gbe- and Yoruba-speaking peoples of Africa were hierarchical societies, their kings and queens were probably chosen from among the high-ranking people of the brotherhood, at least some of whom could also have been distinguished in their countries and kingdoms in Africa. Such an explicit claim to royal ancestry in Africa is revealed in Monte's will.

In 1764 the Brotherhood of Saint Elesbão received final approval for five additional chapters for their bylaws, from the royal council in Portugal that regulated religious bodies throughout the empire, the Mesa de Consciência e Ordens, allowing them to create a requested Empire of Saint Elesbão. The "empire" (like a royal court within a realm) was a hierarchical organization within the brotherhood, headed by an emperor or empress and a court of up to seven kings, who might or might not also have queens.[36] The inauguration of the new empire was probably a Dahomean strategy to manage the internal struggle for power and positions carried on by the minor congregations within the brotherhood, the Mahi grouping among them. The inauguration of those kings, together with the emperor, would allow Dahomeans to elect the emperor and leave the others to elect only kings of lower rank, which would keep power under Dahomean control.[37]

A STRUGGLE FOR SUCCESSION

Monte's death in 1783 promoted a struggle in both Mahi and Mina congregations. Victoria did not submit to Francisco Alves de Souza, and particularly did not submit to the new queen. She decided to fight and keep her existing position as queen of the deceased Monte. Her persistence brought on a long and disruptive conflict within the brotherhood. The conflict generated the documentation upon which this chapter is based.[38]

Francisco Alves de Souza, known as Souza in his lifetime—also a Mahi man and Monte's former regent and designated successor—reported these events, which lasted from 1783 to 1788, in two documents written after he had been enthroned but while he was still involved in the dispute. The first is a long report written in 1786 as a formal classical dialogue and including the draft of a bylaw for a Mahi congregation devoted to the souls of deceased Mahi; the second document is a formal proposal addressed to D. Maria I, queen of Portugal (and Brazil), for a statute authorizing a new Mahi devotional congregation dedicated to Our Lady of Remedies (Nossa Senhora dos Remédios), dated 1788. The second document is signed by Souza, Gonçalo Cordeiro (secretary of the Mahi congregation), and other members.[39]

According to the dialogue (the earlier document), the issue of Monte's succession had split the Mahi congregation. Souza himself headed one faction and Victoria the other. They were fighting over Victoria's refusal to transfer the congregation's treasury chest to the new queen, Souza's wife, Rita Sebastiana. The chest contained the group's monetary assets, and it was a major symbol of prestige and power within the group. The dialogue (1786) did not mention the rule, but the proposal of 1788 gave the queen the privilege of keeping the congregation's treasury in her home, though not permission to make personal use of it. Only the three male councillors, each of whom kept one of its three keys, could open the chest. Unlike the brotherhoods, which the bishopric regulated, congregations did not need to account formally for their funds to any external authority. Subject only to these internal fiduciary standards, congregations were perfect open environments within which to compete.

Since the bylaws of the Brotherhood of Saint Elesbão allowed the election of kings and queens but did not state the qualifications for those offices, the dispute over the titles could have resulted either from the claimed African royal ancestries of the contenders or from their elevated personal positions in the hierarchy of the brotherhood (and, in the case of queens, from being consorts of royal husbands), or from combining any or all of these qualifications in different measures. But while Monte had declared his royal ancestry, his successor, Souza, repeatedly rejected recognition as king. He agreed to accept the title and the crown only after a long debate about hierarchical positions, and against his wishes. Although Souza refused the crown of king of the Mahi, Victoria dreamed of the crown of empress of the Mina Coast, a more elevated rank than she had ever claimed during her royal husband's life. Souza's common ancestry might explain why he so insistently rejected the title of king for himself, arguing that regent was "the proper name for what we do."[40]

Though the initial dialogue provides a good deal of information about the dispute, it remains tantalizingly silent about many important points. Written in an unexpectedly literary style, it should be read carefully to identify the specific circumstances coded in its heated rhetoric. The document is a dialogue between the voices of Francisco Alves de Souza himself and the congregation's secretary, Gonçalo Cordeiro, also a Mahi man.[41] Following the precise model of classical dialogues, Souza and Cordeiro play the roles of master and disciple. Souza's followers, also present in the dialogue, utter a few short sentences. They are all men and designated by their Christian names, and some by their titles in the Gbe and Yoruba languages. Victoria is referred to extensively as the head of the opposing faction but is never given a voice, and not even a name. Souza calls her the widow, perhaps suggesting that her claims to royalty actually derived only from the standing of her deceased husband. In his portion of the dialogue Souza admits she had some male support within the brotherhood. That support allowed her not only to campaign for the position of Mahi queen but also to mount her challenge to become the empress of the Mina Coast within the Mina congregation, where she was supposed to have allies.[42]

Souza's report thus reveals that Monte's absence had created a huge crisis not only within the Mahi congregation but also throughout the brotherhood. He also lets one know, between the lines, that he and Victoria had exchanged mutual accusations. This personal confrontation highlights the fact that the conflict crossed ethnic boundaries, both aligning and opposing individuals and local factions: "She forced people to put a crown on her head, saying she was the queen in such a subtle way that, surprised by her attitude, people flew away in the same day because not only those from the Mahi nation were there, but everyone, those from the Mina coast and other nations."[43] The complexity of the conflict shows that individuals were not encapsulated within rigid "ethnic" collectivities; rather, they moved among these distinctions, organizing personal networks that might not take either country (terra) or nation (nação) as the prime condition connecting people or separating them.[44]

Victoria and Souza fought one another for at least five years (1783–88), perhaps longer. Their conflict extended beyond the brotherhood, revealing not only the local dispute but also links between these African people of low position and high-ranking representatives of the Portuguese crown in Rio de Janeiro and Lisbon. Souza's allies, against his will, denounced Victoria to the Colonial High Court (Tribunal da Relação) in Rio de Janeiro for stealing the chest of the congregation. Once they lost the appeal of the denouncement, Victoria turned against them again. She obtained a copy of the decision of the high court against Souza and took it to the viceroy of Brazil, at the time D. Luiz de Vasconcellos. Victoria and her companions convinced the viceroy to support her position in the dispute. Souza was called before the viceroy to explain his perspectives on the case.[45] With no higher local authority to whom he could appeal, Souza turned then to the queen of Portugal herself, Maria I, in 1788. The last available information about Victoria is this appeal, which was reviewed by the royal bureaucracy in Lisbon, reaching the elevated Overseas Council (Conselho Ultramarino).[46]

THE GENDERED ASPECTS OF THE DISPUTE

Souza appealed to the Portuguese legal system to force Victoria to give the congregation's treasury chest to his own wife, Rita Sebastiana. In the papers detailing the dispute, Rita remains a shadowy figure, no more than a name, with no participation or reported attitudes. If she had her own female allies, as she probably did, they never came onto the scene. The conflict developed directly and personally between Victoria and Souza.

The imbroglio that Victoria provoked represented a challenge to male power within the Mahi congregation, and also within the brotherhood. Souza and his followers had to respond to Victoria's determination to govern them herself, without a male partner to control her. In sum, could there be a queen without a king? According to Cordeiro, secretary of the Mahi congregation and disciple in the dialogue, "the widow should take care of her home and of the soul of her husband because women cannot govern men." Apparently inverting positions, Souza, although the master in the dialogue, asked Cordeiro why not. The secretary-disciple answered that women did not govern men in any other brotherhood, adding that they could be members of the councils, but only for their financial contributions, and emphasizing that this standing did not allow them to rule, since special skills (which he calls male capacity) were necessary to do so.[47]

Interpreting this claim as an argument for male superiority, rather than simply sex-defined complementary forms of participation, Cordeiro associated men with capacity (strength) and women with lack of capacity (weakness). The dialogue thus related men to positive values and women to negative ones in a gendered way. This female lack was then extended to those who supported the queen in her struggle for independent power. Finally, the dialogue introduced another female character, with the aim of demonstrating the inherent inferiority of women: the Virgin Mary, the queen of heaven. Cordeiro argued that even Jesus' mother never governed the Church. As God's designated vicar on earth, Peter, a man, had done so.[48] If Jesus had not chosen his mother as heir, why should the Mahi congregation accept Victoria's claim to such a succession?

Those events took place around 1786, when Maria I, formally queen of Portugal since the death of her father, José I, in 1777, became effectively responsible for governing. She had married her father's brother, who succeeded him as regent, and when her husband died she finally reigned in her own right. Unlike the Virgin Mary, who never governed humanity, Maria I was charged with the secular government of the Portuguese empire. Her accession in 1786 took place in the very same year in which Victoria was defending her position as the queen of the Mahi congregation after the death of her husband, Monte.[49] Thus in 1788, when Souza addressed a petition to the queen of Portugal, those Catholic Mahi congregants had two queens over them: one of them queen in the Christian heaven and the other in Portugal. One could argue about the Holy Mother's weakness before the challenge of governing all humanity but no longer about the Portuguese queen's capacity to govern her Atlantic empire. They also had two African queens among them, Victoria as claimant to her husband's position and Rita Sebastiana as consort of the existing regent, Souza. Souza and his supporters urgently needed an argument to displace the first in favor of the second.

In the dialogue, the argument that finally prevented Victoria from governing the Mahi was centered not on her qualifications as a queen but rather on her behavior as a woman, her highly un-Christian practices of "abuse" and "superstition," powers apparently inherent in her female person: "She made someone put a crown on her head, saying she was the queen. . . . And tell me, is this, or is it not, abuse and superstition?" Souza also mentioned a Bahian crioulo who had been living in Victoria's home since her husband had passed away. By speaking of abuse and superstition, Souza subtly accused Victoria of witchcraft, making use of arguments that could find support both from Christian and African perspectives, since witchcraft was considered dangerous by both. He finally blamed the Bahian *crioulo* for Victoria's improper assertiveness. By mentioning him, Souza returned politics to the control of a male (even if an unqualified outsider), relegating Victoria and all women to secondary roles in politics.[50]

Souza's first act as king of the Mahi congregation was to prepare bylaws. Chapter 3 of the 1788 draft states: "All those who want to affiliate with the congregation (excluding the blacks from Angola) will be tested by the secretary and by the *agau*,[51] that is, the general procurator, to check whether those black men or black women employ abuses and heathen practices or superstition. If it is found or heard that they do, they will not be allowed admittance."[52] The pairing of accusations of immoral attitudes and the practice of witchcraft was reason enough for Victoria not to be accepted as a Catholic queen or even named as a direct contributor to the dialogue, since—according to the rules of the classical dialogue—those lacking moral or other honorable qualities cannot speak or even have their names mentioned.

In sum, Souza's argument is that women could not govern because of inherent moral deficiency and a lack of manly independence. For attempting to violate this norm, Victoria should be punished, and also dishonored, held up as an example to all other women who might dare to subvert the congregational gender hierarchy. This assertion meant that even those women who were rich and contributed significant financial support to the congregation should not aspire to power within the institution but rather submit to the power of men.

PERSPECTIVES ON POWER WITHIN THE MAHI CONGREGATION

The exiled Africans in Rio de Janeiro routinely elected kings and queens within their Catholic brotherhoods. However, in contrast to almost all royal dynasties, they could not transmit their authority to their children, who were considered creole (*crioulos*) and thus disqualified from being African. This contrast between Africans and creoles was one of the reasons why Africans enslaved in Rio developed strong generational cohorts that were evident in many ways, including the strength of the idea of country (*terra*), referring to the place they had come from.

These "country" cohorts also claimed, or were given, distinguishing characteristics or even powers. Coura women in Brazil were reputed to be powerful and dangerous—perhaps "witches" in Catholic terms—and people recognized for the strong links of their powers to religious practices in their homelands. Souza gives no details about Victoria's alleged practices of witchcraft. But other documents from Minas Gerais, where Victoria had lived for about fifteen years, mention a Josepha Coura, an African woman who lived near the gold mines of Paracatu at the same time that Victoria was still in Vila Rica. Josepha dedicated her life to honoring the "God of her country" (*o Deus de sua terra*) with chants and blood. According to denunciations against her, she practiced a kind of dance (i.e., a festival) in which she spoke in the Coura language and made sacrifices over a clay doll that she venerated.[53] Unfortunately, we have no information about worship among people in or around Aledjo-Koura in the eighteenth century.

In Africa, Dahomey, Oyo, and Mahi exchanged women among themselves. Dahomean kings took foreign wives, even foreign *kpojito*, the women in the powerful position of "wives of the leopard" (roughly, mothers of the king). The kpojito of Tegbesu—the Dahomey ruler (r. 1732–74)—was Hwangile, an Aja woman, widow of his father, Agaja. Tegbesu himself had at least two Mahi wives. One of them was a favorite, who used to take care of his treasury.[54] The other wife was Chai, who came to be the kpojito of his son Kpengla.[55] Since Tegbesu reigned to 1774 and

Kpengla from then to 1789, by the time Mahi in the Mina congregation in Rio were carrying on these struggles (1762–88) involving the Mahi and the Dahomean members of the brotherhood, the Dahomean king in Africa had a Mahi wife. The numerous competing wives of the leopard at the Dahomean court made use of witchcraft to attempt to ensure their prospects. To be a "mother" or a "sister" of a Dahomean king was a passport to power, reason enough for them to fight to determine or, at least, to influence the succession of male kings.[56] Dahomean traditions were the core of existing Gbe-speaking people in the brotherhood, since they controlled its major (Mina) congregation, and so Dahomean royal practices framed Souza's petition and statute, even though he was a Mahi.

The documents do not mention the possibility that Victoria might have been sponsoring a male candidate against Souza, just as the Dahomey queen mothers did, but unspecified members of the brotherhood had "crowned" her, and Dahomeans—as the majority of its members— probably were among them. Beyond her political power, she probably also had funds to finance her project. We do not know her occupation or personal wealth, but forty years earlier she had already been able to purchase her freedom for 180,000 réis. In Portuguese legal terms, which she had evidently been careful to take into account, in Monte's will—which she had drafted—she was also his heir, and during the four years since he had passed away she could already have taken possession of her inheritance.[57]

ETHNICITY AND GENDER IN AFRICA AND IN AMERICA

Victoria's male support seems to have involved at least two other members of the brotherhood: António do Couto Suzano and José dos Santos Martins. No information about the first has come to light, but the second came from the Mina coast and, like Monte, was also a barber by profession, and a wealthy and powerful man.[58] Together with Victoria, they were the executors of Monte's will. Souza never mentioned them in the dialogue, nor did their names come out in any document related to the Mahi congregation. Their invisibility in the dispute may represent another name avoidance, beyond its obscuring Victoria's identity, or they may not have acted within the brotherhood in their capacities as representatives of Brazilian political alliances or African ethnic identities. Monte did not always act in an ethnic capacity either. He mentioned neither the Mahi nor the Mina congregations in his will, only the brotherhood. The limited public embrace of ethnicity can be inferred from some peculiar phrasing. Monte says that he came from the Mina coast, although he referred to his Mahi "grandfather." Souza is the one who reinforced Monte's Mahi identity by calling him a true Mahi. Finally, perhaps because Victoria was Coura and not Mahi, both Monte and Souza say only that she is Mina.

The conflict between Souza and Victoria brings out different uses that the competitors made of ethnic issues, which demonstrates that African identities remained strong in their minds but, just as in their homelands, they could invoke them or not, depending on the situation and the advantages they perceived for themselves. This strategic, flexible, and usually political and competitive ability to build networks and to invoke different collective identities extended African ethnic strategies into the challenging circumstances of slavery in Brazil.

Souza and Victoria revealed two different attitudes and political uses of ethnicity in their dispute. Souza reinforced Mahi identity, defending rigid ethnic parameters for the organizational politics of the Mahi congregation. He thus necessarily persecuted Victoria for witchcraft, both as betrayal of the communal solidarity vital in Africa and as Catholic sin, a serious accusation at a time when the Inquisition was still alive in their minds. His attachment to the Mahi ethnic background had, as a corollary, the fact that, even presenting his case in male Christian terms (perhaps from the European Enlightenment), he also believed in the effectiveness of African female witchcraft and feared Victoria. Thus the conventions of the dialogue enabled Souza to denounce her politically without risking a direct mention of personal powers he could not control.

On the other side, Victoria and her allies followed a cross-ethnic strategy allying with other members of the brotherhood, even non-Mina members, like those from Cape Verde, São Tomé, and Mozambique, as one can assume by the sentence above: "not only those of the Mahi nation were there, but everyone, those from Mina coast and other nations." Although she did not rely on normative ethnicity, she made use of subversive and secretive—hence extremely powerful—capacities attributed to the wives of the leopard in particular (Mina-Fon), and which—although I speculate—may have extended to other Mina queens in the brotherhood (Mina-Mahi or Mina-Coura). Victoria, even if from Coura proper, could have borrowed this attitude from the Mahi and Dahomean people with whom she had spent most, perhaps all, of her life.[59]

Souza and Victoria were also deploying Portuguese Catholic terms of gendered legitimacy in their contest for political positions in the congregation and brotherhood. In the emergently modern world of late-eighteenth-century Rio de Janeiro—even if Brazil remained largely a status-based society—men should rule, while women should support. Victoria seems also to have drawn on an African pluralistic model of complementary empowerments inspired by the important roles women had in Dahomey and maybe also among other Gbe people. Souza transcended his uses of Mahi culture and religion by not only adopting the worship of Catholic saints but also embracing new ideas of the Enlightenment circulating in late-eighteenth-century Brazil that gave women "naturally" lower positions than men.[60]

Souza's appropriation of emerging modern standards of gender was certainly a result of the opportunities he had created for himself in Brazil. He was not a freed slave of the usual sort. I could never identify his master or people with whom he might have worked. But he was somehow connected to Enlightened religious (Jesuit) and lay elites of Rio de Janeiro.[61] Those would be the people from whom he could have learned Catholic doctrine, geography, mathematics, and even some Latin, on which he drew to formulate his case as a formal dialogue. Given his evident lack of royal allies in African terms, his educated position in Portuguese terms allowed his allies to make him king of the Mahi congregation, the proper person to represent them to a changing and unfamiliar modern culture.

Since Victoria and Souza had important positions in the Mina congregation at least from the 1750s, they must have been tied to each other for about forty years. In terms of politics Souza adopted the course of reinforcing an ethnic (both African countries and Brazilian nations) framework for politics, but at the same time fighting witchcraft, and ethnic concepts of power among women, in modern enlightened terms. Victoria did not rely strongly on ethnicity, allying people from different ethnic backgrounds. She also managed female witchcraft and a sense of politics, making use of multiplistic African practices of differentiated and combining powers. These contrasting, but also complementing, strategies in Victoria's and Souza's struggle over the assets of the Brotherhood of Saint Elesbão thus open an avenue to understand how Africans in Brazil acted under slavery as individuals and as groups. It also shows how comprehension of the ways in which at least one African woman played her role in so complex a situation in Brazil can help us understand the complexity of slaves' uses of a sort of ethnicity that emerges from a strong representation of the African past. Moreover, this case study shows how slaves used elements from their pasts to deal with radical novelty, both their removal from Africa to America and the changes flowing from the European Enlightenment at the end of the eighteenth century in Brazil.

Souza introduced the emergent enlightened notions of competitive gender, and its exclusionary consequences for them as women, into the politics of the brotherhood as a way of marginalizing an obviously powerful female presence in its still multiplistic politics (thus both African and baroque Catholic Portuguese). The struggle between Victoria and Souza, whatever its legal outcome for the specific contestants—which further research may yet reveal—marked the emergent and enveloping gendered effects of the European Enlightenment, even among African slaves in Rio de Janeiro.

NOTES

1. I follow here the classical work of Joan Wallach Scott, who considers gender in the field of power relationships. Scott, *Gender and the Politics of History*, rev. ed. (New York: Columbia University Press, 1999).

2. On women in West Africa, the chapter relies on Edna Bay's essential work *Wives of the Leopard: Gender, Politics, and Culture in the Kingdom of Dahomey* (Charlottesville: University of Virginia Press, 1998). On the colonial situation, it relies on my own previous work. See Mariza de Carvalho Soares, *Devotos da cor: Identidade étnica, religiosidade e escravidão no Rio de Janeiro, século XVIII* (Rio de Janeiro: Civilização Brasileira, 2000).

3. According to Portuguese law (Ordenações Filipinas, 1603), masters were required to baptize their slaves in the six months following their arrivals from Africa. See Silvia Hunold Lara, org., *Ordenações filipinas, Livro V* (São Paulo: Companhia das Letras, 1999), 99, 309. During the baptismal ceremony slaves received Christian names followed by their nations that corresponded to their large region of origin (Mina, Angola, Mozambique) or to more specific countries (Mahi, Coura, and others). Thus the names Victoria Coura and Ignácio Mina.

4. Banco de Dados da Freguesia do Pilar, Minas Gerais, ID 103340; Patrícia Porto de Oliveira, "Batismo de escravos adultos e o parentesco espiritual nas Minas setecentistas," *X Seminário sobre a Economia Mineira* (Minas Gerais: n.p., n.d), 11.

5. Verger refers to *coiranos* and *couranos*. For *coiranos*, see page 204 and footnote 106, page 209; for *couranos*, footnote 30, page 207. It is not clear whether he considers the two to constitute a single group. Verger transcribes João Basílio's letter: "E se seguio pretender o mesmo Cabo [the Dahomean *agau*] que se lhe entregassem huns negros Couranos inimigos do Rey Daumê, que se dizia estarem na dita fortaleza (Ouidah)" (1743); Pierre Verger, *Fluxo e refluxo do tráfico de escravos entre o golfo do Benin e a Bahia de Todos os Santos dos séculos XVIII a XIX*, 3rd ed. (São Paulo: Editora Corrupio, 1987).

6. Although my research is still in progress, I believe that during the first half of the eighteenth century, probably between the 1720s and the 1740s, a great number of slaves from the northern interior of that region were sold to Portuguese and Brazilian buyers of slaves, who were offering gold along the coast to both European and African traders. For a more detailed analysis see: Mariza de Carvalho Soares,

"Indícios para o traçado das rotas terrestres de escravos na Baía do Benim, século XVIII," in *Rotas Atlânticas da Diáspora Africana: da Baía do Benim ao Rio de Janeiro*, org. Mariza de Carvalho Soares (Niteroi, EDUFF, forthcoming 2007).

7. For the mentioned places, words in italic correspond to African countries in Brazilian colonial documents; words inside parentheses correspond to African places in historical works and modern geography.

8. I thoroughly searched the coastal literature for mentions of the Coura. Robin Law never mentioned Coura as a place or as a people. Law, *The Slave Coast of West Africa, 1550–1750: The Impact of the Atlantic Slave Trade on an African Society* (Oxford: Clarendon Press, 1991). About those people in Rio de Janeiro and Minas Gerais, see Mariza de Carvalho Soares, "A 'nação' que se tem e a 'terra' de onde se vem," *Estudos Afro-Asiáticos* 26, no. 2 (2004): 303–30.

9. G. Parrinder, "Yoruba-Speaking Peoples in Dahomey," *Africa: Journal of the International African Institute* 17, no. 2 (1947), 122–23. On *àlejò* as a term for stranger, see *A Dictionary of the Yoruba Language*, part 2, *Yoruba-English* (London: Oxford University Press, 1975).

10. See Robert Cornevin, *Histoire du Dahomey* (Paris: Éditions Berger-Levrault, 1962), 16–17, 63.

11. Robert Cornevin, *Histoire du Togo* (Paris: Editions Berger-Levrault, 1962), 37.

12. N. L. Gayibor, *Histoire des Togolais*, vol. 1, *Des origines à 1884* (Lomé: Presses de l'Université du Bénin, 1997), 282, 287, 291.

13. Paul Lovejoy, *Caravans of Kola: The Hausa Kola Trade, 1700–1900* (Zaria: Ahmadu Bello University Press, 1980), 34–36.

14. Law, *Slave Coast*, 188.

15. All the names and other important information concerning Victoria mentioned in this chapter were registered along with the legal proceedings necessary to obtain the authorization of the bishopric for Monte's and Victoria's marriage in the Catholic Church, as usual. Arquivo da Cúria Metropolitana do Rio de Janeiro (hereafter ACM/RJ), Habilitações Matrimoniais, Ignácio Gonçalves do Monte.

16. On Mahi in Africa, see J. A. M. A. R. Bergé. "Étude sur le pays Mahi." *Bulletin du Comité d'Études Historiques et Scientifiques de 1'A O F II* (1928); Cornevin, *Histoire du Dahomey*; I. A. Akinjogbin, *Dahomey and Its Neighbours, 1708–1818* (Cambridge: Cambridge University Press, 1967); Jessie Gaston Mulira, "A History of the Mahi Peoples from 1774–1920" (PhD diss., University of California, Los Angeles, 1984).

17. Beyond my personal research on Mahi and Coura, I am grateful to Fernanda Pinheiro and Moacir Maia, who shared their research about Coura and Mahi in Minas Gerais. Since then both have finished their master's dissertations. Pinheiro, "Confrades do Rosário: Sociabilidade e identidade étnica em Mariana Minas Gerais (1745–1820)" (master's diss., PPGH/UFF, Niterói, 2006); Maia, "'Quem tem padrinho não morre pagão': As relações de compadrio e apadrinhamento de escravos numa vila colonial (Mariana, 1715–1750)" (master's diss., PPGH/UFF, Niterói, 2006).

18. "Regra ou estatuto por modo de um diálogo onde, se dá notícia das Caridades e Sufragações das Almas que usam os pretos Minas, com seus Nacionais no Estado do Brazil, especialmente no Rio de Janeiro, por onde se hão de regerem e governarem

fora de todo o abuzo gentílico e supersticioso; composto por Francisco Alves de Souza preto e natural do Reino de Makim, um dos mais excelentes e potentados daquela oriunda Costa da Mina," Biblioteca Nacional/RJ (hereafter BN/RJ); testamento de Ignácio Gonçalves do Monte: Livro de Óbitos e Testamentos da Freguesia do Santíssimo Sacramento, 1776–1784, ACM/RJ, fols. 442v–444.

19. On the slave trade in the Bight of Benin—in Portuguese records, *Costa da Mina* (Mina coast)—in the first half of the eighteenth century, see Patrick Manning's classic "The Slave Trade in the Bight of Benin, 1640–1890," in *The Uncommon Market: Essays in the Economic History of the Atlantic Slave Trade*, ed. Henry A. Gemery and Jan S. Hogendorn (London: Academic Press, 1979), 125–29. For updated numbers, see David Eltis, Stephen D. Behrendt, and David Richardson, "A participação dos países da Europa e das Américas no tráfico transatlântico de escravos: Novas evidências," *Afro-Ásia* 24 (2000): 9–50.

20. Soares, "A nação que se tem."

21. Testamento de Ignácio Monte, ACM/RJ.

22. Cornevin, *Histoire du Dahomey*, 140–42.

23. Mina people were the majority of those who paid for their letters of manumission (*cartas de alforria*). Manolo Florentino, "Alforrias e etnicidade no Rio de Janeiro oitocentista: Notas de pesquisa," *Topoi* 5 (2002): 9–40.

24. Sheila de Castro Faria, "*Sinhás pretas, damas mercadoras*": As pretas minas nas cidades do Rio de Janeiro e de São João del Rey (1700–1850) (Tese de Professor Titular, Departamento de História da Universidade Federal Fluminense, 2004).

25. A. J. R. Russell-Wood, "Prestige, Power and Piety in Colonial Brazil: The Third Orders of Salvador," *Hispanic American Historical Review* 69 (1989): 66–70.

26. A. J. R. Russell-Wood, *The Black Man in Slavery and Freedom in Colonial Brazil* (New York: St. Martin's, 1982).

27. A. C. de C. M. Saunders, *A Social History of Black Slaves and Freedmen in Portugal, 1441–1555* (Cambridge: Cambridge University Press, 1982).

28. The statute passed in 1759 finally allowed the election of Africans from Mina Coast to the Council. For a collection of statutes, including this one, see *http://www.historia.uff.br/labhoi*. For Portuguese brotherhoods, see Didier Lahon, "Esclavage et confréries noires au Portugal durant l'Ancien Régime (1441–1830)," 2 vols. (doctoral thesis, L'EHESS, 2001).

29. For further information see Soares, *Devotos da cor*, ch. 4.

30. The apparent contradiction between the fact that Mahi had no kings and that Monte's grandfather was called a king probably reflects Monte's search for a Portuguese word to define the high prestige and strong power of his ancestor.

31. The Carmelite friars spread the worship of these two saints during the eighteenth century. Saint Elesbão had been a prince in Abyssinia, and Saint Efigênia a princess in Nubia. Both converted and became members of the Carmelite order, which was first created in 1740, and finished building their chapel in 1754.

32. Arquivo da Irmandade de Santo Elesbão e Santa Efigênia/RJ (AISESE/RJ), Compromisso da Irmandade de Santo Elesbão e Santa Efigênia, 1740–1767.

33. Unfortunately, Souza does not make it clear who the Dahomeans he mentioned might have been, whether the prestigious Fon from Dahomey itself or people

of unknown background from the area of the polity. But considering the high position of a king who controlled the Mina congregation and the brotherhood, I strongly suspect they were Fon.

34. Sabaru (Savalu) was a Gbe village inside Mahi land; Dassa was a Yoruba village also inside Mahi land; Agolin (Agonli) was a Gbe village; Za was a Gbe village west of the Zou River. I have no information if they were only villages or if any of them was a walled town.

35. See Pinheiro, "Confrades do Rosário."

36. AISESE/RJ, Compromisso da Irmandade de Santo Elesbão e Santa Efigênia, "Acrescentamento," chs. 1–5.

37. I argue that this is a Dahomean strategy because, based on Souza's description, the Dahomeans were the most powerful group in the Mina congregation and thus controlled the council and dictated the rules. The fact that the empire was able, but not required, to elect queens might be considered a challenge to women who I suspect forced their own presence through yet another set of elections and offices.

38. The possibility of electing unmarried kings and queens was recently described among Coura people in Minas Gerais, at the same period. Pinheiro, "Confrades do Rosário."

39. BN/RJ, "Regra ou estatuto"; Arquivo Histórico Ultramarino, Lisbon (AHU), "Estatuto da Irmandade de Nossa Senhora do Remédio, 1788."

40. BN/RJ, "Regra ou estatuto," fol. 23.

41. Gonçalo Cordeiro was baptized in 1750, in Rio de Janeiro. Like Monte he was a barber. ACM/RJ, Habilitações Matrimoniais, Gonçalo Cordeiro.

42. BN/RJ, "Regra ou estatuto" fol. 43

43. BN/RJ, "Regra ou estatuto" fol. 13.

44. On ethnic boundaries, see Fredrick Barth, Ethnic Groups and Boundaries: The Social Organization of Culture Difference, ed. Barth (Bergen: Universitetsforlaget; London: Allen and Unwin, 1969); Paul E. Lovejoy, "Identity and the Mirage of Ethnicity: Mahommah Gardo Baquaqua's Journey in the Americas," in African Re-Genesis: Confronting Social Issues in the Diaspora, ed. Jay B. Haviser and Kevin C. MacDonald (Tucson: University of Arizona Press, 2006).

45. BN/RJ, "Regra ou estatuto" fol. 43.

46. AHU, "Estatuto da Irmandade." According to A. J. R. Russell-Wood, these appeals of individuals on the behalf of collectivities "revealed the role of the monarch as arbitrator between conflicting interests of corporate groups in the colony" and "constituted tacit recognition of the discrimination inherent to the judiciary." Russell-Wood, "'Acts of Grace': Portuguese Monarchs and Their Subjects of African Descent in Eighteenth-Century Brazil," Journal of Latin American Studies 32 (2000): 307–32.

47. BN/RJ, "Regra ou estatuto," fols. 14–15.

48. Ibid., fol. 39.

49. D. Maria I governed Portugal until 1792, when she was declared insane, and her son became the regent D. João, the future D. João VI. She died in Brazil in 1816. A. H. de Oliveira Marques, History of Portugal (New York: Columbia University Press, 1976), 424.

50. BN/RJ, "Regra ou estatuto," fol. 13.

51. In the Mahi congregation, the agau was a distinguished member of royal court. In Dahomey *agau* is the title of one of the military commanders of the Dahomean army. The modern word is *gau*. Law, *Slave Coast*, 271.

52. BN/RJ, "Regra ou estatutos" fol. 31.

53. Infomation about Josepha can be found in Luiz Mott, "Acotundá: Raízes setecentistas do sincretismo religioso afro-brasileiro," in Mott, *Escravidão, homosexualidade e demonologia* (São Paulo: Ícone Editora, 1998).

54. It is important to highlight that the Mahi queen's custom of keeping the chest in her home was perhaps related to this Dahomean practice. See Bay, *Wives of the Leopard*, 83.

55. Ibid., 152.

56. On royal women, particularly about king's mothers, wives, and sisters, see Bay, *Wives of the Leopard*, 51–56, 71–80.

57. The wills show that brotherhoods usually received a considerable part of the estates of their deceased members. Widowers and widows inherited their partners' belongings. Single women seldom transferred their estates to other women, even to their female slaves. Faria, *"Sinhás pretas."* Nevertheless, it is not clear whether these women actually received their due, since executors were always men and suspected of draining the estates they handled—if not for themselves, then for the brotherhood. Victoria's struggle to keep the chest also represented an ordinary female challenge.

58. When he died in 1800 his estate inventory listed eleven slaves, not all in health, who were assigned a total value of 934,000 *réis*. Arquivo Nacional/RJ, Inventário de José dos Santos Martins.

59. Victoria could never pretend to be a wife of the leopard. She never gave Monte a child, and even if she had, he would have been crioulo, not Mahi.

60. The *Enciclopédie* (35 volumes, edited by d'Alambert and Diderot in 1772) highlights the domestic position of women. Jean-Jacques Rousseau's *Émile* and other eighteenth- century novels refer to motherhood as the most important female activity. Rousseau, *Emílio; ou, da educação* (São Paulo: Martins Fontes, 1995). See also Elisabeth Badinter, *Émile, Émilie: L'ambition feminine au XVIII siècle* (Paris: Flammarion, 1983).

61. On Jesuits, see Dauril Alden, *The Making of an Enterprise: The Society of Jesus in Portugal, Its Empire, and Beyond, 1540–1750* (Stanford: Stanford University Press, 1996). On the effects of the Enlightenment in Rio de Janeiro, see Afonso Carlos Marques do Santos, *No rascunho da nação: Inconfidência no Rio de Janeiro* (Rio de Janeiro: Secretaria Municipal de Cultura, 1992).

4

A PARTICULAR KIND OF FREEDOM

Black Women, Slavery, Kinship, and Freedom in the American Southeast

BARBARA KRAUTHAMER

Enslaved women in the English colonies of southeastern North America in the second half of the eighteenth century frequently responded to the psychic and corporeal ravages of plantation discipline by running away. The majority of these women sought to ameliorate their bondage in short-term respites and so ran off to visit relatives enslaved on nearby plantations, returning eventually to their masters. But other enslaved women fled with little or no intention of returning. Most of these women who sought permanent escape hid out in the anonymity of the bustling port cities of Savannah or Charleston, where they could find employment with either white or free black employers and disappear in the highly mobile and often transitory black population of urban slaves and free black workers and sailors.[1] With approximately one thousand black people living in Savannah and over six thousand in Charleston in the early 1770s, networks of old friends and newly acquired allies offered assistance to women such as Darque, or Darchus, whose face bore the markings of her West African origins and who ran away with her infant child to Savannah, where her master presumed she had taken refuge with her "many acquaintances in and about town." Other women relied on the marketability of their skills in urban settings: Betty fled to Charleston, where she could "hire herself out at needle-work, being an exceeding good seamstress," and Hannah survived there by "selling cakes" in the markets.[2]

A smaller number of these women fugitives, however, ventured even farther. Severing all ties not only to their families but also to the familiar surroundings of the highly commercial plantation environment, they followed rivers and well-worn trade paths inland to present-day western Georgia and northern Florida, then the territory of the Creek Indians. There they sought refuge in the clusters of Creek towns along the Chattahoochee, Coosa, and Tallapoosa Rivers and found a particular kind of freedom from chattel slavery. The Creeks often chose to incorporate these women through marriage and adoption into the extended family networks that made up their individual towns and the Creek society as a whole. As members of Creek kin groups and communities, fugitive women gained powerful allies who protected them from capture and reenslavement by their former masters or colonial authorities.

In the Creek towns that harbored these runaway women, the emancipatory potential of family incorporation—created through adoption, marriage, and, by extension, childbearing—stood in stark contrast to the brutal denials of black women's personal and reproductive lives under chattel slavery. Such prospects made Creek settlements an attractive and feasible destination for enslaved African and African American women in Georgia and South Carolina.[3] The possibility of transcending enslavement through family incorporation in Creek society bears a resemblance to the patterns of liberating servile women in eighteenth-century kin-based societies in West Africa. Paul Lovejoy explains in his comprehensive study of slavery in Africa that wealthy men on the Gold Coast, for example, took slave women as wives, valuing their labor and childbearing capacities as vital sources of wealth. Women and the children born to these unions gained legal freedom, though they remained subordinate to the husband-father and former master. The passage of time and subsequent generations of intermarriage eventually shrouded the slave origins of their descendants.[4]

Given the apparent similarities between the Creek and West African contexts, one might be tempted to juxtapose the two and frame a comparison of the ways in which kinship shaped hierarchical social relations, especially the modes of both enslaving and emancipating women by drawing on the extensive scholarly debates about the meanings and weight of kinship in African systems of captivity and enslavement.[5] Yet, whether kinship and slavery stood as distant points on a continuum or as fundamental antitheses, a comparison of the rules—kinship—that governed interactions reveals very little about individuals' daily lives and the ways in which people interpreted, dismissed, or altered formal standards at any given moment and over long stretches of time. An emphasis on the necessary connections between the subordination of women and social reproduction in West African slave societies, including the avenues to liberation through marriage, highlights the benefits that accrued to household heads but neglects a gendered analysis of social relations and eclipses the complexity of women's roles and the circumstances that prompted women to accept or challenge their positions.

African-born women enslaved in the colonial Southeast drew on a wide range of memories and knowledge when recalling their pasts and imagining futures beyond the confines of chattel slavery. If enslaved women in the Low Country gleaned the similarities between Creek and African patterns of transforming nonkin into kin, so, too, would they have drawn on their nuanced understandings of African female autonomy and well-regarded economic and social roles and their growing awareness of the venerated economic, social, and spiritual positions Creek women held in their own communities. Captives from West-Central Africa comprised nearly 40 percent of the Africans enslaved in the Americas and accounted for nearly half the enslaved population in South Carolina in the 1730s. The ethnic, cultural, and linguistic diversity of peoples from the Congo basin defies broad generalizations about women's roles beyond identifying the widespread importance of women's technical expertise in using the hoe as the primary work tool and the centrality of women's agricultural labor to local trade and subsistence. Women from the Bight of Biafra, another region that contributed significantly to the North American enslaved population, also had a wealth of experiences that informed their understandings of women's prominent and powerful roles in kin-based societies. In Olaudah Equiano's famous account of his capture in Africa and enslavement in the Americas, he writes of Igbo women warriors, fighting to defend his village against slave raiders. Igbo women also controlled local trade relations and retained the money they earned in commercial transactions.

Women's capacity for exercising autonomy and occupying esteemed positions as producers and providers of services, material goods, and social connections in West African kin-based societies is encapsulated in their multivalent roles in public markets. As the principal vendors, as well as producers, of foodstuffs, women oversaw the terms of trade and were remunerated for their produce. In the decidedly female arena of the public market, women dominated social as well as economic interactions. A European observer in the late seventeenth century noted that women's voices filled the air as they preserved history and memory by telling stories to "young people and children [who] listen to such discourse with avid ears and absorb it in their hearts."[6] African women's nuanced understandings of female autonomy and women's well-regarded economic and social roles endured the transatlantic voyage and informed their responses to enslavement, including their decisions to run away. For African women and their American-born daughters enslaved in the eighteenth-century Low Country, the comparison between West African and Creek societies would have been a personal one that considered the possibilities for remaking their lives under more familiar and favorable conditions than those of colonial South Carolina and Georgia.

Enslavement in the Americas rested on legal and social fictions that black people were property, not persons. Following the principles set forth in the seventeenth-century slave codes of Barbados and Virginia, early-eighteenth-century South Carolina lawmakers established slavery as the lifelong and heritable condition of persons of African descent, passed from mother to child. At mid-century, when Georgia's planter-politicians legalized chattel slavery, they modeled their slave code on the laws of South Carolina. Law and custom sanctioned the brutal appropriation of marriage and childbirth by stripping enslaved persons of the common law protections extended to free married adults and parents. This denial of slaves' humanity served the interests of slaveholders and the developing plantation economy by transforming the intimacies of slaves' lives into economic events.[7]

The unions and family relations that sustained couples and communities within slavery also highlighted their vulnerability in the countless moments when they lost loved ones to sale, bequest, or plantation discipline. For fugitive women hoping to navigate the gradual process of achieving full inclusion in Creek communities through adoption and marriage, the experience undoubtedly entailed discord and loss.[8] Enslaved women who distanced themselves from both their masters and fellow slaves by running away to Creek towns sometimes found relief there from the bone-crushing labor of plantation monoculture. However, the permanent refuge from slavery they achieved by securing adoption and thus socially sanctioned positions in the networks of Creek kin groups was a separate matter that entailed long-term negotiation between runaway women and their hosts and created correspondingly permanent places for them to remain.

Creek hosts sought the social and political gains they might derive from runaway women's work and children, but harboring runaway women also promised other, nonmaterial benefits to Creek communities. Concerned about the rapid geopolitical expansion of colonial plantation society, surely Creeks appreciated their potential of retaining fugitive slaves to disrupt colonists' ventures. The fictive and biological kinship ties forged between fugitive women and their Creek hosts promised liberation from chattel slavery, but these intimate relationships nonetheless remained critical sites of contestation for black women in the colonial Southeast and yielded personal dignity, the personal form of freedom relevant to their lives.

WOMEN, GENDER, AND SLAVERY

Studies of slave fugitives in the eighteenth- and early-nineteenth-century Southeast have frequently noted their contacts with Native Americans, but they have focused narrowly on the men who fled. Scholars have devoted much attention, for example, to the insurgent martial solidarity forged between male fugitives and Indian men, who identified each other as allies in the complex webs of alliance and enmity, measured in crucial trade and military partnerships that grew out of colonial geopolitics as the British, French, and Spanish empires vied with one other for territorial and economic dominance in the region.[9] Historian Jane Landers explains that it was the "repeated crosscurrents of raids and migrations across the Southeast" that "acquainted" black and Indian people with the imperial rivalry between the English and Spanish.[10] Informed about Spain's policy of granting sanctuary to runaway slaves from British settlements, fugitives made good use of Spanish Florida's native allies. Seminoles and others often harbored and assisted runaways as they made their ways from British plantations to St. Augustine.

Slaves' escapes to Florida posed multiple problems for South Carolina slaveholders and authorities alike. The economic drain of the property and labor lost to slave flight was compounded by slaveholders' concerns that successful fugitives not only would inspire others to flee but also might take up arms in the ongoing Spanish and Indian attacks against the British. These were not idle fears, as rebellious slave men seized many opportunities to fight Carolina slaveholders by taking part in Indian insurrections against the colony. In 1715, for example, enslaved men joined Yamasee Indians in war against the English, and during the same period the Spanish forces in Florida gladly deployed fugitive slave men as combatants in their raids on Carolina plantations.[11]

Black women are not wholly absent from the scholarship on black-Indian interactions in the colonial Southeast, but their contacts and sustained relations with southeastern native peoples have not been focal points in these studies. Nor have the gendered conditions of women's enslavement been integral to discussions of women fugitives' strategies for remaking their lives by connecting with nearby Indian peoples.

This chapter examines runaway slave women's flight to hospitable Creek communities and their efforts to find permanent liberation from chattel slavery by negotiating labor and marriage relations with Creek kin groups. Tracing runaways' paths to the Creeks is a difficult endeavor, as the sources do not yield this history graciously. Still, it is possible to discern the ways in which enslaved women learned about, fled to, and remained among Creek communities in the eighteenth century. Focusing on both the gendered conditions of enslavement in the colonies and the gendered dynamics of labor, subordination, and kin incorporation in Creek towns not only illuminates an overlooked area of contact between Africans, African Americans, and American Indians but also suggests new ways of thinking about enslaved women's conceptions of slavery and freedom.

Enslaved women's labor, as historians such as Jennifer Morgan have shown, was central to the business of large-scale plantation monoculture and the cultivation of such cash crops as rice, indigo, and cotton. By the eighteenth century Anglo-American slaveholders had reconfigured English gendered meanings of work to legitimate casting enslaved black women and girls ideologically and discursively as "workers," a category previously reserved only for men.[12] Carolina rice planters relied heavily on the skills and knowledge of producing of the grain among African women, especially those from the Senegambia region, and calculated profits in terms of both the commodity crops and the children that enslaved women produced. The resulting routinized exploitation of African and African American women's specialized skills and manual labor supported the rapid multiplication of South Carolina's annual rice exports from under half a million pounds in 1700 to over sixty million pounds by the time of the American Revolution.[13]

Enslaved women's work on the Carolina rice plantations, as in sugar and tobacco fields elsewhere, entailed their use of the hoe to prepare the ground for planting and to weed the growing crops. This relentless backbreaking toil later prompted one antebellum observer to describe them later as "hoeing machine[s]." The most onerous labor associated with rice cultivation, however, was not the cultivation of crops but the pounding of the harvested grains by hand with a mortar and ten-pound pestle. Working at a grueling pace through both day and night, women processed the rice kernels by repeatedly lifting the pestle up and slamming it forcefully down to remove the hulls, work that required both physical endurance and careful attention to the rhythm and force of the pounding to avoid breaking the hulled grains. Enslaved women responded to the arduous work regimes during the growing season by running away temporarily to escape the summertime tasks of hoeing and weeding. Later in the year, after the harvest, incidents of vandalism increased, and the barns housing newly harvested rice were burned as the enslaved determined to disrupt the heightened work regimes "required to process millions of pounds of rice by hand."[14]

Through the latter half of the eighteenth century, profit-hungry Carolina rice planters eagerly moved south onto lands in Georgia beyond the Savannah River. By 1750 the trustees of the Georgia colony had lifted earlier restrictions on landholding, as well as a 1735 ban on importing slaves. These expansive development strategies, coupled with subsequent land cessions from the Creeks and with Britain's 1763 acquisition of Florida from the Spanish, opened Florida to Anglo-American settlement and added over five million acres to Georgia as well.[15] Much of this newly gained territory was ill suited for rice production but instead supported a mix of hunting, agriculture, and livestock-raising prospects that attracted white settlers from the upper South, the West Indies, and South Carolina.[16]

White newcomers in Georgia purchased and imported enslaved people from South Carolina and the West Indies, and within a decade they also began buying slaves directly from the West African coast. Charleston remained the largest importer of enslaved Africans in the North American colonies in the eighteenth century, and over half the enslaved population brought into Georgia between 1751 and 1773 was African born. As the numbers of planters and small-scale white farmers expanded, the enslaved population in the Southeast grew rapidly, increasing from about five hundred in Georgia in 1751 to nearly fifteen thousand by 1773. On the eve of the American Revolution, South Carolina's black majority population totaled over eighty thousand.[17]

This spatial and human expansion of colonial settlement and chattel slavery pushed beyond the periphery of the Creeks' territory, allowing blacks and Creeks to encounter each other more often and placing ever greater strains on the diplomatic ties between Creeks and their aggressive Anglo-American neighbors. Creeks complained vociferously about the destruction that colonists' cattle wrought on their hunting grounds, and colonial officials worried about the Creeks' ability to erode their slaveholdings by harboring fugitives or, up to 1763, giving them safe passage to Florida.[18] Hoping to block the steady flow of runaway slaves from colonial plantations to these nearby Indian settlements in Florida and Georgia, English authorities sought to enlist their Indian diplomatic allies also as slave catchers.

Colonial officials routinely inserted specific provisions for the capture and return of slave fugitives in their treaties with their native neighbors. In the early summer of 1767, for example, John Stuart, the British superintendent of Southern Indian Affairs, met with the Creeks to negotiate trade relations, which necessarily encompassed a discussion of fugitive slaves. Determined to prevent the Indians' territory from becoming an "asylum for Negroes," Stuart insisted that Creeks return the runaways among them to the colonists.[19] Subsequent agreements between South Carolina authorities and Creeks reiterated the demand that the Indians surrender any "Negroes harbored in Creek Country."[20] Southeastern Indians interested in safeguarding their trade and diplomatic ties with the British may not have voiced their reluctance to turn over fugitives, but their continuing willingness to harbor runaways spoke volumes. Although colonial officials repeatedly encouraged Creeks to capture and redeem fugitives, these attempts to control not the enslaved but rather those who might assist them did little to mitigate enslaved women's determination to head for Creek settlements.

The conventional understanding of women's responses to enslavement, based on evidence pointing to its infrequency, has diverted attention from the women who fled. Overall, fewer enslaved women than men ran away. One explanation for this disparity holds that the gendered division of labor on large plantations may have contributed to the lower rates of women's flight. Work assignments took more enslaved men beyond the plantation confines than women and allowed the men to learn about local routes leading away from their masters and enslavement. Enslaved women, of course, hid out nearby or sought refuge with relatives on neighboring plantations or farms rather than attempting to escape slavery forever. Virtually all the historiography that considers women runaways attributes this tendency toward truancy rather than outright escape to women's reluctance to sever the emotional ties that linked family members, especially mothers to their children.[21]

Framing enslaved motherhood as a constraint against escape, however, diverts attention from enslavement's violent negations of maternity. Recurrent instances of women's successful flight, with or without their children, defy the reduction of enslaved women to what Jennifer Morgan has described as the mythic image of "selfless women working endless hours to support their children—mamas with expansive hearts and bosoms and a ferocious protectiveness."[22] Though one cannot ignore the paramount importance of family ties in the lives of the enslaved, maternal desires to care for offspring did not stifle all women's impulses to flee the physically and psychically overwhelming hardships of plantation labor.

Between 1763 and 1790, almost one-third of the advertisements for runaways in Georgia newspapers announced escapes of enslaved women, and the majority of those 273 runaway women fled without children. Only 33 women (12 percent) were reported as having run away with children; 5 women (less than 2 percent) were said to have fled while pregnant, and another 15 escaped (5.5 percent) with both husbands and children. Thus just under 20 percent of the women who ran away during these three decades in Georgia fled with children.[23] In South Carolina women who ran away with children made up an equally small proportion of the escapees, represented by fewer than one-fourth of the runaway advertisements placed in newspapers from the 1730s through 1790.

For the enslaved women in the colonial Southeast, the experiences and expectations of parenting were informed as much by the shattering violence and dislocations of their enslavement and the appropriation of their children as the property of others as by maternal bonds of affection. Both surely factored into women's decisions about when, where, and with whom they would escape.[24] Yet the written record does not tell us whether the majority of fugitive women fleeing without children in these advertisements reflected generally low birthrates among slaves or a determination to quit onerous work routines at the expense of parental ties. Women without children may have favored flight over obtaining emotional and physical relief by cultivating family relations with other slaves. Women recently arrived from Africa, separated from families in their homelands by capture, and too new in the Americas to have formed connections among the enslaved would presumably have tended to fall within this last category.

Enslaved women in the late-eighteenth-century Southeast lived in communities that grew more from arrivals of such new and isolated Africans transported from either the West Indies or West Africa than from natural increase. Whether from the devastating physical toll of rice labor on women's reproductive health and on infant survival, low proportions of women among the enslaved, or the enslaved women's intentional use of contraceptives and abortifacients, low rates of natural increase among the enslaved in Georgia and South Carolina persisted into the late eighteenth century.[25] Over half the West-Central Africans—

who made up nearly 70 percent of the enslaved population in South Carolina by 1739—had been in the colony for less than a decade.[26]

Depressed birth rates in conjunction with high infant mortality rates meant that between 1755 and 1777 the average number of (surviving) children born per enslaved women in Georgia was less than one. According to historian Betty Wood's survey of the inventories of colonial Georgia plantations, 43 percent of enslaved couples who lived together either had no children or had been separated from their offspring by sale or dispersal of the estates of deceased owners.[27] Consideration of these low rates of reproduction and the significant presence of newly arrived and deracinated African women shifts the emphasis in interpreting these data away from gross generalizations about the emotional constraints on women's flight toward the specific hardships and isolation of their lives— their intense labor and limited abilities to form families—that made flight to the Creeks both possible and desirable.

THE PRACTICALITIES OF FLIGHT

Either unencumbered by the burdens of childcare or for other reasons not explained by the historical record, the enslaved women who fled to the settlements of the Creeks ran away either on their own or with only male companions. In the spring of 1769, for example, Sarah, an African-born woman in South Carolina "with her country marks down each side of her face" and filed teeth, ran off with an enslaved boatman named York. Perhaps relying on York's navigational skills to facilitate their escape along the Low-Country waterways, the fugitives made their way to Georgia, where they were "taken up by the Creek Indians."[28] In the autumn of the same year, an enslaved Georgia couple, Harry and Cassandra, ran away from their master and were believed to have gone to "the Indian nation, or to Mobile" along the Gulf coast of West Florida, where Cassandra's family lived. The shrinking territorial distance between white Georgians and the Creeks made slaves' escapes to the Creeks as feasible as running off to family or to nearby urban centers.

Despite Creeks' treaty agreements to pursue and return fugitives, white slaveholders and colonial officials remained dubious that they would regain possession of runaway slaves who reached them. The lieutenant governor of Florida observed in 1771, "It has been a practice for a good while past for negroes to run away from their masters and get into the Indian towns from whence it proved very difficult and troublesome to get them back."[29] Late in 1769 white men captured a fugitive African-born man in the Creek territory some twelve months after he had run away from his master in Pensacola. During his time among the Creeks, he had learned to speak Muskogee and, speaking in the Creeks' language, reported to his captors that his work had mainly entailed gathering firewood for an Indian man, a stark improvement on enslaved men's labor for British masters in Florida, which included clearing swamps, building roads, and toiling in rice fields.[30] Slaveholders paid steep prices even when they succeeded in retrieving runaways; though they re-gained their property, they also brought back a person who had acquired critical knowledge about the location, language, and lifeways of the In-dian settlements.

Information about potential Indian allies and the routes between white plantations and Indian settlements pulsed through the streams of communication that linked enslaved people across the Low Country and kept them abreast of important events and potential destinations for flight throughout the Southeast.[31] Enslaved women who ran away from their Anglo-American masters and headed toward the Creek settlements chose this path because they had an informed awareness of the nearby Indian populations. Early in the eighteenth century, slaveholders had owned both Indians and Africans, who lived and labored side by side. The broad array of racial terminology that Anglo slaveholders used to describe people of African and Indian ancestry in the early eighteenth century attests to the extensive and longstanding intimate connections between the two groups. Subsequent generations of enslaved Africans and African Americans likely gained information about nearby Indian peoples from these fellow bondspeople. When a woman named Mary, de-scribed by her South Carolina master as "mulatto or mustee," ran away in 1771, she fled with the assistance of her "Indian" mother, who lived on a nearby plantation.[32]

Personal relationships like these, however, were only one strand of wider webs linking Africans and Indians in the Southeast. Enslaved women would have gained critical information about the Creeks' loca-tions as well as their social relations and antipathy for brutal domination at the core of chattel slavery simply by listening attentively to conversa-tions among their masters. British trade relations with Creeks also brought a number of enslaved African men into commercial contact with Creeks. English traders living in Creek towns ignored colonial pro-hibitions against keeping slaves at their stores, and enslaved men owned by these merchants and others connected to the Anglo-Indian trade worked as packhorsemen and boatmen. In those they capacities became well acquainted with the locations and languages of Creek towns.[33] As this particular group of enslaved men moved between Creek towns and white communities filled with enslaved people watching for every opportunity to escape, they carried with them information about Creeks that proved highly useful to enslaved women plotting their escapes.

FINDING PLACES

Runaways from the colonies made their way to the Creek towns clustered along the Chattahoochee, Flint, and Apalachicola Rivers in Georgia and the Florida panhandle. Some fled to the towns situated in present-day Alabama on the Tallapoosa and Coosa Rivers, some two hundred miles to the west. Drawing on this geographic dispersal, early British observers distinguished between two principal groups of Creeks, the "Upper Creeks" living on the Tallapoosa and Coosa Rivers and their tributaries and the "Lower Creeks" closer to the Low Country in the Chattahoochee, Flint, and Apalachicola watersheds.[34]

Runaway slave women who reached these Creek towns found themselves in communities composed of hierarchical networks of extended kin groups, or clans. Elaborate rules governed interpersonal relationships and political, economic, and ceremonial responsibilities within and among particular kin groups. Both biological relations and the linguistic idioms of kinship delineated intricate relations of obligation and reciprocity linking Creek townspeople to one another within local communities and also among geographically dispersed towns. Creeks, like other southeastern Indian peoples, viewed outsiders who lacked places in these networks of social, political, and ceremonial relations, such as fugitive slaves, as little more than "dunghill fowl," beings who commanded no respect and were easily disregarded.

At the same time, however, Creek conceptions and practices of kinship had long allowed for inclusion of such outsiders through formal rituals of adoption and marriage that placed the foreigners under the Creeks' control and transformed them into kin who counted.[35] Before and after Europeans' arrival in the Creeks' world, adoption and marriage of women and children captured in wars provided spiritual and physical compensation for losses in these conflicts. In the eighteenth century, marriages of Creek women from powerful clans to British traders not only conferred kinship upon these foreign men but also, and more important from the Creeks' point of view, secured a community's access to the trade goods they could offer. Creeks cemented trade and diplomatic ties also among their own towns by performing gift-exchange ceremonies that linked the contracting parties to each other as kin and bound them to promote one another's political and economic interests. In the latter half of the eighteenth century, as Creeks were increasingly drawn into the complex networks of trade and diplomacy that connected Euro-Americans and Indians, their flexible conceptions of kinship served as a crucial mode of governing relationships with their enslaved African neighbors as well.[36]

Africans and African Americans entered Creek settlements in a variety of roles. Some came as fugitive slaves, others as slaves owned by British traders, and others still as slaves acquired by Creeks. Across the towns dispersed throughout the Creeks' territories, responses to Africans and African Americans varied with individual and local community interests confronting the territorial and political expansion of colonial plantation society. While some Creeks waded into the market economy by taking up commercial agriculture and purchasing African slaves as laborers, others chafed at the dominance and coercive power exercised by colonial planters and politicians and remained skeptical of embracing Euro-American institutions and practices.[37] For Creeks who acquired slaves, however, the old ways did not disappear immediately, and their practices of slaveholding did not simply imitate Euro-American ones.

In the 1770s Philadelphia naturalist William Bartram wrote of his travels through the Southeast and pointed to the complexity of Creeks' slaveholding and to their interactions with black women within the framework of their relations of kin. On the subject of slavery, Bartram noted that the Yamasee captives held as slaves by a Creek chief were permitted to marry Creeks, and their children were considered full and equal members in the society.[38] The Creeks, like other southeastern Indian peoples, had long dealt with war captives in gendered ways: they tortured and executed men while retaining women and children as servants until their transformation into kin. Bartram's descriptions of the Creek towns he visited in the 1770s also reveal the presence of black women as slaves and also as potential kin in Creek families.

Bartram's writings can be read to chart Creeks' changing practices of slaveholding as they moved from retaining Indian captives to acquiring black people as slaves.[39] Bartram focused his attention on Creek ownership of black people as slaves because he hoped to persuade Anglo-Americans of Creeks' potential for conforming to "our modes of civil society," especially men's ownership of private property and participation in the market economy.[40] When reading Bartram and other English descriptions of the complex relations taking shape between Native Americans and African

Americans, it is important to remember that the meaning of the term *slave* is contextual and not easily transposed from the Anglo-American to the Creek context. Rather than clearly documenting the extension of chattel slavery, and thus in Bartram's estimation "civil society," into Creek country, his observations reveal the fluidity of Creek patterns of subordination and thus suggest the ways in which fugitive women may have navigated the path from outsider to kin among the Creeks.

In one instance Bartram described an encounter with a man named Boatswain (also known as James Lawson), the son of a British trader and a Creek woman. Boatswain received the northern traveler into his home, located outside the Lower Creek town of Hitchiti, along the Chatta-hoochee River, and the men enjoyed "excellent Coffee served up in China Dishes by young Negro Slaves." After feasting on corn cakes, bar-becued venison, and assorted sweets, Bartram took stock of Boatswain's agricultural endeavors, approvingly noting that he had close to one hundred acres of fertile land fenced and under cultivation. Those responsible for planting and tending the crops were "his own private family, which consists of about Thirty People, among which were about 15 Negroes." Boatswain thus blended labor acquired through purchase of black women and perhaps the acquisition of fugitives with Creek obligations of family to staff a small but profitable plantation on the margins of the region's growing commercial economy.[41]

Bartram looked with approbation at the composition and organization of Boatswain's household, as it demonstrated not only Creek capacity for commercial pursuits but a Creek man's ability to assume command of Creek and black women's labor. Anglo-American observers usually viewed Creeks' gendered division of labor, matrilineal family order, and willingness to absorb Africans and African Americans into their families as backward and unstable. Bartram, by contrast, saw promise in the gendered and racialized hierarchy of Boatswain's household, implicitly likening it to the ideal southeastern, colonial planter's household in which a constellation of dependents—wife, children, other relatives, ser-vants, and slaves—were subject to capacious, patriarchal authority.[42] The perceived similarities between Boatswain's household and that of colo-nial planters, and even yeomen, however, were largely superficial.

Unlike in the southeastern colonies, the women of African descent in Boatswain's household were not wholly confined by lifelong enslave-ment. Their subordination or dependency was temporary and not inex-tricably linked to skin color, even though by the mid- to late eighteenth century, Creeks had become well acquainted with their Euro-American neighbors' categories of racial classification. Creeks and other southeastern Indian peoples responded to European racial categories by drawing on indigenous color symbolism. The Creeks, for example, understood *red* as the powerful opposite of *white* and thus began referring to themselves as red people as a response to Anglo-Americans' self-identification as whites, not as a description of skin tone. Yet, Creeks often lumped people of African descent in the same categories they used to identify Anglo-Americans, thus marking both primarily as outsiders. Although a small cadre of Creek slaveholders increasingly adopted the Anglo-American equation of blackness with enslavement in the final decades of the eighteenth century, that trend was neither immediate nor universal across Creek country.[43]

Even through the early years of the nineteenth century, many Creeks continued to identify themselves and others as insiders and outsiders, differentiated by kinship and personal relationships, and "cared little whether strangers were black or white."[44] Thus, Boatswain's "family" consisted of female biological relatives and other women in his clan, including those of African descent, who were linked to each other and to Boatswain through Creek understandings of the hierarchical relations of kinship rather than Euro-American conceptions of a permanently, racially stratified household. According to Bartram, several of the black women in Boatswain's family "were married to Indians and enjoy equal privileges with the Indians, but they are slaves until they marry, when they become Indians, or Free Citizens."[45] The complex workings of family ties instead of appearance or African ancestry determined their status, identity, and future prospects in Boatswain's family and the larger Creek community.

While Bartram identified the women of African descent in Boatswain's family as slaves, his descriptions of the kin-oriented route from enslavement to freedom suggests that these runaway women might also have followed this trajectory to permanent liberation from their Anglo masters. Bartram's attentiveness to the "slaves" among the Creeks may also be somewhat deceptive, as many African Americans in Creek country were likely to have been runaways. Creeks, as colonial slaveholders knew too well, routinely "sequestered" these fugitives, refusing to return them to their masters. Outside observers, paying little attention to the dynamics of social relations in Creek communities, viewed these relationships as those of masters and slaves. In the 1790s, for example, U.S. Indian agent Benjamin Hawkins noted with dismay that Sophia Durant, a Creek woman, did not press her slaves to produce ample, marketable crops.

However, he failed to recognize that some of her "slaves" were married to members of her clan and at least one was, in fact, a free black person under her protection.[46]

Although increased intermarriages of Creek women with white men added a patrilineal element to the ways Creeks mapped kin ties in the late eighteenth and early nineteenth centuries, most Creeks continued to trace descent through male relatives in the female line, that is, from a mother's brother (maternal uncle) to her children (as nephews and nieces). By this matrilineal calculus, black women incorporated into Creek kinship groups as subordinates to Creek women and men became eligible for marriage, ensuring their children's lineage and thus positions in clans and towns. Theda Perdue's study of a Cherokee Deer Clan family's adoption of a black woman named Molly in the 1770s makes clear that while southern Indians' ideas about race, property, and slavery were shifting in the late eighteenth century toward an acceptance of Euro-American categories of racial distinction and the ownership of black people as chattel slaves, many native people continued to acknowledge and abide by the primacy of matrilineal kinship.[47]

Yet it would be romantic to imagine that relations of kinship and the transformative power of incorporation proceeded without tension and conflict. Like captive Indian women before them, black women would have performed agricultural work, acquiring the skills that Creeks expected of women. By learning the labor patterns of Creek women and men, outsider women gained more than technical knowledge: they became familiar with the dispersal of power between women and men in Creek clans and towns and the respect given gendered labor.[48] African and African American women in Creek country owed their labor to their host families and, despite the absence of grueling work regimes, nonetheless had little choice about the work they performed.

Did Creek women expect outsider and subordinate women to bear the responsibility for the more onerous and monotonous chores? Similarly, who selected Creek marriage partners for these newly arrived women? The friction, such as negotiations over the daily allocation of work or the selection of a marriage partner, as well as the affection that developed between black women subordinates and their Creek hosts, are not readily apparent in Bartram's writings on life in Creek towns, but they must have been central to black women's experiences of incorporation into Creek society.

Remaining aware of such tensions, however, reminds us of the challenges and choices runaway women faced when they fled to Creek settlements. Definitions of inclusion in Creek society, which entailed clear constraints on autonomy and required outsiders' initial subordinate status and compulsory labor, bore little resemblance to liberal conceptions of civic belonging as "freedom" taking shape in late-eighteenth-century Anglo-America but nonetheless provided more stability than plantation slavery and thus security against the threat of reenslavement in the colonies.

COMMERCIALIZATION IN THE NINETEENTH CENTURY

The American Revolution and the repeated transfers of control over Florida back and forth between the British and Spanish created an unstable geopolitical climate in the Southeast, in which black people there found new opportunities, some of them closer to home, to protect themselves from the multiple modes of violence at the heart of plantation agriculture. During the war, slaves took advantage of the chaos to run away in numbers large enough that one historian has called their flight "a type of slave revolt." British commanders, usually less interested in black liberation than in destroying American patriots' property and economy, nonetheless spurred slaves' flight and offered freedom to those men who served the British forces. In the southeast, the ranks of British forces were comprised of whites, Indian men, and blacks, and their raids on Southern plantations facilitated other slaves' flight and the opening new routes out of chattel slavery and into southern Indians' territories.[49]

One slaveholder in the aftermath of the war, in 1783, placed an ad for the capture of a family of five runaways who had fled four years earlier. The group had retreated from Savannah with Indians just days before the British besieged the city.[50] Slaves' frequent flight during and after the war suggests that, despite some Creeks' growing interest in acquiring black slaves as chattel and participating in the expanding commercial economy of the region, others continued to offer refuge to runaways. In 1786, for example, a large group of runaways—consisting of Juba and her husband, Isaac; Phebe and her husband, Pate; Quahobe and her husband, Battes; Sue, her husband, Ned, and their two young children—fled West Florida for Creek territory to the north.[51]

As Low-Country planters pushed into Georgia's backcountry in the wake of the revolution, the rivers and streams that had formed the core of the Creek territory became major arteries linking new inland cotton plantations to markets on the coast. Facing accompanying pressure from the federal and state governments, Creek leaders, many of whom had distanced themselves from the older models of power sharing and negotia-

tion to participate in slave-based commercial agriculture, ceded communal hunting grounds vital to most Creeks' subsistence. In 1802 they gave
up the central Georgia land between the Oconee and Ocmulgee rivers;
in 1821 they ceded land further west up to the Flint River; and in 1826
they relinquished claims as far west as the Chattahoochee River, which
now marks Georgia's western boundary.[52] The loss of so much territory,
coupled with a poor harvest in 1804 and subsequent shortages of food,
exacerbated divisions within Creek towns and fueled Creeks' discontent
with land-hungry white Georgians.[53] As the newcomers pushed to seize
more land from southeastern Indians, they also pushed to import more
slaves before the Constitution's 1808 ban on the transatlantic slave trade
took effect. Between 1804 and 1807 they brought some forty thousand
Africans into Charleston alone. During the following years, an equally
brutal domestic slave trade would channel hundreds of thousands of
African American slaves from the upper South to the bone-crushing
labor of the cotton plantations that grew up as planters pushed westward
onto Indians' lands.

The interests of many Creeks and runaway slaves thus converged, at
least to the degree that members of both groups were searching for ways
to escape the hardships wrought by this expansion of commercial plantation agriculture in the early nineteenth century. In 1802 an East Florida
planter complained that two of his slave men had run off to the Indians.
In addition, he reported, "an Indian Negro" had stolen a slave woman
and her child. The woman, moreover, had given birth to another child
since she had left her master's plantation.[54]

Neither Creeks nor runaway slave women left accounts of these interactions, but documents generated by slaveholders attempting to regain
ownership of fugitive women provide clear evidence of the significant
extent to which Creeks incorporated black women and their children
into their society. In 1796, for example, a slaveholder from Liberty
County, Georgia, claimed that a "party of Indians" had "inveigled" a
slave couple, Adam and Fanny, away from his plantation and taken them
to a Creek village. While Adam was soon killed, Fanny continued to reside in the town. By 1822 she reportedly had eighteen children and
grandchildren.[55] Fanny clearly had been incorporated into a Creek kinship network, where she had married, borne children, and was living
peacefully. Her integration into the Creek nation—specifically her marriage and reproductive success—attracted the jealous attention of her
master, who sought compensation from the state not only for the two
slaves he had lost but also for the value of Fanny's Creek offspring, thus

creating the record revealing her circumstances. Slaveholders' capacious understanding of their patriarchal rights of ownership over black women's bodies allowed them to bequeath unborn children and even, as in this case, to insist on claiming children born far beyond their plantation confines.[56]

Creeks, intent on safeguarding their political and territorial autonomy, took a dim view of slaveholders' arguments that the children born to fugitive slave women in Creek towns were rightful property of the masters whom slave mothers had fled. Creeks not only refused to surrender fugitive women or their children but also articulated the distinct understandings of descent and identity that lay behind their refusal. In May 1793 the overseer of William Smith's plantation, also in Liberty County, Georgia, noticed that slaves who should have been working in the rice fields were "running in every direction," and he saw Indians leading them away. Seven men and six women had escaped from the plantation: some were eventually retrieved, but several remained with the Creeks. In 1821, when Smith filed suit with the state for compensation for these losses, he indicated that one of the fugitive women, Mary, had had four children who were living among the Creeks. Smith had been unable to gain possession of the children, in spite of his evident close monitoring of their lives, complaining that "the Indians kept them because they were born upon their hands."[57]

The Creeks' insistence on keeping Mary's offspring suggests that she had been woven into their social fabric, despite her initial outsider status, to the extent that she and her progeny were granted the protection afforded to members of the community. When Creeks recognized Mary's children by Creek men as members of their community, they furthermore made clear their rejection of American slavery's oddly parallel definition of descent exclusively through the mother. They also conveyed their utter unconcern with the corresponding American polarized categories of race, in which even a slight taint of African (maternal) ancestry excluded a person from the privileged and paternal status of whiteness.

Creeks continued to accept fugitive slaves into their settlements at least through the early nineteenth century. Some historians have contended that the absence of commercial agriculture among Creeks allowed them to continue their older patterns of retaining fugitive women and other slaves as captives but not as property.[58] Yet such a formulation suggests that Creeks thought only in terms of economic practices rather than with ideas and values about belonging. Even as prominent Creeks adapted their ideas about property to commercialization and grew prosperous with individual ownership, including black people as chattel, these tendencies developed unevenly across time and place. In the late eighteenth and early nineteenth centuries, black people's status varied widely throughout the Creeks' territory, according to richer and poorer Creeks' disparate views and practices of race, kinship, and slavery. Like other southern Indians, Creeks did not immediately or entirely jettison older patterns of kinship and incorporation but continued to rely on clans to give shape and meaning to their social relations even as they simultaneously adopted newer modes of governance, property ownership, and social hierarchy.

The intimacy between Creeks and black women alarmed and infuriated white Southern slaveholders well into the antebellum era. When they looked at the fugitive slaves who gained freedom from chattel slavery in Creek towns, and even at the black slaves whom some Creeks claimed as property, American slaveholders did not see the complex and changing dynamics of kinship and slavery. Instead they saw Creeks as a chaotic, and therefore dangerous, alternative to the theoretically rigid racial and social order that they sought through enslavement. American chattel slavery rested on the abject racial and sexual degradation of African and African American women. The negation of blacks' civic standing through denial of rights as persons extended to whites required the continual policing of boundaries of race. Slaveholders personally and arbitrarily controlled black women's bodies, their physical labor, sexual services, and reproductive potential.[59]

When Anglo-American slaveholders looked at the Creeks' towns, however, they witnessed black women possessing their own bodies, moving freely within the conventions of kin and other relationships and retaining control of much of what they produced. They saw that many Creeks recognized black women's offspring as legitimate children rather than only as added value to their estates, which contradicted all the exclusionary principles of race and property informing the foundations of chattel slavery.

Nothing revealed more clearly whites' failure to understand the alternative forms of freedom that fugitive slave women found among the Creeks than the writings of the men directed by the federal government to take a census of the Creeks in 1832. As pressures built to remove Creeks from the Southeast to the still-undeveloped trans-Mississippi West, the census takers went from town to town throughout Creek territory, recording the names of household heads and tallying the number of men and women in each family, including slaves. At every turn the census takers encountered households that defied the civil and racial scheme of categorization that they brought to their task. They found households in which black women headed families; black women identified, in white terms, as slaves who named free Indian men as husbands; and free men and women who appeared black to the census takers but who labeled themselves Indian. In the end, among the 22,664 people counted in Creek territory, the census enumerated approximately nine hundred black slaves and fourteen free black families, nine of which were headed by women. In one entry, a woman householder named Juba claimed her black husband as one of her five "slaves," recalling the 1786 runaways from West Florida.[60] All the black women family heads in the census claimed black slaves as members of their households, and some indicated that the people counted as slaves in the terms of the federal census were husbands and children in Creek categories of kinship.

African and African American women in the Creeks' territory, like the Creeks who adopted and incorporated them, had their own understandings of what it meant to be enslaved or free. For the African women and their American-born daughters who sought refuge from chattel slavery in the Creek territory in the mid-eighteenth century, the clan-based, matrilineal organization of the Creek world offered freedom of a certain kind—recognized standing in networks of kin and affines—not available in the southern port cities, where they had arrived alone and routinely were isolated again and again through loss of mates and children and other relatives. When recently enslaved women entered Creek towns, they found secure places in communities comparable to those they had left behind in Africa. These women, former slaves, did not somehow recreate their African pasts. Rather, these fugitive women would have found Creek patterns of liberation through protection by responsible patrons—in social as well as gender roles, family structure, and division of labor—not to have been entirely alien or unsatisfying.

In slavery to English planters, women knew all too well that childbearing and other hard-won ties they might build were vulnerable to their masters' ability to destroy them at will through labor demands or sale. By the early to mid-nineteenth century, their American-born daughters were products of the ties of kinship that slave families had nonetheless managed to create, even under the duress of Low-Country plantation slavery. The slave women who ran away to the Creek territory, either on their own or with loved ones, had good reason to recognize that inclusion in Creeks' family and kin relations afforded them a secure refuge from bondage to commercially driven planters, the possibility of enduring families and other connections. Meanings of family or kin relations shaped Creeks' inclinations to retain the fugitive women who arrived in their villages, and the potential security of this particular sort of freedom informed enslaved women's choices to endure the risks of running away. Examining enslaved women's flight from chattel slavery to incorporation in Creek communities suggests the intertwined meanings of family and freedom in the late-eighteenth- and early-nineteenth-century Southeast, not only for the enslaved but also for the planters who held them in bondage and for the Creeks who offered them refuge.

NOTES

1. It is well established among historians of African American slavery that urban settings, especially port cities, beckoned runaways, offering access to employment, contact with other black people, and the possibility of continuing their escape by sea. The First African Baptist Church, founded in Savannah by George Liele, a free black ordained minister, offered runaways a secure hiding place under the floorboards in its basement. For descriptions of runaway slaves in Savannah in the early nineteenth century, see Timothy James Lockley, *Lines in the Sand: Race and Class in Lowcountry Georgia, 1750–1860* (Athens: University of Georgia Press, 2001), 13–15, 118–20. On black Baptists, see Mechal Sobel, *Trabelin' On: The Slave Journey to an Afro-Baptist Faith* (Westport, CT: Greenwood, 1979), especially 188–90, 319. Peter Wood writes that in the early eighteenth century "Charleston harbor became a common locale for runaways." Wood, *Black Majority: Negroes in Colonial South Carolina from 1670 through the Stono Rebellion* (New York: Norton, 1996), ch. 9. South Carolina slaveholders sometimes suspected free blacks in Charleston of hiring runaway slaves. Philip D. Morgan, *Slave Counterpoint: Black Culture in the Eighteenth-Century Chesapeake and Lowcountry* (Chapel Hill: University of North Carolina Press, 1998), 494–97. For discussions of the public markets in Savannah and Charleston, see Betty Wood, *Women's Work, Men's Work: The Informal Slave Economies of Low-country Georgia* (Athens: University of Georgia Press, 1995), ch. 4; Olaudah Equiano writes at length about his time in Charleston and Savannah in 1765 and 1766, not long before he purchased his freedom. Working on a slave ship that regularly made calls in the two southeastern port cities, Equiano hired black men to assist him on the docks and socialized with other slaves in Savannah. Equiano, *The Interesting Narrative and Other Writings*, ed. Vincent Carretta (New York: Penguin Books, 1995), 128–30, 133–40.

2. Lathan Windley, comp., *Runaway Slave Advertisements: A Documentary History from the 1730s to 1790*, 4 vols. (Westport, CT: Greenwood, 1983), vol. 4, *Georgia*, 37; vol. 3, *South Carolina*, 110, 192; Robert Olwell, *Masters, Slaves, and Subjects: The Culture of Power in the South Carolina Low Country, 1740–1790* (Ithaca: Cornell University Press, 1998), 170–71.

3. Tiya Miles, *Ties That Bind: The Story of an Afro-Cherokee Family in Slavery and Freedom* (Berkeley: University of California Press, 2005); Theda Perdue, "Clan and Court: Another Look at the Early Cherokee Republic," *American Indian Quarterly* 24 (2000): 562–69.

4. Paul E. Lovejoy, *Transformations in Slavery: A History of Slavery in Africa* 2nd ed. (New York: Cambridge University Press, 2000), 12–15, 120–23.

5. The debate regarding kinship and slavery is framed by the work of Suzanne Miers and Igor Kopytoff that argues for considering slavery as a continuum of kinship and Claude Meillassoux's position that slavery exists as the direct opposition of kinship. James Brooks's study of captivity, slavery, and kinship in the American southwest adds a new dimension to this debate by suggesting the possibilities of considering slavery and kinship as interrelated and constitutive. Kin incorporation, he argues, makes subsequent denials of incorporation historically and analytically salient. Miers and Igor Kopytoff, eds., *Slavery in Africa: Historical and Anthropological Perspectives* (Madison: University of Wisconsin Press, 1977); Meillassoux, *The Anthropology of Slavery: The Womb of Iron and Gold* (Chicago: University of Chicago Press, 1991); Brooks, *Captives and Cousins: Slavery, Kinship, and Community in the Southwest Borderlands* (Chapel Hill: University of North Carolina Press, 2002), esp. ch. 1. For a feminist-studies response to some of these issues, see Gayle Rubin, "The Traffic in Women: Notes on the Political Economy of Sex," in *Toward an Anthropology of Women*, ed. Rayna R. Reiter (New York: Monthly Review Press, 1975), 157–210.

6. Wilhelm Johann Muller, "Wilhelm Johann Muller's Description of the Fetu Country, 1662–69," in *German Sources for West African History, 1599–1669*, ed. Adam Jones (Wiesbaden: Steiner, 1982), 154.

7. Margaret Burnham, "An Impossible Marriage: Slave Law and Family Law," *Law and Inequality* 5 (1987): 203.

8. In their work on the dynamics of kinship and slavery in East Africa, Justin Willis and Suzanne Miers caution against "the bland implication of a static world of equality and harmony" when considering the ways in which "outsiders of all kinds" might be incorporated into a kin-based society. Willis and Miers, "Becoming a Child of the House: Incorporation, Authority and Resistance in Giryama Society," *Journal of African History* 38, no. 3 (1997): 480.

9. See, for example, Alan Gallay, *The Indian Slave Trade: The Rise of the English Empire in the American South, 1670–1717* (New Haven: Yale University Press, 2002); Kevin Mulroy, *Freedom on the Border: The Seminole Maroons in Florida, the Indian Territory, Coahuila, and Texas* (Lubbock: Texas Tech University Press, 1993); Kenneth Wiggins Porter, *The Negro on the American Frontier* (New York: Arno, 1971); Claudio Saunt, *A New Order of Things: Property, Power, and the Transformation of the Creek Indians, 1733–1816* (New York: Cambridge University Press, 1999), ch. 12; Daniel H. Usner, *Indians, Settlers, and Slaves in a Frontier Exchange Economy: The Lower Mississippi Valley before 1783* (Chapel Hill: University of North Carolina Press, 1992); J. Leitch Wright Jr., *Creeks and Seminoles: The Destruction and Regeneration of the Muscogulge People* (Lincoln: University of Nebraska Press, 1986); Jane Landers, *Black Society in Spanish Florida* (Urbana: University of Illinois Press, 1999), ch. 2.

10. Landers, *Black Society*, 24.

11. Jane Landers's works provide wonderfully detailed accounts of both the imperial rivalry between Spain and Britain as it played out in the Southeast and the complex and shifting relations between blacks, Indians, and Spanish authorities in Florida. Black women are central to Landers's discussion of black life in Spanish Florida, but their interactions with Indians are not the subject of her inquiry. Landers, *Black Society*, esp. ch. 1. In their efforts to foster antipathy between the enslaved and Indians, colonial officials also armed enslaved men to fight against Indians. Gary Nash, *Red, White, and Black: The Peoples of Early North America* (Saddle River, NJ: Prentice Hall, 2000), 310–14; James H. Merrell, "The Racial Education of the Catawba Indians," *Journal of Southern History* 50 (August 1984): 363–84; Martha Condray Searcy, "The Introduction of African Slavery into the Creek Indian Nation," *Georgia Historical Quarterly* 66 (1981): 21–32; William S. Willis, "Divide and Rule: Red, White, and Black in the Southeast," *Journal of Negro History* 48 (1963): 157–76. For a discussion of British attempts to retrieve runaways from the Cherokees, see Miles, *Ties That Bind*.

12. Jennifer Morgan, *Laboring Women: Reproduction and Gender in New World Slavery* (Philadelphia: University of Pennsylvania Press, 2004), ch. 5.

13. For studies of rice production in colonial South Carolina, see Judith Carney, *Black Rice: The African Origins of Rice Cultivation in the Americas* (New York: Cambridge University Press, 2001); Daniel C. Littlefield, *Rice and Slaves: Ethnicity and the Slave Trade in Colonial South Carolina* (Baton Rouge: Louisiana State University Press, 1981).

14. Carney, *Black Rice*, ch. 4, quote from 120.

15. Joshua Piker, *Okfuskee: A Creek Indian Town in Colonial America* (Cambridge, MA: Harvard University Press, 2004), 98.

16. Betty Wood, *Slavery in Colonial Georgia* (Athens: University of Georgia Press, 1984), 92–93.

17. Ibid., 98–99; P. Morgan, *Slave Counterpoint*, ch. 1; Julia Floyd Smith, *Slavery and Rice Culture in Low Country Georgia 1750–1860* (Knoxville: University of Tennessee Press, 1985), ch. 2; Elizabeth Donnan, ed., *Documents Illustrative of the History of the Slave Trade to America*, 4 vols. (Washington, DC: Carnegie Institution of Washington, 1930–35), vol. 4, *The Border Colonies and the Southern Colonies*.

18. The spread of cattle through the region threatened to destroy the local ecosystem on the Creeks' shrinking hunting lands. Cattle both trampled the grasses that fed the indigenous game and drove them off, compromising the availability of food and also diminishing the source of the deerskins that were central to the southern Indians' exchange economy with colonial traders. On the deerskin trade, see Kathryn E. Holland Braund, *Deerskins and Duffels: The Creek Indian Trade with Anglo-America, 1685–1815* (Lincoln: University of Nebraska Press, 1993); Saunt, *New Order*; Piker, *Okfuskee*. On the deerskin trade and other southern Indian peoples, see Richard White, *The Middle Ground: Indians, Empires, and Republics in the Great Lakes Region, 1650–1815* (New York: Cambridge University Press, 1991); Usner, *Indians, Settlers*; Usner, *American Indians in the Lower Mississippi Valley: Social and Economic Histories* (Lincoln: University of Nebraska Press, 1998).

19. John Stuart, quoted in Miles, *Ties That Bind*, 32.

20. Quoted in Daniel E. Meaders, "South Carolina Fugitives," *Journal of Negro History* 60 (1975): 305.

21. Stephanie Camp, "'I Could Not Stay There': Enslaved Women, Truancy and the Geography of Everyday Forms of Resistance in the Antebellum Plantation South," *Slavery and Abolition* 23 (2002): 1–20; Deborah Gray White, *Ar'n't I a Woman? Female Slaves in the Plantation South*, rev. ed. (New York: Norton, 1999). On market women, see Olwell, *Masters, Slaves*, ch. 4.

22. J. Morgan, *Laboring Women*, 113.

23. Windley, *Georgia*.

24. For a comprehensive and insightful discussion of the intricate connections between enslaved women's reproductive lives and chattel slavery, see J. Morgan, *Laboring Women*; Kirsten Fischer, *Suspect Relations: Sex, Race, and Resistance in Colonial North Carolina* (Ithaca: Cornell University Press, 2002); White, *Ar'n't I A Woman?*

25. Carney, *Black Rice*; B. Wood, *Slavery in Colonial Georgia*, ch. 6; Smith, *Slavery and Rice Culture*; J. Morgan, *Laboring Women*, ch. 4.

26. For a discussion of African population trends in North America see Michael A. Gomez, *Exchanging Our Country Marks: The Transformation of African Identities in the Colonial and Antebellum South* (Chapel Hill : University of North Carolina Press, 1998), ch. 6.

27. B. Wood, *Slavery in Colonial Georgia*, 106; Betty C. Wood, "Some Aspects of Female Resistance to Chattel Slavery in Low Country Georgia, 1763–1815," *Historical Journal* 30 (1987): 609; P. Morgan, *Slave Counterpoint*, ch. 1. Jennifer Morgan surveyed the inventories of South Carolina plantations in 1742 and found that the number of women without children was greater than that with children. J. Morgan, *Laboring Women*, 141. For a comparison of birth rates for black and white women, see P. Wood, *Black Majority*, 162.

28. Windley, *Georgia*, 36

29. Quoted in Saunt, *New Order*, 53.

30. Quoted in Robin F. A. Fabel, *The Economy of British West Florida, 1763–1783* (Tuscaloosa: University of Alabama Press, 1988), 28–29. See also Larry Eugene Rivers, *Slavery in Florida: Territorial Days to Emancipation* (Gainesville: University Press of Florida, 2000), ch. 1.

31. Julius Scott, "The Common Wind: Currents of Afro-American Communication in the Era of the Haitian Revolution" (PhD diss., Duke University, 1987); Peter Linebaugh and Marcus Rediker, *The Many-Headed Hydra: Sailors, Slaves, Commoners, and the Hidden History of the Revolutionary Atlantic* (Boston: Beacon, 2000); Jeffrey Bolster, *Black Jacks: African American Seamen in the Age of Sail* (Cambridge, MA: Harvard University Press, 1997); Landers, *Black Society*.

32. Windley, *South Carolina*, 670. Jack D. Forbes, "The Manipulation of Race, Caste and Identity: Classifying Afroamericans, Native Americans and Red-Black People," *Journal of Ethnic Studies* 17 (1990): 1–51.

33. William McDowell, ed., *Documents Relating to Indian Affairs, May 21, 1750 to August 7, 1754* (Columbia: University of South Carolina Press, 1958), 88; *South-Carolina and American General Gazette*, 14–21 January 1771, in Windley, *South*

Carolina, 436; *South-Carolina Gazette*, 23 October 1752, 9 August 1768, in Windley, *South Carolina*, 115, 637. On traders using black boatmen, see P. Wood, *Black Majority*, 114–15, 123–24.

34. Braund, *Deerskins and Duffel*; Gallay, *Indian Slave Trade*.

35. Theda Perdue, *Slavery and the Evolution of Cherokee Society, 1540–1866* (Knoxville: University of Tennessee Press, 1979), chs. 1, 2; Kathryn Holland Braund, "The Creek Indians, Blacks, and Slavery," *Journal of Southern History* 57 (1991): 601–4; Perdue, *Cherokee Women: Gender and Culture Change, 1700–1835* (Lincoln: University of Nebraska Press, 1998).

36. John Reed Swanton, *Social Organization and Social Usages of the Indians of the Creek Confederacy* (1928; repr., New York: Johnson Reprint Corp., 1970); Robert Ethridge, *Creek Country: The Creek Indians and Their World* (Chapel Hill: University of North Carolina Press, 2003), 109–11; Charles C. Jones, *Historical Sketch of Tomo-Chi-Chi, Mico of the Yamacraws* (1868; repr., Millwood: Kraus Reprint, 1975), 45. An extensive body of scholarship examines the ways in which southern Indian peoples defined and mobilized kin relations to navigate their economic and political dealings with each other and with European colonists in the eighteenth-century Southeast.

37. Claudio Saunt, "'The English Has Now a Mind to Make Slaves of Them All': Creeks, Seminoles, and the Problem of Slavery," *American Indian Quarterly* 22 (Winter 1998): 157–80.

38. William Bartram, *Travels through North and South Carolina, Georgia, East and West Florida, the Cherokee Country, The Extensive Territories of the Muscogulges or Creek Confederacy and the Country of the Chactaws* (Philadelphia, 1791); reprinted in Bartram, *Travels and Other Writings* (New York: Library of America, 1996), 166. For a comprehensive discussion of Indian captivity and the changing practices of slavery among southern Indians, see Perdue, *Slavery and Evolution*.

39. Perdue, *Slavery and Evolution*.

40. William Bartram, *Observations on the Creek and Cherokee Indians* (1789; reprint, New York, 1853), reprinted in *William Bartram on the Southeastern Indians*, ed. Kathryn E. Holland Braund and Gregory A. Waselkov (Lincoln: University of Nebraska Press, 1995), 158.

41. Bartram, *Creek and Cherokee Indians*, 186. Claudio Saunt discusses Boatswain as an example of the growing number of wealthy mestizos among the Creeks. Saunt also notes that Boatswain acquired slaves not as private property but in transactions that followed older patterns of reciprocity between powerful men and their subordinates; in one instance, Boatswain received a slave as a "gift" from Indians in exchange for items such as liquor, textiles, and ammunition. Saunt, *New Order*, 55–57.

42. For a discussion of the position of Anglo-American women in colonial households and patriarchal authority, see Kathleen Brown, *Good Wives, Nasty Wenches, and Anxious Patriarchs: Gender, Race, and Power in Colonial Virginia* (Chapel Hill: University of North Carolina Press, 1996); Carole Pateman, *The Sexual Contract* (Stanford: Stanford University Press, 1988), ch. 4; Paula Baker, "The Domestication of Politics: Women and American Political Society, 1780–1920," *American Historical Review* 89, no. 2 (1984): 620–47; Linda Kerber, *Women of the Republic: Intellect and Ideology in Revolutionary America* (Chapel Hill: University of North Carolina

Press, 1980); Kerber, "The Paradox of Women's Citizenship in the Early Republic: The Case of *Martin v. Massachusetts*, 1805," *American Historical Review* 97, no. 3 (1992): 349–78. For a discussion of Anglo-American patriarchal authority that considers interactions between colonists, Native Americans, and African Americans, see Fischer, *Suspect Relations*; Carole Shammas, "Anglo-American Household Government in Comparative Perspective," *William and Mary Quarterly* 53, no. 1 (1995): 104–44.

43. Nancy Shoemaker, "How Indians Got to Be Red," *American Historical Review* 102 (1997): 625–44; Willis, "Divide and Rule"; William G. McLoughlin, "Red Indians, Black Slavery and White Racism: America's Slaveholding Indians," *American Quarterly* 26 (1974): 366–83; Merrell, "Racial Education."

44. Saunt, *New Order*, 116.

45. Bartram, *Creek and Cherokee Indians*, 187.

46. John Moultrie, quoted in Saunt, *New Order*, 53; Benjamin Hawkins, *Letters, Journals, and Writings of Benjamin Hawkins*, ed. C. L. Grant (Savannah: Beehive Press, 1980); Saunt, *New Order*, 121.

47. Perdue, "Clan and Court," 567.

48. Braund, "Creek Indians, Blacks," 602–3; Theda Perdue, "Women, Men and American Indian Policy: The Cherokee Response to 'Civilization," in *Negotiators of Change: Historical Perspectives of Native American Women*, ed. Nancy Shoemaker (New York: Routledge, 1995), 90–114.

49. Sylvia Frey, *Water from the Rock: Black Resistance in a Revolutionary Age* (Princeton: Princeton University Press, 1991), 81; Wright, *Creeks and Seminoles*, 89–93.

50. *Gazette of the State of Georgia*, 15 May 1783, in Windley, *Georgia*, 105.

51. *Georgia State Gazette*, 21 October 1786, in Windley, *Georgia*, 182.

52. Joseph P. Reidy, *From Slavery to Agrarian Capitalism in the Cotton Plantation South: Central Georgia, 1800–1880* (Chapel Hill: University of North Carolina Press, 1992).

53. Saunt, *New Order*, ch. 9.

54. Quoted in ibid., 210. For a similar account of Indians stealing slaves from Georgia planters and then marrying the captive women, see Joseph Le Conte, *The Autobiography of Joseph Le Conte*, ed. William Dallam Armes (New York: D. Appleton, 1903), 19–21.

55. Affidavit of John A. Cuthbert, 8 August 1835, in *Indian Depredations, 1787–1825: Original Claims*, ed. J. E. Hays, 5 vols. (Atlanta: Georgia Department of Archives and History), vol. 2, pt. 1, 17.

56. Jennifer Morgan's *Laboring Women* offers an elegant and pathbreaking analysis of enslaved black women's labor and reproduction in seventeenth-century Barbados and South Carolina.

57. Affidavit of William Smith, 4 June 1821, in Hays, *Indian Depredations*, vol. 2, pt. 2, 628. Thanks to Claudio Saunt for bringing these cases to my attention.

58. Littlefield, *Africans and Creeks*, 44.

59. Burnham, "Impossible Marriage"; Peter Bardaglio, "'Shamefull Matches': The Regulation of Interracial Sex and Marriage in the South before 1900," in *Sex, Love*,

Race: Crossing Boundaries in North American History, ed. Martha Hodes (New York: New York University Press, 1999), 112–40.

60. Parsons and Thomas J. Abbott, *Census of Creek Indians Taken by Parsons and Abbott,* microfilm publication T-275 (Washington, DC: National Archives, 1963); B. S. Parsons to Lewis Cass, 7 September 1832, in J. H. Jonston, "Documentary Evidence of the Relations of Negroes and Indians," *Journal of Negro History* 14 (1929): 37.

5

ENSLAVED WOMEN AND THE LAW

Paradoxes of Subordination in the Postrevolutionary Carolinas

LAURA F. EDWARDS

In the spring of 1829, John Mann fired a gun at Lydia as she was running away from him. Both lived in eastern North Carolina, near Edenton, a once thriving plantation district, then in decline. Lydia was a slave, hired to John Mann by her owner, Elizabeth Jones. Mann was a white man, with the wherewithal to hire a slave but not to purchase one. Mann never denied shooting Lydia. To the contrary, he asserted his legal right to do so. Her disobedience, he claimed, had required discipline, even to the point of death. The North Carolina State Supreme Court later affirmed and amplified Mann's position. "The power of the master must be absolute," wrote Chief Justice Thomas Ruffin, "to render the submission of the slave perfect."[1]

The outcome of *State v. Mann*, though, had been different in Chowan County. Local officials there doubted the legality of John Mann's actions enough to prosecute him on criminal charges of assault. A jury validated those concerns and convicted him.[2] Of course appellate courts in this period routinely overturned lower-court decisions, just as they do now. In that sense, the discrepancy between the two decisions—with Ruffin's endorsement of all masters' absolute rights of property in their slaves and the local jury's recognition of the particular slave, Lydia, as both a person and a woman—is not particularly noteworthy. Yet the difference between

I thank Jacquelyn Hall, Priscilla Wald, Adrienne Davis, Anne Allison, Maureen Quilligan, Gunther Peck, and Dylan Penningroth for their readings of this piece. Special thanks go to Joe Miller for his incredibly engaged and insightful editing.

the two outcomes in this case, at this particular historical moment, does revise the existing interpretative emphasis on enslaved women's exclusion from the emerging legal order in the postrevolutionary United States.

Specifically, the two outcomes of *State v. Mann* express fundamentally different conceptions of the polity, one that included Lydia and one that did not. At the center of Ruffin's decision was a distinct conception of the state, with sharply delineated boundaries of inclusion and exclusion, consonant with federal political principles, particularly the protection of individual property rights. In *Mann*, Ruffin fit slavery into those national guarantees, based in gender and in race, which made free white men the paradigmatic citizens of the new republic. Ruffin uprooted John Mann from context, extrapolating from him to everyone within the abstract legal category of master—that is, men with property rights in slaves. That allowed Ruffin to make this one man's rights representative of the rights of everyone in that privileged legal category: each had the same bundle of rights that were distributed universally and uniformly to everyone designated master.

Ruffin's decision also affected the legal status of other groups. The extension of master's rights ate into those of all slaves, represented through Lydia, who were left with a much smaller bundle at their disposal. By implication, the decision also inhibited white women in the category of wives, since Ruffin's conflation of property rights and authority over persons further removed the legal powers of master from them. Because the state was bound to protect rights, their distribution directly differentiated the abilities of the people in the categories he created to mobilize the law on their behalf: people with rights, like John Mann, could make claims in law, while people without rights, like Lydia, could not. It was no coincidence that Ruffin focused his decision on the legal status of Mann, not on Lydia's physical injuries. To the extent that Ruffin acknowledged Lydia at all, it was to urge more vigilant oversight of slavery by community members, outside the formal mechanisms of law as Ruffin envisioned them. Lydia's plight had no place within the abstract legal categories he laid out in his decision.

In that recommendation of community oversight, however, Ruffin acknowledged another important institutional dimension of law at this time, namely the legal dynamics—both formal and informal—outside the appellate court. Although Ruffin drew a sharp line between abstract law and the engaged members of a local community, like Edenton, the distinction was not as apparent in the actual operation of local courts. At the time, most legal business was conducted in local courts below the

appellate level—which included magistrates' courts that held prelimi-
nary hearings and tried minor matters as well as district courts that held
jury trials and heard serious felonies. Unlike the abstract realm of the
appellate court, these local venues were firmly rooted within specific
communities of real people. In the latter, both the legal process and its
underlying logic blurred the line between the people of the community
and legal principles. Cases hinged on direct knowledge of the participants, and decisions were reached through face-to-face interactions. The
process took this form because the legal system dispersed authority over
law widely, made legal claims contextual, and defined a just outcome in
terms of the implications for the specific people involved rather than the
protection of abstract legal rights.

In Edenton, for instance, Lydia was a slave, but not an abstract slave.
She was not even *just* a slave. Similarly, John Mann was a specific free
white man, not an abstract representative of all those in that group. In
fact, his conviction suggests that jurors did not think him a particularly
good representative of white men at all. In that sense, John Mann's conviction was exceptional. But it was not an exception to the practice of
law in local courts, which routinely acknowledged not just slaves' humanity but also their identities as women and men. That was because the
identities were relational, formed through connections with others in
the community. Lydia was a particular enslaved woman, who belonged to
a particular person and who had relationships with others in the community also. Where those relationships tied Lydia into the community,
John Mann's relationships did not. He was a poor white man whose bad
reputation effectively isolated him as a person who did not fulfill his role
within the intricate social networks that formed the local community. As
such, when the local court found John Mann guilty, they found a particular man guilty. The outcomes of this and other similar cases did not
alter slaves' legal position or undermine the rights of white men. That
was because such cases were based on slaves' position as subjects whose
social connections still positioned them as marginalized members of
hierarchically ranked communities. Of course, localized law could just
as easily sanction the most inhumane violence against slaves. That kind
of consistency, however, was not the point, since the operative logic
characterized each case as a discrete event, the outcome of which did not
necessarily affect other cases.

These two conceptions of the state—one in which law was an abstrac-
tion and the other in which the rule of law was realized through concrete
relations within the community—coexisted in the postrevolutionary

South. Although historians of slavery usually turn to appellate decisions, like *State v. Mann*, as definitive expressions of "the law," they represented only one strand of the emerging legal order. The localized legal culture represented in the handling of *Mann* in Edenton formed a historically important, although historiographically neglected, element in the pattern. This chapter explores the dynamics in this localized legal culture, focusing particularly on bondswomen in North Carolina and South Carolina.[3] The system was highly gendered, but in ways that acknowledged the places of enslaved women and other marginalized people. Through their marginalization, all these people were connected to the community and, by extension, to law. No similar connection existed at the appellate level, where universal categories based in gender, race, and property did not— and could not—acknowledge enslaved women's presence without undermining the law's privileging of adult, free, white males, as it operated in that arena. In focusing on enslaved women's connection to the state, this chapter intends to complicate and deepen our understanding of the practices of living with slavery in the postrevolutionary U.S. South, without minimizing the oppression of the slave system. The point is that inequality is maintained through different practices in different contexts, with profound implications for what people can do and how they can do it. At this particular historical juncture, the slave South's local legal systems were simultaneously oppressive and inclusive—the hierarchies of local communities also provided the means of potential inclusion, a situation that contrasted sharply with the oppression of slavery as an abstract institution, rendered in categorical terms as it was emerging in this period at the appellate level. As a result, enslaved women had a direct relationship to the law within the communities where they lived, a position that enabled them to shape local legal processes, without experiencing liberation.

AN INFORMAL LEGAL HERITAGE MOVING TOWARD NATIONAL LAW

Enslaved women do not occupy center stage when it comes to scholarship on slave law in the United States. Historians have tended to focus on the formal, civic exclusion of all slaves as appellate decisions and statutes defined it, contrasting that situation with the principles of political inclusion emergent—at least in political rhetoric and constitutional theory—throughout the rest of the nation. One result is that the scholarship has focused on the law's effect on slaves, rather than slaves' effect on law. Recently, historians have taken up the latter issue, considering slaves' imprint on market transactions and civil cases, matters in which slaves were legally positioned solely as property and, therefore, most circumscribed, at least in theory. Yet, even as these analyses brilliantly reveal how slaves shaped those dynamics, the conclusions still tend to characterize their influence as indirect, and necessarily so owing to their formal exclusion from law.[4] Slave law itself forms another barrier in analyzing the relationship of enslaved women, as women, to law. That body of law, as defined in statutes and appellate decisions, made no distinction between men and women, a gender blindness that has reinforced the historiographical tendency to have male slaves stand in for all slaves in scholarship on slave law. The effects are evident in the work on enslaved women in North America, where historians have done a remarkable job uncovering the legal constraints imposed on these women as well as the details of their work, the meaningful relationships in their lives, and their resistance to individual masters—as other papers in this volume indicate. The work nonetheless defines bondswomen's lives in terms of productive and reproductive labor within the social realm of individual plantations, rather than as subjects of legal or political history.[5]

Running through these historiographical issues is the persistent power of historical narratives that conflate inequality with civic exclusion and that associate the effective exercise of guaranteed civil and political rights with personal agency and social progress. Recent work has begun to shift from those paradigms.[6] Yet much of the literature still rests on the assumption that slavery was the primary source of civic exclusion in South, perpetuating regional forms of inequality at odds with national principles of inclusive equality. That emphasis on legal disability, although often unacknowledged, shapes historical narratives in profound, if unintended ways. Above all, it tends to cast enslaved men and women as outsiders to law and the state, bound by something akin to historiographical chains, immobilized by historians' obsession with the denial of civil status. These narratives of civic exclusion do have great analytical value in their ability to highlight the problematic position of slaves within a functioning liberal order and modern nation-state—one based on universal principles of contract, property rights, and individualism, upheld by a centralized, but democratic, government that protected personal rights and thus encouraged individual initiative. Yet because the point of comparison is the position of free people within a modern nation-state, these narratives also obscure slaves' active roles in times and places where the government institutions and liberal ideology usually associated with that state form were not fully realized, or necessary.

The postrevolutionary South did not meet the conditions associated with a modern nation-state. Although other historians have made that observation, they have done so in the context of debates about southern exceptionalism, in which the region's ideological commitment to slavery explains both the underdevelopment of state institutions and slaves' civic exclusion. This chapter uncouples slavery and the modern state, to push beyond narratives that focus on slavery's exclusions. It places the dynamics of slavery in a different context—a region in the throes of profound political transition and enmeshed in conflicts over how law and government should work.[7] Although these questions of state formation may seem far removed from enslaved women, they are not. In fact, they are essential in both complicating narratives about slavery and understanding enslaved women's relationship to law and the developing state. When the postrevolutionary slave South is considered from this perspective, it is clear that slavery was not the only source of inequality either in that region or in the nation as a whole. Nor was it slavery per se that excluded enslaved women from law or the community.

The principles now associated with modern nation-states were very distant from law in the postrevolutionary Carolinas. After separating from Britain, legislatures in North Carolina and South Carolina restructured their state governments to locate basic institutions and authority over them in local communities. Law played a crucial role in government in the South and elsewhere in that form, as recent scholarship in legal history has noted. It was not only a popular, participatory forum where people worked through community conflicts but also the primary arena for dealing with a range of public issues that were later moved to other parts of state government—from community policing and poor relief to public health and economic regulation.[8] In the Carolinas the law's basic institutional structures were heavily tilted toward local control, despite institutional changes that were slowly solidifying the state's purview over their authority.[9]

The content of law was also localized, in the sense that local jurisdictions had considerable discretion in defining its meaning in any given matter. Like most states, North Carolina and South Carolina entered the postrevolutionary period without an inclusive collection of the statutes. That relative incoherence at the state level speaks volumes about the ad hoc and highly personal nature of law at the time. Although reformers spearheaded efforts to collect and to coordinate their statutes soon after the Revolution, with the intent of turning them into a coherent body of law representative of the state, they failed to achieve that result, because existing statutes had never been intended for that purpose. In the broad areas left uncovered, legislators invoked common law—in the open-ended sense that combined case law and local custom. But that did not provide uniform answers either, since common law was an unstable set of inconsistent, often conflicting principles the inherent ambiguities of which were magnified in practice by a decentralized legal structure that allowed for multiple interpretations in their application.[10]

Within this localized system, central legal concepts that historians usually track only in legislative halls and high judicial chambers continued to be interpreted locally, reflecting the dynamics of local communities. Many different interpretations could and did flourish in this legal system without compromising its integrity—in the most basic sense of its functionality. The situation frustrated reform-minded critics, who hoped to rebuild their states around principles now associated with a modern nation-state. These critics, Thomas Ruffin included, were part of a national network of lawyers who worked to systematize law and government throughout the new republic. They saw law in scientific terms, as an internally consistent set of universally applicable principles. They also tended to support the centralization of legal authority to ensure uniformity in the law's content and application, although many still believed that the system should allow room for local outcomes that might achieve justice in particular circumstances, even if at the expense of those rules. They defended their proposals with singular zeal and bombastic rhetoric, based in a decidedly Whiggish perspective that characterized the ad hoc and highly personalized nature of community-based law as outdated relics of receding, illogical, and unenlightened times—a mere prologue in the progressive journey that led inevitably to a more perfect union, defined by their vision of abstract and categorical law.[11]

These reformers have had a greater effect on the historiography than they did on law in their own states at the time. Accepting the reformers' criticisms, historians once routinely portrayed law and the legal process in the slave South as dysfunctional, backward, or both. Although subsequent scholarship has rehabilitated the integrity of the region's legal system, elements of the reformers' recidivist vision still shape the historiography. In particular, historians tend to base their research on the assumption that southern legislatures and appellate courts defined a unitary law for "the state," just as reformers said they should. They tend to see the localized legal system as an outdated holdover from the past, instead of a recent creation, based in Revolutionary ideology, allowing for the local discretion over law promised in English tradition but unjustly denied by imperial authorities. They also accept the pejorative bifurcation of law and custom that reformers asserted, in their efforts to distinguish undependable local outcomes from their vision of the law as uniform and controlling.

Most of all, historians have lost sight of the influence of people on law and government in this period, although recent work is recapturing those dynamics.[12] The essence of both was people, in a very literal sense. These people were not "the people" of an abstract civic order composed of legally categorized individuals, some of them accorded full civil and political rights, protected by the state at the expense of others. Rather, the process and content of law depended on the concrete circumstances of actual people's lives. This personalism did not make localized law more responsive or humane, let alone just, for the local process was no more democratic in its dynamics nor egalitarian in its outcomes than the complex and evanescent social rankings that ordered local communities. People mattered because the localized legal system of the Carolinas required them to be there physically: where the appellate courts favored by reformers made decisions based on legal abstractions, without even the presence of those involved, local courts could not operate without people. Those people included enslaved women.

LAW AT WORK IN THE COMMUNITY

Rooted in specific communities, localized law reflected both the intricate hierarchies of community life *and* the fluid social dynamics that complicated those hierarchies. The inclusion of enslaved women within these networks meant that they, too, found their ways into local legal practices. At this level of the system, *State v. Mann* was a typical criminal case, because it crystallized complex webs of ongoing human interaction in one dramatic moment. Most local court cases began long before conflicts reached a legal official, let alone a courtroom. Immediately following an incident, the parties directly and indirectly involved began weighing its legality informally. Magistrates' hearings, the first institutional level of the legal system, blended those informal deliberations with formal law. Magistrates conducted their business in houses, yards, stores, and taverns, where their proceedings took on the flavor of neighborhood gatherings. What people said, though, carried formal legal significance: they formed the basis through which magistrates resolved most minor confrontations and determined how conflicts would acquire broader and more serious overtones in the formal legal system.[13]

Magistrates had a great deal of discretion in determining whether disputes would be formally denominated legal or not. The magistrate who heard the complaint against John Mann, for instance, could have sent everyone home and done nothing at all. He could have facilitated a settlement outside of court. He could have encouraged Elizabeth Jones, Lydia's owner, to pursue a civil suit to obtain damages for property loss. He could have issued a peace warrant against John Mann, labeling his actions as a potential, yet unrealized, public offense. John Mann then would have secured bond for his good behavior but would not have incurred any criminal penalty unless he broke the peace thereafter. In this particular case, though, the magistrate pressed criminal charges, which turned Lydia's injury into a serious offense against the public order and moved the evaluation of John Mann's actions to the next level of the legal system.[14]

Given the several options and the ambiguous nature of the offense, criminal charges were not an obvious course of action. As in so many other cases, the magistrate's determination reflected his direct knowledge of the specific people involved. Those details do not always appear in the documents, although they were clearly in play just beneath the surface, subtly shaping the official record. In Lydia's case, for instance, her owner, Elizabeth Jones, may have insisted on prosecution, and the magistrate may have agreed out of personal regard for her. The seriousness of Lydia's injuries, although the case documents do not describe them, may have buttressed Jones's demands. The fact that both Lydia and her owner were women may have shaped the magistrates' evaluation. It also may have been details about John Mann that swayed him. He might have considered any man capable of shooting at an unarmed female—slave or not—to be despicable enough to deserve criminal prosecution. Or, given John Mann's reputation as a rabble rouser, prone to drink and violence, the magistrate may have deemed him undeserving of the leeway he might have given more respectable white men in similar circumstances.[15]

In making such decisions, magistrates relied heavily on the people who came to hearings and who gave *information*, a term that applied to both physical evidence and verbal testimony. Informants' identities, which in turn depended on their relationships within the community, were as important as the information they gave. Above all, information was expected to be subjective, and it was valued for that reason. For instance, the subjective meanings attached to information invalidated charges in a rape case from up-country South Carolina. Tried about the same time as *State v. Mann*, this case ended very differently, even though it involved a white woman, Lucretia Campbell, who accused a slave named Sam of rape. In addition to testimony, the magistrate and jury considered the state of the defendant's clothing. But they never saw the clothes in question. It was what people said about them that mattered, with some claiming they were "smutted" with signs of sexual activity and others insisting they were not. Informants mixed descriptions of the physical evidence with their assessments of Sam and Lucretia Campbell: they "saw" the clothes differently because of their own relationships to the people who had worn them.[16]

Magistrates evaluated information through the character of the informant. The notion of character was closely related to honor or credit, terms that were often used interchangeably. Character reflected other indices of status, such as gender, race, or property ownership that defined a person's position within the community. As such, white men with property were thought to be inherently more credible than anyone without property, or any woman or anyone of African descent. Beyond that, credible white men's information—opinions, really—literally *created* truth. What they said could validate or invalidate a charge, elevating their versions of events over others. Those dynamics regularly brought in information from people who had no direct knowledge of the actual crime, as in Sam's trial. His owner called two white men to testify to Sam's good character, even though they knew nothing of the incident in question, pitting them against the less credible Lucretia Campbell and turning the tables on a situation where her words would otherwise trump those of an enslaved man.[17]

In the context of local communities, the close relationship between personal character and this kind of socially determined truth did not automatically validate the information of all white men or exclude the information of every slave, free black, or white woman. So, too, in localized legal culture. There, generic status marked only the potential of character. For that potential to acquire specific meaning, individuals had to demonstrate the associated attributes and others had to acknowledge them— character had to be lived through a person's relationships with others. The importance of social witnessing was why it was so common to include testimony about the reputations of all parties involved in a case. Such background was believed necessary for evaluating accounts, a practice that suggests how contextual and multivalent both character and the truth were: because the facts of the case did not exist apart from contexts, personal knowledge of people was essential in evaluating whatever they said had happened.[18] It was thus possible that certain slaves could have greater standing to establish truth than particular whites, in some circumstances. In effect, that is what the two white men who testified on behalf of Sam did. In establishing his good character, they gave credibility to his claim to innocence over the accusation of a white woman whose poverty and dubious reputation made her word complementarily questionable.

Some slaves also gave information to magistrates and testified in court, on occasion even in cases involving whites. More commonly, though, slaves' information came into institutional legal forums through the mouths of whites, in a dynamic analogous to the one Ariela Gross describes in civil cases, in which whites used slaves' bodies and actions as evidence.[19] In criminal matters, slaves' words regularly appeared in court, because the credibility of the original information did not matter as long as a credible person presented it. That was how Sam's wife came to play a decisive role at her husband's rape trial, although she was never sworn in and was never even identified by name. Other white men related facts attributed to her: that Sam's clothes were unsoiled and that he had been with her all night. Even if they made up what they attributed to her, their own reputations ensured that these men could make an enslaved woman's words believable to the other propertied white males.[20]

The process mirrored social hierarchies, rooted in slavery and gender, which allowed white male household heads to appropriate the words of slaves and other dependents just as they claimed labor and property. It also reproduced the ambivalent social conditions of slavery, in which white owners demanded slaves' subordination to the point of negating their individuality in some regards while expecting slaves to act independently in others. In criminal matters involving slaves, it was clear that neither slave owners nor other whites knew much about slaves' daily activities. That left slaves as the only ones who could provide evidence, even when the incident happened to involve a white person—as in Lucretia Campbell's case. All that created obvious difficulties for slaves when they became enmeshed in criminal matters, where formal law positioned them as extensions of their masters: although they were the ones with information, whites could not attain it directly. The ambiguity of the slaves' very imminent presence but their civic absence in formal categories of law also created difficulties for owners, who had significant financial and social capital invested in their slaves. A trial and conviction entailed financial losses. As recent scholarship also has pointed out, masters had their own reputations and identities tied up in their slaves. A slaves' trial exposed the owner to public scrutiny, which could compromise his reputation.[21] Obviously, then, what whites attributed to slaves did not necessarily reflect what slaves would have said, had they been able to say it themselves. It is nonetheless significant that whites attached value to information attributed to slaves, depending on the repute of the attributor. A white person needed to validate a slave's information. But that white person also needed that slave to be a source.

All these legal dynamics were about white men and their reputations. However, the fact that words acquired credibility simply because credible whites spoke them also created possibilities for slaves to influence legal deliberations. Cases in which whites prosecuted slaves for slander are suggestive.[22] In law, slaves' words were not supposed to be given credit. In practice, they mattered a great deal, because rumors made their way through the community and acquired credibility along the way. As people heard gossip and passed it along, the source became increasingly obscure and increasingly irrelevant. Therein lay the power for slaves, for their words acquired credibility as they went in the ears and out the mouths of white people. That happened so easily and often that rumors had acknowledged standing in local legal proceedings as common reports—information about a person that was widely acknowledged to be true, even though substantive proof was lacking.

This ebb and flow—a cultural process of creating consensus from conflict—informed all legal deliberations at the local level. The information produced and conducted through community networks was inseparable from the information that people brought to magistrates' hearings and that thus became legal evidence and testimony. The dynamics that turned reported circumstances into common reports also drew enslaved women into the legal process, even when they could not participate in formal legal institutions. That was how Sylva, who lived near Camden, South Carolina, managed to implicate her overseer in her own death in 1822. The conflict began when Sylva intervened to protect her son from their overseer's lash, and the overseer turned on her instead. Within minutes, Sylva's master had heard about the incident and called the overseer to explain himself. The only way he could have found out so quickly was through Sylva or another slave who witnessed the event. Although the overseer managed to justify his actions at that initial encounter, the interview opened up more general suspicions about him. Gossip spread all the more rapidly because three white men, who happened to be visiting Sylva's master at the time, witnessed the accusations and the overseer's response. Sylva, whose health declined after the whipping, kept the rumors alive. She made the seriousness of her injuries known, emphasizing the connection between her illness and the whipping. Her complaints were loud enough and frequent enough to reach beyond her plantation and into the neighborhood, where they became common report by the time of her death.[23]

At the inquest the overseer confessed immediately and voluntarily to Sylva's death. At that point, he had little choice. As his statement indicates, reports of the incident, from Sylva's perspective, had already circulated so widely that he could not deny what he had done. The jurors at the inquest accepted his responsibility for Sylva's death without question. All that may have been because neither the overseer nor the coroner's jury expected any legal penalty to result from the decision: a coroner's jury could find a person responsible for a death without attaching criminal charges, and that is what happened in this case. Even so, the outcome was not ideal for the overseer. The verdict established that he had killed a slave, hardly a ringing recommendation in his line of work and one that left him liable for civil charges. Beyond that, the process opened him to public scrutiny and, ultimately, public condemnation. That, too, was evident in the outcome of the case.

Local hierarchies, structured by gender and property, shaped the decision. For one, the result reflected credible white men's power to make decisions about others. If the jurors—all propertied and white, of recognized social standing—thought it had been Sylva, and not the overseer, who acted inappropriately, the verdict would have been different. Her death would have been laid to "misfortune," as the deaths of so many other slaves were. Yet the jurors used their authority to discipline the overseer in an act that demonstrates both the contingency and contextuality of gender-based authority: while all white men *could* have it, not all actually exercised it to the same degree. In this instance, then, the same hierarchies that subordinated enslaved women as a group made this one bondswoman, Sylva, visible and influential. It was not just his propertylessness that worked against the overseer. Nor was it just Sylva's attachment to a prominent, wealthy white man that determined the outcome. Instead, it was also a complicated convergence of the overseer's reputation and Sylva's efforts, within a very specific, local context. As discussions about the event circulated, community sentiment coalesced around Sylva's version of events, not the overseer's. That version then became the one validated in law. Had Sylva not worked to publicize her version of the incident, the outcome would have been different.

ENSLAVED WOMEN AND THE LEGAL PRINCIPLES OF LOCALIZED LAW

The *outcomes* of cases form no particularly logical pattern outside the highly localized dynamics and rankings of the communities in which they were tried. By contrast, the legal *process* that guided the adjudication of these cases did follow well-defined legal principles. Those principles, however, were not articulated in statutes and appellate cases. They were based in the traditions of common law, echoed in the pages of justices' manuals and other legal materials that built on those traditions, and expressed in the dynamics of the local legal process itself. Both statute and case law, for instance, were either silent or unclear about the status of violence against slaves. Local officials nonetheless proceeded with criminal charges in such instances by drawing on common-law rules, outlined clearly in justices' manuals, that gave all subjects a recognized presence in law and a direct connection to the state. The rubric was highly gendered, subordinating all subjects to a sovereign, public body in the same way that slaves and other domestic dependents were subordinated to their male heads of household. The metaphorical public body was represented first through the king of England and then, after the Revolution, "the people," through the agency of the state—although what form that state should take was still in question in this period. Violence against subjects became crimes only when the effects reached beyond the individual victim's body to disrupt the body of that metaphorical public and its "peace," an open-ended legal term that expressed the notion of mutual trust that was so central in this understanding of the public order. Clear-cut instances of murder, rape, and mayhem placed the perpetrators beyond the pale of community trust and were, by definition, criminal acts. But not all acts of violence rose to that level of collective threat. For it was the disruption to the peace and not the injury to the private individual that distinguished criminal matters. Other incidents were either dismissed or dealt with in law as civil cases, a categorization that confined the issues only to the affected individuals. Although tried in legal arenas that were public, civil cases were classified as "private" matters in law, in contrast to the "public" legal dimension of criminal cases.[24] It fell to local magistrates to determine when violence breached the peace, disrupted the public body of the state, and became a crime against all the people. In Lydia's case, the magistrate thought the implications of John Mann's actions had ramifications for the community that reached beyond her owner and could not thus be rectified through a civil suit. That decision was tied to his evaluation of incident, based on what he knew about Lydia and John Mann. Not all violence against slaves represented a threat to the peace; this incident did because of those involved. John Mann had to answer to the larger public as well. Lydia and her injuries thus became legally visible as a public wrong.

This logic gave priority to the peace of the public body—or state—over any individual, regardless of legal status. As such, it allowed for violence against slaves and other domestic dependents to enter the courts as crimes. Beyond that, this legal logic recognized slaves and other domestic dependents as members of the peace and subjects of the state—a status they shared with free white men. For instance, free white men were subjects, even though they had recognized rights as individuals. So were white women and children, even though they did not have the full array of rights and were subjected as domestic dependents within the households of their husbands and fathers. And slaves were subjects as well, although their rights were even more limited and their legal subordination to their masters took on the most repressive forms.[25] Yet, despite their different degrees of marginalization, all subjects were members of the peace and answered to the laws of the state. That meant even masters and husbands were subject to the state through the mechanisms of law. Nor did free white men's property rights in aspects of their slaves', wives', and children's lives imply authority over them to the exclusion of external legal oversight. Not only were all subjects responsible to the state, but the state also acquired a basic responsibility for them and their protection, even in the absence of individual rights. That logic allowed violence against slaves that offended the state's interest in public order to enter the courts as crimes against the people and the peace of the state, if not against the slaves themselves.

In fact, subjects acquired a recognized presence within the state *through* their positions of marginalization. Slaves' standing, then, had multiple dimensions. They were subject to their masters, in ways that all but eliminated their agency in formal law. That same status, however, also established their position as subjects of the state and thus made them subject to state jurisdiction—a direct connection between slaves and the peace of the state mediated through law, although not based in their position as legally recognized individuals who claimed rights in their own names or who occupied positions of equality with others in the polity. Consequently, officials could legally separate slaves from their masters and acknowledge slaves' places within local public orders on a case-by-case basis, without extending individual rights or other elements of civil status to slaves as a group. Those legal multiplicities of slaves' status converged to draw unique boundaries around each case. Local officials could affirm one slave's interests and limit those of one white man without turning that circumstantial assessment into a statement about all slaves and all white men in all like conditions. That is what happened

in Lydia's case at the superior court. Recognizing Lydia's injuries as resulting from a crime did not alter her legal status or that of any other
slave. Similarly, convicting John Mann did not predict the court's treatment of other white people who assaulted other slaves.[26]

Yet, even though Lydia and other slaves could not claim categorical
rights in their own names, they could move out from under the legal
purview of their masters and acquire a more direct, if momentary, relationship to the state as subjects. The outcome in Lydia's case in the
Chowan County court thus achieved the intent of common-law proceedings: acknowledging slaves as subjects, within the broader goal of
capturing—or creating—the consensus of the community. Of course,
Lydia's injuries were not the basis of the crime. It was the public body—
the state—that had been violated through the violence her body experienced. That legal logic nonetheless rendered enslaved women's assaults
legally visible and linked them to the peace of the state.

AND THE WOMEN

Both the practice and the logic of the localism of law meant that enslaved women mattered in it. Their attempts to define acceptable behavior, personally, in terms of what others did to them and of what they
themselves could do had strong resonance within the system, on at least
two levels. In the narrow sense, they shaped specific legal matters. But,
given an institutional context that rooted so much authority over law in
local areas, enslaved women's efforts acquired broader legal meanings as
well. In those cases where enslaved women acquired a public presence
and forced the state to respond to them, their ideas found their way into
the content of law as well, because the law's content was not defined
solely in appellate decisions and statutes. Those dynamics, then, can cast
court cases involving enslaved women in a light that threw long shadows
across the legal system.

Take, for instance, the case of Violet, an up-country South Carolina
slave accused of assaulting a white woman.[27] The details of the case come
through the Burgesses, the white family in whose household Violet was
working and who had every reason to portray her actions as anomalous.
According to the Burgesses, the incident began when Polly Burgess, the
mistress, ordered Violet to stop what she was doing and perform another
task instead. Violet ignored her. Polly then threatened to strike Violet if
she did not obey. Violet "came at" Polly. In response, Polly tried to strike
Violet with an axe handle. But Violet hit Polly, jolting the improvised

weapon from her hands and knocking her to the floor. Polly's daughters then came to the rescue, helping her to her feet. Violet struck her down again. That brought Polly's husband, Thomas, into the fray, although he did not fare much better. According to the Burgesses, Violet put up such a fight that it took Thomas, Polly, and all their daughters to subdue her. Even that was not entirely successful. After Thomas tied her up and struck her ten blows with a whip, Violet untied her bonds, left the house, and stayed away for several days. Thomas Burgess filed assault charges soon thereafter.

Yet Violet's actions seem reckless only when the Burgesses' account and the outcome in a formal legal forum is elevated over Violet's version and the community context, which lurk just beneath the surface of the Burgesses' carefully constructed account. As that context suggests, Violet had every reason to believe that she could limit the authority of Thomas Burgess's family and even censor their treatment of her. She was actually the property of John Burgess, Thomas Burgess's father, who had recently loaned Violet to his son and daughter-in-law. John, Thomas, and Violet all seem to have understood the transfer as a limited one, moving her place of residence and giving Thomas temporary use of her labor, without granting him the authority of her master. The court proceedings, which treated Thomas as an injured third party and not as Violet's master, conform to that presumption. So do the participants' actions.

The Burgesses' description suggests that their own response to Violet in fact was measured, based in the recognition that they had limited authority over her. That would explain why Thomas, his wife, and daughters had so much trouble subduing her. That also would explain why she escaped so easily afterward. Even more telling, however, is that after Thomas whipped her, he went to his father to ask permission to continue punishment. His father refused either to let his son punish Violet further or to punish her himself, although the records do not reveal why. So Thomas, utterly unable to resolve a domestic matter within the family, followed the only remaining course, filing legal charges against Violet. That solution did result in her punishment, but it came at a cost: Thomas Burgess had to air the details of the incident in public, which exposed both his dependence on his father and his impotence in governing his own household.

More than that, Thomas Burgess did not have a clear-cut case, given the context. If Violet had transgressed accepted social practices, so had Thomas and Polly—perhaps more than Violet, although in different ways. That John Burgess refused to discipline Violet or allow his son to do so speaks volumes on this score. So does the testimony of Thomas's family. As one of the Burgess daughters later described it, Violet had "generally done as she pleased" when she had lived with John Burgess. She could have meant it as an accusation, not unlike her mother's statement that Violet "thought she was an eaqual [sic]." But the daughter's words likely contained a grain of truth as well. It could be possible that these comments were freighted with sexual overtones. If Violet had an intimate relationship with the father, John Burgess, that might explain his support for her. On the other hand, if Violet had a sexual relationship with the son, Thomas Burgess, that might explain his wife's resentment, Thomas's muddled response, and his father's refusal to engage in the resulting mess.

Or it could be that Violet's ties were gendered in another way. As a slave with a long-standing relationship with the Burgess family, she may have established intimate—if conflicted—ties to the Burgesses through all the domestic services that enslaved women so often provided to the families of their white masters. Those kinds of intimacies could have complicated the conflict's dynamics just as easily as explicitly sexual ones. The evidence, unfortunately, remains tantalizingly silent on these issues. What the evidence does establish is that Violet had done very much as she pleased a great deal of the time. She seems to have expected that she would exercise considerable discretion over the labor she performed, hiring out her own time and doing specified tasks for her master when and as she saw fit. She seems also to have expected to come and go freely. None of this would be unusual, particularly in the South Carolina up-country where Violet lived.[28]

The fight that landed Violet in court was not the first confrontation between her and members of Thomas Burgess's family. After moving to their farm, she had continued to act on privileges she had exercised in John Burgess's household. The son's family had tried to change that, leading to conflict on several occasions. Yet Violet remained resolute, for good reason. Since Thomas and Polly Burgess were not her owners, they did not necessarily have the authority to institute such major changes in her life. Only John Burgess did—if Violet recognized it in anyone at all. Reading the Burgesses' testimony through the lens of personal patronage and family patriarchy in operation within the community context, it is easy to see the fight from an angle from which Violet appears less as the unpredictable and invincible aggressor and more as a stubborn woman who felt justified in her actions and who expected others to support her, because of who she was—a particular bondswoman with a particular history in a particular family. In fact, the outcome would have been different had Thomas Burgess accepted his father's refusal to punish Violet further. Violet evidently did not guess that Thomas Burgess would defy his father's wishes, question his custom, and try to mobilize another version of law to trump family authority.

Violet's presence was apparent in the institutional arena of the court, even though she could not appear there to recount her version of events. The proceedings began with a statutory ultimatum: "Violet a negro slave the property of John Burgess is put upon her trial for inflicting a grievous wound on a white person, Mrs. Polly Burgess, the commission of which is a capital offence punishable by death, Acts of 1844 and 34"—the latter a somewhat mystifying statutory reference that serves to underscore the localized nature of law.[29] The local court nonetheless interpreted the statutes creatively, emphasizing the seriousness of the wounds Violet had inflicted. The entire tone of the proceeding also suggests the presence of doubts about the propriety of the Burgesses' conduct. That Violet had struck Polly Burgess was not enough. Every member of the Burgess family who testified carefully justified the use of force. They claimed that it was Violet who was out of control—wildly out of control. They, by contrast, were the hapless victims of Violet's unprovoked, vicious, and life-threatening attack. They barely survived, even though they outnumbered Violet and had a gun. But how believable was that?

The trial transcript suggests that the Burgesses' version was not, in fact, very believable. Violet nonetheless struck a white woman, and the jurors would not sanction that, even if they did not agree completely with the Burgesses' actions. She was found guilty and sentenced to fifty lashes. Violet clearly overplayed her hand and thereby experienced a tragic loss with definitive, lifelong consequences. To the extent that the court exercised restraint in punishment, it was probably as much to preserve John Burgess's property as to censure Thomas Burgess or to support Violet. Nonetheless, that misjudgment does not erase Violet's palpable presence in shaping the case or the context of recognized family responsibility that led her to think that she could play a hand in the first place. The results for the larger legal principles, moreover, are even less certain. The verdict did not necessarily indicate a vindication of the Burgesses' irresponsible approach to slaveholding, the defeat of those customary rights that Violet sought to preserve, or a victory for law as defined in opposition to custom. That the Burgesses had to go to such violent lengths to assert their will over Violet and that Violet went to equally violent lengths to defend her actions suggest the opposite.

STATE LAW VERSUS MEN — AND WOMEN

Violet and Lydia have a great deal in common. In some ways, they both conformed to the image of slaves as property conveyed in Thomas Ruffin's rendering of *State v. Mann*. Violet, like Lydia, can appear as a victimized woman who fled personal oppression, since she was unable to evade it, let alone challenge it directly. Both women's victimization was then legitimized in public law. Yet, while injured, Violet was neither silent nor passive. There is no reason to believe that Lydia was any different, even though the court records provide no evidence that she defended herself aggressively, as Violet did. The handling of Lydia's case as a public, criminal matter and its outcome favorable to her in the local court strongly suggest that her version of events did have influence, even if they came into the court through her mistress or another white person.

Although neither Violet's nor Lydia's case resulted in stunning legal victories for enslaved women, they tell us a great deal about these women's expectations of the legal process. They acted as if they *thought* they were included within the legal system, to the extent that they could influence the localized dynamics that permeated the process. Given the decentralized structure of the legal system, those expectations had solid basis in fact. Enslaved women and men played key roles in defining offenses against them as crimes and in holding white people responsible for those acts, even though they could not use law directly, as whites could. Above all, enslaved women pushed legal officials and other whites to treat them as particular individuals who were women—not as the abstractions of property or even slaves. In Lydia's case, the local court agreed, labeling what Mann did as criminal assault against a woman thus recognized as a member of the public order. It was only after the case was removed to the appellate court that John Mann won. It was only at this level of formal law that Lydia became a paradigmatic slave, silent and without agency in a formative era of national law.

Two very different constructions of patriarchy shaped the two outcomes in *State v. Mann*. At the appellate level, the authority of patriarchs derived from their abstract rights, which they possessed as individuals in isolation from connections to either their dependents or their communities: all white men could claim patriarchal authority, regardless of who they were, how they conducted themselves, and what others thought of them. In fact, acknowledging differences among white men would undermine the logic of law and governance, making rights contingent and undermining the most basic national political principles. Similarly, acknowledging that slaves had a connection to categorical law of this sort might imply that they had individual rights like those idealized and attributed exclusively to white men.

By contrast, at the local level patriarchy always had particular male faces within law. More than that, patriarchy required the presence of other people to have any meaning at all. Not only was white men's patriarchal authority based in concrete ties to their dependents, they also acquired standing in the community through their handling of those relations. Other whites had to see and acknowledge a master's authority for it to have social currency and to translate into status. Those dynamics, in turn, bring new meaning to concepts that have become almost axiomatic in the scholarship on the postrevolutionary slave South, namely paternalism and the implied reciprocity in the master-slave relationship. It was not just that masters owed food, clothing, and protection in return for slaves' labor and loyalty. What slaves did and what happened to them reflected back on their masters, either enhancing or detracting from their master's social standing. Similarly, masters' reputations extended back to their slaves, allowing slaves to use those strengths and weaknesses to their own benefit.

Scholars also have noted this mutual, profoundly lopsided dependence in other contexts. But in the specific context of the postrevolutionary South it had particularly profound implications for slaves' relationship to law and the state. In a system where the basic structures of governance were still so localized, slaves were connected to law because they were connected to their masters and, through them, to the local community. Within this system, slaves were subordinate, but not just as pieces of property under their masters' control. Rather, because slaves' humanity was required to demonstrate their masters' authority and establish their standing, it had to be acknowledged. As a result, slaves also had faces, as particular men and women.

Enslaved women could thus claim a place in law, as women. Yet that place was the result of gendered connections created through a particular form of patriarchal power that also denied enslaved women individuality and independence in law, precisely because they were both slaves and women. That kind of womanhood would acquire new, problematic dimensions as southern states developed along national legal principles, focusing on rights as individual possessions and on categorical abstractions. Such a system separated patriarchs from context—and from the people, including enslaved women, who gave their authority meaning. It thus reduced the personal responsibility that local community standing had imposed on them. The importance of gender to state structures and the fact of bondswomen's subordination in law did not change. But the results profoundly altered the logic and dynamics of inequality, not only rendering enslaved women invisible in law and within the state but also erasing a past in which their presence had been not only possible but also necessary.

NOTES

Abbreviationations

NCDAH   North Carolina Department of Archives and History
SCDAH   South Carolina Department of Archives and History

1. *State v. Mann*, 13 N.C. 263 (1829).

2. *State v. Mann*, no. 1870, Supreme Court Original Cases; *State v. Mann*, 1829, Slave Records, Chowan County; both in North Carolina Department of Archives and History (hereafter, NCDAH).

3. Although the chapter focuses on only a few cases, it draws on extensive runs of local court records (totaling about five thousand cases) as well as statutes, appellate decisions, other government documents, newspapers, and manuscript collections from North Carolina and South Carolina, 1787–1840. The local court records are from Kershaw District, Anderson/Pendleton District, and Spartanburg District, South Carolina Department of Archives and History (hereafter, SCDAH); Orange County, Granville County, and Chowan County, NCDAH.

4. Ariela Gross, *Double Character: Slavery and Mastery in the Antebellum Southern Courtroom* (Princeton: Princeton University Press, 2000); Walter Johnson, *Soul by Soul: Life inside the Antebellum Slave Market* (Cambridge, MA: Harvard University Press, 1999).

5. The classic work is Deborah Gray White, *Ar'n't I a Woman? Female Slaves in the Plantation South* (New York: Norton, 1985).

6. See, for example, Steven Hahn, *A Nation under Our Feet: Black Political Struggles in the Rural South from Slavery to the Great Migration* (Cambridge, MA: Harvard University Press, Belknap Press, 2003).

7. The analysis draws on work that questions the centrality and inevitability of the nation-state's development. See Benedict Anderson, *Imagined Communities: Reflections on the Origins and Spread of Nationalism* (London: Verso, 1983); Etienne Balibar, "The Nation Form: History and Ideology," in Balibar and Immanuel Wallerstein, *Race, Nation, Class: Ambiguous Identities*, trans. (of Balibar) by Chris Tyler (London: Verso, 1991), 86–106. The analysis also owes a debt to scholarship emphasizing the gendered nature of state building: see, for example, Bonnie Smith, *The Gender of History: Men, Women, and Historical Practice* (Cambridge, MA: Harvard University Press, 1998).

8. William J. Novak, *The People's Welfare: Law and Regulation in Nineteenth-Century America* (Chapel Hill: University of North Carolina Press, 1996).

9. William J. Adams, "Evolution of Law in North Carolina," *North Carolina Law Review* 2 (1923–24): 133–45; Walter Parker Stacy, "Brief Review of the Supreme Court of North Carolina," *North Carolina Law Review* 4 (1925–26): 115–17; Donald Senese, "Building the Pyramid: The Growth and Development of the State Courts System of Antebellum South Carolina, 1800–1860," *South Carolina Law Review* 24 (1972): 357–89. See also Lauren Benton, *Law and Colonial Cultures: Legal Regimes in World History: 1400–1900* (Cambridge: Cambridge University Press, 2002).

10. Efforts to collect and coordinate statutes were distinct from later codification movements, which involved a more comprehensive approach to overhauling the law. The specific dynamics emerge from legislative debates, as covered in state newspapers; see, in particular, the *Raleigh Register*, the *North Carolina Gazette*, and the *Charleston Courier*. See also Charles M. Cook, *The American Codification Movement: A Study of Antebellum Legal Reform* (Westport, CT: Greenwood, 1981).

11. These assumptions pepper the introductions to statute collections and legal treatises, all of which were written by reformers.

12. See: Gross, *Double Character*; Joshua D. Rothman, *Notorious in the Neighborhood: Sex and Families across the Gender Line in Virginia, 1787–1861* (Chapel Hill: University of North Carolina Press, 2003); Dianne Miller Sommerville, *Rape and Race in the Nineteenth-Century South* (Chapel Hill: University of North Carolina Press, 2004).

13. These patterns emerge from the local court records and conform to procedures in justices' manuals. See John Haywood, *The Duty and Office of Justices of Peace . . . According to the Laws of the State of North Carolina*, 2nd ed., rev. and corr. (Raleigh: printed by William Boylan, 1808); John Faucheraud Grimké, *The South-Carolina Justice of Peace* (Philadelphia: printed by R. Aitken and Son, 1788).

14. Haywood, *Duty and Office of Justices of Peace*; Grimké, *South-Carolina Justice of Peace*.

15. Other cases from Chowan County suggest that John Mann's reputation was bad.

16. *State v. Sam*, 1830, case 50, reel 2916, Court of Magistrates and Freeholders, Trial Papers, Anderson/Pendleton District, SCDAH. An "information" was one of the ways to establish a criminal charge in British law. See Arthur P. Scott, *Criminal Law in Colonial Virginia* (Chicago: University of Chicago Press, 1930), 72–75. In practice, in the postrevolutionary Carolinas, *information* seems to have acquired a broader definition, encompassing all the evidence given at the investigatory hearing.

17. *State v. Sam*, 1830. Also see Barbara Shapiro, *"Beyond Reasonable Doubt" and "Probable Cause": Historical Perspectives on the Anglo-American Law of Evidence* (Berkeley: University of California Press, 1991).

18. Dylan Penningroth, notes similar practices in former slaves' property claims and finds African cultural echoes in them; but such practices were pervasive among western Europeans as well. Penningroth, *The Claims of Kinfolk: African American Property and Community in the Nineteenth-Century South* (Chapel Hill: University of North Carolina Press, 2003)

19. Gross, *Double Character*, 122–52.

20. *State v. Sam*, 1830.

21. Gross, *Double Character*, 98–121, 122–52; Johnson, *Soul by Soul*.

22. Such cases appeared frequently in the South Carolina slave court records, 1787–1850.

23. Inquest on negro Sylva, 1822, Court of General Sessions, Coroner's Inquisitions, Kershaw District, SCDAH.

24. The logic is apparent in justices' manuals, the one kind of legal source justices and other legal officials were most likely to have; those manuals were based in long-standing common-law practices.

25. Nancy Fraser and Linda Gordon, "A Genealogy of Dependency: Tracing a Keyword of the U.S. Welfare State," *Signs* 19 (1994): 309–36. Recent work in women's history uses the concept of dependency to highlight connections among power relationships based in race, class, and gender.

26. In the court term that John Mann was convicted, Joseph McKiel (who served on Mann's jury) was acquitted for assaulting another slave: *State v. Joseph McKiel*, 1829, Criminal Action Papers; *State v. Joseph McKiel*, October 1829, Minute Docket, Superior Court, 1828–38; both Chowan County, NCDAH. McKiel was in the general assembly, a justice of the peace, and a militia colonel. *Edenton Gazette*, 27 January 1829.

27. *State v. Violet*, 1854, case 160, reel 2921, Trial Records, Magistrates and Freeholders Court, Spartanburg District, SCDAH. Further information and quotes in this section come from this source.

28. The court records establish these patterns. See also Ira Berlin and Philip D. Morgan, eds., *Slaves' Economy: Independent Production by Slaves in the Americas* (London: Frank Cass, 1991); Loren Schweninger, "The Underside of Slavery: The Internal Economy, Self-Hire, and Quasi-Freedom in Virginia, 1780–1865," *Slavery and Abolition* 12, no. 1 (1991): 1–22.

29. It was a 1740 statute that applied the death penalty to slaves who "grievously wound, maim or bruise any white person." See Thomas Cooper and David J. McCord, eds., *The Statutes at Large of South Carolina*, 10 vols. (Columbia: printed by A. S. Johnston, 1840), 7:405.

3

Rebuilding Lives in the Caribbean

Emancipation and Its Aftermath

6

PRICING FREEDOM IN THE FRENCH CARIBBEAN

Women, Men, Children, and Redemption from Slavery in the 1840s

BERNARD MOITT

In the nineteenth century, more than in previous times, enslaved people in the French Caribbean—primarily women who, along with children, were the major beneficiaries of manumission throughout slavery—freed themselves through *rachat* (redemption), by buying back their freedom from slave owners for a fixed sum. They were encouraged to do so by the enactment of new laws and state initiatives that made redemption more attainable than before. Not all slave owners accepted rachat. Indeed, most were hostile to redemption, the end result of which was usually the loss of valuable slave labor. Thus, the number of enslaved persons, female and male, who acquired freedom through rachat was statistically small, as was the number of formerly enslaved persons compared to the total population enslaved in the French colonies. However, neither the hostility nor the reluctance of slave owners deterred enslaved people from pursuing this path to liberation, and their demands for redemption remained high until the end of slavery in 1848.

This essay explores rachat mainly among enslaved women in Martinique, Guadeloupe, and French Guiana. Redemption was an important means of self-liberation for enslaved women and their kin—mostly their own children. Enslaved women of all ages, principally women of mixed African and European descent—including those in Martinique, Guadeloupe, and French Guiana—engaged in redemption as an antislavery act.

This chapter builds on Bernard Moitt, *Women and Slavery in the French Antilles, 1635–1848* (Bloomington: Indiana University Press, 2001).

Though different from other antislavery acts such as armed resistance, acts of poisoning aimed at destroying slave owners, their slaves and animals, and *marronnage*, or slave flight, the practice of rachat demonstrates that women and men still resisted slavery in the same manner "as well as in ways which gender and differential allocation of tasks made possible."[1]

Although the study of rachat is worthy of scholarly pursuit, scholars have largely ignored the phenomenon. That neglect is baffling because French authorities in the Caribbean were preoccupied with regulations governing manumission throughout slavery. Even so, the number of enslaved persons who redeemed themselves through self-purchase was limited, and the small numbers may have a bearing on research interest. Apart from the works of Victor Schoelcher and Josette Fallope, there is little else on self-purchase. In a recent essay on gender and emancipation in the French Caribbean, Sue Peabody examines the paths to freedom that enslaved took but gives scant attention to self-purchase.[2] An exploration of rachat or redemption can provide important glimpses into a dimension of slavery—the struggle for freedom—and enhance our understanding of the multidimensional nature of manumission.

SLAVE LAWS AND MANUMISSION

Redemption was one of many ways in which people enslaved in the French Caribbean acquired freedom. Thus, this phenomenon can best be examined and understood if it is analyzed in the context of manumission. In the French Caribbean many enslaved people took matters into their own hands by engaging in marronnage, by litigating, or by seizing freedom collectively by force, as in Saint Domingue (now Haiti) in the 1790s. Other individuals gained liberty as a result of bequests, by performing meritorious acts, or by serving in the local militia for a prescribed period. Still others, mostly women, secured freedom through marriages to free persons—a rare occurrence—and through informal conjugal relations with white males. Indeed, conjugal relations were behind most of the de facto manumissions (*libre de savane* or *libre de fait*) that slave owners granted mostly to mixed-race enslaved women and their mixed-race children, as I have shown elsewhere. As such manumissions were given without the authority of the state, the libres de fait lacked legal and appropriate documents attesting to free status. These modes of manumission remained virtually unchanged during slavery.[3] To be sure, there were variations in law from colony to colony due to the enactment of local ordinances. Royal ordinances normally applied to all the French colonies, but political events in the colonies sometimes thwarted their local effects. Also, it goes without saying that legislation had different impacts on male and female slaves, as we shall see.

Before the promulgation in 1685 of the Code Noir (lit., black code)—a French code governing slavery—the rules governing manumission had not been firmly established in law. Therefore, the granting of freedom had been somewhat arbitrary and usually left up to slave owners, who favored mixed-race women and their children. This tendency remained a contentious issue in slave society. Indeed, French authorities attempted to circumvent the problem of their status by prohibiting miscegenation, particularly between white males and black females. At the same time, they enacted ordinances aimed at creating strict boundaries between slave and free, taken roughly as equivalent to white and colored. After 1685 the French administration adopted an increasingly stringent policy limiting the granting of manumission.[4]

The Code Noir established, for the first time, clear guidelines on manumission. Under article 55, slave owners twenty years of age or older could free their slaves without giving reasons or seeking consent from their parents. Under article 9 manumission was also possible in cases where male slave owners had one or more children by slave concubines. If such a slave owner was unmarried, he was required to marry his concubine in the Catholic Church, by this act freeing her and her progeny. But the state could not compel slave owners to marry their slave concubines. Under the Code Noir a slave family could gain liberty if a slave owner contravened article 47, which prohibited the break up of a slave family if all its members were the property of the same owner and the children were under fourteen years of age. The Code Noir notwithstanding, metropolitan and local amendments aimed at reducing the number of mixed-race individuals in society, while limiting their civil and political rights, were restrictive and curbed manumission.[5] In particular, enslaved women and their mixed-race children, who were viewed as illegitimate products of concubinage, became the focus of the amendments and the motivation for legal reform.[6]

Throughout the eighteenth century, French authorities, both in France and the colonies, were preoccupied with manumission, particularly with regard to the legitimacy of acts of freedom. The number and tone of the amendments that were introduced after 1685 is proof of this. In a royal ordinance of 1713 that applied to the French colonies, Governor Raymond Balthazar Phélypeaux of Martinique ruled that all slave owners had to obtain written permission from the authorities whenever they wished to free their slaves. His primary concern was that enslaved people were paying their owners to set them free unofficially. In a comment aimed principally at women, Governor Phélypeaux had mentioned a few years earlier that some enslaved people engaged in any activity, however infamous, to obtain manumission—a possible reference to prostitution on the part of enslaved black women. He continued, "We must put a halt to this overly free method of manumitting slaves by introducing an ordinance that will henceforth prohibit any colonist from freeing male or female slaves . . . without the permission of the Governor General or the Intendant, who must first examine the reasons for manumission. If they determine that the reasons are justified, they will register the manumission with the [Superior] Council; if they find the reasons to be unacceptable, they will reject them, and the slave will not be granted freedom."[7]

French authorities were determined to control manumission as much as possible. What constituted a legitimate demand was theirs to decide. But the constant renewal of measures over the eighteenth century and beyond shows that it was difficult to guarantee enforcement. In 1736, for example, a royal ordinance that applied to all the French colonies, reinforced previous measures and carried the severe penalty of confiscation and sale of slaves, with proceeds going to the crown.[8] At the same time, members of the clergy were forbidden to baptize children of women of color as if they were free, unless there was proof of free status.[9] In an ordinance of 1786 in Martinique, these measures were renewed at a time when enslaved people apparently went before priests to have their children baptized as free. As a corrective measure, the ordinance called for compliance with the ordinances of 1713 and 1736. A legitimate baptism required that priests verify that the mothers of black and mixed-race children who came before them had been baptized and had obtained freedom through administrative acts. Further, verification had to be provided in writing from the governor or intendant and recorded in baptismal registers. The rule pertaining to verification also applied to notaries, who could not legitimize any act of liberty without abiding by it. Contravention of this particular measure carried a penalty of one thousand *livres d'amende*—a cash penalty—and suspension of the notary's license for a year.[10]

Although the number of enslaved people who acquired freedom continued to increase in spite of these measures, they were not significant until after 1830, when the pace of manumissions picked up. Two causes are worth highlighting by way of explanation. First, a new administration in France, the July Monarchy of 1830, pushed to some degree by a stronger antislavery movement, was more willing to confront slavery head-on. Second, the plantation economies of the French Caribbean became more integrated into the global economy and declined as a result of increased competition in the sugar market.[11] During the 1830s the colonial economies of the French Caribbean were in crisis, much as had been the British Caribbean colonies from the late eighteenth century. Add to those external stresses increased restlessness among the enslaved populations, which resulted in a serious revolt in Martinique in February 1831. On this occasion the enslaved staged a general insurrection, seeking to torch and pillage the town of Saint Pierre and massacre its white inhabitants. Armed with cutlasses, the slaves terrified the planter class, who drew comparisons to the slave insurrection of 1791 in Saint Domingue that had ended slavery there twelve years hence.[12] Consequently, the viability of the French slave economies came into question. The result was an attempt to ameliorate slavery. Almost immediately, discriminatory statutes to which the *gens de couleur* (free people of color) had been subjected since the eighteenth century—including measures that prohibited them from purchasing arms and practicing professions such as medicine and surgery—were withdrawn.

French authorities then turned to the enslaved population. Under a royal ordinance of 1 March 1831, they dropped the fee for individual liberty patents (certifications of freedom), which cost as much as three thousand French francs. This measure facilitated manumission for enslaved people who wanted to purchase their freedom but had limited access to cash. The 1831 ordinance was followed by a royal decree of 12 July 1832 that permitted all categories of enslaved people not covered by previous legislation to bid for freedom through sponsorship by a patron, usually a slave owner.[13]

RACHAT

The Code Noir made no mention of self-manumission by rachat, but neither did it prohibit self-purchase. Self-redemption was therefore possible at the discretion of slave owners, and it remained so until the last years of slavery. Major changes came in the 1840s. In 1840, the Commission de Broglie, headed by the Duke of Broglie, submitted two reports on amelioration commissioned by the French administration. The reports recommended gradual rather than immediate emancipation. The minister of the navy and colonies in Paris, Baron de Mackau, took advantage of the Broglie commission to expand the parameters of freedom. Under the Mackau Law of 18 July 1845, enslaved people were permitted to legally possess cash and to purchase their freedom and that of their parents, grandparents, spouses, and children, as long as slave owners and the enslaved could agree on an acceptable price. Such transactions constituted a "cordial redemption" (*rachat amiable*) in which the enslaved person often paid the slave owner by installments. If no such agreement was possible, a commission composed of judicial officials of the Royal Court (*Cour Royale*) in each colony fixed the price. This procedure was called a contentious redemption (*rachat forcé*). However, under a royal ordinance of 23 October 1845, slave owners and others had a period of six months to contest the commission's price by filing a complaint with the state treasury. In any case, an enslaved person redeemed contentiously had to work for a free person for a period of five years and abide by restrictive conditions bordering on indentureship. But there were, in theory at least, safeguards against abuse.[14]

French sources indicate that the average price fixed by the colonial commission was about 1,200 francs. One, a document in the archives of Martinique that gives no information about the author or date of publication, notes that a member of the Conseil Colonial of Martinique complained (during a sitting of 5 June 1846) that the colonial commission was not acting in the interest of slave owners because slaves were being priced below 1,200 francs. But the *procureur général,* the chief legal administrator in the French colonies, stated that the price of freedom set by the commission in Martinique and Guadeloupe from 1836 to 1846 was usually higher than that of cordial redemptions.[15] According to Josette Fallope, 1,200 francs—the price set by the commission in Guadeloupe—was well over the 900-franc value of a mature adult enslaved person, especially at a time when the prices of enslaved people were declining due to economic downturn in the French colonies and the pending abolition of slavery.[16] In a similar vein, the French abolitionist Victor Schoelcher accused the commission of being overly generous in setting prices higher than slave owners expected.[17] No systematic guidelines were used to determine prices, but price data show that sex, age, and profession were important variables. Indeed, enslaved Africans engaged in professions that slave owners deemed most valuable, such as those practiced by young skilled males, were highly priced. Thus sugar boilers, slave drivers of the first field gang, artisans (all of whom were males), in addition to women cooks, housekeepers, and those engaged in health care, were especially valued. By the 1840s the slave population in Martinique, Guadeloupe, and French Guiana was highly creolized, but slaves with professions were always valued, as Karol Weaver demonstrates in her recent book on enslaved women healers in Saint Domingue during the eighteenth century.[18]

In 1847, the sixty-two-year-old sugar boiler, Oreste, owned by the woman Amédée Maillet of François, Martinique, paid the commission 1,900 francs for his redemption—a high price in view of his advanced age. But the slave woman, Joséphine, redeemed her two-year-old son from Maillet for only 300 francs. The commission pegged a thirty-year-old slave driver, Laurent, at 2,500 francs; a thirty-one-year-old mason, Désir, at 2,000 francs; a thirty-six-year-old carpenter, Elydée, at 2,400 francs; and a forty-year-old cook, Etienne at 2,000 francs. Women—including the Countess De Grenonville of François, who may well have been reluctant to let Etienne go—owned all the enslaved in this transaction except for Désir.[19]

Those who worked in the fields were at the bottom of the occupational hierarchy among the enslaved, but some still paid substantial prices for their redemption. Such was the case of the thirty-three-year-old African-born Melchior, who purchased his freedom in 1848 from his owner, Brono-Charlery Pousset of Trinité, Martinique, for 1,500 francs.[20] Melchior used his own funds, a remarkable achievement, given that he must have arrived in Martinique after 1815, when French slave traders resumed trafficking illegally in slaves.

Other transactions show that the sixty-one-year-old field woman, Solitude, owned by Pierre Lagodière of Lamentin, Martinique, deposited 500 francs with the commission. Born in the United States, the woman Clarise, a fifty-four-year-old housekeeper in Saint Pierre, bought freedom from her owner, Barlama, for only 300 francs. But the commission fixed the price of redemption for forty-year-old Laurencine, an enslaved female servant of the woman Dathy Morestin of Saint Pierre, at 1,600 francs. These examples, along with a list of other enslaved people whose prices the Martinique commission fixed and published in May 1847, show that males generally paid more for their freedom than did females. Often, the commission priced women and their children as a single unit, but they were still priced lower than men.

These high prices for rachat baffled Victor Schoelcher, who took the commission to task for its "handiwork," which he believed discouraged enslaved people from self-redemption. Drawing upon examples from French Guiana, he argued that the commission's valuation of redemption was excessive and arbitrary. There, the commission estimated a fifty-nine-year-old woman, Clérence, at 1,100 francs; the seventy-eight-year-old Mélanie, at 150 francs; and a sixteen-year-old female at 1,700 francs.

Schoelcher also pointed out that "Urbain, a poor leper who was incapable of rendering service to his female owner, and whose mother wished to deliver him from slavery, was estimated at 600 francs!"[21]

Schoelcher may not have been aware that personal relationships between the enslaved and the slaveholding class resulted in private deals and lower prices, particularly in the case of females. In March 1848, Euphanie, a twenty-six-year-old mixed-race female domestic from Saint Pierre, obtained her freedom from her male owner, Seraphin-Fédéric Sainte-Rose, for 432 francs, a low price for a female of her youth.[22] Similarly, in January 1848, Théoline, an eighteen-year-old mixed-race woman, aided by Joseph Martialis, paid a modest 775 francs to obtain freedom for herself and her four-month-old son, Georges, from Louis Laurent, a baker in Saint Pierre.[23] In some cases, the terms of the rachat involving slave women were not made public. So no figure was attached to the 1848 advertisement announcing that Louisia, a thirty-five-year-old mixed-race enslaved woman, had purchased freedom from Adolphe Zinzo, a butcher in Saint Pierre.[24]

As general abolition approached, the French parliament (Chambre des Députés) voted 400,000 francs to accelerate the manumission process through grants to slave petitioners. This aid, which amounted to between 100 francs and 700 francs per enslaved person depending on the age and profession of the enslaved, was intended to supplement redemption fees. Martinique received 122,000 francs, which partially covered the redemptions of 284 enslaved people, of whom 100 were field hands, 76 domestic slaves, and 108 people of diverse professions. Of the 284 enslaved people, only 62 (22 percent) were males; 87 (31 percent) were females, and 135 (48 percent) were children.[25] Aside from the evident bias toward women and children, the grant was intended to assist "necessary cases." For example, 217 of the 284 enslaved people (76 percent) were judged according to criteria of conduct, morality, industry and labor. Indeed, enslaved people had to provide the privy council (Conseil Privé) in each of the colonies with a letter from a parish priest attesting to good conduct. Forty-five enslaved people were assisted because they fell under the category "marriage, family unification and legitimization of children." Interestingly, although mistreatment of enslaved people was rampant, only two of them were aided because of abuse by owners. Thus there is merit to Fallope's contention that there was strategic partiality in the granting of state aid, in that it went mostly to enslaved people who, once freed, would be inclined to marry and remain as field workers.[26]

In Guadeloupe 462 enslaved persons, of whom 137 (30 percent) were males, 169 (37 percent) females, and 156 (34 percent) children, benefited from the colony's subsidy of 149,000 francs. The enslaved contributed 92,523 francs toward their own redemption. French Guiana's share of the funds amounted to 23,000 francs, and the enslaved there contributed 13,988 francs. The remainder of the funds—106,000 francs—went to the French colony of Bourbon (now Réunion) in the western Indian Ocean, where enslaved people contributed 65,915 francs. These statistics show that state aid, however meager, enabled more women than men to obtain manumission through rachat. The significance of children, who accounted for the highest percentages in all three groups, can hardly be overlooked. Nor can the fact that some women obtained redemption along with more than one child, a common occurrence from 1845.[27]

Even in the absence of state aid, enslaved people still gathered the necessary funds to assure their rachat. How did they do this? The means by which enslaved people acquired cash in slave society remains largely unexplored. It is widely known that enslaved women were the ones who cultivated most of the slave gardens on land allotted by the planters. They sold some of the produce from their gardens at markets—usually held on Sundays in the French Caribbean, although the Code Noir forbade work on that day. Both Hilary Beckles and Barbara Bush have explored the role of women in independent cultivation and in the internal market economy of the British Caribbean. With reference to Jamaica and Barbados, Beckles argues that "slaves fought for the right to be legitimate, autonomous economic agents, as this was the only way to preserve aspects of the commercial heritage they had brought to the New World." Furthermore, "it was the slave women, African-born and Creole, who, from the beginning, dominated numerically the huckstering business in Barbados. They stamped their mark so indelibly upon this activity that it is associated with them even today."[28]

As in Barbados, enslaved women in the French Caribbean were also associated with employment in taverns, which provided resources that they used to purchase their freedom. The story of the La Palu sisters of Martinique is a good example of how such women accumulated resources: "While decrying slaveowners whose relations with slave women resulted in illicit manumission, the colonial administration became entangled in its own web when a liaison between the Intendant Vaucresson and the black slave woman Babet became a public scandal in Martinique in Martinique in the period 1711–13. Babet was one of three sisters called the La Palu sisters, after the name of the family who once owned them.

In Saint-Pierre, the sisters ran a successful tavern and lucrative retail enterprise with merchandise obtained from buccaneers."[29]

In spite of their wealth, the La Palu sisters were not able to secure Babet's freedom. There are, however, other examples of the means by which slaves acquired cash. Seamstresses in Martinique, in particular, did a lucrative business practicing their craft on the plantations. In Saint Domingue, enslaved women kept chicken coops, which allowed them to sell eggs and chickens in the colony. Among the libres de fait, who were mainly women, there were those who operated far from the confines of the plantation, both in urban and rural areas, as petty traders, selling everything from *pacotille* (scavenged trash) to women's makeup. Others engaged in task work on plantations. Their activities allowed them to gain cash, part of which they shared with their owners as a condition of their semifree status. Some women gained such resources through prostitution. They rented rooms in Saint Pierre in Martinique, but the authorities soon caught on, and introduced a series of regulations from 1765 aimed at cracking down on unlicensed bars and taverns and owners who permitted their slaves "to wander about on their own or to rent dwellings on the pretext of carrying on a business or other activities."[30]

Fallope has cited French archival sources that hint at administrative skepticism about slave resources. Administrators did not think that the amount of money the slaves put toward their redemption matched their level of savings. In a letter to the minister of the navy and colonies in April 1847, the governor of Guadeloupe wrote, "Most often, blacks in slavery conceal the amount of money they have amassed and obstinately refuse to divulge the level of their savings. It is not unusual to see nonfree persons who possess slaves and employ them to their own benefit. Others practice lucrative professions and, in so doing, gain much more money than the sum they are required to pay their masters."[31]

Slaves could not own other slaves, but there are cases in slave society where enslaved women, in particular, occupied positions within the plantation household that allowed them to exploit the labor of other slaves in much they same ways as slave owners did. Such was the case of Old Doll, a slave woman on the Newton plantation in Barbados in the eighteenth century. Beckles states that "from the mid-eighteenth century to the closing years of slavery one family of slave women, Old Doll, her three daughters and her niece, dominated the housekeeping occupation on the estate. . . . They rejected arduous manual labour and socialized with free white persons, both black and white."[32] Indeed, "Old Doll's family not only had access to slave attendants, but they also 'owned' slaves who waited on them."[33]

Given the conditions of slavery, it is reasonable to assume that it took time and ingenuity to accumulate resources. The long-term commitment to freeing themselves may explain why a significant number of the redemptions in the French Caribbean involved mature slaves and not the young. Also, enslaved women were in better positions to accumulate resources, as their owners granted them more passes to leave the plantations than they did to men. Women, more so than men, were also engaged in occupations that allowed them to accumulate cash.

Between 1845 and 1846 fifteen enslaved persons out of a total of 205 in Guadeloupe and fourteen out of 295 in Martinique paid for their rachat without support from government. In Guiana, six enslaved persons benefited from state aid, while twenty-six bought their own freedom. As in rachat with state aid, gender distinctions could be observed. Proportionally more women than men engaged in this type of rachat, no doubt because they sought a greater prospect of freeing their children in the process or soon after they procured freedom for themselves. But there were other women, mostly elderly, who may have had children but who could redeem only themselves. In March 1847, Marianne, a fifty-three-year-old merchant formerly owned by the widow Fonclair Lapeyre of Saint Pierre, visited the colonial treasury to deposit the price set by the commission—1,100 francs. That same year, the forty-year-old woman, Laurencine, owned by the woman Dathy Morestin, also of Saint Pierre, deposited 1,600 francs at the colonial treasury to buy freedom for herself and her two children, Eugène and Roselie. Other redemptions in 1847 included a sixty-one-year-old field hand, Solitude, owned by Pierre Lagodière of Lamentin, Martinique, who paid 500 francs, and Jeannine, a fifty-nine-year-old domestic of widow Anquetil de Braincourt of Saint Pierre, who purchased her freedom for 600 francs. In February 1848, just months before emancipation, the commission fixed the price of redemption for Eléonide (Labrune) and her one-year-old son, Philippe (Forès), both owned by Sylvanie (Marie-Claire) of Fort-Royal, Martinique, at 1,000 francs. Eléonide deposited 600 francs, and the state put up the remaining 400 francs. As Philippe was omitted from a previous declaration of liberty, the procureur général freed him by a special decree issued on 2 February 1848.[34]

The fact that the colonial commission had to settle so many disputes over rachat suggests that slave owners and enslaved people clashed over prices. After 1845, contentious, as opposed to cordial, redemption was the norm, most of the latter being between enslaved males and male slave owners. It seems curious that the fifty-six-year-old black domestic enslaved woman, Sainte-Rose, of Basse-Pointe, Martinique, made a point of counting out loud the 300 francs she gave to her owner, Rose-Adéle Jeannot, in what was listed as a cordial redemption.[35] A close examination of rachat in Martinique, where more data are accessible, reveals that women slave owners were less likely than men to settle amicably with enslaved women over redemption. In this regard, as in others, they had no special consideration for women in bondage.

Using 1846 as a benchmark, the French administration sought to demonstrate that rachat had succeeded in inducing the enslaved to compensate their owners for their freedom. To do so, it compared statistics in 1846 with those of the previous five years (1841–45). As table 6.1 indicates, 1,010 enslaved people were manumitted in Martinique in 1846. From 1839 to 1845, the annual average number of enslaved persons manumitted was 749. The corresponding figures for Guadeloupe and French Guiana were 577 and 70 respectively. Thus, for Martinique, the administration boasted that in 1846, there were 261 more manumissions than the annual averages for the years 1841–45. Likewise, there were 577 and 107 more manumissions in Guadeloupe and French Guiana, respectively. This emphasis on the growing numbers of redemptions masked the reality that Martinique's 1,010 manumissions in 1846 represented only 0.4 percent of the island's total slave population of 275,339. Besides, most of the manumissions counted were still the result of legislation introduced in 1832.[36] That the number of manumissions in 1847 fell by 25.5 percent from 1846 indicates a pattern of slight surges following the introduction of new legislation (as in 1832 and 1845) but no dramatic and sustained increases. Interestingly, Baron de Mackau, author of the Mackau Law, also

Table 6.1. Manumissions in the French Caribbean, 1846

	MARTINIQUE	GUADELOUPE	FRENCH GUIANA
Voluntary (1832 law)			
Rachat amiable (cordial redemption)	637	978	135
Voluntary (1839 law)	78	7	0
Slaves in France	0	80	10
Rachat forcé (contentious redemption), with state aid	281	34	26
Rachat forcé, without state aid	14	16	6
Totals	1,010	1,115	177

Source: Bernard Moitt, Women and Slavery in the French Antilles, 1635–1848 (Bloomington: Indiana University Press, 2001), 170.

reported a strong rachat demand in early 1847, especially from Martinique, where more than 1,000 individuals had signed up with the commission. De Mackau rightly took this relatively large number to be an indication that "all those slaves are in possession of either all or a part of the funds for their redemption."[37]

From beginning to end, then, manumission was limited. In a royal ordinance of 12 October 1847, King Louis Philippe authorized the manumission of 218 urban and rural enslaved persons—the majority of them women—of whom 36 were from Martinique, 41 from Guadeloupe, 119 from French Guiana, and 22 from Bourbon. This decree was less an act of benevolence than a matter of necessity. In 1847, Baron de Mackau explained that several landed properties on these islands had come into the hands of the colonial state through repossessions, and with them, their enslaved labor forces, mostly field hands. As these acquisitions had virtually coincided with the 1845 legislation on rachat, the state could hardly stand back from its own policy of negotiating manumissions for any who requested them. De Mackau expressed concern about the prospect of crime amongst those thus emancipated and its impact on planters, but he noted that the first batch of 126 had been freed in 1846 without incident.[38]

The data on redemption in the French Caribbean in the 1830s and 1840s indicate that enslaved women opted for freedom irrespective of their material and social conditions. They also suggest that women were willing to enlist the help of French authorities, if necessary, when a transaction involving rachat went awry. Such was the case of Annoncine of Guadeloupe, who was freed in 1833, under the terms of the will and last testament of her owner, Madame Avril. On 12 March 1847, Annoncine wrote to the minister of the navy and colonies in Paris complaining that under article 47 of the Code Noir, her four prepubescent children should have been freed along with herself but had not been. She cited the celebrated Virginie Affair of 1844, in which the formerly enslaved Guadeloupean woman Virginie won a judgment in the French Supreme Court, which had ruled that minors could not be alienated from their mothers, under article 47 of the Code Noir.[39]

In this suit, Annoncine explained that she had purchased one of her children, Alfred, but her attempts to purchase Exilie and Fontenelle—a twenty-six-year-old daughter and seven-year-old grandson—were thwarted by their owner, Madame Roujol, a widow in Basse-Terre. Roujol had set the price of the rachat at 1,800 francs. Annoncine struggled to find that sum but managed to come up with only 1,300 francs and turned to the state for the remaining 500 francs. Attorney General Bayle-Mouillard of Guadeloupe turned down her request on the grounds that Exilie was a bad egg (*mauvais sujet*). Madame Roujol, along with the merchant firm Stedmann et Compagnie of Basse-Terre, claimed that the 1,300 francs that Annoncine had deposited with a notary in Basse-Terre represented money for merchandise extended on credit to Exilie, in effect a commercial loan. Annoncine then claimed that the attorney general had in effect condemned her daughter, who had no desire to acknowledge a debt she alleged was fictitious, to perpetual servitude. She reminded the minister of the navy and colonies that her daughter had launched legal proceedings against her accusers to clear her name and that the Royal Court of Guadeloupe had ruled that the charge against her had no merit.[40] Indeed, it is unlikely that Exilie, as an enslaved woman, would have been allowed to accumulate such a debt on her own account. It seems obvious that Madame Roujol did not wish to free her captives.

But why had Annoncine originally attempted to purchase her children's freedom rather than go to the courts directly on the basis of article 47, on which she subsequently rested her case? She could not have done so in 1833, but in 1847 she could have profited from the precedent-setting Virginie case of 1844. It seems almost certain that for enslaved people, rachat yielded quicker results than litigation. However, they turned to the courts when it suited them. So it is no wonder that when Annoncine failed to gain freedom for her children through rachat, she asked the minister to use the Virginie case as a precedent, so that her children could be declared legally free. As in the Virginie case, the Supreme Court of Guadeloupe (Cour de Cassation) upheld article 47, but legal battles were often long, and outcomes were never certain.[41]

The Martinican woman Marie Sainte Platon is one of the few enslaved women who struggled to free her husband as well as her children and herself. Her case also reveals her strong, resilient character. In 1840, Marie Sainte, aged forty-six years, purchased her freedom from the owners of the plantation Casse-Cou for 1,000 francs. She and her common-law husband, François, with whom she shared thirteen children and grandchildren, had been enslaved there since birth. She was duly provided with her freedom papers. The drama began when Marie Sainte and François legitimized their union in the Catholic Church, after they had properly sought and received permission from Desvergers de Chambray, one of several co-owners of the plantation and the representative who had authorized Marie Sainte's rachat.

None of the other co-owners of Casse-Cou objected to the marriage, but one of them, Madame de la Pommeraye, opposed Marie Sainte's bid to free her husband, children, and grandchildren. Under the terms of an ordinance of 11 June 1839, an enslaved person who contracted marriage with a free person attained outright and legal freedom, as did the children they had had previous to the marriage. In any case, three of their children, Marie Luce, age sixteen; Hedwige, fourteen; and Anatole, ten should have been freed under article 47 but had been separated from Marie Sainte upon her rachat. On the basis of these decrees, Marie Sainte brought her case before the lower court (*tribunal de première instance*) of Saint Pierre. On 26 May 1846, Judge Maynier of that court ruled in her favor and freed all the parties. But that decision was not the end, for Madame de la Pommeraye and five other co-owners appealed the case, which eventually went to the Royal Court, which declared the marriage null and void.

Marie Sainte then took her case to the Supreme Court, which in 1847 ruled in her favor—five years after she had first brought her case. The Supreme Court chided the Royal Court for hearing a case brought by a minority of the co-owners, who, by their absence, had signaled their agreement with the initial judgment. The Court went on at length about the marriage of Marie Sainte and François, which suggests that opposition to their freedom hinged on its legitimacy. However, the Court deemed the marriage valid under the Code Noir, which permitted the marriage of enslaved people with their owners' consent, holding that Desvergers de Chambry, who alone had actually given permission for the marriage to go ahead, had acted behalf of the other co-owners. The marriage could not be annulled, either for lack of proper consent or for failure to observe formalities. The law of 11 June 1839 guaranteed manumission of a legitimately married enslaved couple and their children, whether or not they were prepubescent. Therefore, the Court affirmed that the application of article 47 was superfluous in this case.[42]

The picture of enslaved women and redemption that emerges from the legal records of the French Caribbean shows that enslaved people, principally mixed-race women as in previous times, manifested a strong desire for freedom through rachat and other means, even on the eve of emancipation in 1848. Women had some advantages over men in acquiring freedom through self-purchase, but these advantages were not always evident. The pursuit of rachat required ingenuity and the will and courage to stand on one's own against the odds. That women sometimes seized the opportunity to use the law—a tool designed primarily to oppress them—to gain redemption, must certainly mean that they saw the law as a means of turning the tables on their oppressors. Freedom from bondage at a price was desirable and worth fighting for, even when slavery was on its last legs.

NOTES

Abbreviationations

ANC   Archives Nationales, Colonies
ANSOM   Archives Nationales de France, Section Outre-Mer, Aix-en-Provence
JOM   *Journal Officiel de la Martinique*

1. Moitt, *Women and Slavery*, 125.
2. Sue Peabody, "*Négresse, Mulâtresse, Citoyenne:* Gender and Emancipation in the French Caribbean, 1650–1848," in *Gender and Slave Emancipation in the Atlantic World,* ed. Pamela Scully and Diana Paton (Durham: Duke University Press, 2005).
3. See Bernard Moitt, "In the Shadow of the Plantation: Women of Color and the *Libres de Fait* of Martinique and Guadeloupe, 1685–1848," in *Beyond Bondage: Free Women of Color in the Americas,* ed. David Barry Gaspar and Darlene Clark Hine (Urbana: University of Illinois Press, 2004), 37–59.
4. Ivan Debbasch, *Couleur et liberté: Le jeu de critère ethnique dans un ordre juridique esclavagiste,* vol. 1, *L'Affranchi dans les possessions françaises de la Caraïbe: 1635–1833* (Paris: Dalloz, 1967), 22–27.
5. *Le Code Noir ; ou, receuil des règlements rendus jusqu'à présent* (Paris: Prault, 1767; reprint, Basse-Terre: Société d'Histoire de la Guadeloupe, 1980), 33–34, 51, 55.
6. See Pierre Baude, *L'affranchissement des esclaves aux Antilles Françaises: Principalement à la Martinique du début de la colonisation à 1848* (Fort-de-France: Imprimerie du gouvernement, 1948), 19–23; Gabriel Debien, *Les Esclaves aux Antilles Françaises, XVIIe–XVIIIe siècles* (Basse-Terre: Société d'Histoire de la Guadeloupe, 1974), 377.
7. ANC, 8A 18, F18, 3 June 1711.
8. ANSOM, Fonds Généralités, carton 666, dossier 2845, 12 July 1832.
9. Pierre Dessales, *Les annales du conseil souverain de la Martinique,* 2 vols. (1786; reprint, Paris: L'Harmattan, 1995), 1:374–75.
10. "Ordonnance de MM. les Général et Intendant concernant les soi-disant libres de les libertés non-registrées," 10 September 1789, in M. Durand-Molard, *Code le la Martinique,* 5 vols. (St. Pierre: Impr. de J.-B. Thounens, fils, 1807–14), 4:157. In the eighteenth century, the colonial livre was worth about twelve sols; one sol was worth about twelve deniers (about twelve U.S. cents). See Moitt, *Women and Slavery,* 178n29.
11. See Josette Fallope, *Esclaves et Citoyens: Les noirs à la Guadeloupe au XIXe siècle dans les processus de résistance et d'intégration,1802–1910* (Basse-Terre: Société d'Histoire de la Guadeloupe, 1992), 247–49; Dale Tomich, *Slavery in the Circuit of Sugar: Martinique and the World Economy, 1830–1848* (Baltimore: Johns Hopkins University Press, 1990), 53–75; Christian Schnakenbourg, *Histoire de l'industrie sucrière en Guadeloupe aux XIXe et XXe siècles,* vol. 1, *La crise du système esclavagiste (1835–1847)* (Paris: L'Harmattan, 1980), 124–36.
12. See Moitt, *Women and Slavery,* 131.

13. Victor Schoelcher, *Des colonies françaises: Abolition immédiate de l'esclavage* (1842; reprint, Basse-Terre: Société d'histoire de la Guadeloupe, 1976), 305.

14. ANSOM, Fonds Généralités, carton 40, dossier 316; "Rapports, débats, correspondances diverses concernant les lois des 18 et 19 juillet, 1845" (Paris, 18 July 1845); JOM, 26 May 1847, 1; 9 February 1848, 1.

15. Archives Départmentales de la Martinique, "L'affranchissement des esclaves aux Antilles françaises."

16. Fallope, *Esclaves*, 292.

17. Victor Schoelcher, *Histoire de l'esclavage pendant les deux dernières années*, 2 vols. (1847; reprint, Pointe-à-Pitre: Emile Désormeaux, 1973), 2:19–26.

18. Karol K. Weaver, *Medical Revolutionaries: The Enslaved Healers of Eighteenth-Century Saint Domingue* (Urbana: University of Illinois Press, 2006).

19. See "Compte rendu des lois des 18 et 19 juillet, 1845, sur le régime des esclaves, la création d'établissements agricoles par le travail libre," JOM, 26 May 1847, 1. See also JOM, 12 May 1847, 1; 15 May 1847, 1 ; 26 May 1847, 1; Fallope, *Esclaves*, 292; Schoelcher, *Histoire de l'esclavage*, 2:19–26.

20. JOM, 6 May 1848, 1.

21. Schoelcher, *Histoire de l'esclavage*, 2:19.

22. JOM, 6 May 1848, 1.

23. JOM, 23 February 1848, 3.

24. JOM, 12 February 1848, 1.

25. Here and below, percentages do not total 100 due to rounding.

26. ANSOM, Fonds Généralités, carton 40, dossier 316 (19 July 1845); JOM, 26 May 1847, 2; Fallope, *Esclaves*, 293.

27. JOM, 26 May 1847, 2; Fallope, *Esclaves*, 293.

28. Hilary Beckles, *Natural Rebels: A Social History of Enslaved Black Women in Barbados* (New Brunswick, NJ: Rutgers University Press, 1989), 73; Barbara Bush, *Slave Women in Caribbean Society, 1650–1838* (Bloomington: Indiana University Press, 1990), 46–50.

29. Moitt, *Women and Slavery*, 153.

30. Moitt, "Shadow of the Plantation," 55.

31. ANSOM, Fonds Généralités, carton 163, dossier 1327, cited in Fallope, *Esclaves*, 293n155.

32. Beckles, *Natural Rebels*, 65–66.

33. Hilary Beckles, *Centering Woman: Gender Discourses in Caribbean Slave Society* (Princeton: Markus Wiener, 1999), 132.

34. JOM, 6 March 1847, 2; 14 April 1847, 1; 9 February 1848, 1; Fallope, *Esclaves*, 293; Baude, *Affranchissement*, 96.

35. JOM, 19 June 1847, 2.

36. See Moitt, *Women and Slavery*, 151–72.

37. JOM, 26 May 1847, 1; Tomich, *Slavery*, 83.

38. JOM, 26 May 1847, 3.

39. See Moitt, *Women and Slavery*, 163–66.

40. Schoelcher, *Histoire de l'esclavage*, 2:128–29.

41. Ibid., 2:129.

42. ANSOM, Fonds Généralités, carton 372, dossier 2197 (1848), 4–16.

7

SLAVE WOMEN, FAMILY STRATEGIES, AND THE TRANSITION TO FREEDOM IN BARBADOS, 1834–41

LAURENCE BROWN AND TARA INNISS

Between 1807 and 1834, Barbados was the only sugar colony of the British Caribbean in which an expanding plantation economy coexisted with a naturally increasing slave population. The demographic structure of the island's slave population of creoles, their work regimes, and the pronatalist measures of individual planters fueled rising birthrates during the 1820s.[1] However, this apparently mutually reinforcing relationship between reproduction and economic production was transformed with the abolition of slavery, as the women who made up the majority of the enslaved workforce in Barbados faced new coercive pressures resulting in intense labor conflict and a dramatic surge in infant mortality. The white elite of Barbados constructed this latter crisis as caused by the failings of black motherhood, but these debates over the ill-effects of emancipation on former slaves also provide fresh evidence of the family strategies that slave women used to negotiate freedom.[2]

Three-quarters of the slave population of Barbados in 1834 lived concentrated within sugar plantations, although the island's low-lying landscape and extensive road network enabled them considerable mobility.[3] Interactions between slaves on different estates could occur during periods

---

The authors thank the University of the West Indies (Cave Hill) for a research grant that funded this research. They are also grateful to Christine Barrow, Gwyn Campbell, Joseph Miller, and the participants at the Fourth Avignon Conference on Slavery and Forced Labour who offered valuable comments and encouragement.

of labor when enslaved women and men were hired out individually or placed in jobbing gangs to supply extra labor elsewhere. More often, in the hours after work slaves would seek company and relationships with those on neighboring estates. On the Codrington plantations it was reported that "the Negroes are in the habit of leaving the estate on those Saturdays, and visiting and wandering about the country, and often not returning till monday [sic] morning in time for work."[4] Such complaints were common in the decades before emancipation, as on the Seawell estate, whose manager encouraged intermarriage among slaves within the plantation, "as it hinders them from running out of the Estate at night, which they do sometimes, to a great distance to visit each other."[5] Enslaved women often took partners from another estate, and such "visiting" remote relationships could characterize the majority of families within an individual plantation.[6]

While visiting relationships were conditioned by the possibilities of slave mobility that existed within Barbados, the increasing creolization of slaves on the island had fueled the development of extended family units during the eighteenth century. As a visitor to the island, Frederick W. Bayley described how in the 1820s, "The houses appropriated to the negroes are built in a cluster, families reside together."[7] Family units were not only concentrated in single dwellings but also located in adjacent households focused around "yards." It was these "clusters of households of maternal kin" that provided enslaved women with extended support networks of grandmothers, mothers, and daughters together with fathers, uncles, brothers, and sons—all within the plantation.[8]

With emancipation in 1834, the visiting relationships and family yards established by women and men during slavery in Barbados faced intense coercive pressures. Only Antigua enacted the immediate abolition of slavery; Britain's other West Indian colonies adopted a transitional period of "apprenticeship," in which children under six were freed but the majority of the enslaved population remained bound to their owners as apprentices for four to six years.[9] In Barbados, this meant that 14,047 children, or 17 percent of the island's enslaved population, were liberated (see fig. 7.1).[10] The creation of families divided between freed and still-enslaved understandably provoked an atmosphere of conflict and hostility, rather than one of peaceful evolution to a new free society.

The period of apprenticeship was also marked by an intensification of coercion as planters sought to extract the maximum labor return from their former chattels before they were fully liberated. Planters across the region revoked customary rights and entitlements that slaves had established

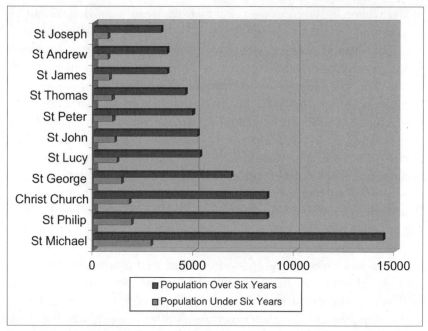

Figure 7.1. Slave population of Barbados in 1834. *Source:* W. K. Marshall, ed., *The Colthurst Journal,* 237

to provision grounds, accommodations, and family care. Even such prona-talist policies as reduced work regimes or increased food allowances for pregnant mothers, developed in the early 1800s as part of attempts at amelioration, were directly reversed.[11] All these measures heavily affected enslaved women, who faced intensifying coercive pressure to continue offering not only their own labor in the cane fields, but also that of their children. As a result, apprenticeship in the British West Indies may per-haps best be seen as a prolonged battle between planters seeking to main-tain or reconstruct the slave family as a production unit for their estates and apprentices with their own visions of freedom and family relationships.

Planters and managers divided their work force according to the diffi-culty of labor that needed to be performed. Able-bodied adult men and women, organized into the first and second gangs, usually performed the hardest plantation tasks such as cane holing and dunging. As soon as children were deemed able to work (usually at age four or five), they en-tered the third gang, commonly referred to as the hog-meat gang or pot gang, moving into the second gang as they grew older and stronger. The 1834 emancipation of children under the age of six resulted in severe strains on slave families as planters attempted to maintain their third gangs of child labor.[12] Reports by stipendiary magistrates from across the British West Indies repeatedly testify to parents' refusals to apprentice their children on the plantations.[13] In Barbados, police magistrates stressed the "decided aversion" of families to any continuation of estate labor by their children, as parents preferred to "keep them at home for their own purpose."[14] Faced with such opposition, and unable to use force to retain child labor in their fields, planters resorted to more indirect means of coercion. Plantation owners in the Americas had long concentrated food allocations to working slaves, a practice that resulted in widespread child malnutrition. Thus, as free children in Barbados ceased plantation labor, they were increasingly denied access to estate resources.[15]

British abolitionists Joseph Sturge and Thomas Harvey, who visited Barbados at the end of December 1836, reported,

> The free children are much neglected. After 1834 many of the planters turned them off the estates, provoked by the disappointment of their expectation that the parents would consent to apprentice them; an expectation which was baffled by the perseverance of the mothers, acting under the advice of the Governor, Sir Lionel Smith. This extreme measure against the free children, was happily not persevered in; but cases have recently occurred, where it has again been resorted to. On the estates of a once humane resident proprietor, the children are taken care of in the estates' nurseries as before; but in the vast majority of instances, they are neglected. . . . The mortality amongst them has been very great since 1834. The boon of freedom granted, as if in mockery to their helpless infants, has proved a source of misery and bitter persecution to the negro mothers.[16]

Sturge and Harvey thus stressed the degree to which planters in Barbados denied access to food, medical care, clothing, and education to those children who failed to work on the estates.[17]

While younger children therefore depended for survival on the strained resources of their families, their older siblings continued to labor on the plantations as apprentices. In January 1838, for example, children still represented nearly a fifth of the recorded working population at the Drax Hall estate.[18] With the end of apprenticeship there was a second withdrawal of child labor, although not as absolute as the reports of stipendiary magistrates portrayed it. While other officials decried the absence of children laboring on the estates, Joseph Evelyn, the police magistrate for Christ Church, noted at the end of 1839, "I am happy to say that the labourers are beginning to feel the *necessity* of rearing up their children in habits of industry."[19] Control over access to such basic necessities as food and shelter replaced the legal constraints of slavery as new tools of coercion for those who wanted to restrict the emancipated population—both adults and children—to plantation production.

That British abolitionists seeking the end of apprenticeship publicized the plight of the free children is not surprising, given their earlier focus on the family unit in demonstrating the damaging impact of slavery.[20] Their moral critique of Atlantic slavery as corrupting family life resulted in abolitionists conceiving of emancipation in terms of liberating women from estate labor and transferring them into the private sphere of domesticity.[21] They therefore welcomed the postemancipation flight from the fields by women as a form of natural retreat into the home, where they would be supported by their husbands' labor. However, such a vision of gender relations was distant from the experiences of enslaved women and was almost impossible to achieve under the economic and social constraints of postemancipation society.

For emancipated Barbadian women, the intensification of estate labor under apprenticeship continued well into the era of legal freedom. In the decades before emancipation, the Barbados plantocracy had often claimed that the island's increasing population was a product of their benevolent paternalistic management and amelioration polices.[22] However, they displayed little of either of these qualities during apprenticeship. The plantation records of Drax Hall in Barbados reveal that in 1836 almost a fifth of the female apprentices working on the estate were pregnant.[23] All these women were listed as field laborers, including Mary Bellah, who despite her pregnancy had been hired from an outside contractor to work in the first gang. While contemporaries would later emphasize the extent to which women withdrew from plantation production after 1838, immediately after emancipation many Barbadian women found that continuing field labor was one of their few options to provide for their families.[24]

The necessity of providing labor at subsistence wages to maintain residence on the plantation had a powerful impact on black family strategies, that resulted in gendered labor patterns in which females toiled in the fields to avoid eviction from homes or provision grounds while their male partners sought wage labor off the estates.[25] However, planters in Barbados were much more successful in making estate labor a condition for continued residence on estate land after emancipation than their neighbors in the Windward Islands.[26] The police magistrate for St. John noted that, though children had been almost wholly removed from agricultural work, "It rarely occurs however that the Women withdraw themselves from field labour, but on the contrary are more regular as attached Estate Labourers—The Husband generally roves about or lives on a different Estate."[27]

Both coresidential family yards and visiting relationships came under increasing strain in 1838 and 1839, when a wave of evictions swept over Barbadian estates as planters sought to retain their control of labor relations. Henry Pilgrim, police magistrate for St. John reported, "I have never been called upon to investigate complaints on account of the undue occupation of houses by Labourers; the planters having generally themselves dislodged such occupants."[28] However, these ejectments, like prosecutions for such offences as trespass and vagrancy, provide a means for mapping family relationships established during slavery that reached beyond plantation boundaries.[29]

In one case, Nanny Sue, with her three-year-old child and three-month-old child, were ejected from the Locus Hall estate because she was physically unable to cut or load cane.[30] She was the third generation of her family born and raised on the plantation. Evicted from the home that had been built by her deceased husband, she also lost the allotment of land that she had planted in potatoes. At Niels plantation, a woman "far advanced in pregnancy" also lost her house (built partly from savings) and the half an acre of land she rented from the estate.[31] After her eviction, she sought refuge with an uncle on the same estate, who already had her children staying with him. As a result, he was also ejected from the plantation. Brothers, sisters, uncles, aunts, and grandparents resident on the same estate could thus draw on the familial strength formed under slavery. However, common residence on the same estate also left such families more exposed to postemancipation pressures such as eviction.

Another case of ejectment that reveals the strength of extended family connections was heard before the Barbados Court of Appeal. It involved Molly Cuffs and her sister Queen, both of whom had resided on the Vaucluse estate. Queen had spent three weeks off the estate visiting her husband in St. James, claiming that she remained with him for that extended period because she was sick. While Queen was absent, Molly's home was repeatedly searched by the estate bookkeeper, who accused her of "habouring" her missing sister.[32] When Queen returned to the estate, she and her child were ejected from her sister's house. Queen's eviction shows why some couples maintained relationships beyond the borders of the plantation after emancipation. As during slavery, it was possible for women and men to gain a measure of autonomy in their lives through choosing partners or maintaining connections with kin living elsewhere. The continuation of this family strategy shows perhaps how little the social and economic constraints of estate life had changed with freedom.

At the same time that the *Liberal*, a local radical newspaper, was publishing these accounts of evictions in the immediate wake of slavery it was also reporting on the considerable food shortages affecting Barbados. These concerns over food supply resulted in an islandwide survey by the police magistrates, which generally acknowledged that there were fewer agricultural provisions available in 1839 than during slavery.[33] The magistrates tended to blame poor weather conditions and the refusal by laborers to work or to buy provisions as the main causes of the shortage.

However, their reports showed that there were more profound causes. In the final months of 1838, with the uncertainties of emancipation, most estates had concentrated on planting sugarcane and had cut back considerably on growing ground provisions to feed their workforce.[34] This important shift in production was as much a rejection of older pretensions to paternalism as was the revocation of customary slave rights to housing and land. While J. R. Ward has argued that figures showing rising importation of foods in postemancipation Barbados reflect improving consumption and living standards for ex-apprentices;[35] local newspapers and stipendiary magistrates describe a very different situation. For most black families the period between 1834 and 1841 was marked by a prolonged crisis over access to ground provisions and other basic necessities.

That contemporaries saw a direct correlation between supplying food and controlling labor is reflected in comments such as those made by magistrate Henry Pilgrim about St. John at the end of 1839: "The Labourers of this district, for the last twelve months, in consequence of the price of food having remained at a standard beyond the price it bore during the apprenticeship, and immediately subsequent have given a more continuous labour than heretofore, and are generally working willingly."[36] The following year in St. Andrew, magistrate James Bascom wrote, "I think the relation of employer and laborer would be considerably improved and be rendered more permanent, if the laborers located for continuous service received an allowance of food from the employer each day that they labor, the experiment has been tried by some and works successfully; it is true that the laborers generally refused it when first emancipated, subsequent experience and the scarcity of 1839 has produced a different impression with many."[37] Ultimately, it was the absence rather than the supply of food that became the mechanism for regulating the postemancipation labor market. In densely populated Barbados the impact of the decrease in cultivation of basic food crops on the estates was exacerbated by a three-year drought that followed the end of apprenticeship in 1838.[38]

The extent to which postemancipation conflicts over labor relations were also conflicts over familial relationships is perhaps most clearly expressed in the debate that developed in Barbados in 1841 over child mortality. As Robert Schomburgk reported,

> In the year 1841, 596 cases in an aggregate of 1000 were deaths of children between the first and tenth year. This number struck me as so astonishing, that I made inquiries whether it was to be ascribed to an epidemic, but I was assured by several of the clergy that no epidemic raged that year, and that it could only be ascribed to the neglect of their offspring by mothers among the lower classes. In the year 1841, emigration from Barbados to Guiana and Trinidad had reached its height; some mothers left their children with relations who perhaps did not take much care of them; but much more numerous instances occurred where the father of the child emigrated and left the burden of the child to the mother, who, thus, abandoned to her own resources, had not the means of providing for its sustenance or attending to its necessities.[39]

In this passage, "neglect" by the mother or "abandonment" by father were the prime cause of the spectacularly high numbers of infant and child deaths in postemancipation Barbados. However, while Schomburgk's comments accurately expressed the pejorative perspective of the local white elite, they leave silent the context of planter policies that generated this vision of the unstable and unreliable black family.

In mid-June 1841 the governor of Barbados, Sir Evan Murray MacGregor, died in office. Within a fortnight he was replaced by the lieutenant governor of Tobago, Major-General Henry Darling, who was far more sympathetic than his predecessor to the local planters' attempts to limit working-class emigration from Barbados to the cane fields of Trinidad and British Guiana.[40] In the years immediately following emancipation, the high wages on offer in these southern territories during crop time attracted several thousand Barbadian migrants and stirred fears of a labor shortage among the Barbadian elite.[41] As a result, Darling requested the archdeacon of Barbados, Thomas Parry, to investigate the reported rise in infant mortality since emancipation. In early 1836, Parry had publicly campaigned against the mortality caused by estate ejection of children during apprenticeship, but five years later the island's elite were arguing that such deaths were caused by parental abandonment.[42]

Relying on parish burial records, Parry's report showed that the total of deaths was three times higher over the summer of 1841 (541 burials) than for the preceding three summers (which averaged 185 burials).[43] In laying the archdeacon's report before the Barbados House of Assembly, Darling directly linked this mortality with emigrating workers' abandonment of their families, adding that he expected "the Legislature will not hesitate to provide by suitable enactment against a continuation of the evils to the community."[44] Not surprisingly, given the assembly's concern with limiting the flow of laborers from Barbados, its members quickly passed a law obliging intending emigrants to prove that their family would be supported properly during their absence.

While similar legislation against emigration was also enacted across the Leeward Islands (also experiencing considerable labor emigration), in Barbados the explicit justification in alleged abandonment for such a law was dubious at best.[45] Darling's arguments when presenting Parry's report were based on a highly selective reading of the text. Archdeacon Parry had in fact reported that parish clergy blamed the severe mortality of 1841 on five main causes:

1. The prevalence of epidemics though not violence, such as Whooping Cough, Dysentery, and Low Fever, combieed [sic] with

2. Want of adequate care, arising sometimes from ignorance, sometimes from necessity, and occasionally it is feared, from less worthy motives, and [lack of] suitable nourishment arising from the distress consequent upon the long drought which prevailed from October 1840 to September 1841, causing great scarcity and dearth of provisions.

3. Want of regular and timely Medical Assistance, arising from negligence, or from inability to meet the expenses combined with unwillingness to accept of the aid proffered by directors of Estates.

4. Want of attention in administering the Medicines, when prescribed, or giving Medicine without proper advice.

5. Emigration of Fathers, throwing the whole burden of supporting the children upon the Mother, and obliging them to leave

their children unattended in order to work for their support (This
is alleged only from hearsay, not from actual observation).[46]

Darling, in attributing infant mortality exclusively to parental deser-
tion, relied on the fifth point of the report alone, even though Parry had
qualified it as based only on rumor. The acting governor glossed over far
more substantial causes of mortality, especially the severe food shortages
and lack of medical care, which in the wake of slavery were fundamental
and deleterious to working-class life. Darling stated, "it may not perhaps be
within the means of the Legislature to provide a remedy" to such causes,
presumably because they were assumed to be "natural" and not a product of
planter actions reinforced by the assembly's own coercive legislation.[47]

As Parry recognized, parishes where child mortality soared so dramatically during the summer of 1841 were also those most plagued by food
shortages (see fig. 7.2). The severe drought of 1840 and 1841 had its
strongest impact on the parishes of St. Phillip, Christ Church, St. John
and St. Joseph, where it caused near famine conditions for the laboring
poor. It was deprivation due to drought, not emigration, that fueled the
dramatic escalation of child deaths in these parishes. Richard Steckel's
argument that infant mortality "is particularly sensitive to conditions in
the first and last trimesters" of pregnancy may also explain this high mortality.[48] For Barbadian women coming to term in the summer of 1841,
their whole pregnancy would have been affected by the protracted food
shortages. Malnutrition also had a severe impact on the health of Barbadian children, especially given their greater nutritional requirements
than adults.[49] Almost two years before the drought of 1841, W. S. Austin,
the police magistrate for St. Joseph, reported that in several parishes
on the island a "considerable and undue mortality among children, and

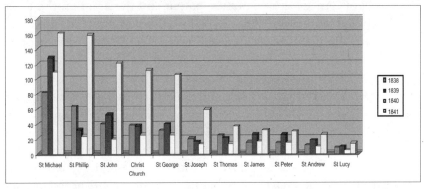

Figure 7.2. Recorded child burials for the period July to September, 1838–41.
Source: Barbados Archives, House of Assembly Minutes, 1841

especially younger ones, has occurred, which no reigning epidemic has oc-
casioned."[50] Austin's testimony highlights that the specter of child mortality was not a product of 1841 events but had been emerging steadily in
the wake of emancipation.

The "astonishing" child mortality of 1841 was not a temporary crisis,
though it was certainly worsened by the extreme drought of that summer, nor was it simply a result of the two waves of plantation evictions
that occurred after August 1834 (of young children) and August 1838 (of
adults).[51] Rather it was the product of seven years of labor conflict, in
which planters attempted to counter the specter of black independence
by using their ex-slave's needs for family subsistence and shelter as means
to force them to provide field labor. While arguing that the high death
rates for black children were caused by parental abandonment, Barbadian authorities remained silent about the extent to which local planters
and the colonial state had undermined black families. Amid the many
social tensions after emancipation, children became one of the main ca-
sualties of an island agricultural economy focused on export markets
rather than on feeding its own population. While adult emigration for
seasonal employment or permanent settlement may have strained family
resources in Barbados in the early 1840s, the most significant factor elevating infant and child mortality was the rapid revocation of planter paternalism after the abolition of slavery in 1834, in which customary allowances of accommodation, provisions, and health care were reversed
and made conditional on estate labor. As a result, legal freedom was accompanied by a radical decline in living conditions that pushed many
Afro-Barbadian families to the edge of subsistence.

Planter attempts to recast labor relations at emancipation were reinforced by the colonial state's attempts to dictate the social mores of black
laborers. Concerned with plantation output and the drain on the labor
supply, and reluctant to recognize their role in pushing families toward
starvation, colonial officials attacked mothers and fathers for neglect-
ing their children. Legal freedom transformed the debate over the relationship between production, reproduction, and paternalism that had
dominated abolitionist politics, and had resulted in planters using pro-
natalist allowances to legitimize slavery before 1834.[52] During the decade
that followed abolition, women faced ever increasing material pressures
to remain in field labor, and the toll this took on their own bodies and
their children's lives was identified by the new paternalist state as originating from black moral failings rather than the new political economy of
emancipation. The transition to freedom in Barbados was therefore

marked by intense physical hardship, in which the extended family strategies and relationships developed among households and across estates during slavery were both tested and reinforced. In these circumstances, women emerged as the brokers of freedom—charged with responsibility not only for uniting families after emancipation but also for protecting and sustaining them against the planter and state coercion that followed.

NOTES

1. B. W. Higman, *Slave Populations of the British Caribbean, 1807–1834* (Kingston: University of the West Indies Press, 1995), 75, 311, 374–75.

2. Herbert G. Gutman, *The Black Family in Slavery and Freedom, 1750–1925* (New York: Vintage Books, 1976).

3. Higman, *Slave Populations*, 50.

4. Regulations of the Society for the Treatment and Religious Instruction of Slaves, 1829, USPG C/WIN/BAR 5 C/COD/70, Rhodes House, Oxford.

5. List of and Report on the Negroes at Seawells, 1796, Newton Estate Papers MS 523/ 292, University of London Library.

6. Higman, *Slave Populations*, 369. Visiting relationships could also be created by the separation of families through sale.

7. F. W. Bayley, *Four Years' Residence in the West Indies* (London: William Kidd, 1830), 369–70.

8. Christine Barrow, "'Living in Sin': Church and Common-Law Union in Barbados," *Journal of Caribbean History* 29, no. 2 (1996): 249.

9. For an account of attempts at family reunification in Antigua in 1834, see Keithlyn B. Smith and Fernando C. Smith, eds. *To Shoot Hard Labour: The Life and Times of Samuel Smith, an Antiguan Workingman, 1877–1982* (Scarborough: Edan's Publishers, 1986), 29.

10. John Bowen Colthurst, *The Colthurst Journal: Journal of a Special Magistrate in the Islands of Barbados and St. Vincent, July 1835–September 1838*, ed. W. K. Marshall (New York: KTO, 1977), 237.

11. Bridget Brereton, "Family Strategies, Gender, and the Shift to Wage Labour in the British Caribbean," in *The Colonial Caribbean in Transition*, ed. Bridget Brereton and Kevin Yelvington (Kingston: University of the West Indies Press, 1999), 79–81.

12. Henry Drax, "Instructions for the Management of Drax-Hall, and the Irish-Hope Plantations: To Archibald Johnson by Henry Drax Esq," in *A Treatise upon Husbandry or Planting*, ed. William Belgrove (Boston: printed by D. Fowle, 1755), 65; William Dickson, *Letters on Slavery* (1789; reprint, Westport: Negro University Press, 1970), 12; Richard S. Dunn, "A Tale of Two Plantations: Slave Life at Mesopotamia in Jamaica and Mount Airy in Virginia, 1799 to 1828," *William and Mary Quarterly* 34, no. 1 (1977): 47.

13. Brereton, "Family Strategies," 81–82.

14. Brathwaite to Russell, attached Police Magistrates Reports, 1 October–31 December 1839 for St James & St Michael, Colonial Office, National Archives, London (hereafter, CO), 28/140, 17 June 1841.

15. Richard H. Steckel, "A Peculiar Population: The Nutrition, Health, and Mortality of American Slaves from Childhood to Maturity," *Journal of Economic History* 46, no. 3 (1986): 733–34; Tara Inniss, "From Slavery to Freedom: Children's Health in Barbados, 1823–1838," *Slavery and Abolition* 27, no. 2 (2006): 251–60.

16. Joseph Sturge and Thomas Harvey, *The West Indies in 1837: Being the Journal of a Visit to Antigua, Montserrat, Dominica, St Lucia, Barbados and Jamaica* (London: Hamilton Adams, 1838), 132–33.

17. Ibid, 135.

18. Drax Hall Increase and Decrease Book, 1 January 1836, Drax Hall Day Books 1836–1838, Z9/1/2, Barbados National Archives, Bridgetown.

19. Brathwaite to Russell, 17 June 1841, attached Police Magistrates Reports, 1 October–31 December 1839 CO 28/140; emphasis in original.

20. Higman, *Slave Populations,* 303–7; Barbara Bush, "Hard Labour: Women, Childbirth and Resistance in British Caribbean Slave Societies," *History Workshop Journal* 36 (1993): 5.

21. Brereton, "Family Strategies," 102–4.

22. The claimed success of such "breeding" policies in the exceptional population growth of Barbados needs to be evaluated in a much broader environmental, biological, and economic context that includes analysis of changes in infant mortality as well as the range of other factors affecting fertility. Higman, *Slave Populations,* 348–52, 375–77.

23. Drax Hall Increase and Decrease Book, 1 January 1836.

24. Brereton, "Family Strategies," 83.

25. Ibid., 98–99.

26. Bentley Gibbs, "The Establishment of the Tenantry System in Barbados," in *Emancipation II: Aspects of the Post-slavery Experience in Barbados,* ed. Woodville Marshall (Bridgetown: National Cultural Foundation/Department of History, University of the West Indies, 1987): 23–45.

27. Grey to Stanley, 3 October 1842, attached Police Magistrates Reports, CO 28/144.

28. Brathwaite to Russell, 17 June 1841, attached Police Magistrates Reports, 1 October–31 December 1839, CO 28/140.

29. Sturge and Harvey, *West Indies,* 148.

30. *Liberal* (Bridgetown), 20 March 1839, 3.

31. *Liberal,* 29 June 1839, 2.

32. *Liberal,* 13 March 1839, 3.

33. *Liberal,* 20 April 1839, 1–2.

34. Brathwaite to Russell, 17 June 1841, attached Police Magistrates Reports, 1 October–31 December 1839, Reports for St John, St Joseph, St Andrew, Speightstown and Holetown, CO 28/140.

35. J. R. Ward, *British West Indian Slavery, 1750–1834: The Process of Amelioration* (Oxford: Oxford University Press, 1988), 244–48.

36. Brathwaite to Russell, 17 June 1841, attached Police Magistrates Reports, 1 October–31 December 1839, CO 28/140.

37. Brathwaite to Russell, 17 June 1841, attached Police Magistrates Reports, 1 July–30 September 1840, CO 28/140.

38. Grey to Stanley, 3 October 1842, attached Police Magistrates Reports for Christ Church, CO 28/144.

39. Robert H. Schomburgk, *The History of Barbados* (1848; reprint, London: Frank Cass, 1971), 75–76.

40. Ibid, 491; Darling to Russell, 30 June 1841, CO 28/140.

41. Dawn Marshall, "Migration within the Eastern Caribbean, 1835–1980," paper presented at the Conference on Cultural Contacts and Migration in the Caribbean Barbados, April 1984, 7–14; George Roberts, "Emigration from Barbados," *Social and Economic Studies* 4 (1955): 3.

42. Hilary McD. Beckles, *A History of Barbados: From Amerindian Settlement to Nation-State* (Cambridge: Cambridge University Press, 1990), 97.

43. Schomburgk, *History of Barbados*, 491.

44. House of Assembly Minutes, 6 December 1841, Barbados National Archives, 72.

45. Bonham Richardson, *Caribbean Migrants: Environment and Human Survival on St. Kitts and Nevis* (Knoxville: University of Tennessee Press, 1983), 81–82.

46. House of Assembly Minutes, 6 December 1841, Barbados National Archives, 73.

47. Ibid, 72.

48. Richard H. Steckel, "A Dreadful Childhood: The Excess Mortality of American Slaves," in *The African Exchange: Toward a Biological History of Black People*, ed. Kenneth F. Kiple (Durham: Duke University Press, 1987), 207.

49. M. Behar, "Disturbances of Nutrition: 'Protein-Calorie Malnutrition,'" in *Diseases of Children in the Subtropics and Tropics*, ed. D. B. Jelliffe (London: Edward Arnold, 1970), 161.

50. Brathwaite to Russell, 17 June 1841, attached Police Magistrates Reports, 1 October–31 December 1839, CO 28/140.

51. Melanie Newton, "'New Ideas of Correctness': Gender, Amelioration and Emancipation in Barbados, 1810s–50s," *Slavery and Abolition* 21, no. 3 (2000): 121–24.

52. B. W. Higman, "Slavery and the Development of Demographic Theory in the Age of the Industrial Revolution," in *Slavery and British Society, 1776–1846*, ed. James Walvin (Baton Rouge: Louisiana State University Press, 1982), 164–94.

8

FREE BUT MINOR

Slave Women, Citizenship, Respectability, and Social Antagonism
in the French Antilles, 1830–90

MYRIAM COTTIAS

One of the first measures proclaimed by the Second Republic on 25 February 1848 in Paris was to abolish slavery in the French colonies. The initial decision was made final on 4 March, and the law enforcing its application was ready on 27 April. Within two months, slavery was to be abolished in the French colonies. Except for its terseness, nothing was surprising about this measure . News of the emancipation had been circulating for months among the populations of the French colonies, terrifying some and giving others cause to rejoice. In the feverish atmosphere of the towns of the islands, it was becoming obvious that the government had delayed too long in applying the decree. Impatience gained the upper hand among the enslaved and bloody uprisings exploded. Under pressure from the slaves' workshops in Prêcheur and Saint Pierre in Martinique, the governor, Claude Rostoland, decided to apply the decree as of 23 May before the official arrival of republican *commissaire-général* Perrinon.[1] From then on, the distinction between free people and slaves had no further formal effect. The French colonies contained neither "free nor slaves but [only] citizens."[2]

The republicans thus gave political and social equality, full citizenship,[3] the right to salaried work, access to land, education, and respectability, as defined by the criteria of the period, to the newly liberated slaves, who numbered 87,752 persons in Guadeloupe, 19,375 in Guyana, and 72,859 in Martinique. The most significant aspect of this event from the point of

Translated by Gwyn Campbell.

view of the age-old colonizing nations was without a doubt that emancipation concurrently and immediately established universal suffrage in the French colonies. In 1848, in fact, in a movement of "social inclusion" (Pierre Rosanvallon's term for it[4]) the right to vote was unconditionally granted to all men above the age of twenty-one. Freedom and social equality were key words of the French Second Republic, but this same principle had an important impact on gender relations, for it also gave women only a subordinate legal status. Under the new civil legislation, forged at the heart of the French state and based on the Napoleonic Code, women became minors. They were, for example, excluded from the vote, one of the primary rights of a citizen. The spirit of the law thus constituted a distinct status based not on civil standing (slave versus free) but on gender. Whereas in slave owning societies, men and women could, from an economic standpoint, be interchangeable,[5] under the new legal and ideological order, women became chattels under the authority of men.

From the July Monarchy period (1830–48) to the Second (1848–70) and Third (1870–1914) Republics, in the ideological framework concerning marriage and women there was no break in the extent to which the republican political organization relegated women to the periphery of social movements. The impact of this ideology, combined with freedom, consolidated the inner oppositions in the French Antilles based on social and color status. According to their social and color status, some women became able to fight for respectability and others were stigmatized by the French creole term *poto mitan*.[6] How did a political system based on nominal equality create such social antagonisms?

THE PATRIARCHAL CONTEXT OF LIBERTY VERSUS LONG-STANDING OPPOSITION TO MARRIAGE

If the granting of civil liberties seemed to have constituted a major turning point in a debate that had raged without resolution since the end of the eighteenth century,[7] there was nevertheless a certain continuity in terms of the moral content of liberty between Philanthropist Monarchy and Republic. In 1848 the French Republic, which wished to forge a new and unified political community, imposed conditions on the granting of citizenship specified first under the July Monarchy. Since 1828 politicians, Christians,[8] and philanthropists had debated what precisely liberty should entail for the slaves in the French West Indies. For them, it was essential to direct and structure a population created as part of the new society of a unified state. The moral content of the status of a republican citizen was paradoxically inherited from the philanthropic monarchy. Since 1828 the abolitionists who were preparing for emancipation legislated over colonial societies. They did not know whether emancipation should be gradually introduced, accompanied by the patronage of the former slaves, as when prisoners or workers in France were freed, or whether it should be introduced abruptly and immediately.

In the context of the general moralization of French society, the welfare state (*l'état providence*) took on the job of resocializing all marginalized outcasts, including workers, prisoners, and slaves. Slavery then became a social evil that must be remedied.[9] The same evils were stigmatized: loose morality, vagabondage, vice, sexual unions outside marriage. The same rules are applied. The same men (Victor de Broglie, François Guizot)[10] debated these problems, and the results took the same form on both sides of the Atlantic Ocean. In 1832 legislation outlawed branding prisoners and subjecting them to humiliating punishments and amputations. A year later, on 30 April 1833, the punishment of slaves by mutilation and branding was also outlawed. When liberty was at issue, prisoners and workers as well as slaves were patroned, that is, assigned to sponsors—a kind of parole.[11] Moreover, the same models were employed to structure, organize, and correct these populations by distancing them from vice. At the center of this system was the "family," considered the highest guarantee of virtue by moralists of the nineteenth century. The family was attributed a rehabilitative function, curing social evils, and a normative function, enabling society to find its unity.[12] In the abolitionists' discourse the individual was supposedly able to be treated through applying mechanical rules and simple causal relationships, such as those linking the repression of deviance, the organization of work, and marriage. The path toward so-called full citizenship was traced along these lines.[13]

At that time, the family that "offered a necessary base, a minimum support for the maintenance of social order" was a patriarchal one.[14] Male power was held to be the remedy for all social pathologies. From this viewpoint, slaves constituted a population that, like prisoners, the mentally ill, and notably the working class, should be subjected to the methods for social improvement being tested by the social-scientific community of the era. Slaves, like all social "deviants," should be brought into the curative context of families organized and led by men—simultaneously husbands to wives and fathers to children.

In order to validate fully the notions of republicanism and citizenship, the concept of the (patriarchal) family as the basic institution of society was, from the time of the French Revolution, allied to two other concepts, those of work and property.[15] For instance, in 1832 the Society for Christian Morality (Société de la Morale Chrétienne) established a "committee for the redemption of black female slaves in French colonies" in order to give them "the advantages enjoyed by citizens," namely the right to freely acquire property and marry.[16] Some years later, in order to calm a West Indian slave population feverishly awaiting liberty under the soon-to-be-declared decree of general emancipation, the rules governing citizenship were expanded. The main principles of these changes were included in the declaration issued to plantation slaves on 31 March 1848, two months before the emancipation measure, by Husson, a Martinique creole and "interior director" (home secretary) in the provisional government. The declaration illustrates the main values attributed to "freedom":

> When you wish to demonstrate your joy, cry out:
> LONG LIVE WORK!
> LONG LIVE MARRIAGE!

Liberty, guaranteed by the goodness of former slave owners, was thereby nothing more than the synthesis of work (for men) and marriage (for women).[17]

Marriage was presented as a core aspect of citizenship; it was the foundation of the family, it made work possible and efficient, and it stabilized property. However, the fundamental relationship between marriage and family posited by abolitionists posed a major problem for slaves. In slave communities, the absence of family, or at least the lack of a family structured around a male and officially registered through an act of marriage, for abolitionists formed one of the basic reasons to criticize the slave system. The humanism they developed was founded on a very Eurocentric view of society and mankind. According to abolitionists, the "licentiousness of the slave population" reflected "the absence of marriage" and thus the absence of social regulations. It was vital that they first tackle the question of marriage for the slaves to be freed. Furthermore, marriage should be celebrated in civil rather than religious fashion in order to extract the former slaves from the arbitrary power of their masters and so permit them access to citizenship. As the Naval Ministry declared in 1836: "There are very few slave couples that have been united religiously, and these are the only unions to which one could apply the term *marriage.*"[18] Civil marriage long remained the primary focus of abolitionists, who consistently offered lengthy arguments to demonstrate that it was necessary in order to ensure male authority, and thus social order.

They held that marriage in slave communities was nonexistent because women slaves became prostitutes or were raped by slave owners: "Please explain why a Negro slave should marry when his wife could be raped and when paternal power becomes the slave owner's prerogative."[19] In such arguments, the victim was always portrayed as the male slave, as abolitionists had no consideration for women's experiences of rape; in some cases, it was obvious to them that women had agreed to sex. It was the man who suffered from the power of the slave owner, who—in taking his wife—had mocked him: "I must again testify that many Negroes, pressured by their priest to marry, would reply: 'I'm not so stupid, for my master would take my wife the day following the marriage.'"[20] And another source asks, "Moreover, why would the slaves themselves not retreat from the thought of marriage? What would marriage be for them while they remained slaves? In other words, what is a woman who belongs to her master rather than to her husband? And in what state are children over whom the authority of the father is subject to the whims of the planter, who is their owner?"[21]

According to the abolitionists, the male slave could not exercise authority over his wife and children, because he was not their owner.[22] They backed such arguments with examples of enlightened slave owners who introduced firm rules of female conduct that made female slaves responsible to male heads of families. For instance, it was reported that an "intelligent man," the owner of a plantation, took measures to enforce "law and order." He "decided first that Negro females belonged to their menfolk" and that "from that moment no female slave would be touched on the plantation other than by slaves. He himself gave the example and maintained it with the utmost rigor among the free men on the plantation."[23] Security and prosperity were based on such authority.

The male slave was a victim of a slave system that, in failing to recognize his true position as a "man," permitted a dissolution of moral codes[24] that affected men as much as women. As Victor Schoelcher, the leading abolitionist in France, asserted, "Let us remember that Negroes [women] rarely get legally married for the simple reason that marriage would impede the licentiousness habitual to them, or more precisely because, deprived of all knowledge of social principles, incapable of raising their slave mentality to conceive of such a moral aim, they instinctively resort to concubinage as the most natural condition."[25] A later report imposed republican stereotypes on a black population in order to characterize slave men: "The black is sensual, lax, idle; he doesn't wish to go to the trouble of finding a wife who suits him; in his private life, he finds it difficult to submit to rules. If in his work he is a slave, in his tastes, fancies, and desires he wants to be free and independent. He wishes to live in a state of nature, and marriage is generally for him a responsibility and source of worry from which he liberates himself in not submitting to his master's control."[26]

Therefore, in the reorganization of colonial societies around ideals of civic responsibility the abolitionists and republicans assumed the task of reestablishing masculine power through founding nuclear families that they considered to be the universally acknowledged fundamental unit of civic society. To this end, the government of King Louis-Philippe in 1839 voted the sum of 650,000 francs for the Fund for Moral Improvement (Fonds de Moralisation) for the moral instruction and protection of slaves. The "moral improvement" of slaves should be achieved thanks to "the growth in the number of clergy, primary school teachers, and public magistrates."[27] The church, public education, and the law should guarantee for the state that its policy in this regard be successfully executed. A royal edict concerning the moral and religious education and continued supervision of slaves was proclaimed on 5 January 1840.[28] This decree, of a monarchy allied with the church, envisaged monthly visits to plantations by the clergy and special catechism lessons at least once a week. These conditions were reiterated in the so-called Mackau Law of 18 July 1845, which made morning and evening prayers obligatory for slaves, as well as religious instruction once during the week as well as on Sundays and holidays. It also established an educational scheme for slaves aged between eight and fourteen years under the direction of Catholic brothers and nuns. The reiteration of these measures reflected the probably minimal extent to which they had been applied in practice. For instance, whereas the Colonial Council of Martinique claimed that the Mackau Law "had been achieved unassisted" because "the true philanthropy of settlers had since time immemorial been responsible for implementing such measures,"[29] on-the-spot witnesses reported that the application of the law in reality was limited. It was noted that from 1840 the money earmarked for the religious education of slaves was transferred into general church funds. Thus, in 1841, the minister for the colonies "complained that these funds had been channeled into the education of the white classes."[30]

Despite the chaos arising from attempts to apply the Mackau Law, and white settlers' resistance to it, after 1848 abolitionists adhered to the

centrality of religion, marriage, and the patriarchal family in the reconstruction of slave society and its transformation to liberty throughout the
nineteenth century. In the eyes of Martinique's legislators, the power
of newly emancipated males had to be consolidated, and their women-
folk had to be convinced of the necessity of that need! The newly emancipated population would thus be focused around a patriarchal family
over which the male, as envisaged in the 1805 civil code for colonies,
would dominate.

A ruling on slave marriages, proposed in 1846 but never applied, reflected the concern of the era over promoting the moral education of
slaves and the ideological framework envisaged for emancipation. In the
proposed text, the male slave would become superior to the woman, who
was described as a "perpetual minor" living under his authority. Within
marriage she lost all rights over her possessions and her children, because
"the father exercised the exclusive rights of paternal authority" and
could "bring actions both to disclaim paternity and contest the legitimacy of an infant slave."[31]

From 1848 the civil code was applied to all citizens in the colonies
and its "sound principles" spread by parish priests (for they accorded with
the teachings of the church), by colonial governors when visiting the
plantations, and generally by all colonial administrators. On 20 June
1850, Councillor Garnier reported in his diary a case that provoked him.
To make the point that men should assume personal moral responsibility
in this postabolitionist society, and with no indications other than the
following sentences, Garnier gave the example of a son accused of hit-
ting his mother. He also condemned women of color. In May 1848 he
wrote, "These poor women of color have attitudes, expressions that
would wake desires in an old man the most cooled by years." In June
1850 he implicitly put blame on Antillean women at the same time as he
recalled the moral frame of emancipation:

> We had to judge a son accused of having hit his mother. There
> were no witnesses present. The son's reputation is very good,
> that of the mother very bad. He was acquitted. Judge B delivered
> to this young man an exhortation that lessened the bad effect
> that the acquittal might produce: "The court was saddened that
> you willingly hit your mother. However, your favorable record
> and your modest comportment during these sad proceedings were
> the determining factors in your acquittal. Never forget that a
> son should respect and protect his mother in all circumstances.

> Don't lose sight of the fact that it was your illicit relations
> with Rosélia that have led you to this sad state of affairs. Leave
> the irregularity, uncertainty, and disappointments of concubi-
> nage in the past and in the shameful practices of slavery. With
> liberty, the child of security and good habits, and in assuming
> the status of French citizen, aspire to the dignity of marriage, a
> civil contract that the Christian religion has elevated to the
> rank of a sacrament."[32]

In the nineteenth-century institution of marriage in the West, the male was the mediator between women and children on the one hand and the state on the other. The woman was confined to the private sphere, whereas the male concentrated on the public sphere. With the establishment of the republic, this same division of responsibilities was very rapidly imposed on the newly enfranchised. Immediately following emancipation, electoral lists, on which only males were registered, were established in order to prepare for municipal elections and voting for the Constituent Assembly. "Universal" suffrage[33] excluded women, who under slavery had been employed in a variety of ways and had participated di-rectly in the public sphere.[34] For example, in 1842 the list of women be-tween the ages of fourteen and sixteen to be enfranchised showed that 88 percent were engaged in public, commercial activities such as dressmak-ing (22 percent), farming (26 percent), domestic service, and laundering. At the Lamentin estate, a similar female public presence was evident: 38 percent of the women freed between 1833 and 1848 were dressmakers, 16.5 percent agricultural workers, and 16 percent tradeswomen.[35] Such economic independence, even within the coercive framework of slavery, gave women the means to negotiate their relations with men, or at least to create a "free space"—even a tiny one—that they could control. Their resistance to marriage, in addition to other, older forms of such resis-tance, could have emanated from this relative autonomy.

From the seventeenth century onward, observers had noted the "an-tipathy" slaves had shown toward the Christian institution of marriage.[36] Besides the fact that this formalization of individual male-female unions had no meaning for slaves, because it did not correspond with alliances established between families or with the exchange of goods ("For slaves, marriage did not imply joint ownership: The interests of each [partner] were entirely distinct"[37]), or even with a particular type of protection of-fered by the slave owner, it encountered very real feminine resistance, as recorded in documents from the seventeenth to the nineteenth centuries.

In fact, the reasons for slaves' resistance to marriage given in the seventeenth century were repeated during the nineteenth century. In 1682, Father Mongin had sought

> the reasons for their [the Negroes'] refusal [to marry], something that certainly had nothing to do with a dowry, for they possessed absolutely nothing in the world. Both [men and women] protested that they had other relations, ones that marriage would not force them to abandon. The male says that the woman that I want to give him is a "hen": she claims, to the contrary, that he is cruel and too lazy to collect and sell goods in order for them to earn their daily bread. Many protest that they still have no hut, nor the means to celebrate the wedding festivities, that neither comes from the same area nor is of the same age, and many other pretexts of a similar nature that I have much difficulty in rebutting.[38]

In the 1840s, in addition to slave owners raising objections to the marriage of slaves from different plantations, many female slaves also objected to marriage. One "Negress" claimed that "marriage made men too despotic," while in concubinage "women dominated men whom they found more generous,"[39] and while "marriage was fine for whites, should they marry and be beaten by their husbands it would be impossible for them to leave their spouses."[40] For female slaves, it appeared that their ability to be autonomous (inasmuch as their enslavement permitted) and to escape from the constraint of male power was primary. There was thus female resistance to unions in which "the Negro took a wife only so that she might serve him; he considered her to be his house-servant; often they fought; [and] marriage did not prevent the husband from having concubines—and his example was followed by the wife."[41] Moreover, the laws proclaimed at the time of the general emancipation in 1848 in no way modified most women ex-slaves' skeptical opinions about marriage, although they may have convinced some others.

THE FIGHT FOR RESPECTABILITY, OR RELATIONS BETWEEN NEWLY EMANCIPATED AND LONG-LIBERATED EX-SLAVES

Following the abolition of slavery, some ex-slaves had their very reserved opinions of marriage confirmed. The conventions established by the civil marriage ceremony of the new republic and application of relevant portions of the civil code (*code civil*, or Napoleonic Code) responded to the aspirations of only a portion of the population. For the remainder, the benefits accruing from marriage, such as ownership of property, did not interest newly enfranchised women. In fact, pro-marriage campaigns conducted at the time of the abolition of slavery, and the application in 1851 of the law of 10 December 1850, attempted to promote marriages among the poor, legitimize those children formerly considered illegitimate, and return illegitimate children who had been placed in institutions to their mothers.[42] These measures encouraged a rise in the nuptial rate to around 10.6 per thousand on Martinique and 11.7 per thousand on Guadeloupe between 1845 and 1854. Who married in this period? What is the social profile of these women and men? Were they newly freed persons? To answer these questions, we must study the enfranchised, a polymorphous group whose composition varied over time.

In fact, throughout the colonial epoch, a growing group of slaves—mostly females—gained their freedom either through a proper process of enfranchisement or through the ratification of manumission.[43] From 1660 to 1722, this group grew from 1.2 percent to 18.6 percent of the "free" Martinique population, rising further to 40 percent by 1802 and to 80 percent by 1845. From the seventeenth century to 1831, approximately 60 percent of these *affranchis* were women. Despite *bon ordre* legislation methodically passed at the close of the eighteenth century to prevent the preferential enfranchisement of women as a cover for "immoral" master-slave relations, and a rise in the enfranchisement tax for female slaves from six hundred livres in 1745 to two thousand livres in 1775, women remained a numerically significant element among the *groupe des libres* (ex-slaves).

This female majority among the free was reinforced everywhere after 1830, due to pressure from the antislavery movement. In fact, after interminable debates in Paris between 1832 and 1845 over whether the emancipation of slaves should take place gradually or rapidly, three main laws were enacted that facilitated the registration of certain enfranchised groups to begin a reorganization of colonial societies. Each law permitted a new group to emerge and become part of the *libres de couleur* (free colored).[44] For that reason, this category increased annually by an average of 24.6 percent on Martinique and 15 percent on Guadeloupe during the period 1832–45. The stability of the colonist class in Martinique created more opportunities for slaves, especially women, to purchase their own freedom.

As a result, with the first main law on emancipation—the Edict of 12 July 1832, which recommended that "in the colonies, no administrative tax will be levied on enfranchisements"—40 percent of those *libres de fait* between 1832 and 1836 on Martinique and Guadeloupe were women. They had routinely been manumitted for a long time by their masters, but because of the administrative tax they were not registered as free people. Because libre de fait was a status gained mainly by women who lived many years with their masters, statistics show that they were not young. In the Martinican small village of Trois-Îlets, the average age was forty-three years.[45] Moreover, taken together with their children, for Martinique, Guadeloupe, and French Guiana, they constituted 75.6 percent of the ex-slaves who gained *de fait* (de facto) or *patronné* liberty.[46]

The second royal edict, of 11 June 1839, established *de droit* (de jure)[47] enfranchisements. This law affected slaves who intended to marry, sole legatees, children of a slave mother by her master, and slaves closely related to their owners (e.g., parents who were slaves of their children, slaves who were siblings of their master, etc.). Of this new group, female adults accounted for 67 percent on Martinique (with an average age of thirty, according to *Bulletin officiel de la Martinique*), 55 percent on Guadeloupe, and 70 percent in French Guiana. In these three colonies, 80 percent of those liberated in 1839 were women and children.

By contrast, the third and last law before general emancipation in 1848, the Mackau Law of 18 July 1845, gave slaves the possibility of redeeming themselves at prices mutually agreed upon by the slaves and masters or, if no accord was reached, at a price established by a colonial commission established with four hundred thousand francs from Louis-Philippe's government to finance this operation. Of the ex-slaves enfranchised under this law, women comprised 56 percent on Martinique, 68 percent on Guadeloupe, and 72 percent in French Guiana.

These laws thus progressively integrated women into the free colored group during the nineteenth century, though the reasons for their enfranchisements changed through time. The profiles of the women freed in each successive stage were different. The first group of the women enfranchised were older and gained manumission after a long time. The next two groups to be freed were younger and had proportionally fewer children. Given these differences, we might ask if the different means of achieving liberty produced different forms of conjugal relations. Also, did there exist distinct conjugal strategies associated with particular forms of enfranchisement? And at least, did the different manumission laws serve to further stratify society?

A longitudinal study of women freed during the nineteenth century at Trois-Îlets[48] shows how only a part of the "unions" were legitimized through the civil ceremony of marriage.[49] Trois-Îlets was a village in southwestern Martinique associated with the cultivation of sugarcane and with pottery making. In 1837 the village had 1,368 inhabitants, 32 percent of whom were "free." Following the application of the new laws on enfranchisement, this population grew profoundly. From 1831 to 1848 a third of the population under the age of fourteen, 81 percent of people over the age of sixty, and 44 percent of the women between the ages of fourteen and sixty were newly freed.

Before analyzing marriages of the newly emancipated of Trois-Îlets, it is necessary to define the concept of marriage with further precision. In fact, it was not the ceremony of marriage that signified the start of male-female unions occurring during the woman's child-bearing years but rather the birth of children. Beginning the analysis with the birth of the first child shows how marriage took place in a women's life cycle according to the date and type of emancipation. Although on a general level only a minority of the newly emancipated women chose to marry, the proportions varied depending on their type of liberty. Approximately 25 percent of women liberated before 1832 married subsequently, eleven years after the birth of their first child. Twenty-one percent of women freed between 1832 and 1848 married twenty-one years after the birth of their first child. Of the first group, 59 percent were single mothers, slightly less than the corresponding 68 percent in the second group. Seventeen percent of the first group had their children recognized by the father, as against 11 percent of the second group. In addition, the two groups adopted different matrimonial strategies.

In effect, women gaining their freedom before 1832 overwhelmingly practiced a sort of "homogamy" by marrying men also freed before 1832. Likewise, in their turn, their children avoided marrying newly freed ex-slaves. On 6 July 1840, Félicité Robertine, a free mulatto whose father was a landowner, married Arnaud Joseph Balaire, a free mulatto whose father was also a landowner. Until 1841 all marriages at Trois-Îlets united long-liberated ex-slaves, except for the marriage on 22 November 1831, three months after the emancipation of her partner, of the *capresse* (lit., someone considered 25 percent black) Cécile, formerly owned by Thomas Montout.

Those emancipated between 1832 and 1839 started to enter marital unions only after 1841. Nancy, a dressmaker aged forty-four years, freed on 13 January 1834, on 19 March 1841 married Ambroise Boye, a fisherman aged forty-two years, who had been enfranchised on 4 June 1833. On 18 May 1841, Camille Lauret, sixty-two, who had been emancipated on 28 January 1840 and had no stated occupation, married fifty-four-year-old Célestin, a master wheelwright who had gained his liberty on 24 December 1833. Another social category of newly freed ex-slaves was emerging. From 1841 to 1846, 83 percent of marriages at Trois-Îlets were between members of this group. Official marriage ceremonies had to wait until both parties had been liberated, as reflected in the high average ages of those marrying (47.5 years for women, 59.6 for men).

Following general emancipation, a tendency toward restratification thus developed. While a distinct division existed between long-freed slaves (those emancipated before 1832) and the newly emancipated from 1832 to 1846, the dividing line between the two groups shifted with time to distinguish those liberated before and after 1848 (the Emancipated of '48). All women liberated in the general emancipation measure of 1848 married men similarly liberated in that year, whereas those liberated before 1848 married others who had gained their freedom previously. The same trend toward consolidation of groups defined by the timing of their freedom appears in the documentation of legal recognition of paternity. Fathers freed before 1848 tended to recognize paternity of children born to women who gained their liberty also before 1848. This tendency is confirmed throughout Martinique, where of 421 marriages between ex-slave couples that occurred in 1858, only 129 (31 percent) were between "newly emancipated" and long-freed ex-slaves.[50] A distinct social division between earlier—and later—enfranchised ex-slaves was beginning to emerge.

If a division developed among those who had access to marriage, there was also a rupture between freed women in positions to uphold the ideology of marriage and citizenship and other women definitively excluded from such respectability because they lived in a state of concubinage. At Trois-Îlets on Martinique during the nineteenth century, of women who gave birth outside marriage, 68 percent remained unmarried, forming matrifocal households. This high percentage of unmarried mothers reflected the overall trend as noted in censuses that reveal the numbers of those "excluded" from marriage. The nuptial rate for the newly freed on Martinique increased from 1.9 percent to 10.6 percent between 1835–44 and 1845–54 (when the rate for Guadeloupe was 11.7), only to fall to 4.9 on Martinique and 5.4 on Guadeloupe by 1855–66, and further still by 1877–81 to 3.4 on Martinique and 3.2 on Guadeloupe.[51] After the decisions to marry by those who were in a position to do so under the emancipation measure of 1848 (accounting for 65 percent of marriages between 1849 and 1863), few couples registered their unions from the

1860s. Throughout the nineteenth century the proportion of "natural" births (to use the terminology of the time) to legitimate ones was very stable. From 1845 to 1865 natural births accounted for approximately 61 percent of all infants born on Martinique and Guadeloupe.[52] That proportion grew later in the century due to the economic crisis of the 1880s and to industrialization, peaking at 70 percent in 1885[53] and consolidating and stressing the different social attitudes and divisions within French colonial societies in the Caribbean that the republican model of equality did not reverse.

On the other hand, from the ranks of those emancipated before 1848 emerged an element of the "colored" population able, through marriage and other means, to adhere to the strict criteria necessary to become "good citizens" specified by the Republic of 1848. By adhering totally to these themes, the republican islanders on Martinique completely confused the issue of the legitimacy of unions with their political legitimacy. The adoption of this ideology was total and something of a caricature. For example, in the Saint-Pierre newspaper, Les Colonies, birth announcements took on a highly specific form: the names of legitimate children were published along with the total number of natural children, born outside marriage, who represented the majority of live births![54] For them, citizenship and family were indivisible concepts.[55] Leading republicans tried to recognize the development of an ideology of respectability within this group,[56] in which marriage played a central role. The women of this group could accept the status of minors because valued respectability that up to then had been the monopoly of "whites" counterbalanced this relative disability. Thus, "while practicing the love of God and the honest things,"[57] the elite among the women of color reinvested in the public sphere. Women of the colored elite reentered the public sphere demonstrating "honesty" and the "love of God." Rather than protest noisily in the streets, as had the newly emancipated females,[58] they worked to improve moral conditions through sociétés de bienfaisance (charities) and sociétés mutuelles (societies of solidarity), in which they promoted maternal and family values.

The first voluntary sociétés de bienfaisance developed on Martinique from 1882, with the aim of alleviating human suffering and misery and working toward the birth of a new era of progress. Two distinctly female sociétés de bienfaisance followed quickly, both in 1899; the Union of the Ladies of Prêcheur[59] (Union des Dames du Prêcheur) and the Association of the Ladies of Charity (Association des Dames de la Charité) at Sainte-Marie. Later, in 1901, the Ladies' Saint-Louis (Saint-Louis des

Dames) and the Female Provident Society (Prévoyance des Femmes) at Fort-de-France. In 1893 the Ladies' Sisterhood (Fraternité des Dames) was founded at Saint-Pierre, followed by the Working Women's Union (Union des Ouvrières), and a few years later by the Ladies Improvement Society (Progrès des Dames) and the Association of the Ladies of Charity (Association des Dames de la Charité). The aim of all was to safeguard the physical and moral health of their members and of members' families through helping children in distress, visiting the sick, delivering mutual aid vouchers, and paying a portion of the medical expenses of the underprivileged.[60] Subscriptions (about two francs a month for active members and three francs for honorary members) enabled these associations to assume responsibility for the cost of medical visits and medicines for its members; one hundred francs was also allotted toward the funeral costs of family members, and between fifty and two hundred francs to households with newborn babies.

In the eyes of the "man of color" Césaire Philémon, vice president of the Federation of Mutual Aid Societies, these early associations had constituted "the first female emancipation movements."[61] But what was described as a positive action and as participation of the women in the public sphere had other consequences for the social standing of the members. Endorsing this model, the colored elite stigmatized those who failed to adopt the values laid down for structuring society. At the end of the nineteenth century this group—mainly composed of women—began to be described as pathological. Through the republican prism, the stigma was put on these unmarried women, not only by administrators, governors, and colonists but also by the local colored elite. A dual movement of aversion and attraction developed.

On the one hand, the aversion and the tendency to reject those who failed or did not conform to normative values can be explained in part by the need of the colored elite to erase some of their own family histories, in which "illegitimacy" played a role. For them, this past must be forgotten because to do so was a condition of consolidating their success and fulfilling the promise of their social recognition.[62]

On the other hand, but not in a contradictory way, gradually, the model of the courageous mother was established, a woman facing life alone and managing both economic and domestic affairs (e.g., child care). Such a model was emphasized strongly, while the colored elite defined the "temporal destiny" of their daughters as a "mission of law, love, and charity."[63]

In this dual movement, the image of the "courageous mother" was magnified, as in "La glaneuse," a poem written in 1900 with a lyricism reminiscent of Zola's description of working-class life: "What could she do? Her child should have woken. Had she not counted on the sap of the plant to calm this infant who was biting his pillow, pale with hunger, seething with anger against his absent mother?"[64] Later writers from the colored elite also portrayed the figure of the "courageous mother," explaining her in terms of slavery: "Also, her chief qualities are rectitude, meekness, loyalty, unselfishness, a profound and sincere faith, devotion to the point of sacrifice, and a love of the family and of children. She subjects herself to the harshest of work and exerts herself to the utmost so that certain life rituals, such as baptism and the first communion of the child that she often raises alone—a reflection of a *'free union,' the fruit of slavery* which was widely practiced in the country until a few years ago and which has sadly left many unfortunate women with four, five, and sometimes six children to raise."[65]

She was also condemned by, and isolated in, her poverty. This is shown, for example, in 1945 by the women of the Feminine Group (Rassemblement Féminin), who declared it the "social obligation" of well-off women to "first throw off old prejudices and lazy habits in order to better understand [women of a] social milieu different from theirs" and to establish charitable works (*l'œuvre des layettes*) for "less evolved fellow citizens," above all for married women.[66] Women not officially married had to be recommended by both spiritual and lay authorities.[67] Yet were the elite in French colonies really unaware that the unmarried state, rather than constituting a social anomaly,[68] or reflecting conjugal instability,[69] highlighted the difficulty of erasing age-old antagonisms?

The discourse of the republicans of 1848 on the family and marriage presented only inadequate change from that of the preceding July Monarchy. It joined, on the contrary, a wider perspective that exceeded the borders of France and its colonies. In the nineteenth century, as in the twentieth, the whole Western world credited marriage and the family with an organizational function of society: these two institutions define status, identity, and rights, as well as nationality, filiation, and inheritance of possessions.[70] The application of this ideology in the colonial and postabolitionist era nevertheless received particular declensions. Indeed, the republican French national project cancelled the racial question under the excuse of universalism,[71] while slave societies had rested on this division. It is not a question here of building a strict contrast between metropolis and colony, because the interactions between these two political entities—including on the racial question—were constant, as Fred Cooper and Ann Stoler have shown.[72] It is rather a question of showing the sexual effects of the republican emancipation in the French Antilles. Emancipation put equality at the heart of all social processes while practicing the political disparity of gender and the stigmatization. With the application of the Napoleonic Code to the whole colonial population, the "natural" children born out of wedlock, for example, who enjoyed legal equality with legitimate children since 1793, are characterized as bastards, illegitimate children, without rights. The line of civil exclusion built around moral notions was repositioned in 1848. Marriage produced full citizenship—that is, citizenship aligned with the moral values promulgated by the metropolis. In these conditions, even with underestimated rights, only the women of the elite of color were able to attain the republican ideal. They also practiced what Lucette Valensi calls a "therapy of forgetting."[73] Indeed, through the period of slavery, the sexuality of the women slaves and of free women of color produced a discourse on their immorality, their lasciviousness, their consensual and active prostitution.[74] The colonial power—that is, the law that prevented their marriage with "white" men, or the practices of the colonists that did not favor unions within the slave population—discredited them. On the contrary, the abolition of slavery allowed the women of the social elite to buy back their honor. This "respectability" had to counter the stigmas of their history. Nevertheless, it surreptitiously reconstructed lines of social and racial exclusion. By adhering to the Western moral model prescribed by the metropolis, the elite of color, and particularly the women of this group, assumed the cultural idioms of the dominant.[75] Without taking into account the agency of the poorest women, the speech and the practices of the feminine elites established them as other. In a continuous effort to be recognized as full citizens (men and women) by the former class of the dominant, the elites of color agreed to disqualify all the poor classes and, in particular, poor women and the mothers of children born out of wedlock.

Borrowing a sociological concept used recently to analyze the contemporary phenomenon of suburbs in France,[76] we can say that using marriage as a differentiating factor (*différentialiste*) ethnicized poorer women, that is, relegated them to total otherness: their identity was rooted in the slave past, without possibility of exceeding their subordinate status. In discourses, these "pathological" women, poto mitan, were excluded from the social competition around the citizenship that the republic had introduced into the French colonies and that was going to structure their history until the law of *départementalisation* of 1946[77] and beyond.

NOTES

1. Likewise, the decree took effect on 27 May 1848 in Guadeloupe and, according to the official calendar, on 10 June 1848 in Guyana.

2. Governor of Martinique, 23 May 1848.

3. Reciprocally, any Frenchman convicted of "possessing, purchasing, or selling slaves" lost his French citizenship. See decree of 27 April 1848, art. 8.

4. Pierre Rosanvallon, *Le sacre du citoyen: Histoire du suffrage universel en France*, Paris: Gallimard, 2001.

5. Arlette Gautier, *Les sœurs de solitude: La condition féminine dans aux Antilles, du XVIIIe au XIXe siècle* (Paris: Editions Caribéennes, 1985); Bernard Moitt, *Women and Slavery in the French Antilles, 1635–1848* (Bloomington: Indiana University Press, 2001); Sue Peabody, "*Négresse, Mulâtresse, Citoyenne*: Gender and Emancipation in the French Caribbean, 1650–1848," in *Gender and Slave Emancipation in the Atlantic World*, ed. Pamela Scully and Diana Paton (Durham: Duke University Press, 2005), 56–78.

6. Christiane Veauvy and Laura Pisano, *Paroles oubliées: Les femmes et la construction de l'Etat-nation en France et en Italie, 1789–1860* (Paris: Armand Colin, 1997), 1. *Poto mitan* (std. Fr., *le pilier du milieu*, "the pillar of the place") designates a woman on her own with children, sustaining her own home.

7. On 4 February 1794, the National Convention declared, "Slavery is abolished in all colonies; in consequence, it is decreed that all men, without distinction of color, resident in the colonies, are [henceforth] French citizens and enjoy all the rights guaranteed under the Constitution." See Jean Meyer, Jean Tarrade, Annie Rey-Goldzeiguer, and Jacques Thobie, eds., *Histoire de la France coloniale* (Paris: Armand Colin, 1991), 402. Nevertheless, this decree applied only to Guadeloupe and French Guiana, as, with the blessing of its settlers, Martinique came under British rule.

8. For the religious history of the French West Indies, see Philippe Delisle, *Renouveau missionnaire et société esclavagiste: La Martinique, 1815–1848* (Paris: Publisud, 1997).

9. The economic variable is certainly part of this development, as shown by researchers such as Robin Blackburn in *The Overthrow of Colonial Slavery* (Berkeley: University of California Press, 1988).

10. Alexandre Moreau de Jonnès (1778–1870) can be added to the list, for he wrote on slavery as well as on poverty and delinquency in laborers. Moreau de Jonnès, *Recherches statistiques sur l'esclavage colonial et sur les moyens de le supprimer* (Paris: Impr. de Bourgogne et Martinet, 1842).

11. See the Penal Code of 1810 on liberated criminals.

12. Michel Foucault, *Surveiller et punir: Naissance de la prison* (Paris: Gallimard, 1975), 300–301; Patricia O'Brien, *Correction ou châtiment: Histoire des prisons en France au XIXe siècle*, trans. Myriam Cottias (Paris: Presses Universitaires de France, 1988).

13. See Myriam Cottias, "De la moralisation des esclaves à la citoyenneté dans les Antilles françaises (Martinique, Guadeloupe)," in *Mujer y familia en América Latina, siglos XVIII–XX*, ed. Susana Menéndez and Barbara Potthast (Málaga: Asociación de Historiadores Latinoamericanistas Europeos, 1996), 135–52.

14. Jacques Donzelot, *La police des familles* (Paris: Minuit, 1977), 87.

15. The preamble to the Constitution of 4 November 1848 (art. 4, sec. 2) notes that "Family, Work, and Property form the basis of the French Republic."

16. Société de la Morale Chrétienne, *The Committee for the Redemption of Female Negro Slaves in the French Colonies* (Paris: Société de la Morale Chrétienne, 1832), 2.

17. Pierre Dessalles notes in his journal that the title of the text "written in Creole and in French" publicizing the freedom of slaves received more attention than its content. Dessalles, *La vie d'un colon à la Martinique au XIXè siècle: Journal, 1848–1856* (Fort-de-France: Désormeaux, 1984), 29; see also Richard Burton, *La famille coloniale: La Martinique et la mère patrie, 1789-1992* (Paris: L'Harmattan, 1996).

18. Ministère de la Marine et des Colonies, *États de population, de cultures et de commerce relatifs aux colonies française* (Paris: Ministère de la Marine et des Colonies, 1836), 61.

19. "Tableau de la situation actuelle des esclaves dans les colonies françaises d'après les dernières publications officielles," *L'abolitionniste français*, January–February 1844, 44.

20. "Rapport du procureur du Roi de Fort-Royal (octobre 1842)," in Ministère de la Marine et des Colonies, *Exposé général des résultats du patronage des esclaves dans les colonies françaises* (Paris: Imprimerie royale, 1844), 574.

21. *Martyrologe colonial: Tableau de l'esclavage aux colonies françaises* (Paris: Pagnerre, 1848), 19.

22. Interestingly, between 1830 and 1848, some French female authors used anti-slavery rhetoric in their denunciation of the situation of women. See, for example, Jenny Derouin, *Profession de foi* (Paris: by author, 1832); Claire Demar, *Appel d'une femme au peuple pour l'affranchissement de la femme* (Paris: by author, 1832). In anglophone countries, protestant feminists commonly compared their fight for liberty with that of slaves: See Jean Baubénot, "De la femme protestante," in *Histoire des femmes en Occident*, ed. George Duby and Michelle Perrot, 4 vols. (Paris: Plon, 1991), 1:206–7.

23. Ministère de la Marine, *Exposé général*, 575.

24. See Myriam Cottias, "La séduction coloniale: Damnation et stratégies: Les Antilles, XVIIe–XIXe siècle," in *Séduction et sociétés*, ed. Cécile Dauphin and Arlette Farge (Paris: Seuil, 2000), 125–39.

25. Victor Schoelcher, *De l'esclavage des noirs et de la législation coloniale* (Paris: Pagnerre, 1833), 47.

26. Ministère de la Marine, *Exposé général*, 571.

27. *Bulletin officiel de la Martinique*, 1846, 107.

28. "Ordonnance du Roi sur l'instruction morale et religieuse et pour le patronage des esclaves," *Bulletin officiel de la Martinique*, 1840.

29. Colonial Council of Martinique, session of 19 May 1846.

30. "Tableau de la situation actuelle des esclaves," 42.

31. Ministère des Colonies, *Proposition de loi sur le mariage des esclaves* (Paris: Ministère des Colonies, 1846), title 2, ch. 3, arts. 20, 28.

32.Alphonse Garnier, *Journal du Conseiller Garnier à la Martinique et à la Guadeloupe, 1848–1855*, ed. Gabriel Debien (Fort-de-France: Société d'Histoire de la Martinique, 1969), 233.

33. See Gilbert Pago, *Les femmes et la liquidation du système esclavagiste à la Martinique à 1848–1852* (Fort-de-France: Ibis Rouge Éditions, 1998), ch. 3.

34. Moitt, *Women and Slavery.*

35. "Tableau des affranchissements," *Bulletin officiel de la Martinique*, 1833–48.

36. See Jacques Bouton, *Relation de l'établissement des Français depuis l'an 1635 en l'île de la Martinique, l'une des Antilles de l'Amérique: Des mœurs des sauvages, de la situation et des autres singularités de l'île* (Paris: S. Cramoisy, 1650).

37. Ministère de la Marine, *Exposé général,* 584.

38. Marcel Châtillon, "Copie de la lettre du P. Jean Mongin, missionnaire de l'Amérique à une personne de condition du Languedoc écrite de l'île de Saint-Christophe au mois de mai 1682," *Bulletin de la Société d'Histoire de la Guadeloupe* 61–62 (1984): 90.

39. "Rapport du procureur du Roi de Marie-Galante," in Ministère de la Marine, *Exposé général,* 579.

40. Ministère de la Marine, *Exposé général,* 580.

41. Ibid., 585.

42. Louise Tilly and Joan Scott, *Les femmes, le travail et la famille* (Paris: Rivages, 1987), 121.

43. Jacques Adélaïde-Merlande, *Histoire générale des Antilles et de la Guyane* (Paris: L'Harmattan, 1994).

44. See Jacques Adélaïde-Merlande, "Problèmatique d'une histoire de l'esclavage urbain–Guadeloupe, Guyane, Martinique (1815–1848)," *Bulletin de la Société d'Histoire de la Guadeloupe* 65–66 (1985): 10–32.

45. "Tableaux des affranchissements," *Bulletin officiel de la Martinique*, 1832–36.

46. In other words, those who gained manumission but whose masters refused or were unable to pay the *affranchisement* tax.

47. *De droit* in this case means that no opposition to freedom could exist because the king and the administration decided which situations automatically provided freedom.

48. See Myriam Cottias, "Trois-Ilets de la Martinique au XIXe siècle: Essai d'étude d'une marginalité démographique," *Population* 4–5 (1985): 675–98.

49. Under the republican regime, civil marriage took priority over religious marriage and was the one recognized by the state.

50. *Notices statistiques* (Paris: Imprimerie Nationale, 1859).

51. The nuptial index used is the number of marriages in relation to the adult population (14–60 years of age), multiplied by 1,000. For Martinican slaves the index was 0.9 per thousand in 1839 and 1.1 per thousand in 1847.

52. Including, before 1848, the birth of slave and "free" children.

53. "État civil du 9 au 18 septembre 1885," *La défense coloniale,* 20 September 1884, 4.

54. The theme of legitimacy was dealt with in the newspaper on a regular basis. For example, it published Paul Rouget's novel *La faute de Jeanne* in two installments.

55. Burton, *Famille coloniale.*

56. See, for example, Delisle, *Renouveau missionnaire,* 271.

57. Société des Femmes Schoelchériennes de Fort-de-France, in Victor Schoelcher, *La vérité aux ouvriers et cultivateurs de la Martinique suivie de rapports, décrets, arrêtés, projets de lois et d'arrêtés concernant l'abolition immédiate de l'esclavage* (Paris: Pagnerre, 1849; reprint, Lausanne: Editions du Ponant, 1985).

58. Dessalles, *Vie d'un colon,* 42, 81.

59. Prêcheur is an area of Martinique.

60. See Myriam Cottias and Annie Fitte-Duval, "Femmes, famille et politique dans les Antilles françaises de 1828 à nos jours," *Caribbean Studies* 28, no. 1 (1995): 75–100.

61. Césaire Philémon, *La Société, la solidarité et le mouvement mutualiste à la Martinique* (Fort-de-France: Imprimerie du Gouvernement, 1941).

62. , "L'oubli du passé 'contre la 'citoyenneté': Troc et ressentiment à la Martinique (1848–1946)," in *1946–1996: Cinquante ans de départementalisation outre mer*, ed. Fred Constant and Justin Daniel (Paris: L'Harmattan, 1997), 293–313.

63. Vincent Allègre, "speech," *La défense coloniale*, 9 august 1884, 4.

64. Quoted by Césaire Philémon, *Galeries martiniquaises* (Paris: Exposition Coloniale Internationale, 1931), 250.

65. André Delaunay-Belleville, *Choses et gens de la Martinique* (Paris: Debresse, 1963), 188, 190; emphasis added.

66. Anon., *La femme dans la cité* (Fort-de-France: Le Rassemblement Féminin, 1945), 3.

67. Ibid., 3.

68. For an anthropological view of this, see, for example, Stéphanie Mulot, "Je suis le père, je suis la mère" (PhD diss., Paris, EHESS, 2000).

69. See Christine Chivallon, *Espace et identité à la Martinique* (Paris: CNRS, 1998).

70. André Burguière, *Histoire de la famille* (Paris: Livre de Poche, 1994). For more recent views, see Suzanne Desan, *The Family on Trial in Revolutionary France* (Berkeley: University of California Press, 2004), 17; Jennifer Ngaire Heuer, *The Family and the Nation: Gender and Citizenship in Revolutionary France, 1789–1830* (Ithaca: Cornell University Press, 2005); Nancy Cott, *Public Vows, A History of Marriage and the Nation* (Cambridge, MA: Harvard University Press, 2002).

71. It would be more precise to say that French universalism had implicit racial overtones associating the French nation with the color white. See Myriam Cottias, "Le silence de la nation: Les 'vieilles colonies' comme lieu de définition des dogmes républicains," *Outre-mers* 90 (2003): 338–39.

72. Frederick Cooper, Ann Laura Stoler, eds., *Tensions of Empire: Colonial Cultures in a Bourgeois World* (Berkeley: University of California Press, 1997).

73. Lucette Valensi, *Fables de la mémoire: La glorieuse bataille des trois rois* (Paris: Seuil, 1992).

74. Cottias, "Séduction coloniale."

75. Ann Laura Stoler, *Carnal Knowledge and Imperial Power: Race and the Intimate in Colonial Rule* (Berkeley: University of California Press, 2002), 23.

76. Abdelmalek Sayad, *L'immigration, ou, les paradoxes de l'altérité* (Brussels: De Broeck, 1991); Jacqueline Costa-Lescoux, "L'ethnicisation du lien social dans les banlieues françaises," *Revue européenne des migrations internationales* 17, no. 2 (2005): 123–38.

77. In 1946 Guadeloupe, Guyane, Martinique, and Réunion became French *départements* and thus no longer were French colonies. The same laws were supposed to be applied in the islands as they were in continental France.

4

Representing Women Slaves

Masters' Fantasies and Memories in Fiction

9

DEVIANT AND DANGEROUS

Proslavery Representations of Jamaican Slave Women's Sexuality,
ca. 1780–1834

HENRICE ALTINK

Slave women's sexuality has long attracted the attention of historians. American historians first researched this field in the late 1960s, most notably Winthrop Jordan in his seminal work *White over Black*.[1] In the 1980s American feminist scholars provided evidence that slave women's sexual relations with white men were primarily based on force to do away with the myth presented by planters and their supporters that bondswomen were scheming jezebels and took readily to the prostitution of their bodies.[2] Using, among others, Foucault's argument that the "deployment of sexuality . . . engenders a continual extension of areas and forms of control," they argued that the sexual exploitation of bondswomen was as much a means of control as the whip and that it made female bondage worse than male bondage.[3]

Scholars of slavery started to research the sexuality of Caribbean slave women only from the late 1980s. They initially focused also on sexual coercion and bondswomen's resistance against it.[4] It was difficult for them, however, to debunk the myth that slave women were sexually promiscuous because scholars lacked primary sources in which (ex)slave women described their sexual abuse. Nevertheless, they succeeded in providing an alternative account of the sexuality of female slaves by comparing proslavery remarks about the sexuality of bondswomen with abolitionist

A different version of this article was published as "Forbidden Fruit: Pro-Slavery Attitudes towards Enslaved Women's Sexuality and Interracial Sex," *Journal of Caribbean History* 39, no. 2 (2005): 201–35.

accounts and anthropological data. More recently they have, like some of their North American counterparts, started to pay attention to the meanings that these contemporary observers attached to slave women's sexuality. Several scholars have addressed the stereotype of the scheming jezebel in late-eighteenth-century proslavery writings and have begun to explore abolitionist counterconstructions of bondswomen's sexuality.[5]

This chapter expands on these sound beginnings by examining representations of the sexuality of female slaves in a wide range of materials, including literary sources, that Jamaican planters and metropolitan defenders of slavery produced between 1780 and 1834.[6] These authors focused on bondswomen's sexuality not only because it was inextricably connected, in very practical terms, to one of the main threats to the viability of the plantation system—the failure of the slave population to produce naturally—but also because its moral overtones featured prominently in abolitionist attacks on the slave system. As purity was considered priceless for females in the metropolitan society of the day, the sexual abuse of female slaves was an excellent means for abolitionists to demonstrate that slavery reduced people—particularly women—to a less than human condition and that it also corrupted slaveholders because it seduced them from living up to the metropolitan norm of masculine restraint.

Slave men's sexuality did not feature as extensively as slave women's in proslavery writings because it constituted less of a threat to the social order. The paucity of white women in Jamaica meant that slave men satisfied their sexual needs first and foremost with the females enslaved with them.[7] Bondswomen, on the other hand, had both voluntary and involuntary sex with white men, which resulted in colored offspring. As large numbers of these colored slaves grew up and were set free, many white islanders regarded slave women's interracial sexual relations as threatening their superior status in society. It is no surprise, then, that the proslavery construction of female slaves as sexually deviant drew especially on bondswomen's relationships with white men.

THE SEXUALLY DEVIANT SLAVE WOMAN

English ideas about sexuality in the late eighteenth and early nineteenth centuries confined permissible sex to the married procreative couple but differentiated the inherent sexualities of males and females.[8] It had been assumed that men had strong sexual desires that were beyond their control, but after the turn of the century men were increasingly urged to control and ration these passions within increasingly circumscribed avenues.[9]

The norm of female sexuality changed even more. For centuries, women had been regarded as the lascivious sex; lust originated with them, and men were merely victims of their wanton sexual power. To make possible the Victorian domestic ideology that located women firmly in the home and defined them as devoted wives and mothers, women were urged to control their sexual urges both before and after marriage. Gradually, female chastity came to be seen as an inner virtue rather than a discipline imposed by men. It was asserted that women did not have an innate sex drive and that their sexual feelings were invoked only in marriage through love. By the early nineteenth century, the ideal of the naturally passionless woman was firmly established.[10]

Proslavery writers simultaneously constructed bondswomen as the threatening deviants from this model of inherent female sexual passivity in their discussion of slave women's acknowledged sexual relations with white and slave men. First, they argued that female slaves began sexual activities at an early age. Second, they claimed that they changed partners frequently as they continued. Third, they believed that they preferred more than one partner at the same time.[11] The argument that lent most support to the construction of the sexually deviant bondswoman, however, was that female slaves eagerly prostituted their bodies. The overseer in the proslavery novel *Marly* (1828), for instance, expresses his surprise at the readiness with which slave women offered themselves or their daughters to him.[12]

Two theories were put forward to explain why bondswomen deviated from the norm of restrained female sexuality. The first, adhered to primarily by those who resided on the island (hereafter, Jamaican writers), was that female slaves were naturally promiscuous.[13] The second theory, which was advanced less often, attributed their lack of sexual purity to various external pressures. Resident Anthony Davis, for instance, blamed it on nonconformist missionaries, the most prominent symbols of humanitarianism and abolition on the island. In 1832 he alleged that a missionary in Spanish Town had urged slave women in his congregation to raise money to build a chapel in New Zealand by "the prostitution of their bodies."[14] Only a few defenders of slavery acknowledged that the brutalities of slavery might have contributed to bondswomen's promiscuity. Former plantation bookkeeper J. B. Moreton expressed this possibility in his guide to prospective estate personnel, entitled *West India Customs and Manners* (1793): "I say if the most virtuous woman now in England had been tutored like blacks, a slave in like manner, she would be as lascivious and as common as any; and again, I say if blacks were tutored from their infancy in England, they would be as virtuous as white women."[15]

Considering these two diametrically opposed theories of deviance as innate and acquired, it is not surprising that the proslavery debate about the sexuality of women slaves contained competing representations of bonded females as both property and as human beings: the *scheming black jezebel* that is the immoral and evil temptress, and the *potentially virtuous female slave*. These two representations of slave women's sexuality both characterize them in terms of their sexual relations with white men. First, short-term relations initiated by a black or, as was more common, a colored[16] bondswoman, who was generally referred to as a prostitute. It was argued that she started the relationship solely to obtain material favors and that she did everything possible to hurt her white partner immediately after he gave her money or gifts. These damaging interracial liaisons contrasted with the long-term relationships initiated by white men with the consent of the slave woman, who was referred to as a housekeeper. Like the prostitute, the housekeeper's innate appetite for material goods was provided as the main reason why she entered such a relationship.[17]

The percentage of colored slaves provides a rough-and-ready indicator of the prevalence of these two types of interracial sexual relations on the island. In 1817, there were about 30,000 whites in Jamaica and 300,000 slaves, including 36,000 coloreds.[18] A population of 24,000 adult white men, then, leads to a colored slave (presumably descendant)/white adult male (presumed paternity) ratio of 1.5. Compare this ratio to the North American mainland at the same time, which had a white population of 8 million and a slave population of 1.5 million, including 150,000 coloreds. An adult white male population of about 2.8 million means that there were only on average 0.05 colored slaves per one white male.[19] Thus, even at this rough estimate, the incidence of mixed offspring per available white father in Jamaica was thirty times that in North America.

While all proslavery writers presented both the prostitute and the housekeeper as scheming jezebels, they regarded the domestic arrangement as more of a threat to Jamaican society than casual liaisons. They raised four objections against housekeeper relationships. First, they threatened the social order because they led to "spurious offspring."[20] By this characterization they meant that owners set a large percentage of colored slaves free in recognition of their white paternity or special and personal services and that these free coloreds upset the delicate balance of power on the island, which—as the ending of slavery as the prime civic distinction loomed—was increasingly based on skin color. During slavery, the highest rungs of the social ladder belonged exclusively to the small number of white islanders. The large numbers of blacks—enslaved and free—were at the bottom of the ladder, while those of mixed parentage occupied a middle rank, even though many of these had gained economic positions similar to or even exceeding those of the whites.[21]

Second, spurious offspring posed a threat to the productivity of the estates, as colored slaves were generally exempted from heavy labor in the fields and employed around the main house.[22] Third, slave housekeepers endangered the stability of the estates because they managed to obtain "complete ascendancy and sway" over their white men and, as Moreton argued, became "intolerably insolent to subordinate white men."[23] This objection should be seen in light of the tendency of Jamaican slaveholders to bequeath property and wealth to their free colored offspring. The legitimate sons and daughters and other relatives of these men generally argued that the slave mistress had persuaded the deceased to include his colored offspring in his will and hence was to blame for their own limited inheritances.[24]

From the 1820s, Jamaican writers ceased to focus on the slave prostitute and presented her housekeeper counterpart less as a scheming jezebel than as a potentially virtuous woman, albeit one in slavery. This accommodating shift was a direct response to abolitionist attacks on the loose sexual mores of white Jamaican men. From the mid-1820s, abolitionists contended that all interracial sexual relations were the result of male force and—by extension—the moral depravity of white men in Jamaica. To demonstrate the planters' and the estate officers' deviation from the metropolitan norm of male sexual restraint, they not only emphasized that these men gratified their sex drives outside such legitimate channels as marriage, but also that married slave women ranked as high among their victims as unmarried female slaves. For them, the sanctity of marriage was so great as to extend even to unions among slaves.

Several Jamaican writers pointed out that no force was involved, as slave women were keen to become housekeepers because of the material and immaterial benefits bestowed upon them, and that the bondswomen who engaged in sex with white men were young and single.[25] Their strongest argument in favor of such housekeeper relations, however, was that they mirrored the monogamous, stable, and affectionate relationships of English middle-class men and women. One local resident, for example, argued that housekeepers were "faithful and attached, and, in hours of sickness, evidenced all the kindness and affection of wives."[26] To emphasize that love rather than lust underpinned housekeeper relations, Anthony Davis mentioned that most estate officers did their utmost to have their housekeepers accompany them to new places of employment.[27] Thus in the late 1820s and early 1830s, some proslavery writers argued that both slave women and white Jamaican men lived up to, rather than deviated from, the metropolitan norms of sexual restraint and domestic fidelity.

The greater prominence of the potentially virtuous bondswoman in the proslavery discussion about interracial sexual relations by the mid-1820s accompanied a stronger denunciation of more casual sexual relations between the races. This discourse focused on the socially and politically destabilizing effects that the offspring of interracial unions had in a society increasingly polarized in terms of "race" and called upon slave women and white men not to cross the color line to satisfy their sexual desires. Cynric Williams, a visitor to Jamaica, urged for instance that white estate officers should bring "a wife from England" and that female slaves should marry "black men rather than commit adultery with white ones."[28]

The stronger denunciation of interracial sex was a direct response to the growth of the free population after abolition of the slave trade in 1807. This potentially politically challenging population consisted largely of colored people, as colored slaves, more often than ones regarded as black, were allowed to purchase their freedom or were manumitted after their master's death in recognition of paternity or special services. Between 1810 and 1830 the number of free men and women increased from 7.3 to 10.6 percent of the total population of the island.[29] This growth in numbers was accompanied by increased public assertiveness: from 1815 freedmen held regular meetings in Kingston and petitioned the House of Assembly (the Jamaica legislature) to extend their social and political rights. These political initiatives reached a climax in 1830 with the establishment of the first freedman newspaper, *The Watchman*, which became the major organ to attack the racial discrimination on the island.[30]

The growing and increasingly visible free population threatened not only the social but also the economic status of the white islanders, especially that of the nonslaveholders, as freedmen were usually highly skilled and thus competed with white tradesmen. Several proslavery writers suggested that a legal ban on sex between white men and bondswomen would go some way toward containing the threat posed by the growing free population. Other writers argued, however, that such a ban would do little to stop the growth of the existing freed population, as existing slave law stipulated that anyone four or more generations removed from black ancestors was free.[31] They advocated instead endogamy within each of the six "castes" that made up Jamaican society: white, mulatto (white and black), mustee (white and quadroon), quadroon (white and mulatto), sambo (mulatto and black), and black.[32]

Endogamy was most clearly advocated in the anonymously published novel *Hamel, the Obeah Man* (1827), probably written by Cynric Williams.[33] The highly pejorative representations of slave women in this novel demonstrate not only that black female bodies were simultaneously despised and desired but also the extent to which the proslavery debate about female slaves' sexuality wove race, sex, and gender together. The novel's main character is Roland, a white missionary. While he tries to incite the slaves of a plantation to plan a rebellion and establish a black king, he falls in love with Joanna, the white daughter of the plantation owner. Roland's assistant, Sebastian, a free mulatto man, is in love with Joanna's personal servant, a quadroon bondswoman called Michal. Michal, however, has set her heart on the missionary, Roland, thus transgressing the established racial boundaries.

It is especially the inset story of the mulatto Sebastian's futile attempts to court the quadroon Michal that conveys the novel's message not to blur the color line. Sebastian realizes, shortly after his first meeting with Michal, that because of his skin color his hopes to win this slave woman's heart are in vain: "Quadroon damsels do not look for beauty in the youth of their own colour; their first ideas of admiration or love are devoted to the genuine white breed, either native or imported, to which they are themselves indebted, as they think, for the charms of their own persons, and all the favour they find in the eyes of those who sigh for their affections."[34]

The author presents Michal's sexuality as an ardent deviation from the metropolitan norm of female sexual restraint mainly by comparing her with her virtuous white mistress, Joanna. Whereas Joanna does not even entertain Roland's advances, Michal actively tries to woo him so as to become his housekeeper. Like earlier proslavery writers, the author presents this manipulative move as devoid of the love that respectable English middle-class girls were supposed to entertain toward their suitors: "this young girl is in love with some white gentleman—for they always aspire: *ambition* goes hand in hand with love."[35] This representation of Michal as an immoral temptress coexists, however, with descriptions of her physical appearance as similar to white women, which the *Westminster Review* described as "not displeasing":[36] "Her skin was nearly as white as that of any European, of a clear and animated hue, the roses glowing upon her cheeks— . . . and her forehead was shaded by some of the prettiest brown curls that ever graced the brows of a Quadroon damsel . . . the long black eyelashes which like portcullises, guarded those portals of her heart, or mind, or genius, . . . had been designed by nature with such attention to symmetry, and to what we have learned from our ancestors to consider beautiful."[37]

Arguably the author eroticized Michal in order to ease his guilt of being sexually attracted to a colored woman. Colored women, especially the most light skinned, were far more sexually desirable than black women to white men, not only because they were seen as more aesthetically pleasing but also because they were considered more refined, as they were generally employed around the house rather than in the field. As a result of the growth of the freed population and the shift in the metropolitan norm of male sexuality toward containment (if not restraint), sexual attraction to colored bondswomen had become a less acceptable desire by the mid-1820s. The author could thus give vent to his sexual fantasies about light-skinned female slaves by providing elaborate accounts of their beauty.

It is, however, also possible to read the author's eroticization of Michal as a means through which he expressed his anxieties about the fragile status of white Jamaicans. Quadroon women posed far more of a threat to Jamaica's social structure than other colored women, first because they were so similar to white women in appearance that they could easily pass among strangers as white, and second because the offspring of their relations with white men were four generations removed from their black ancestors and hence legally became members of the troublesome population of free coloreds.

The discussion in *Hamel* of slave women's sexualities supports Patricia Mohammed's contention that by the early part of the nineteenth century "black women's centrality in production and reproduction may have very well been shared or superseded by [that of] mulatto women."[38] In this novel, black women feature only secondarily in the account of Roland's attempt to stir some slaves up into rebellion—averted by the obeah man Hamel—and representations of them compare unfavorably to those of the more fully delineated colored women slaves. Not only does the author omit references to black women's physical appearance, he also rarely gives them names and refers to them mainly in derogatory terms: "The missionary was no sooner left alone with the *black dame* than the latter asked him if he was hungry or thirsty, and offered him all she had to offer in the shape of refreshments. 'Black *woman*,' said he, '*mistress Hamel*, or by what other name shall I address you? *Negress! sister in the spirit!* . . . Tell me *mistress—mammy*, I should say—are you the only wife of Hamel?"[39]

Thus while black bondswomen in the novel, like their colored counterparts, are presented as dangers to the social order, their danger is not linked to their sexuality but rather to their submissiveness to black men; they docilely obey their male partners' orders to help overthrow the plantation regime. In fact, the allusion to polygyny in the last line of the quote seems to suggest that the author regarded black men's sexuality as a greater threat to plantation society than black women's. Early proslavery verse and fiction lends further support to the idea that by the mid-1820s proslavery writers had come to displace their main fears more on to colored than black slave women. This literature presents the sexuality of both black and colored bondswomen as a deviation from the metropolitan norm of virtuous restraint. The song "Me Know No Law, Me Know No Sin," which is included in Moreton's guide, demonstrates the lack of sexual restraint attributed in the late eighteenth century to black slave women:

> *Altho' a slave me is born and bred,*
> *my skin is black, not yellow:*
> *I often sold my maidenhead*
> *To many handsome fellow.*[40]

The treatment of the sexuality of bondswomen in *Hamel, the Obeah Man,* suggests, then, that by the 1820s proslavery writers did not just contrast slaves, regardless of color, to English middle-class men and women but also distinguished behaviors among the defined degrees of race in Jamaica. They attributed to each racial category a set of internal characteristics, such as intelligence or laziness, as well as sexuality for females. These were used together with visible signs, such as skin color and hair texture, to rank the castes in a hierarchy. In other words, by the 1820s skin color had become the primary signifier of human difference for white Jamaicans, and sexuality the defining characteristic of women.[41]

Although these two images of bondswomen, the scheming jezebel and the potentially virtuous woman, jostled for power in the proslavery debate about interracial sex, fears of the former became more prominent in the 1820s and dominated the debate throughout the period. Considering the immediate threats to the socioeconomic standing of Jamaican writers—first in the form of the abolition of the slave trade and later in the increase in the free population—it is unsurprising that these writers were more likely to present the negative image of the scheming jezebel than were their metropolitan counterparts. The latter resorted more often to the potentially virtuous woman, not only because they were influenced more than Jamaican writers by the metropolitan discourses on feminine virtue and masculine sexual restraint but also because they hoped to defend the institution of slavery against abolitionist attacks by appealing to the slaves' virtuous potential. Metropolitan writers were convinced that grand-scale amelioration of the slaves' condition was the best solution to save the plantation economy. White islanders, on the other hand, were of the opinion that the survival of Jamaica's plantations required not an extension but rather further limitations of the slaves' autonomy through coercive restraint and physical punishment. The image of the scheming jezebel lent itself, of course, much better to the justification of this project than did the passive potentially virtuous woman.

The two images of slave women's sexuality served a variety of purposes. These images first had to express and thereby control the major fears that troubled the authors—including declining output of sugar and the growth of the freed population—which were exacerbated by the abolitionist attacks on the slave trade and slavery. Proslavery writings on the sexuality of bondswomen thus support the argument advanced by various scholars that times of social upheaval and instability, such as wars and large-scale immigration, witness an excessive public concern about sexual morality, especially that of women.[42] Before 1770 planters and others whose interests were closely tied up with then relatively prosperous Jamaican plantations had not expressed concern about the sexuality of female slaves. While the majority glossed over this issue, some presented slave women's sexuality as a positive rather than a negative feature. One such was Isaac Teale, whose 1765 poem "Sable Venus" described bonded females as sensual creatures.

Sonya O. Rose, who has examined strong denunciations of women's sexual morality in various historical instances, has concluded that discourses about the sexual morality of women intensify "when establishing unity of identity has become especially important to a community."[43] Her argument also seems to explain why the proslavery debate after 1770 expanded to incorporate bondswomen's sexuality. The development of organized abolition forced the diverse group of proslavery writers to assume a degree of unity to avert legal action that could undermine their social and economic standing. Jamaican and metropolitan writers appealed to the sexuality of slave women because of the broader political culture in which they were engaged but developed it contrastingly according to the two political contexts, West Indian and English, in which they lived.

ATTEMPTS TO CONTAIN THE SEXUAL DANGER

Another important function of the two images of slave women's sexuality was of course to justify interracial sex at a time when race became a defining feature of Englishness. Sexual relations across African and European backgrounds were a common and accepted feature of Jamaican society. By presenting the bondswoman as a scheming jezebel, white men on the island could deny responsibility for their casual relations with slave women. Such a woman was inherently wanton and lured innocent white men in order to fulfill her insatiable sexual appetite. On the other hand, the potentially virtuous female slave was used in the 1820s and 1830s to justify the widespread practice of housekeeper relationships on the island. White islanders used these two images not only to justify their interracial sexual encounters to the outside world but also to themselves. As Trevor Burnard has shown in his study of the Jamaican slaveholder Thomas Thistlewood, interracial sexual relations were more often forced than consensual.[44] In order to avoid regarding their sexual violation of bondswomen as a sin or as evidence of less than civilized instincts, white men must have told themselves that slave women were not human beings but lustful savages indestructible under their assaults. The two images, then, were to a large extent shaped by real interracial sexual relations. The background of widespread interracial sex on the island poses the question whether the increased prominence of the potentially virtuous woman in the 1820s in the debate about female slaves' sexuality expressed less permissive attitudes toward this heritage on the part of white men on the island.

Principled proposals to control the sexual behavior of bonded females were advanced especially in the late eighteenth and early nineteenth centuries, when the abolitionist debate peaked. They aimed to encourage monogamous sexual relations among slaves and discourage cross-plantation unions. In 1831, James Simpson, a manager of several plantations owned by absentee planters, declared that both objectives could best be achieved by "locking up and securing the female sex from all intercourse with the male sex at night."[45] His proposal was clearly based on the idea that slave women were naturally promiscuous. Another suggestion was to offer female slaves a reward, such as a small sum of money or a furnished cabin, upon formal marriage; that is, a marriage solemnized by an Anglican minister.[46] It was not the representation of the scheming jezebel or the potentially virtuous companion that underlay this proposal, however, but rather that of a maternal but practical jezebel—that is, a bondswoman who would remain sexually pure but only if she was generously compensated for the exchange of her trade in sexual favors for a responsible life of raising children.

Several proslavery writers felt that these schemes to make slave women cohabit with slave men from their own estates would succeed only if accompanied by measures to curtail the intrusive and disruptive sexual practices of white estate officers. One strategy proposed toward this end, which clearly built on the metropolitan idea that marriage domesticated men's sexual passions, was to employ only married white men as estate officers. However, this would have significantly increased a planter's expenses, as he had to build houses and other facilities to accommodate the wives and children of married employees and had to pay family wages. As the profit margin on sugar, by far Jamaica's most important export commodity, dropped between 1763 and 1782 from 8.9 to 3 percent, it is no surprise that it had become common practice by the late eighteenth century to employ only single men on estates.[47] Planter and historian Edward Long, who advocated the employment of married men as early as 1774, acknowledged that this method to reduce interracial relationships depended on making the few white, single women on the island "more agreeable companions, more frugal, trusty and faithful friends" than such dangerous bondswomen as the "housekeeper."[48] The scheming jezebel who underlay Long's proposal also supported planter James Adair's suggestion to prevent slave women from offering sexual favors to whites under threat of severe punishment.[49]

Moreton, on the other hand, supported his proposal to curb interracial sex with a representation of female slaves otherwise found only in abolitionist discourse, namely that of the innocent victim. He proposed to protect bonded women's "virtue and chastity" through a law that would fine white men, mainly hired estate officers, for having sex with them.[50] Long, Adair, and Moreton, then, all illustrated yet another form of displacement in proslavery writings about slave women's sexuality, namely shifting uncontrolled male sexuality away from virtuous planters on to immoral white estate officers.

It is surprising that so few of these proposals were adopted by individual planters and also that they were not debated extensively in the assembly. Planters were reluctant to adopt marriage reward schemes for their slaves primarily because they perceived formal slave marriage as a threat to their control over their labor forces; formal slave marriage was a contract and thereby gave slaves a legal identity other than exclusive obedience to a single owner, while the promise of husband and wife to protect and obey threatened further to divide the slaves' loyalty.[51] The planters' apparent reluctance to act legally to combat interracial sex made Jamaican slave society stand out from the slave societies on the North American mainland.[52]

By the early eighteenth century practically all the colonies in North America had adopted laws that discouraged sexual relations between whites and blacks. Virginia was the first to do so. In 1662 it made "fornication with a negro man or woman" a crime punishable by a fine. Thirty years later, it issued a law that made interracial marriage illegal by banishing the white partner from the colony.[53] This sequence of legislation was supported by social practice. Kirsten Fischer's recent examination of slander suits in North Carolina indicates, for instance, that local gossip about casual sexual relations with bondswomen could severely compromise a white man's sexual reputation.[54]

The majority of the white Jamaican population, by contrast, did not frown on white men, married or single, who had casual or long-term sexual relations with female slaves. For instance, in 1823 former resident John Stewart remarked that "every unmarried man, of every class, has his black or brown mistress, with whom he lives openly" and that "his white female friends and relations think it no breach of decorum to visit his house."[55] Moreover, the assembly never banned interracial marriage nor did it, unlike the North American colonies and some other Caribbean islands, adopt laws that fined white men for having sex with slave women. The only act inhibiting interracial sexual relations passed by the assembly was the death sentence for the rape of bondswomen, introduced in 1826. This measure was a radical prohibition, as no other New World slave society of the time had legal codes that made the rape of slave women a crime.[56] Not a single white man ever appeared in court under the terms of this act, but this judicial silence should not be seen as an indication that it succeeded in discouraging interracial sex. Rather the absence of complaints reflects the complicated and intimidating process that the act imposed on slave women to have a white man convicted under its terms. Whites accused of abusing slaves in other ways were usually acquitted in colonial courts, and the responsibility imposed on the complainant also exposed the violated female slave to the risk of corporal punishment by local justices if her allegations were not proven.

The 1826 rape act was not a response to calls to criminalize interracial sex in order to limit the growth of the freed population but rather a device to please the abolitionists and the government at home. In May 1823, as a result of abolitionist campaigning, the House of Commons in

London had adopted a set of resolutions intended to ameliorate the condition of slaves in the West Indies in preparation for abolition. These included a proposal to admit slave testimony in courts of law, a program to encourage religious instruction and marriage, and a ban on flogging females.[57] The assembly declined when asked in November 1823 to enact these proposals for local implementation, because it saw them as a step toward imminent emancipation.[58] Instead it passed the 1826 rape act to convince the London government that Jamaican planters were willing to improve the condition of the slaves and thus ward off future interference in their affairs. The act simultaneously was meant to deny the abolitionist emphasis on the planters' inhumane conduct toward their slave women.

The relaxed attitude of the Jamaican planting class toward interracial sex becomes even more puzzling given the threats to their socioeconomic status, which their North American counterparts did not experience and which were exacerbated by interracial sex. Two reasons seem to explain why planters did not actively try, either in the assembly or on their plantations, to curb interracial sex. Studies on the regulation of interracial sex in colonial North America have shown that the criminalization of interracial sex was strongly linked to a leveling of sex ratios among the white population. For example, in 1625 there were four white men to every white woman in Virginia. In 1662, when the colony passed its ban on interracial marriage, men made up only 60 percent of the total white population.[59] The balancing of sex ratios among whites was accompanied by a rise in the social and familial status of white women, which enabled a wife to keep any liaisons between her husband and black slaves out of public notice and allowed her to refuse to accept possible offspring of these discreet, or hidden, unions.[60]

Throughout the period under discussion, there were about four men to every one white woman in Jamaica.[61] This low ratio of white women provided, along with the significant (40 percent and more) numbers of females among the huge slave majorities, the demographic opportunity for interracial unions. It also worked against the development of cultural mores against interracial sex, a task deemed most suitable for women because of their supposed moral superiority, and left most white men on the island without one of the most powerful cultural constraints on their alleged powerful sexual energy: marriage. Recent studies of white Jamaican society during slavery have shown that while their metropolitan counterparts increasingly began to control their sexual passions, many white Jamaican men continued to adhere to the interlinked ideas that it was essential to release the male libido in unrestrained relations with the other sex, because it was a powerful and otherwise potentially destructive natural force, and that sexual prowess was the main test of manhood.[62] This increasingly anachronistic faith in their own animality combined with the paucity of white women largely explains why the planters in the Jamaican assembly did not legislate against their own sexual liaisons with bondswomen.

A second and more important reason for the planters' disinclination to tackle interracial sex is that it brought short-term economic benefits to their estates. First, it enabled them to increase their labor force at no extra cost through the offspring of their own or their employees' sexual unions with slave women, because children took the enslaved status of the mother. After 1807 this economic consideration became an important reason for not acting against interracial sex. Second, tolerating white estate officers' sexual liberties with female slaves could serve as a means to keep them on the estate at a time when white employees were in short supply.[63] Third, interracial sex helped planters control their labor forces, since forced interracial sex, even more than flogging, demonstrated to bondswomen that the planter's power (and that of his officers) was absolute. Consensual sex with housekeepers, on the other hand, enhanced the stability of the estates as the jobs, clothing, housing, and other gifts bestowed on these women and their colored children set them apart from the rest of the slave community and thus enlarged the divisions within the slave community.

The proslavery debate about slave women's sexuality did not much affect sexual practices between white Jamaican men and bondswomen. Most white men did not internalize the idea that gained prominence in the 1820s that female slaves could be as virtuous as white women, and they continued to force bonded women into having sex with them. The yawning gap between word and deed suggests that we should read the local residents' discussion about slave women's sexuality, like that of the metropolitan writers, as a displacement of other political and cultural concerns. The ongoing discussion served first to allay residents' fears about the failure of the slave regime due to a growing free population, abolitionist attacks on their slave management and masculinity, declining profits, and, as suggested in Hamel, potential slave revolt. Second, it served to shift responsibility for these political, social, and economic threats away from the residents themselves. It is possible that for some local planters, writing about female slaves' sexuality served as a substitute for real sex with bondswomen and thus as a means to live up to the metropolitan norm of male sexual restraint in deed, if not in fantasy. For most resident planters, however, sex with the women they enslaved remained a more important means to displace their fears about the future of their enterprises than writing about it.

It can be argued that sex with bondswomen also served as a form of displacement for white estate officers. Considering that many men at the time continued to regard sexual prowess as a key marker of masculinity, these local whites, whom the planters dismissed as lesser men, may have had forced sex with slave women to counteract this demeaning treatment. The proslavery writers' displacement of fear, blame, and aggression thus functioned at multiple, powerful levels, each of which served to overcome a sense of threatened masculinity at slave women's expense. That they singled out female slaves for this purpose is not surprising, as it is often an available, vulnerable person with noticeable differences who is chosen as the object of displaced fears and aggression.[64] Moreover, because of their gender, and assumptions about female docility, slave women were regarded as less likely than slave men to resist abuse.

Considering the multiple purposes served by the scheming jezebel, it is no surprise that this image did not subside with the appearance of the potentially virtuous slave woman in the 1820s. These contradictory images of bondswomen coexisted in proslavery discourse throughout the 1820s and early 1830s because proslavery writers had different ideas about how to avert abolitionist attacks and were also located in different political settings. Although Jamaican writers resorted more to the scheming jezebel and metropolitan writers more to the potentially virtuous woman, it needs to be stressed that some writers, including Moreton and Cynric Williams, relied on both, sometimes even within the space of one work. This ambivalence illustrates most clearly the contradictory nature of proslavery discourse.

However, not only was proslavery discourse on the island changing, complex, and contradictory but it also engaged with broader metropolitan discourses on gender, race, and sexuality. Proslavery writers used the discourse of white female sexual restraint as the yardstick against which they contrasted slave women's sexual aggressiveness. Both extremes of the proslavery representations of female slaves' sexuality, jezebel and the virtuous housekeeper, however, also helped shape the metropolitan discourse on sexuality. The construction of the naturally passionless white woman in the late eighteenth century was made possible by displacing female sexual aggression to women defined as other. As Sander Gilman has shown, by the turn of the century not only the white prostitute but also the scheming black jezebel served this purpose.[65]

The two images helped furthermore to vitalize the metropolitan discourse on race by sexualizing it; that is, they helped make sexual deviance one of the key characteristics defining the inferiority of people of African descent. These two complementing processes—the racialization of sex and the sexualization of race—have not yet relinquished the power they gained then over British and North American fantasies of domination, sexual or—it may be suggested—military. Various studies have pointed out, for instance, that black women in Africa and the diaspora are still regarded as naturally promiscuous and immoral and as a result suffer rape and other forms of sexual abuse by both white and black men.[66] Accounts of the spread of HIV in Africa, furthermore, link sexual excess and racial inferiority in the minds of contemporary politicians, journalists, and even scientists as firmly as they did in the minds of the proslavery writers.[67]

Although proslavery representations of bondswomen's sexuality shaped metropolitan discourses on gender, race, and sex in profound and lasting ways, even more intense were the overwhelmingly negative effects they exerted on Jamaican slave women, the convenient objects of the male fantasies that formed the modern world. The sexual abuse that underpinned these representations, however, led not only slave women but also slave men to perceive the planters' power as absolute. The sexual abuse of female slaves was thus critical to the maintenance of slavery itself, while bonded women's misrepresented sexuality was a specific female extension of modern slavery's pervasive misrepresentation of human beings as property.

NOTES

1. Winthrop Jordan, *White over Black: American Attitudes toward the Negro, 1550–1812* (Chapel Hill: University of North Carolina Press, 1968).

2. See, for instance, Angela Y. Davis, *Women, Race, and Class* (New York: Random House, 1981); Deborah G. White, *Ar'n't I a Woman?: Female Slaves in the Plantation South* (New York: Norton, 1985).

3. Michel Foucault, *The History of Sexuality*, vol. 1, *An Introduction* (Harmondsworth: Penguin, 1990), 106.

4. See Rhoda E. Reddock, "Women and Slavery in the Caribbean: A Feminist Perspective," *Latin American Perspectives* 12, no. 1 (1985): 63–80; Hilary McD. Beckles, *Natural Rebels: A Social History of Enslaved Black Women in Barbados* (London: Zed Books, 1989); Barbara Bush, *Slave Women in Caribbean Society, 1650–1838* (London: James Currey, 1990); Marietta Morrissey, *Slave Women in the New World: Gender Stratification in the Caribbean* (Lawrence: University Press of Kansas, 1989).

5. See Hilary McD. Beckles, "Female Enslavement and Gender Ideologies in the Caribbean," in *Identity in the Shadow of Slavery*, ed. Paul E. Lovejoy (London: Continuum, 2000), 163–82; Verene A. Shepherd, "Gender and Representation in European Accounts of Pre-emancipation Jamaica," in *Caribbean Slavery in the Atlantic World: A Student Reader*, ed. Verene A. Shepherd and Hilary McD. Beckles (London, James Currey, 2000), 702–12; Barbara Bush, "'Sable Venus,' 'She Devil' or 'Drudge'?: British Slavery and the 'Fabulous Fiction' of Black Women's Identities, c. 1650–1838," *Women's History Review* 9, no. 4 (2000): 761–89.

The representation of slave women as scheming jezebels was not confined to North America and the anglophone Caribbean. See, for instance, John Garrigus, "Race, Gender, and Virtue in Haiti's Failed Foundational Fiction: La Mulâtre comme il y a Peu de Blanches," in *The Color of Liberty: Histories of Race in France*, ed. Sue Peabody and Tyler Stovall (Durham: Duke University Press, 2003), 73–94. Today, the scheming jezebel is one of the main dominant white interpretations of black female sexuality. On the impact of this image on the sexual lives of black women, see Patricia Hill Collins, *Black Feminist Thought: Knowledge, Consciousness, and the Politics of Empowerment* (New York: Routledge, 1991), ch. 4.

6. Metropolitan defenders of slavery included plantation owners, merchants, former estate officers, and also men and women who had no direct interest in the plantations but were convinced that Britain's prosperity depended on slavery.

7. Although not abundant, there is evidence that slave men had sexual relations with white women, especially lower-class white women. See, for instance, Trevor Burnard, "'A Matron in Rank, a Prostitute in Manners': The Manning Divorce of 1741 and Class, Race and the Law in Eighteenth-Century Jamaica," in *Working Slavery, Pricing Freedom: Perspectives from the Caribbean, Africa and the African Diaspora*, ed. Verene A. Shepherd (Kingston: Ian Randle, 2002), 133–52.

8. On this new norm of sexuality, see Jeffrey Weeks, *Sex, Politics and Society: The Regulation of Sexuality since 1800*, 2nd ed. (London: Longman, 1993).

9. Tim Hitchcock, *English Sexualities, 1700–1800* (Basingstoke: Macmillan, 1997), 100, 108; John Tosh, *A Man's Place: Masculinity and the Middle-Class Home in Victorian England* (New Haven: Yale University Press, 1999), 45–46.

10. G. J. Barker-Benfield, *The Culture of Sensibility: Sex and Society in Eighteenth-Century Britain* (Chicago: University of Chicago Press, 1992), 325–47, 366–73; Leonore Davidoff and Catherine Hall, *Family Fortunes: Men and Women of the English Middle Class, 1780–1850* (London: Routledge, 1992), 401–3.

11. Bryan Edwards, *The History, Civil and Commercial, of the British Colonies in the West Indies*, 2 vols. (London, 1793), 1:80.

12. Anon., *Marly; or, a Planter's Life in Jamaica* (Glasgow, 1828), 133.

13. See, for instance, Jesse Foot, *Observations Principally upon the Speech of Mr. Wilberforce . . .* (London, 1805), 96; [J. Stewart], *An Account of Jamaica, and Its Inhabitants . . .* (London, 1808), 276.

14. [Anthony Davis], *The West Indies* (London, 1832), 26.

15. J. B. Moreton, *West India Customs and Manners* (London, 1793), 160. For similar remarks, see Hector McNeill, *Observations on the Treatment of Negroes in the Island of Jamaica* (London, 1788), 41; Maria, Lady Nugent, *Lady Nugent's Journal: Jamaica*

One Hundred Years Ago Reprinted from a Journal kept by Maria, Lady Nugent, from 1801 to 1815, ed. Frank Cundall (London: Published for the Institute of Jamaica by Adam & C. Black, 1907), 118.

16. The term *colored* refers here not only to offspring of black-white unions but to all mixed offspring.

17. Matthew Gregory Lewis, *Journal of a West India Proprietor, kept during a residence in the island of Jamaica* (London, 1834), 78; Moreton, *West India Customs*, 77; McNeill, *Treatment of Negroes*, 41; Nugent, *Journal*, 40.

18. Barry W. Higman, *Slave Population and Economy in Jamaica, 1807–1834* (Cambridge: Cambridge University Press, 1976), 139–53: Higman, *Slave Populations of the British Caribbean, 1807–1834* (Baltimore: Johns Hopkins University Press, 1984), 147–48.

19. This calculation is based on the assumption of a 50/50 sex ratio and a 30/70 child/adult ratio in the white population. Figures for the white and slave populations are from 1820. Robert W. Fogel and Stanley L. Engerman, *Time on the Cross: The Economics of American Negro Slavery* (Boston: Little, Brown, 1974), 132; Joe William Trotter Jr., *The African American Experience*, vol. 1 (Boston: Houghton Mifflin, 2001), app. 13. The fertile female slave/white adult male ratio also supports the idea of a higher incidence of interracial sex in Jamaica than on the North American mainland. In Jamaica there were 3.6 fertile slave women to one white adult male, whereas in North America there were only 0.19.

20. See, for instance, [Stewart], *Jamaica and Its Inhabitants*, 200.

21. Gad Heuman, "The Social Structure of the Slave Societies in the Caribbean," in *The Slave Societies of the Caribbean*, vol. 3 of *General History of the Caribbean*, ed. Franklin W. Knight (Basingstoke: Macmillan, 1997), 138–68.

22. Nugent, *Journal*, 118; McNeil, *Treatment of Negroes*, 42; [Stewart], *Jamaica and Its Inhabitants*, 200.

23. Ibid.; Moreton, *West India Customs*, 77.

24. See Gad Heuman, *Between Black and White: Race, Politics, and the Free Coloreds in Jamaica 1792–1865* (Oxford: Clio, 1981), 6, 28; Christer Petley, "Boundaries of Rule, Ties of Dependency: Jamaican Planters, Local Society and the Metropole, 1800–1834" (PhD diss., University of Warwick, 2003), ch. 7; Trevor Burnard, *Mastery, Tyranny, and Desire: Thomas Thistlewood and His Slaves in the Anglo-Jamaican World* (Chapel Hill: University of North Carolina Press, 2004), ch. 7.

25. See, for example, James McQueen, *The West India Colonies: The Calumnies and Misrepresentations Circulated against Them by the Edinburgh Review* (London, 1824), 230–33; Alexander Barclay, *A Practical View of the Present State of Slavery in the West Indies* (London, 1827), 100.

26. A Resident, *Sketches and Recollections of the West Indies* (London, 1828), 231.

27. [Davis], *The West Indies*, 70.

28. Cynric Williams, *Tour through the Island of Jamaica from the Western to the Eastern End in 1823* (London, 1827), 56, 310.

29. Higman, *Slave Populations of the British Caribbean*, 380–84.

30. Heuman, *Between Black and White*, chs. 2–3; Robin Blackburn, *The Overthrow of Colonial Slavery, 1776–1848* (London: Verso, 1988), 424–26.

31. The law was enacted in 1733. Higman, *Slave Populations of the British Caribbean,* 147.

32. Edward Brathwaite, *The Development of Creole Society in Jamaica, 1770–1820* (Oxford: Clarendon, 1971), 167.

33. *Westminster Review,* April 1827, 445.

34. *Hamel, the Obeah Man,* 2 vols. (London: Hunt and Clarke, 1827), 1:77.

35. Ibid., 193; emphasis added.

36. *Westminster Review,* April 1827, 460.

37. *Hamel,* 195–96.

38. Patricia Mohammed, "'But Most of All Mi Love Me Browning': The Emergence in Eighteenth and Nineteenth Jamaica of the Mulatto Woman as Desired," *Feminist Review* 65 (2000): 43.

39. *Hamel,* 83–88; emphasis added.

40. Moreton, *West India Customs,* 154.

41. The proslavery writers' six-caste hierarchy was one of several attempts at the time to theorize the differences between human beings based on visible and invisible signs. As Roxann Wheeler has shown, many metropolitan men and women continued to rank human beings on the basis of older criteria, such as Christianity, civility and rank. Wheeler, *The Complexion of Race: Categories of Difference in Eighteenth-Century British Culture* (Philadelphia: University of Pennsylvania Press, 2000). By the mid-nineteenth century, however, these older theories were no longer in use and theories that explained human variety in terms of race drew increasingly upon science to explain and justify race hierarchies. It could be argued that the growth of the free coloreds in the 1820s sped up the process in white Jamaican society of regarding skin color as the most important marker of racial identity.

42. See, for example, Karen Binhammer, "The Sex Panic of the 1790s," *Journal of the History of Sexuality* 6, no. 3 (1996): 409–34.

43. Sonya O. Rose, "Cultural Analysis and Moral Discourses: Episodes, Continuities, and Transformations," in *Beyond the Cultural Turn: New Directions in the Study of Culture and Society,* ed. Victoria E. Bonnell and Lynn Hunt (Berkeley: University of California Press, 1999), 217–38.

44. The planter kept a diary for thirty-seven years in which he recorded 3,852 acts of sexual intercourse with 138 slave women. A significant number of these acts were forced and served as punishment. See Burnard, *Mastery, Tyranny,* 156–60.

45. As mentioned in his statement before the 1832 Select Committee on the Extinction of Slavery. *Parliamentary Papers* (hereafter, *PP*), 1831–32, vol. 20, 393.

46. See, for example, James M. Adair, *Unanswerable Arguments against the Abolition of the Slave Trade* (London: 1790), 161. Nonconformist marriages exceeded formal marriages in number but, as in the mother country at the time, were not legally recognized.

47. John R. Ward, "The Profitability of Sugar Planting in the British West Indies, 1650–1834," *Economic History Review* 31, no. 2 (1978): 197–213.

48. Edward Long, *The History of Jamaica* (London, 1774), 330.

49. Adair, *Unanswerable Arguments,* 161.

50. Moreton, *West India Customs,* 155.

51. See Henrice Altink, *Representations of Slave Women in Discourses on Slavery and Abolition, 1780-1838* (New York: Routledge, 2007), ch. 4.

52. For a good overview of the regulation of interracial sex in colonial America, see A. Leon Higginbotham Jr. and Barbara Kopytoff, "Racial Purity and Interracial Sex in the Law of Colonial and Antebellum Virginia," *Georgetown Law Journal* 77, no. 6 (1989): 1967–2029.

53. Paul Finkelman, "Crimes of Love, Misdemeanors of Passion: The Regulation of Race and Sex in the Colonial South," in *The Devil's Lane: Sex and Race in the Early South*, ed. Catherine Clinton and Michele Gillespie (New York: Oxford University Press, 1997), 127–31. The Virginia laws criminalized both sexual relations between whites and blacks and those between whites and Native Americans. These laws, like those in other colonies, aimed primarily at preventing the sexual pollution of white women.

54. Kirsten Fischer, *Suspect Relations: Sex, Race, and Resistance in Colonial North Carolina* (Ithaca: Cornell University Press, 2002), 149–55. For similar accounts see Joshua D. Rothman, *Notorious in the Neighborhood: Sex and Families across the Color Line in Virginia, 1787–1861* (Chapel Hill: University of North Carolina Press, 2003); Laura F. Edwards, "Enslaved Women and the Law: Paradoxes of Subordination in the Post-revolutionary Carolinas," *Slavery and Abolition* 26, no. 2 (2005): 305–26 (reprinted, slightly edited, in this volume).

55. J. Stewart, *A View of the Past and Present State of the Island of Jamaica* (Edinburgh, 1823), 173.

56. In some societies, such as Brazil, sexual abuse could be invoked in claims for manumission. Slave women in these societies, then, had some means of legal redress in case of abuse. See, for instance, Keila Grinberg, "Freedom Suits and Civil Law in Brazil and the United States," *Slavery and Abolition* 22, no. 2 (2001): 55–82; Alejandro de la Fuente, "Slave Law and Claims-Making in Cuba: The Tannenbaum Debate Revisited," *Law and History Review* 22, no. 2 (2004): 339–70.

57. Blackburn, *Overthrow*, 422.

58. *PP* 1824, vol. 24, 427, 452.

59. Finkelman, "Crimes of Love," 127–31.

60. See, for example, Carl N. Degler, *Neither Black nor White: Slavery and Race Relations in Brazil and the United States* (New York: Macmillan, 1971), 238–39.

61. This estimate of the white sex ratio is based on parish records from the late eighteenth and early nineteenth centuries and provided to me by Christer Petley.

62. Burnard, *Mastery, Tyranny*, ch. 3; Petley, "Boundaries of Rule," ch. 7. Recent studies on early modern masculinity have argued that sexual control of women was key to manhood. See, for example, Alexandra Shepard, *Meanings of Manhood in Early Modern England* (Oxford: Oxford University Press, 2003).

63. The estate Worthy Park, for example, employed a total of eighty-five officers between 1783 and 1796. Since there were usually between five and ten whites on an estate at any one time, this suggests a very rapid turnover. Heuman, "Social Structure," 154.

64. For a good introduction to displacement theories, see Tom Douglas, *Scapegoats: Transferring Blame* (London: Routledge, 1995). Their role in the reproduction

230   HENRICE ALTINK

of the slave labor force and the growth of the freed colored population—two major
fears of the proslavery writers—explains of course also why proslavery writers singled
out slave women rather than slave men. This chapter, then, supports the thesis in
Hilary McD. Beckles's *Centering Woman: Gender Discourses in Caribbean Slave Society*
(Kingston: Ian Randle Publishers, 1999) that slave women were central to the discourses on slavery and abolition in the late eighteenth and early nineteenth centuries.

65. Sander Gilman, *Difference and Pathology: Stereotypes of Sexuality, Race and
Madness* (Ithaca: Cornell University Press, 1985).

66. See, for example, Davis, *Women, Race*; Barbara Bush, "History, Memory,
Myth? Reconstructing the History (or Histories) of Black Women in the African Diaspora," in *Images of African and Caribbean Women: Migration, Displacement, Diaspora*, ed. S. Newell (Stirling, Scotland: Centre of Commonwealth Studies, University of Stirling, 1996), 3–28.

67. See, for example, David Spurr, *The Rhetoric of Empire: Colonial Discourse in
Journalism, Travel Writing, and Imperial Administration* (Durham: Duke University
Press, 1996), ch. 5.

10

THE CONDITION OF THE MOTHER

*The Legacy of Slavery in African American Literature
of the Jim Crow Era*

FELIPE SMITH

A public discourse about the dangers of "hidden blackness" influenced much of the legislation that reduced African Americans to second-class citizenship within a few decades after emancipation. The existence of many individuals thus defined as being of mixed race, but who were physically indistinguishable from relatives defined as white, caused many to feel that the future of America as a "white" Western nation was threatened if enough of these suspected hidden hybrids could evade the barriers of race then being erected and pass as white. According to Joel Williamson, when the rates of mulattoes among both slave and free nonwhite populations began to mushroom just before the Civil War, the convention that any traceable amount of black blood made the individual "all black" developed among whites distrustful of the allegiance and good intentions of "racially mixed" people.[1] From the mid-nineteenth century on, pioneers in the pseudosciences of essentialized racial difference also began to warn that intermarriage would destroy the very fabric of American civilization.[2]

A new definition of race, the so-called one-drop rule, thus crept into common usage and challenged the efficacy of existing laws that classified individuals' race according to a maximum fraction of black blood allowable to be considered as white. As early as 1865, but accelerating throughout the former slave states, beginning in the first decade of the twentieth century, this one-drop definition of race became encoded into restrictions on interracial contact of any sort in public accommodations, in educational opportunity, in voting privileges, and particularly through interracial marriage.[3] The aim was to quarantine African Americans so as not to "pollute" the public and private spheres where pure "white" Americans conducted their lives.[4]

That the very presence of African Americans was potentially polluting was the manifest message of this late-nineteenth-century race hysteria. Consider the hyperbolic language of this anecdote about the tragic discovery made by two Virginia newlyweds: "At the end of a year a boy child is born to them, but, horror of horrors, it is found to be as black as coal, and with hair as kinky as the veriest young Congo that a negress of that race ever gave birth to in Africa. . . . [H]er first child was simply a reversion to the black ancestry on her maternal side, and had inherited the Ethiopian characters, and among them the black skin and kinky hair."[5]

What drove this obsession with the unseen single drop of black blood was fear of a reversion in some succeeding generation to an atavistic, primordial African phenotype antithetical to the aesthetic ideals and intellectual requirements of the modern, industrialized democracy that white Americans saw themselves becoming. According to Thomas Dixon Jr., author of the racist novels on which the Ku Klux Klan propaganda film *Birth of a Nation* was based, "One drop of negro blood makes a negro. It kinks the hair, flattens the nose, thickens the lip, puts out the light of intellect, and lights the fires of brutal passions. The beginning of negro equality as a vital fact is the beginning of the end of this nation's life. There is enough negro blood here to make mulatto the whole Republic."[6]

Dixon's language pointed horrifically to full citizenship for African Americans as the beginning of the causal chain that would end with the destruction of America. Dixon and others, despite advocating Jim Crow quarantine statutes based on one-drop definitions of racial caste status as a first step in the removal of African Americans from national life, felt that utter extermination or at least expulsion would ultimately become necessary to save the republic from the otherwise fatal consequences of its broad promises of rights and freedoms.[7]

Beyond the obvious aversion to the African blood flowing in the veins of the American body politic, note that in the example of the Virginia couple quoted above, the source of racial pollution is the mother. This focus on the maternal sources of the stain of blackness harks back to the beginnings of racial classifications in the colonies, where definitions of slavery and race as maternally inherited had set the newlyweds' dilemma in motion. Maternal descent trumped paternity as a source of identity, and for slaves alone, as absolutely as the polluted African blood thus conveyed disabled the offspring. In the aftermath of slavery, many states and localities enacted laws using race to define differential access to citizenship privileges and public spaces (e.g., public conveyances and accommodations, commercial and entertainment venues, religious and educational

institutions) and giving the force of law to previously informal rules of social preference toward white citizens. This system, familiarly referred to
as Jim Crow segregation, reinscribed an inferior social status for recently
freed citizens of African descent that, at its worst, replicated slavery's
forced labor and physical violence, and, at its least intrusive, circumscribed their freedom of movement.[8] Through Jim Crow segregation, the
language and logic of the earliest attempts to define slave status through
the "condition of the mother" survived into the era of freedom—indeed
thrived tragically. Thus, Jim Crow discrimination represented a de facto
return to a hereditary caste system based in slavery's racial coding of the
populace. In the face of overwhelming white popular support for this
movement and its attendant race mythology, African American writers
Pauline E. Hopkins and Charles W. Chesnutt constructed thoughtful fictions examining the social consequences of racial identity (including the
denial of citizenship rights and entitlements) conferred by matrilineal
descent for African Americans.

Hopkins and Chesnutt dramatized and criticized public panic about the
polluting effects of "one drop of black blood" as the "return" of an original African (slave) mother to reclaim her unsuspecting progeny into Jim
Crow's confinement, virtually a return to slavery itself in the exclusion
and isolation that it brought. These African American writers invoked
this motif of the inopportune return to the despised racial caste identity
of the mother to explore the tragedies of the ethical crises of African
Americans coming to terms with racial and national identities often depicted as being in conflict. Central to their narratives were the dilemmas
of biracial African Americans, many of whom by education and occupation belonged to the relatively comfortable group that W. E. B. Du Bois
described as the talented tenth, and who experienced overwhelming
temptation to withdraw from affiliation with darker counterparts increasingly reduced to the "natal alienation" and the "social death" of
slavery that Jim Crow's designers had intended.[9]

Hopkins and Chesnutt and writers like them transformed the trope of
the African mother's return from condemnation to a despised social status into a moment of unambiguous embrace of black identity, racial
pride, and race agency on the parts of previously ambivalent mulatto he-
roes and heroines. They thus inaugurated one of the earliest tropes of
modern African American literature: affirmation of pride in an imposed
identity designed to shame African Americans as heirs to slavery. In the
process they transformed the very meaning of slavery from a badge of
dishonor, which disqualified African Americans from full participation

in the national society, into certification of the virtues that had enabled group survival through the centuries of slavery's "social death" and that would subsequently affirm and strengthen the generations of African Americans to come.

THE CONDITION OF THE MOTHER

The background as to why mothers figured crucially in scenes in which racially ambiguous individuals were unmasked as "black" goes back to the earliest slave statutes in Virginia. In 1662, the Virginia colony enacted a statute of *partus sequitur ventrem* to address the difficulty of assigning places to the offspring of unions between black and white, already well on the road to being taken presumptively as slave and free, in a rigidifying and increasingly complex society: "Whereas some doubts have arisen whether children got by any Englishman upon a negro should be slave or ffree, . . . all children borne in this country shal be held bond or free only according to the condition of the mother."[10] According to Joel Williamson, the Virginia assembly in 1662 "wrenched itself away from the English rule that the child followed the status of its father" in an attempt to clarify the social identity of the growing number of mixed-race children in the colony through enslavement.[11]

The full import of exclusion eternally over the generations that this partus sequitur ventrem language established comes through in a review of the earliest stages in the definition of slavery in the North American colonies. For example, in 1652, William Whittington had sold to John Pott "one Negro girle named Jowan; aged about Ten yeares *and with her Issue and produce duringe her (or either of them) for their Life tyme. And their Successors forever.*"[12] These chilling lines stipulated with ominous finality female reproductivity as both a contractual commodity and a legal basis for proprietary claims to the future fecundity of all offspring of the female slave child until the exhaustion of the maternal line. Ownership of the black womb enabled the Virginia colonials to freeze the condition of the mother into a permanent and utterly unambiguous racial space: all black wombs were forever collapsed into one primordial mother, passing her original enslavement on in perpetuity, without regard to the status of the fathers of their children. White men were correspondingly forever relieved of acknowledging or caring for their now legally black progeny.

One famous contributor to the ignoble Virginia tradition of stalking the descent lines of African American women was Thomas Jefferson, who worried about the dangers of emancipation and subsequent racial intermarriage on the grounds that black women were physically repulsive even to black men and that African women had mated with apes.[13] Another in that line of Virginia scholar-aristocrats, an influential post–Civil War historian of Southern race relations, Philip Alexander Bruce, used his family's huge Virginia plantation as a laboratory for observing what he described as the "evolutionary regression" of emancipated blacks. According to Bruce, the new opportunities promised by emancipation had not lessened the probability of black regression into savagery; emancipation had made their prospects worse by removing the former slaves from the "civilizing" influences of slavery. Bruce felt that degeneration was particularly true of black women, who, he claimed, were dramatically regressing in physical character since the end of slavery due to their decreasing sexual contact with white men. "Into this class, all the females of the race are slowly merging, which fact, when fully accomplished, will produce an unpleasing appearance and temper that will be universal."[14]

What was scandalous in all the pseudoscientific race theory that shaped national laws for more than a century is the way that scholar-racists like Jefferson and Bruce based their radical schemes of expulsion or enslavement of African Americans on aesthetic and moral disparagement of black women's bodies. Discounting the question of Jefferson's relationship with Sally Hemings, both Jefferson and Bruce as historians of Virginia had to have known (and therefore had to have suppressed the information) that their own state's laws regulating the condition of the mother were irrefutable evidence that there had never been a time in American history when African women had been too hideous to attract the amorous attentions of white men.

If one drop of black blood could spawn an "atavistic, regressive, pure African" offspring, then neither the womb of the original black slave mother, the source of that one drop, nor the social identity associated with it, could ever be escaped. The "atavistic" child was the essence of that original slave mother, prone to unending and innumerable returns to reclaim mixed-race individuals into the descent line reaching back to "mother" Africa, the material manifestation of the legal fiction that blacks were unfit for civilization. Marital unions involving any racial hybrid were thus haunted by the aesthetic and moral stigma of an "original African slave mother," lurking like a biological time bomb in the mythical and inescapable one drop. Black writers like Hopkins and Chesnutt, in keeping with their intervention into this late-nineteenth-century discourse of race, and consistent with the developing literature of America's otherwise multiethnic melting pot, sought to recast the racial hybrid from

Dixon's image of the diseased American body politic into a model of a utopian comprehensively ethnically inclusive future.

THE MOTHER'S RETURN IN CHARLES W. CHESNUTT

The African American woman's experience during and after slavery caught the imagination of black authors of both genders in the 1890s. Already, slave narratives like Harriet Jacobs's *Incidents in the Life of a Slave Girl* (written as Linda Brent, 1861) and Elizabeth Keckley's *Behind the Scenes; or, Thirty Years a Slave and Four Years in The White House* (1868), and novels like William Wells Brown's *Clotel; or, The President's Daughter* (1853) (based loosely on rumors of Thomas Jefferson's paternity of slave children) and Harriet Wilson's *Our Nig; or, Sketches from the Life of a Free Black, in a Two-Story White House, North* (1859) had educated earlier generations about the dilemmas of women in slavery and the precarious nature of emancipated life for freed women. By the turn of the century, black authors had tapped into late Victorian angst about women's social condition and, encouraged by the growth of an educated African American middle class in the North, had begun to reflect the concerns of the women's movements battling the moral, social, and educational legacies of slavery. Nearly forty years after Brown's *Clotel* had dramatized the tragic fate of a slave-born daughter of President Jefferson, imprisoned in a slave pen symbolically positioned between the Capitol and the White House,[15] Frances E. Watkins Harper's *Iola Leroy* (1892) refashioned the "tragic mulatta" heroine from victim of social injustice to social activist. Harper depicted the educated freed woman as missionary teacher in the American South, as indeed many graduates of the newly created colleges and normal school for the education of African Americans had become.[16] Harper gave added emphasis to the ideal of racial uplift by making Iola's choice of a black identity an entirely voluntary one achieved through the sacrifice of the greater social rewards her white appearance afforded.

Charles W. Chesnutt's stories and novels of the "color line" continued this trend of probing the drama of slavery's tangled genealogies in an era increasingly paranoid about establishing clear racial boundaries. Born in 1858 of free persons of color from North Carolina, both of whose grandmothers were of mixed race, and whose grandfathers were probably white, Chesnutt fantasized as an adolescent about identifying as white but opted instead to live as African American. He worked in postwar North Carolina in his twenties as the principal of the State Colored Normal School in Fayetteville but later settled in Cleveland, Ohio, establishing himself as a stenographer and as a local-colorist author of some repute.[17] In his 1899 story "Her Virginia Mammy," Chesnutt uses a black mother figure to illustrate the stigma of African descent in color-line politics. Faced with a decision about whether or not to marry the suggestively named John Winthrop (who of course can trace his ancestry back to the *Mayflower*), Clara Hohlfelder withholds her consent until she can ascertain that her status as "Miss Nobody, from Nowhere" will do no harm to John's elevated social standing. The "Virginia mammy" who returns into Clara's life at this crucial moment of anticipating progeny of her own and who provides the links to Clara's past is, of course, her real mother, though Clara's adoption by a German immigrant couple has secured for Clara herself a respectable place in the white world.

The mammy, who calls herself Mrs. Harper, gambles that she can settle Clara's nagging doubts about her worthiness to marry Winthrop by speaking out as an authority on Clara's respectable background, without revealing Clara's maternal African descent. She assures Clara of the social acceptability of her white relations (they turn out to have been a landed Virginia clan known as the Staffords), while withholding information about the slave condition of her mother, Mary Fairfax, saying only that Mary "*belonged* to one of the first families of Virginia [FFV], and in her veins flowed some of the best blood of the Old Dominion."[18] When Clara attempts to tell her intended that her fears of some disreputable past that might becloud her matrimonial happiness have proved unfounded, John sees what she cannot—that the woman she calls her Virginia mammy is in fact her biological mother. What Clara takes as a sign of her elevation to John's social plane—her FFV mammy now more than a match for his *Mayflower* antecedents—John sees more accurately as her profound social liability. Amazingly, Mrs. Harper wordlessly appeals to John not to tell Clara, pleading that it is ultimately Clara and not he who has to be protected from the taint of blackness.

John, aware that Clara's fear of a "dark" family secret that would disqualify her to be his wife is an actuality, must make a decision about how matrimony with a woman of African and slave descent would affect himself and his heirs. Having already rather whimsically boasted that as a sign of his love, he would marry Clara even if she were colored, like her dance students, John makes good on his declaration, agreeing to bestow the Winthrop name upon Clara as a protection against her and society's paranoid obsession with racial ancestry. John's indifference to the stigma of the black slave mother as a potential complication of his children's future reveals, ironically, his "true" aristocrat's self-assurance, a gesture mirroring Clara's father, who had stood firm against his family out of love for Clara's African American mother. As a tangible link to the slave past, Mrs. Harper disguises the condition of the mother behind the euphemistic signifier *mammy,* implicitly reminding white Southerners that even their claims to the social elite derived from their relation to a black mother figure, perhaps also their own black mothers. The story finally turns on the *necessity* of Clara's being kept ignorant of her mother's racial origin in order to preserve her happiness, since we are given every assurance that Clara would never have consciously disavowed her true racial heritage for personal advancement.

In an 1898 short story, "The Wife of His Youth," Chesnutt crosses the racial divide to tell of a "Blue Vein" society of racially mixed but white-appearing African Americans in "Groveland" (Cleveland), whose "custodian of standards" and "preserver of . . . traditions," "Mr. Ryder," comes face to face with a ghost of the past on the night he plans to announce his engagement to Molly Dixon, an attractive young light-complected widow. "Ryder" has changed his name from Sam Taylor and has shed a Southern rural past for a new life in the Northern city, where he becomes the spokesman for the near-white social group determined to preserve its store of Caucasian genetic traits against the day when whites will intermarry with them freely. Ryder's summation of the choices of affiliation facing the Blue Veins certifies that they understand clearly that the newly fashionable one-drop theory of race was aimed at reducing what had been an ambiguous classificatory system into a rigid binarism: "Our fate lies between absorption by the white race and extinction in the black. The one doesn't want us yet, but may take us in time. The other would welcome us, but it would be for us a backward step. . . . [W]e must do the best we can for ourselves and those who are to follow us. Self-preservation is the first law of nature."[19] In order to preserve the advantage of their white racial features in a land that openly reviled bodies with a single drop of black blood, the Blue Veins have tacitly agreed to exclude any dark-skinned people, who would make more likely the feared "backward step" to the original African phenotype. Thus, Ryder's betrothal to the fair-skinned Molly solemnizes Blue Vein endogamy as attempted exorcism of the condition of the mother.

The ghost from the past who arrives to disturb the engagement banquet is 'Liza Jane, the woman who had been Ryder's common-law slave wife in his former incarnation as Sam Taylor, though Sam himself had never been a slave. When 'Liza Jane appears at the door of the house of her long-departed Sam, on the very day of Ryder's betrothal party, she does not recognize Ryder as the man in the picture that she has carried with her for twenty-five years. Even Ryder must examine his face in a mirror to determine if any trace of Sam Taylor remains. Ryder must decide whether to reveal himself to this "wife of his youth" or to ward her off as the toothless black hag that his pretensions have made of her: "she seemed quite old; for her face was crossed and re-crossed with a hundred wrinkles, and around the edges of her bonnet could be seen protruding a tuft of short gray wool. . . . And she was very black,—so black that her toothless gums, revealed when she opened her mouth to speak, were not red, but blue. She looked like a bit of the old plantation life, summoned up from the past by the wave of a magician's wand."[20]

To emphasize the spectral quality of 'Liza, Chesnutt makes her a "blue gum," a "regressive type" credited with the power to poison anyone she bites, as Ryder's affected blue veins have poisoned his relationship with the woman he had once known in her most intimate capacities.[21] As Werner Sollors has pointed out, 'Liza seems more a "mother (or even grandmother) figure"[22] than a spouse for the more youthful-appearing Ryder, who in fact had been younger than 'Liza at the time of their marriage. The collapsing of time through the generations effected by the condition of the mother could not be clearer. 'Liza's motherliness reflects more than just her embodiment of the past. It also signals the condition of the mother repackaged via the one-drop rule that threatens all the Blue Veins with entrapment in the state-defined racial caste system.

Ryder publicly acknowledges 'Liza as the wife of his youth, a choice in favor of ethical obligation to the past, and to himself, over social "mobility and upward drift" toward an imagined future.[23] Ryder does the "right thing" in renouncing his current youthful fiancée for the old hag, who, despite her devotion, has no *legal* claim to Ryder. Principle and self-affirmation thus triumph over the rule of unjust law. Ryder's voluntary embrace of the condition of the mother, for a woman not even the mother of progeny of his, seems on the surface to be a blow to the self-preservationist agenda of the Blue Veins against the ancient claims of the blue gums. But Ryder's act also owes something to the fact that 'Liza was the one who had saved him from being sold into slavery unlawfully. 'Liza thus returns to bring the enslavement that she averted in his past through facilitating his escape, shackling him to the "backward step" of low-caste affiliation.

There is something funereal in Ryder's manner as he introduces 'Liza as his wife, because by renouncing the younger, whiter bride for 'Liza, he has resigned himself to the extinction of his own lineage in her withered womb, against all his instincts for self-preservation. Yet Ryder's renunciation of the fair Molly suggests that his intention to marry her after decades of bachelorhood may have been more the result of an ideological obligation to "preserve" his Caucasian features by mating with a woman "whiter than he, and better educated"[24] than a sign of any deep affection for his intended bride. In making Ryder's choice a decision to "preserve" an ideal of honest self-affirmation less self-interested than mulatto eugenics, and one endorsed by the assembled Blue Vein community in contrasting and guiltily deceptive "white" terms, Chesnutt argues for public certification of the slave mother's virtues, by means of which the "race" has persevered as such, beyond slavery, as the necessary gesture demanded of African American leadership in an era that witnesses the public demonization of African descent.

By contrast, Chesnutt's 1900 novel *The House behind the Cedars* presents yet another male faced with the dilemma of embracing or rejecting the stigma of slavery in the body of a woman. In a morality tale that ends tragically for the offspring of slavery's genetic entanglements, the wellborn white suitor George Tryon, unlike John Winthrop, fails to live up to his boast that he would love Rena Walden even if she were mixed race, like the mulatto servant girl Mimy. When Tryon eventually learns of Rena's African ancestry, "love . . . [gave] place to astonishment and horror."[25] His imagination spurred on by a newspaper article that assured its readers of the latest scientific proof that "the smallest trace of Negro blood would inevitably drag down the superior race," Tryon suffers a nightmare vision revealing Rena's "true" nature: "In all her fair young beauty she stood before him, and then by some hellish magic she was slowly transformed into a hideous black hag. With agonized eyes he watched her beautiful tresses become mere wisps of coarse wool, wrapped around with dingy cotton strings; he saw her clear eyes grow bloodshot, her ivory teeth turn into unwholesome fangs."[26] Poisoned by the lurid images of the one drop transforming Rena into the original slave mother, Tryon abandons her to a fate that predictably ends in death. For Chesnutt, the onus for righting slavery's wrongs to women is on men, both white and African American, as each racial allegory forces on them an individual test of the heart over the prejudices of the popular imagination, the only cure for the stigma and outcast status of slavery's maternal line.

THE MOTHER'S RETURN IN *HAGAR'S DAUGHTER*

Pauline E. Hopkins made no less a substantial contribution than Chesnutt to the literary challenge to the ghost of slavery past (and Jim Crow present) haunting the African American maternal line. A Northern-born writer from a prominent family of both clergymen and musical performers, Hopkins had come of age in postwar Boston, an important crossroads of New England intellectualism and African American social activism. As a playwright and later a fiction writer, Hopkins reflected the inspiration of her childhood encounters with icons of midcentury abolitionism, William Wells Brown and Frederick Douglass, and a broad community devoted to women's uplift.[27] Hopkins's novel *Hagar's Daughter*[28] stages key scenes of racial unmasking as imagined confrontations with the condition of the mother debased by slavery. Hopkins draws on the biblical figure Hagar as the archetypal slave mother—Abraham's concubine through whom the legitimate Hebrew nation cannot be accomplished.[29] Setting much of her story in Washington, D.C., accents the national import of the discovery of hidden blackness in three prominent socialites of the nation's capital. In the novel's first section, which takes place on the eve of the Civil War, the ne'er-do-well St. Clair Enson, son of a prominent family of Maryland planters, returns to the home of his older brother, Ellis Enson, accompanied by a slave trader named Walker. They come armed with the information that Hagar, Ellis's young wife and the adopted daughter of the deceased owners of the Sargeant plantation immediately adjacent to the Enson estate, unknown even to herself, has black ancestry and is in fact a slave. Because Walker has papers proving his legal ownership of Hagar, he forces Ellis to pay for his own wife's freedom. Yet it is not until Walker raises his further legal claim to Ellis and Hagar's daughter that Ellis understands the full meaning of slavery defined through the mother.

> "As for the pickaninny—"
> "What!" thundered Ellis, "the child, too?"
> "In course," [*sic*]) replied Walker, . . . "the child follows
> the condition of the mother, so I scoop the pile."[30]

Ellis's introduction to the true meaning of slavery, despite his lifelong association with a large plantation with many slaves, arises out of this recognition of the alienating intent of the rule of the condition of the mother with reference to the two people whom he thinks of as his nearest kin. Ellis's paternity is entirely irrelevant to legal possession of mother and child because the trader Walker's titular claim to Hagar's womb supersedes Ellis's marital (and also quasiproprietary) rights as her husband. After a long night of anguish, Ellis decides he will give up everything for his wife, intending to remarry Hagar and to resettle with her in Europe to escape the racism peculiar to the United States. Before he can put that plan into action, however, Hagar has to grapple with the meaning of *the condition of the mother* to her own mother, to herself as daughter of a slave, as mother to her child, and to her own image of herself: "Could it be true, or was it but a hideous nightmare from which she would soon awake? Her mother a slave! She wondered that the very thought did not strike her dead. With shrinking horror she contemplated the black abyss into which the day's events had hurled her. . . . Her name gone, her pride of birth shattered at one blow! Was she, indeed, a descendant of naked black savages of the horrible African jungles? . . . Her education, beauty, refinement, what did they profit her now?"[31] When Hagar sees her slave maid, Marthy, for the first time after this revelation, her response is to scrutinize anxiously the girl's "black skin, crinkled hair, flat nose and protruding lips" as if looking into a mirror. When she does eventually see her own face in a mirror, Hagar's response is to smash the glass, now that the visage of the naked savage of the jungle lurks behind the image of the white woman she had thought herself to be. Hagar, to whom slavery had always seemed just, takes immediate recourse in manic self-repudiation to deny the denigration that she experiences.

Later in the novel, after a lapse of twenty years during which Ellis, Hagar, and the child Jewel have become separated and reunited by various plot contrivances, Hagar's true identity is revealed again to a Washington social world that Jewel has reentered under a different identity, passing as Hagar's stepdaughter. Cuthbert Sumner, Jewel's wealthy aristocratic husband, offspring of the New England abolitionists, feels sympathy for Hagar's polluting maternal ancestry but is determined to separate Jewel from her "stepmother" before public suspicion of the matrilineal chain can call Jewel's ancestry into question. Cuthbert confronts Ellis Enson, back from the "dead" over his decision to remarry Hagar twenty years later, to return with her to Enson Hall, and to acknowledge her publicly as his wife. In the conversation between abolitionist-descended Sumner and Enson, the reformed Southern aristocrat and former slaveholder, Hopkins locates the source of white paranoia over intermarriage in the indelible condition inherited from the African mother, as Cuthbert protests, "'But my dear Enson, you do not countenance such a—such a—well—terrible action as a wholesale union between whites and blacks? Think of it, my dear man! Think of our refinement and intelligence linked to such black bestiality!'"[32]

When Ellis reminds Cuthbert of his own prior infatuation with Aurelia Walker, the quadroon daughter of the former slave trader Walker, Cuthbert reacts predictably, unaware of the discovery in store for him about his own wife, Jewel: "'I think that the knowledge of [Aurelia's] origin would kill all desire in me,' replied Sumner. 'The mere thought of the grinning, toothless black hag that was her foreparent would forever rise between us.'"[33] Jewel's subsequent discovery that she is Hagar's daughter, not her stepdaughter, by the condition of *her* mother links her to the original black hag of Cuthbert's imagination and sets in motion a crisis for the young couple that repeats her parents' experience with the ultimate divisiveness that the one-drop rule added to the disabling condition of the mother. Hopkins's novel ironically contrasts the Southern aristocrat's ability to transcend his antebellum racial prejudices and redeem his beloved from the stigma of slavery with the racial mythology to which the postemancipation Northerner, Cuthbert, falls prey. He cannot clearly see Jewel as an individual, only as a specter of the original slave mother, and abandons her to a tragic early death.

For Hopkins, then, the outcast status of African Americans after the Civil War is in some ways more pernicious, having become a national mania, rather than a sectional peculiarity. Like Chesnutt, Hopkins would later shift the question of how to address the lingering stigma of slavery to the personal decisions of African Americans themselves.

REDEMPTION IN THE MOTHER'S RETURN

In a short story that shadows Chesnutt's "The Wife of His Youth," Pauline Hopkins similarly made the mulatto male's decision to return to the black mother figure a testament to the slave mother's successful transmission of the transracial human virtues of selflessness and fidelity. In "The Test of Manhood" (1902), at age eighteen Mark Myers deserts his mother, "who could not be mistaken for a white woman," leaving the South to pass in the North as white.[34] He becomes the fabled poor boy who makes good, earning money in real estate and rising in his employer's law firm after five years of apprenticeship, though he is periodically troubled by thoughts of his mother, who, like 'Liza Jane, has ventured to the North in search of him. As the red-turbaned Aunt Cloty, she eventually becomes the pet social rehabilitation project of Katherine Brown, the daughter of Mark's unsuspecting white employer and the woman he loves. On Christmas Eve, Katherine inadvertently effects a reunion of mother and son when Mark goes to visit her at her home with the intent of proposing a marriage that would seal his transition to white society and secure the futures of his eventual children. In the act of announcing his engagement to Katherine, Mark encounters Aunt Cloty, who unthinkingly unmasks him by claiming him as her son. The effect of this revelation is devastating: "Mark stood as if carved in stone, in an instant he saw his life in ruins, Katherine lost to him, chaos about the social fabric of his life."[35] But defiantly, he embraces his mother, formally renouncing any claims to marriage with Katherine and the life of material ease that was to have been his future for the chaos and ruin of black life in the Jim Crow South to which he must return.

Hopkins's Christmas story, with its black ghost of slavery past, locates in an ironic epiphany of madonna and child the inevitability of the return of the condition of the mother as an ethical crisis for African Americans. Mark's physical whiteness bespeaks Aunt Cloty's dalliance with, or victimization by, a white man, and so Mark's acknowledgment of "Aunt Cloty" connotes his symbolic acceptance of responsibility for the stigma of the sexual transgression that produced his marketable racial ambiguity. His dilemma is that his dream of social ascent must come to terms with the shame of concubinage that grew out of slavery's colonization of the black female womb and produced him. Mark must bridge the "gulf he saw yawning between them" in their social stations by a voluntary return to the mother.[36] Unlike Mr. Ryder, another "white" recalled to his maternal blackness, Mark's return to the black mother here redeems the socially debased condition of the mother without terminating the maternal descent line, since nothing prevents his future marriage to an African American woman. But like Ryder, Mark's embrace of an unequivocal African American social identity reclaims an intended truant back into the struggle for race advancement.

Yet Pauline Hopkins clearly wanted to move beyond the notion that the slave mother's rehabilitation from slavery's injustices required a male champion. For her, refiguring the shame of slavery conveyed through the black mother could be better accomplished by redefining Africa itself, making the black mother the repository of an African spirituality of classical proportions. In her first novel, Contending Forces (1900), Hopkins had been dubious about any cultural carryovers from Africans on the continent to African Americans, with the anxious exception of conjuration at which she scoffed as a lingering African barbarism.[37] But in Of One Blood,[38] Hopkins revised her previous doubt about residual African spiritual power to make it a striking means of valorizing the image of African motherhood. In this speculative fiction of the "lost civilization" genre, the surviving populace of the ancient African kingdom of Meroe, a center of mystical practices and older than Ethiopia itself, hides in the underground city of Telassar, awaiting the return of a redeemer king descended from their long-lost ruling clan. The novel's hero, an African American with extrasensory powers named Reuel Briggs, has been passing in America for white and is in pursuit of a medical degree at Harvard. But he finds himself compelled by faltering financial circumstances to accept a position in an archaeological expedition, where he digs deep into hidden pasts that will lead him to this lost African city and to a recovery of his familial heritage. Reuel reacts to the discovery of his origins with a reflection on the folklore about his heritage and the maternal origins of previously unexplained extrasensory powers, and a birthmark: "It was a tradition among those who knew him in childhood that he was descended from a race of African kings. He remembered his mother well. From her he had inherited his mysticism and his occult powers. The nature of the mystic within him was, then, but a dreamlike devotion to the spirit that had swayed his ancestors; it was the shadow of Ethiopia's power."[39]

The physical birthmark he possesses eventually reveals him as the redeemer king of Meroe, but more important is the spiritual mark of Africa that has sensitized Reuel to the supernatural. In his medical research, Reuel has been obsessed with "what might be termed 'absurdities' of supernatural phenomena or *mysticism*."[40] His interest in psychic phenomena becomes focused on the strange case of Dianthe Lusk, a featured soloist of the celebrated black Fisk Jubilee Singers, who appears to Reuel in a vision before he ever actually sees her on stage in the flesh. When the actual Dianthe turns up in the hospital where Reuel is training, stiffened to a catatonic condition after a train derailment, Reuel calls on a power that he has "stumbled upon" in his quest to understand the paranormal, "the reanimation of the body after seeming death."[41]

In her trancelike state, Dianthe speaks of mystical powers of her own: "I see much clearly, much dimly, of the powers and influences behind the Veil, and yet I cannot name them. Some time the full power will be mine; and mine shall be thine."[42] Her cryptic utterances, a prophecy that only her restoration to her true self will fully empower Reuel, leads Reuel to describe her condition as a "*dual* mesmeric trance."[43] The dual sources of enchantment in Dianthe's life are clearly inspired by W. E. B. Du Bois's metaphorical construct of a "double-consciousness" effected by the socially constructed "veil of race." Du Bois described this essential conflict of postemancipation African Americans as an internalized, distorted self-image absorbed from Jim Crow America ("a world that looks on with amused contempt and pity"⁴⁴) that obscures self-awareness and acceptance of that self.

The resolution of Dianthe's paradoxical and ironic comatose double consciousness, which Reuel sensationally achieves, will involve a complex return of the condition of the mother through Dianthe's zombielike psychic enslavement. The primary source of the psychic bondage of Dianthe's unconscious consciousness is her legacy from the slavemaster-scientist Aubrey Livingston, who haunts her family's past. Livingston, a deceased slave owner, was the father of the second Aubrey Livingston, currently Reuel's Harvard schoolmate, confidant, secret antagonist, and (predictably, given the genre) also the brother of Reuel and Dianthe as well. Hopkins's complex gloss of Du Boisian double consciousness involves two sources of mesmerism, however: one perverse, deriving from the necromancy of the unholy race science of the slaveholder-father, the other benevolent, from the maternal line of African spiritual power.

Thus Reuel, Dianthe, and the second Aubrey, antagonist and unknown brother, share the positive and negative spiritual potentials of both parents. The young Aubrey, drawn more toward the malignant science of the father than to the benign influence of the mother he never knew and desiring the spotlight for himself after Reuel's celebrated re-animation of Dianthe, relates at a social event how his father would entertain his party guests by placing a young slave girl named Mira into a trance, making her perform tricks and render prophecies. Thus, Dianthe's trancelike condition, attributed to despised "mother" Africa, is actually also a legacy inherited from the sorcery of her consummately respectable white father.

The slave girl Mira of Aubrey's story is in fact the mother of Dianthe, Reuel, and Aubrey. It is Mira, descendant of the ruling dynasty at Meroe, who provides the countervailing spiritual resources to the still potent mesmeric influence of the slavemaster Aubrey Livingston. Mira's complicated legacy includes as well Dianthe's visible African descent, the family's experience of slavery in America, and their origin in African royalty. Mira enters the story in the form of a second, inner "voice" that haunts Dianthe's singing, invoking the racial trope of "bondage in Egypt" as a lived familial experience. The vehicle of this revelation is the Old Testament–derived African American spiritual "Go Down Moses," which Dianthe sings one evening after Reuel has departed on the archeological expedition to Africa that will eventually lead him to the hidden city of Telassar. Mira's voice is detectable *within* Dianthe's as she sings in "a weird contralto, veiled as it were, rising and falling upon every wave of the great soprano, and reaching the ear as from some strange distance. The singer sang on, . . . the echo following it."[45]

The external agent of Dianthe's discovery of her personal past is her maternal grandmother, Aunt Hannah, a woman previously unknown to her but "the most noted 'voodoo' doctor or witch in the country." Aunt Hannah reveals that the power by which Mira shadows Dianthe's voice and life is the legacy of their family's consecration to the ancient Egyptian god Osiris. Her quest to reconnect the missing pieces of family knowledge lost during the shattering experience of slavery parallels Reuel's African expedition, but with an important distinction. Even though Reuel fulfills the role of the adventurer-hero who discovers his royal lineage and ascends to his destined throne, significantly Dianthe does not need to travel to discover her identity, the bad and the good of it. Rather, she needs only to reconnect with her maternal line, extending from royalty through American slavery into the hopeful present.

But after suffering sexual abuse from young Aubrey during Reuel's absence in Africa, Dianthe dies, another victim of slavery's lingering legacy of exploiting black womanhood. To some extent, even the three siblings' incestuous triangle (Reuel and Dianthe marry before his departure on his expedition but do not consummate the relationship) had dual origins in dynastic antiquity and in the still prevalent concubinage of African American women in the South into the twentieth century. On her deathbed, Dianthe addresses Aunt Hannah as Mother and relates to her a prophetic vision of ancient African continuities: "A very golden cloud is printed with the fleecy words of glory: 'I will return.'"[46] The significance of this return, Hopkins suggests, is the eventual revelation of Africa's primacy in world civilization, a revision of racist doctrines that based transatlantic slavery, the one-drop paranoia, and the entire racial caste system on the lie that Africans were incapable of achieving civilization and were inherently incompatible with it. The mystical mother's return therefore is simultaneously the African spirit's triumph over the slave-master's enchantments; a dramatic refiguration of the doctrine of the condition of the mother, reversing its humiliating reimposition of slave status on the mother's descendants, and a reclamation of the slave mother's children for a unifying ideal of Africa as redemptive mother of all world civilization.

Hopkins's and Chesnutt's allegories of elective and involuntary racial classification within and across the color line of Progressive Era America assessed the colonial slave statutes' self-perpetuating, ineradicable legacy of social caste formation through the condition of the mother. They highlighted the personal ethical dilemmas of caring and attachment deriving from imposed caste identity. The virulent race consciousness facing the black talented tenth no doubt at some level included themselves and their own decisions to affirm their own African heritages from Africa. They sought to provide a basis for proud elective affiliation with Africa as African Americans by deconstructing, and thus revealing the utterly false premises of the Jim Crow doctrine of unproblematically "separate origins, separate destinies." In focusing on the tangled genealogies growing out of the long history of the intimacy of the relationships of slavery that the condition-of-the-mother statutes had created, they made the point that caste distinctions based on race are absurd. "No man can draw the dividing line between the two races, for they are both of one blood!"[47]

Their generation of African American writers thus paved the way for the more celebrated Harlem Renaissance through their committed articulation of the meaning of slavery as validation of African American worthiness for full participation in the social and political life of an otherwise claimed white America. Each seized the received history of racial mixing under, and as a central result of, slavery as an opportunity to challenge the Progressive Era's unexamined nostalgia for the antebellum South as a time of physical as well as legal separation, and to rehabilitate the slave mother as a figure of redemptive race consciousness and a potential source also of national racial reconciliation.

NOTES

1. Joel Williamson, *The Crucible of Race: Black-White Relations in the American South since Emancipation* (New York: Oxford University Press, 1984), 32. Note: The shifting designations of racial identity require judicious qualification, as populations became reclassified by statute or by common usage. Understanding that race is a scientifically discredited system of biological classification, I will continue to use terms such as "race," "black," "white," "mixed," "mulatto," and so on as appropriate to the historical circumstances, sometimes within quotes to indicate particularly ironic, arbitrary, or implausible applications, but most often not.

2. See, for example, George W. Stocking Jr., *Race, Culture, and Evolution: Essays in the History of Anthropology* (Chicago: University of Chicago Press, 1982), 49–51.

3. Pauli Murray, ed., *States' Laws on Race and Color* (Cincinnati: Women's Division of Christian Service, Board of Missions and Church Extension, Methodist Church, 1951, 21, 39, 90, 173, 237, 356, 428, 443–34, 462. See also Virginia R. Domínguez, *White by Definition: Social Classification in Creole Louisiana* (New Brunswick, NJ: Rutgers University Press, 1994), 26–36.

4. Williamson, *Crucible of Race*, 464–65.

5. Robert W. Shufeldt, *The Negro, a Menace to American Civilization* (Boston: R. G. Badger, 1907), 95–96.

6. Thomas Dixon Jr., *The Leopard's Spots: A Romance of the White Man's Burden, 1865–1900* (New York: Doubleday, Page, 1902), 242.

7. John S. Haller, *Outcasts from Evolution: Scientific Attitudes of Racial Inferiority, 1859–1900* (Urbana: University of Illinois Press, 1971), 210.

8. Williamson, *Crucible of Race*, 224–58.

9. W. E. B. Du Bois, "The Talented Tenth," in *Writings by W. E. B. Du Bois in Non-Periodical Literature Edited by Others*, ed. Herbert Aptheker (Millwood, NY: Kraus-Thomson, 1982), 17–29. See also Orlando Patterson, *Slavery and Social Death: A Comparative Study* (Cambridge, MA: Harvard University Press, 1982), 13.

10. Michael J. Cassity, *Legacy of Fear: American Race Relations to 1900* (Westport, CT: Greenwood, 1985), 22.

11. Joel Williamson, *New People: Miscegenation and Mulattoes in the United States* (New York: Free Press, 1980), 8.

12. Winthrop Jordan, *White over Black: American Attitudes toward the Negro, 1550–1812* (Chapel Hill: University of North Carolina Press, 1968), 75; emphasis added.

13. Thomas Jefferson, *Notes on the State of Virginia* (1785; reprint, New York: Harper and Row, 1964), 133. See also Jordan, *White over Black*, 229.

14. Philip Alexander Bruce, *The Plantation Negro as a Freeman: Observations on His Character, Condition, and Prospects in Virginia* (New York: G. P. Putnam's Sons, 1889), 84.

15. William Edward Farrison, introduction to *Clotel; or, The President's Daughter: A Narrative of Slave Life in the United States*, by William Wells Brown (New York: Citadel Press, 1969), 7–11.

16. Angela Y. Davis, *Women, Race, and Class* (New York: Vintage, 1983), 99–109.

17. Williamson, *Crucible of Race*, 61–70.

18. Charles W. Chesnutt, *Collected Stories of Charles W. Chesnutt*, ed. William L. Andrews (New York: Penguin, 1992), 127–28, emphasis added.

19. Ibid., 105.

20. Ibid., 106–7.

21. Newbell Niles Puckett, *Popular Beliefs and Superstitions: A Compendium of American Folklore from the Ohio Collection of Newbell Niles Puckett*, ed. Wayland D. Hand, Anna Casetta, Sondra B. Thiederman, 3 vols. (Boston: G. K. Hall, 1981), 1:401.

22. Werner Sollors, *Beyond Ethnicity: Consent and Descent in American Culture* (New York: Oxford University Press, 1986), 159.

23. Ibid., 160.

24. Chesnutt, *Collected Stories*, 104.

25. Charles W. Chesnutt, *The House behind the Cedars* (New York: Collier, 1969), 127.

26. Ibid., 133.

27. Hanna Wallinger, *Pauline E. Hopkins: A Literary Biography* (Athens: University of Georgia Press, 2005), 19–29.

28. Serialized in *Colored American Magazine*, 1901–2.

29. Genesis, chs. 16, 21.

30. See Pauline Hopkins, *Hagar's Daughter*, in *The Magazine Novels of Pauline Hopkins* (New York: Oxford University Press, 1988), 55–56.

31. Ibid., 57.

32. Ibid., 270.

33. Ibid., 271.

34. Pauline Hopkins, "The Test of Manhood," in *Colored American Magazine*, December 1902, 115.

35. Ibid., 119.

36. Ibid., 115.

37. Pauline Hopkins, *Contending Forces: A Romance Illustrative of Negro Life North and South* (1900; reprint, Carbondale: Southern Illinois University Press, 1978), 198.

38. Serialized in *Colored American Magazine*, 1902–3.

39. Pauline Hopkins, *Of One Blood*, in *Magazine Novels*, 558.

40. Ibid., 442; emphasis in original.

41. Ibid., 464.

42. Ibid., 475.

43. Ibid., 471; emphasis in original.

44. W. E. B. Du Bois, *The Souls of Black Folk* (1903; reprint, New York: Bantam, 1989), 3.

45. Hopkins, *Of One Blood*, 502.

46. Ibid., 613.

47. Ibid., 607.

5

Historiographical Reflections on

Slavery and Women

11

RE-MODELING SLAVERY AS IF WOMEN MATTERED

CLAIRE ROBERTSON AND MARSHA ROBINSON

For some time within the ever-expanding field of historical studies of slavery, many scholars have understood that women slaves often outnumbered men. Most slaves in the contemporary world are women. Although most of the world's slaves were and are women they have been invisible or nearly so in much scholarly discourse on slavery. Scholars of slavery across several continents have noted this absence and have urged systematic inclusion.[1]

In this chapter we will examine the roots of this invisibility in an eclectic sample of influential works on slavery from recent decades and show how inclusion of women and gender is transforming scholarly models of slavery. We draw on studies from around the world that offer gendered analyses from feminist theory and women's history, in particular, bringing insights from studies of the Americas into dialogue with those from other continents. Our goal is not simply to add women to the mixture in order to achieve mainstream status but rather "to offer a new geometry which locates the female experience within the pivot rather than on the tangent."[2] Making women's experiences the fulcrum of the field puts into question certain conventional models. Thus our aim is to use gender as an analytical tool to re-model slavery in ways that reflect women's distinctive experiences as slaves and participation as slave owners and slave users.

GENDERING SLAVERY STUDIES

As Monique Deveaux has stated, "In many societies, men's freedom (privilege, etc.) is contingent upon women's unfreedom."[3] Gender is thus deeply implicated in most systems of unfree labor, since any privileges or higher status accruing to slaves went to men, even when most of the unfree were women. Women's history has shown the value of gendering historical analysis, which means, according to Joan Scott, acknowledging that "relations between the sexes are a primary aspect of social organization . . . , that the terms of male and female identities are in large part culturally determined . . . , and that differences between the sexes constitute and are constituted by hierarchical social structures."[4] Slavery, as David Brion Davis noted, is a central institution in history, and we would add that it remains so to the present day.[5] The unfree labor of women in particular has been, and still is, a fundamental characteristic of many societies. For Gerda Lerner, the slavery of women in antiquity provided, in fact, the model for enslaving men.[6]

Insights gained from women's history and feminist theory have nonetheless been rare in slavery studies. While historians of women maintain that history is solipsistic without the inclusion of women and gender in every aspect, there has been a pervasive tendency to leave gender analysis to those doing women's history. Indeed, the number of articles focusing on women or gender in the journal *Slavery and Abolition* increased only from 7.1 percent in the 1980s to 7.9 percent between 1990 and 2002. Similarly, fewer than 1 percent of the entries in the most comprehensive bibliography of slavery in 1980 focused on women or gender, while in 2002 that number had risen to only 4.4 percent.[7] For every study that included women or gender, at least ten others did not. Here we have highlighted works notable for their inclusion of women and/or gender (even if sometimes tangentially), while critiquing others that do not, although they may be otherwise highly valued. We are not insisting that every scholar focus exclusively on women and/or gender, but—with Joan Scott—we believe that the inclusion of women and gender analysis enriches any history.

REASONS FOR THE INVISIBILITY OF WOMEN
AND GENDER IN SLAVERY STUDIES

The causes of the widespread omission of women and gender from most works on slavery vary, going beyond the default suggestions that there has been a paucity of women scholars in slavery studies or that men sometimes run into difficulties when they try to interview women as sources. More important has been the assumption that women's history is trivial, an attitude noted in the 1990s by Patricia van der Spuy and Bridget

Brereton in the historical literatures on slavery in the Cape Colony (South Africa) and the Caribbean respectively.[8] Mary Helen Washington noted somewhat earlier a double layering of patriarchal neglect regarding U.S. slave narratives written by women, wherein not only had scholars ignored women but the narratives of male ex-slaves also diminished or omitted reference to women's roles. Frederick Douglass, for instance, wrote as if his escape was solitary, when he could not have succeeded without the help of a free black woman. Washington noted that women, who were less likely to be literate, had written only 12 percent of the then known narratives and concluded, "the life of the male slave has come to be representative even though the female experience in slavery was sometimes radically different."[9]

Another reason little attention was paid to women and gender for so long in the slavery literature is that males predominated in much of the Atlantic slave trade. Anglo-American chattel slavery in the Americas dominated slavery discourse. Scholars assumed that New World plantation owners preferred males for heavy agricultural labor and that Euro-American demand determined the heavily male sex ratio in the trade.[10] However, the fact that more men than women were exported to the Americas was due as much to Africans' preferences for retaining women as to Americans' preferences for men as workers. American slave populations did not reach parity in the sex ratio until the time of the Revolution in the British North American colonies, and in the Caribbean sometimes not until after emancipation in the 1830s. Thus, the assumption that most slaves in the Americas were male was correct for much of the history of African slavery there. Also, while women and children predominated among enslaved Native Americans, scholars have not always made them principal subjects of analysis.[11]

G. Ugo Nwokeji has ably shown that this sexual imbalance in the maritime trade requires gendered analysis of the origins of the trade in Africa. Almost half the deportees from the Bight of Biafra from 1650 to 1700 were women, an unusually high ratio for the transatlantic trade. Work roles in Africa generally determined who was exported, he argues, and since men there did more agricultural work than elsewhere, they were less likely to be sold. However, the number of women exported from the Bight diminished later because male Aro traders preferred to retain slave women for their own use.[12]

Women have also been omitted from historical scrutiny because the slavery literature has focused on more formal, public forms of slavery, where more male slaves were involved. Thus, North American–style chattel slavery was best documented and most visible, whereas pervasive female slavery within the privacy of large households elsewhere around the world remained much less well documented. Further, the tendency to mask enslavement of women by designating them with kinship terms or claiming employed servant status for them rather than "possession" in a legal sense makes it difficult to tease their presence from sources accepting of these terms. In colonial India, northern Nigeria, and elsewhere, the British assured the male leaders of newly colonized peoples that their abolition of slavery would not affect domestic "servants." Even though both sexes were eligible for manumission, since women were normally under male control it was more difficult for women to leave their owners unless they were accompanied by a male partner. British men, ostensibly committed to liberating slaves as part of the "civilizing" mission, nonetheless traded submission to colonial rule by colonized local men for allowing them to retain control over free and enslaved women.[13]

MODELS OF SLAVERY

This essay examines conventional models of slavery in light of their utility for analyzing women as slaves, slave-owners and slave users, in three sections, each dealing with a particular prominent aspect of these models: first, women's particular status and rights (or lack of same) among slaves; second, the work that women do or did as slaves; and finally, issues regarding identity, agency and construction of ideals of citizenship as they affected women slaves, based on their degrees of alienation or assimilation, ethnicity, race, work, religion, sexuality and gender. Emphasizing these three axes allows us to analyze conventional models of slavery to account for their omission of gender and women within a historiographical framework, and also to illustrate the insights added by gendering the analysis of slavery.

Status and Rights of Women Slaves

Many early studies focused on the legal status as property and denial of the rights of citizenship to (implicitly male) slaves. The definitions of slavery used prioritized civic alienation and the limited degrees of assimilation that enslaved men could attain. Other definitions of slavery defined slaves' exclusion socially by their kinlessness. Orlando Patterson assumed that slavery entailed natal alienation and "social death."[14] Further insights came from Africa and Asia. Suzanne Miers, Igor Kopytoff, and James Watson stressed that types of slavery could be arrayed along a continuum from extreme natal alienation and total absence of rights, as in North American chattel slavery, to slavery as a means of assimilating outsiders into societies. Asian and African societies accorded them places and rights, as with male slaves designated as heirs to family estates in imperial China, and in many African and Native American examples.[15]

One of the first approaches to considering women's status as slaves in particular came with Gerda Lerner's hypothesis that slavery in the ancient world might first have been practiced on women before being extended to a deprived status for men. Her model of slavery prioritized the enslavement of women as the "cultural invention of slavery," [which] "rested as much on the elaboration of symbols of the subordination of women as it did on the actual conquest of women."[16]

At the same time Angela Davis in *Women, Race and Class* in 1983 contested the invisibility of women in U.S. slave families as described by major writers on U.S. slavery in the early 1970s: Eugene Genovese, John Blassingame, and Herbert Gutman. She focused on the economic value of slave women's work, the sexual abuse of enslaved women, and punishments for women that were equal to men's. She also raised such issues as identity for women slaves; the dominant white ideology as it affected slave women; housework as an area of autonomy for them; their resistance to slavery; and how slave women's roles affected white women abolitionists' views.[17] Davis, along with Jacqueline Jones and Deborah Gray White, thus laid the basis for a research agenda concerning women and slavery that went beyond the negative emphasis on exclusion characteristic of the status or rights approach.[18]

This agenda was absorbed only slowly into the general literature. In 1991 Orlando Patterson in *Freedom in the Making of Western Culture* developed Lerner's insight by showing that Greek and Roman ideas of civic rights, or freedom, were rooted in the prior experience of slavery, including that of women. "Women played a decisive role in the Western social invention of personal freedom. I now find it extraordinary that this fact had not been previously established [*sic*]. What is more, women continued to play a critical role in the history of this element of freedom, continuously reconstructing a distinctively feminine version of the value after men had embraced and refigured it in its now more familiar negative form."[19]

In 1997 Robin Blackburn's *The Making of New World Slavery* revisited much of the terrain covered previously by David Brion Davis, who in *Slavery and Human Progress* (1984) had pointed out the coincidence between chattel slavery and the expansion of capitalism, which he framed as "progress." Blackburn recast Davis's progress into "modernism" and, widening the range of associations of modern slavery in the Americas, linked it also to instrumental rationality, nationalism, and the nation-state's racialized perceptions of identity, administrative bureaucracies and modern tax systems, and communications, consumerism, individualism, and self-awareness.[20] These insights of Davis, Blackburn, and Patterson have been enriched and reanchored to women's history by those of the feminist theorist Linda Alcoff, who noted that ideas of freedom, selfhood, empowerment, reason, and truth are constituted also through concepts of sexual difference.[21]

In the usual U.S. chattel slavery model, slaves' legal inability to own property is a defining element of their utter lack of rights. However, in some societies slaves had the right to own property to the point that some, although they had the means to free themselves, found buying slaves to be a better means for advancement. In southwestern North America and many African societies, for instance, enslaved women could own slaves.[22] An appropriate term for this type of slavery might be patron-client, because slaves had a degree of autonomy and property rights similar to those of clients within a patron-client system. Even within U.S. chattel slavery, some slaves negotiated, or owners preferred, an arrangement with some characteristics of patron-client slavery. Such slaves accumulated property and manumitted themselves through self-purchase rather than by running away or awaiting the owner's will. Even though their legal status denied them rights to their own persons, their de facto condition included limited customary rights entailing a degree of autonomy in their choice of residence and disposal of earnings. They owed their owners a portion of their wages and often lived apart from them. Although this clientlike status applied more often to male slaves with skills to sell than to women, some women purchased their freedom with profits from growing and marketing produce, or wages earned as cooks, seamstresses, weavers, or hawkers, as noted by Ira Berlin for the Chesapeake area of Virginia and Robert Olwell for Charleston market traders.[23]

Work on women enslaved in Spanish American colonial territories has been particularly important in challenging the notion of the inherent propertylessness of slave women. Christine Hünefeldt's *Paying the Price of Freedom* documented the "myriad and diverse mechanisms that slaves created in anticipation of freedom and despite the resistance of slaveholders" in colonial Lima, Peru. These mechanisms primarily involved women slaves. Less valued for unskilled hacienda manual labor, they were allowed to move to town and initiate the eventual manumission of their families, using wages and profits from trade and aided by Spanish laws that allowed slaves to force owners to set a value on them and free them if they could raise the sum contracted. Hünefeldt's analysis of women's roles in enslaved families avoids stereotyping women as either victims or as matriarchs.[24]

Sandra Lauderdale Graham in *House and Street: The Domestic World of Servants and Masters in Nineteenth Century Rio de Janeiro* pointed out nuanced degrees of acknowledged rights of Brazilian slaves and refused to draw a sharp distinction between free and enslaved female domestic servants. All could earn wages, were subjected to the same authority of male and female exploiters of their labor, and were treated similarly. They also created social networks transcending their differing civic standings and developed other female strategies to aid self-manumission, like those noted by Hünefeldt. Legal redress for sexual impositions or extreme physical abuse was possible; servants, enslaved or not, could even testify in court. Graham's study thus reveals another Latin American context where slavery merged into clientship, a phenomenon enabled for women, in particular, by a heritage of Spanish legal forms granting them certain rights not common in the British tradition.[25] Jane Landers's *Black Society in Spanish Florida*, and Larry Rivers's *Slavery in Florida* explore the similarly varied statuses of enslaved and free black women from the Spanish colony from the seventeenth to the early nineteenth century.[26] By highlighting the agency of individual women slaves in particular, such studies demonstrate the superficiality of definitions of slavery based primarily on notions of absolute status or rights.

The borderlands between Mexico and the American Southwest displayed dynamics useful for gendering slavery studies. James Brooks's *Captives and Cousins* stresses that Spanish enslavement of Native American women in far northern Mexico in the nineteenth century furthered their assimilation. Brooks alludes to the slavery continuum regarding social assimilation identified by Miers and Kopytoff in documenting a wide variety of servile statuses among Spanish captives held by Native Americans. One of his most valuable theoretical contributions is to point out that servile statuses were not singular; bondspersons could, at the same time, inhabit more than one position on the continuum. However, Brooks overemphasizes the similarities between Native American and Spanish forms of slavery by underplaying the extreme brutality of gang rape inflicted on Native American women by Spanish settler men in the process of enslaving them; Native Americans seem to have inflicted no comparable trauma on the Spanish settler women they captured.[27]

In West African communities debtors often transferred people to creditors as "pawns," that is, as human pledges or collateral for debts they owed; the pawn's work paid the interest on the debt. Women and girls were, of course, more useful for this purpose than men because of their productive and reproductive (domestic) labor; hence young females formed the great majority of people pawned. Commonly, a female pawn would eventually marry a male member of the creditor's family. Omission of the bridewealth expected by the debtor's family canceled the debt. Pawnship was also a frequent method by which women ended up enslaved when creditors did not respect legal differences between the status of pawnship, a limited form of indentured labor for a defined term, and slavery, or labor for an indefinite term. Some creditors sold pawns.

Gender roles severely impacted British emancipation of slaves in early-twentieth-century northern Nigeria, as documented by Ibrahim Jumare in the Sokoto caliphate. A 1901 British ordinance allowed all slaves to redeem themselves, but males were more likely than women to be able to take advantage of this opportunity by presenting themselves to the colonial officials charged with documenting these claims. Women slaves more often were trapped within domestic households by converging Islamic sharia and British notions of domesticity. If such women had escaped, they would have left behind their children fathered by a free man. Female slavery ended only in 1936, when the British finally officially outlawed slavery.[28]

The legal status of the children of slave women was a key element in every system of slavery. Whether those children were free and equal, or free but lower in status than children of two free parents, or born into full enslavement as in the United States, they posed problems not only for women attempting to escape slavery, who faced great difficulties in taking them along, but also for owners' lineages and families with regard to maintaining clear boundaries between slave and free. In Islamic systems from the eighth-century Abbasid era on, as described by Ehud Toledano and Judith Tucker, a slave woman who bore her master or one of his free relatives a son, in particular, was supposed to be manumitted on the death of her master and was often freed earlier. Women whose masters married them were also freed and might become members of the ruling elite, with accompanying dowries. Women in these cases left the status of slave for that of wife, and motherhood could be a means for social mobility.[29]

Uncovering the history of women, including those in slavery, has now become a preoccupation of some scholars of classical Greece and Rome. Whereas K. R. Bradley's work on Roman families and slavery barely mentioned women, Sarah Pomeroy's *Goddesses, Whores, Wives, and Slaves* pioneered a sharp focus on women.[30] In the collection of essays edited by Sandra R. Joshel and Sheila Murnaghan, *Women and Slaves in Greco-Roman Culture: Differential Equations*, the framing query regards the correlation of, or disjunction between, the status of woman or wife and that of slave. Such work not only problematizes issues of status and rights but also examines symbiotic relationships between slave and free women.[31]

One of the most important contributions of the literature on status or rights for women and slavery has been the suggestion that the servitude of women sheds light on other forms of legal subordination. If Lerner posited that women's slavery in the ancient world was a model for slavery in the modern Western world, Susan Mosher Stuard saw medieval women's "domestic" slavery, unhindered by laws, also as a precursor for plantation slavery in the Americas. For women more than for men, gradations of servitude are relevant; the statuses of free, freed, pawned, indentured, junior wife, concubine, maidservant, "free" worker, client, and chattel slave shaded into each other and/or represented different stages within a woman's assimilation and maturation, or both.

The servitude of women also sheds much light on the complex hierarchy of kin and nonkin relations within households. As Nell Painter pointed out, "hierarchy by no means precludes attachment." Although some white women in the United States had authority over black slaves, their own unquestioning obedience to white men served as a model for the subservience of slaves. "Ideals and practices of servitude, family and religion [were] linked in this cultural system."[32] Slave, freed, and free women must be included in our analysis, since slaves were or are not isolates, and all persons are affected by, and in turn affect, women's overall status in a society. More studies on relationships among free, freed, and slave women are needed, especially outside of the Americas.

Finally, the omission of gender analysis hinders problematizing the status or rights of female workers in modern global industries, who, through lack of skills and/or other opportunities, trickery, sale by their parents, kidnapping, migration loans, and so forth, may become slaves. They are locked behind factory doors or worksite fences and subjected to health-damaging, numbingly repetitive processes, and demanding production quotas in situations where unionization and strikes are prohibited by the police. These women workers' fertility is controlled through mandatory use of contraceptives and through abortions. Kevin Bales has called their status slavery.[33] Curiously, however, he did not gender his analysis, nor did Elaine Pearson in a special issue of the *New Internationalist* entitled "The Burden of Slavery," although all her specific examples were women.[34] Clearly we need a gendered history both to analyze this phenomenon and formulate means of abolishing such oppression.

The Work of Women and Slaves

The second aspect or axis of slavery under consideration here is enslaved women's work, including sex work. The chief problems in many scholarly writings on this subject involve, on the one hand, its invisibility or trivializing its value, and on the other, assuming that women slaves were wanted mainly for sex or concubinage, which sex was not viewed as being work but as their exclusive use.

Historiographically, the strongest focus on work, though not on women, has come from those influenced by Marxist models emphasizing labor as constituting social value. In the 1960s Walter Rodney traced the origins of slavery in Africa to the influence of capitalism through the European Atlantic slave trade.[35] In contrast, in 1987 Robert Miles in *Capitalism and Unfree Labor: Anomaly or Necessity?* made slavery a necessary part of precapitalist modes of production.[36] The strength of Miles's Marxist analysis, focused on Caribbean slavery, lies in his adding racism to the materialist category of exploitive relations of production, but his marking of chattel slavery as an aspect of primitive accumulation, because it is or was unpaid and therefore not contributory to capital formation in a strict Marxist sense, consigns much of women's work in any political economy—even modern capitalism—to a precapitalist limbo. Despite their diverging emphases, both of these slavery models in Marxist theory omitted gender analysis and women.

Beginning in the 1970s feminist theorists, including Angela Davis and others, revised Marxism accordingly. They broadened the definition of women slaves' work and emphasized its value by theorizing that the unpaid labor of both free and enslaved women in many contexts, particularly domestic ones, increases the surplus value, or profitability, of men's paid labor while slave labor increases capitalist profits for both genders.[37] This profitability is one explanation for why slavery in its contemporary forms became increasingly prevalent in the twentieth century. Contemporary slavery results from high population densities within subordinated economies made possible by an international trade in food products and by the endless profit seeking of multinational corporations. Going into the twenty-first century, most of the world's slaves are women or girls, as they have been historically.[38]

Beyond historical North American and Caribbean slavery, where the majority of enslaved males performed the least skilled, most menial labor, in other systems higher proportions of enslaved men performed skilled labor, filled key military roles and could have substantial political and/or bureaucratic power, as in North Africa, China, and elsewhere.[39] Enslaved women, however, were usually confined to low-level jobs, which could nonetheless be skilled. Stuard's study of medieval European slavery filled a gap in the literature between Roman and American plantation slaveries by showing continuing "domestic" slavery for women; many women slaves on rural estates were used in textile production in *gynaecea*, female-staffed factories.[40] Eurocentric notions of women have ignored or undervalued the worth of women's productive labor, slave and free. Jennifer Morgan sees this phenomenon as a twentieth-century historiographical artifact not shared by New World slave owners in the seventeenth century, who valued women highly as laborers and exploited their labor accordingly.[41] The pervasive assumption that all women's work was (valueless) housework is evident in U.S. nineteenth-century abolitionist use of the trope of female domesticity. Some abolitionists objected that slavery forced women to do work unsuited to their tender natures, as did Marx to women working in mines.[42]

Robertson and Klein, influenced by Claude Meillassoux,[43] highlighted work as a key factor in women's enslavement in Africa. They recognized the predominance of women among the people enslaved in Africa, in contrast to the male majorities sold into the Atlantic trade, and argued that women slaves were kept in Africa more than men because:

1. Women were in demand as slaves primarily for their reproductive and productive labor (both domestic and agricultural), and only secondarily for their biological reproductive functions;

2. The demand for women slaves was linked closely to the high labor value of free women, whose labor slave women usually replaced or enabled, and who often were the primary users, supervisors and owners of women slaves;

3. The demand for women slaves hinged secondarily on their utility for expanding the numbers of people within kinship systems;

4. Free women's social structural and economic vulnerability made them more likely to be enslaved than free men;

5. And finally, colonial-era emancipation of slaves favored men because: women slaves were more likely to have been

assimilated within their owners' lineages; women slaves had
more difficulty than men in acquiring the money needed to
achieve self-emancipation; and especially because free and
slave women were more likely to be involved in labor-intensive
unskilled occupations than men, while colonialism drew more
men off into skilled and/or wage labor.[44]

Free women in eighteenth- and nineteenth-century trading towns
along the West African coast had well-established rights to own and control property independently of men. Accordingly, some particularly successful women traders, far from being victims, themselves dealt in slaves.
More commonly, free women owners and users of slaves controlled much
of the labor in systems where most of the slaves were women and sometimes were able to improve their situations economically and socially by
doing so.[45] Elsewhere, when most free women were arguably property
themselves, elite women often profited directly from the labor of slaves
who performed tasks they otherwise would have had to do themselves;
in some cases women increased production of textiles and other wares by
using female "factory" slave labor. Thus, the labor value of women slaves
could be a key factor in supporting elite status for free women, who, because of systemic disabilities in acquiring capital and hiring labor for wages,
depended more on slave labor than men did, and undoubtedly rooted their
identities in ideas of superiority connected to avoidance of menial labor.

The harem assumption that militated against analyzing slave women as
workers is the premise that slave women's sexual functions are not work;
this we have called the harem assumption. Joseph Miller's *Way of Death*,
for example, followed the common practice of including women slaves in
eighteenth-century Angola primarily as reproductive pawns for wealthy
men. Despite widespread evidence showing that slave women's fertility
was substantially lower than free women's and the inability of slave
women to produce legitimate heirs, Miller claimed that "harems of wives"
(he did not distinguish between slave and free wives) were forced to bear
more children than other free women. Women's prominence in agricultural labor in Africa, since Europeans began describing African labor systems in the fifteenth century, is attributed to increased (male) slavery
caused by the Atlantic slave trade, whereas the usual dominantly female
farming systems seem to have made women's labor more highly valued
and men more readily exportable.[46]

The harem assumption focus on women as reproducers has sometimes
made invisible the significant range of productive labor performed within

Islamic harems, as described by Leslie Peirce and Fatema Mernissi.[47] In spite of the importance of women's labor, their use as concubines is often assumed to explain the predominance of women in the slave trades to Muslim areas of Africa and beyond. Paul Lovejoy in *Transformations in Slavery* argued that prices for women slaves in the Sokoto caliphate were generally higher than for men because they were in demand as concubines. He also noted that birthrates among enslaved women were low, leaving us to conclude that enslaved African women were sex workers who must have used abortifacients or had high rates of sterility due to STDs. However, Lovejoy acknowledged that women were also the principal agricultural workers in the Sokoto caliphate, which undoubtedly enhanced their value.[48] Patrick Manning, who attempted to grapple with the situation of women slaves at a time when most did not, nonetheless also assumed that harems were only about sex rather than considering that one reason most harem women bore fewer children than other women was that their primary duties did not include sex work.[49] What work might enslaved women have performed in harems? Mohammed Ennaji pays specific attention to the training of slaves, including women, to do jobs beyond characteristic domestic work, such as chefs, musicians, and storekeepers in nineteenth-century Morocco.[50]

European women's narratives of enslavement in North Africa at the time of the Barbary Wars in the early nineteenth century also implicitly challenge the sexual emphasis in the harem assumption. Abolitionists wishing to whip up fervor against this "white slavery" sought usefully sensational narratives of harem owners' rapes of white women, only to be disappointed when they found tales of menial drudgery and pressure to convert to Islam. Paul Baepler assumed that "a female captive in an Algerian seraglio . . . would be forced to recount her rape" and was skeptical about the lack of sex work in two white female captivity narratives. Similarly, in the North American Southwest, Brooks expected sexual assault to be a prominent part of Spanish women's narratives of captivity among Native Americans and accepted that the captives' denials of rape might have been true, but only "given the stigma attached to cross-racial rape."[51] He thus leaves in place the general impression of enslavement of women as primarily sexual in aim.

Graham's study of domestic servants' work in Rio de Janeiro has perhaps the most detailed look at the high economic value of enslaved women's labor.[52] Judith Carney also questioned the assumption that slave women's work was valueless, based on the assumption that it was largely unskilled. She pointed out that "African-born slaves provided crucial expertise in the rice cultivation system" in South Carolina. Mainly women did the dehusking of the rice by hand, but eventually, with exponential growth in demand for their product, this task was degendered and men were trained to perform it.[53]

In many African and Asian slave systems the value of the labor of girls and women slaves was highest for the free women who owned and used them, since that labor replaced free women's labor and/or expanded its profitability. Edna Bay has demonstrated that women in slavery in the kingdom of Dahomey were involved in a whole range of occupations, from farmers and miners to soldiers, advisors to kings, queens, and queen mothers.[54] The overweening importance of women's agricultural work in Africa suggests that the Muslim ideal of secluding free women might have heightened demand for women slaves, who did not have the same status constraints that prevented free women from working outside the home.

Overstressing the sexual functions of women slaves also produces an exclusive emphasis on rape and/or slave breeding. Abolitionist tracts in the United States sometimes stressed bondswomen's sexual vulnerability, while contemporary cinematic representations of slavery are notable for this emphasis. *Sankofa, Amistad,* and *Beloved* all present slavery for women as primarily a problem of lack of control over their sexuality and biological reproduction. The sexual violence entailed in some forms of slavery is undoubtedly one of its most abhorrent aspects. It is also useful, however, to move beyond disgust to evaluate how sexuality impacted slave women's work. Some slave women's sexual services were routinized as prostitution, while some bondswomen might have viewed less organized sex as work. Various slave women's narratives, such as the one by Harriet Jacobs, indicate the prevalence of sexual harassment and rape as a prominent aspect of domestic servitude.[55] However, systems in which owners controlled the bodies of their slaves closely were often also systems in which systematic maltreatment and lack of provision for childrearing vitiated any systematic efforts at slave breeding. Indeed, in the United States and elsewhere, routine whipping and other physical abuse of pregnant bondswomen in connection with their agricultural or domestic work suggest that their work was more valuable to their owners than their utility as breeders.

The high value of slave women's work, as well as its invisibility as domestic labor, also explains why slavery for women often was abolished well after the emancipation of men, de facto or de jure, as we have seen. Gendered labor demands also have contributed to the present resurgence of slavery for women. In general, then, modeling slave women's work, especially beyond the Americas, needs to include many forms of production located within, as well as outside of, households, as well as sexual services.

Identity, Agency, and the Construction of Ideals of Citizenship

The third axis of slavery, social identity, especially as it connects to agency, has roots going back to Hegel and more recently has come to prominence in academic studies, following a strand introduced by Orlando Patterson with regard to male slaves. Slaves' social identity is often based by scholars on their degrees of agency and assimilation to specific societal ideals of citizenship. From slaves' own perspectives, they may find other identities based on ethnicity, race, work, and/or religion. Gender is also important for identity but much less documented for slaves outside of the United States.[56] However, in West Africa Sandra Greene made excellent use of oral history stretching back to the seventeenth century to develop a sensitive appreciation of identities among the Anlo-Ewe of the Gold Coast as related to outsider-insider status and to slave heritage.[57]

Ideas of freedom related to slaves' efforts at emancipation also might have played a strong role in identity formation.[58] The identities of slaves and their owners were related, since they were often mutually constructed. What this dialectical process means is that, like eighteenth-century Enlightenment men who constructed their identities as primary and women's identities as "other," slave owners might have seen slaves as "other," but slaves and owners alike both constructed oppositional identities. Notions of citizenship have been negatively affected, so far as women are concerned, by the assumption heavily influenced by male thought of the Enlightenment that premised full citizenship on masculinity; men were seen as the only fully human, rights-bearing individuals, as opposed to women, their adjuncts.

Linking this section to the preceding one on work, Hegel pointed out that slaves' (and other workers') subjectivities are mediated through their labor in creating new objects as expressions of self, as well as through the slaves' recognition of their shared relationship to the master.[59] Ira Berlin and Phillip Morgan drew on these intellectual roots to emphasize how slaves' identities could be influenced by their assessment of their work.

> Slavery was first and foremost an institution of coerced labor . . . work was both Adam's curse—unrelenting toil from which they derived but few benefits—and a source of personal satisfaction and political self-assertion. The act of creation, which even onerous and exploitative work entailed, allowed slaves to affirm

the humanity that chattel bondage denied. By making something
where once there was nothing, slaves discredited the masters'
shibboleth that they were simply property, countered the daily
humiliations which undermined their self-esteem, and laid claim
to the fruits of their labor for themselves and their posterity.[60]

In fact, the first gendering of identity of slaves by scholars focused on
slave men, who were "emasculated" when forced to do "women's work"
and deprived of control over women. Two assumptions are evident here:
first, that all women were controlled by men, and second, that property
status for the slave entailed complete loss of the rights and honor that
constitute identity.[61] Angela Davis again led the way to shift the focus of
scholarly discussion to the construction of identities of women slaves.
She looked particularly at areas of work where women slaves in the
United States had a certain autonomy as a possible source of pride, and
hence identity, for them. Robertson found a sense of identity in U.S.
women's ex-slave narratives preeminently rooted in performance of public, as opposed to domestic, work, even to the point of their constructing
motherhood in terms of that labor.[62] In Africa women—slave and free—
produced food to feed their families and sell in markets, along with other
goods manufactured at home. Men wanted wives who were good workers; indeed, male material prosperity was largely based on the number of
wives men could secure to increase the goods and children under his
control, and children in turn became labor and pawns for making alliances with other men through arranged marriages.

Slave women's identities are also strongly related to their degree of
agency, which is a core element in historical treatments of slavery in establishing their status as actors.[63] Pervasive in many studies of slavery is the assumption that women, enslaved or free, lacked agency. Hence they may be
referred to as only pawns (literally or figuratively) within a system.[64] Treating women in these passive terms goes back, among other roots, to the
structural societal analyses characteristic of anthropological studies of the
1950s and 1960s. For example, Claude Lévi-Strauss made incest taboos
within "kin" groups of related males and their exchanges of women among
themselves the fundamental building blocks of society.[65] If women's agency
was a casualty of this exclusive emphasis on male initiative, so was that of
men in some societies who were or are comparably "exchanged" through
female authority and matrilocality. The assumed passivity of women was
an extension to other parts of the world of early modern and nineteenth-
century European laws that confined full rights of citizenship to men and

made most women effectively the property of males. An unstated social Darwinist assumption prevailed that all history consists of the unfolding of male superiority and power in various guises of patriarchy, within which women are invariably seen as disempowered.

The intertwined statuses of slave and free women in many slave systems requires closer consideration of the agency of free women as well. Although a growing literature regarding the Americas has taken into account the agency of free white women as slave users and owners,[66] a paucity of literature elsewhere leaves interactions between women of slave and free statuses in obscurity. An exception is Margaret Strobel's pioneering study of slave and slave-owning female-dominated households among Swahili women in Mombasa.[67] However, when Peter Haenger mined Basel Mission archives from the mid-nineteenth-century Gold Coast, where women predominated both as slaves and as slave users, he was more interested in the Basel missionaries' impact than in a gendered analysis of their interactions.[68]

If women had agency as owners of slaves, so also—though to varying degrees—did women as slaves. Rosalind Petcheskey noted that "slave culture, in rebellion against the laws of property, generated an ethic and practice of bodily self-determination."[69] A large and long-running literature on the resistance of slaves has included women in the last twenty years or so. Much of it concerns the United States, but two exemplary treatments of women resisters in the Caribbean, following Lucille Mathurin Mair's pioneering study, are Hilary Beckles's *Natural Rebels: A Social History of Enslaved Black Women in Barbados* and Bernard Moitt's *Women and Slavery in the French Antilles, 1635–1848*.[70] Beckles especially pointed out the success of self-emancipation efforts of some slaves and their activism in abolition movements.[71]

In three collections of articles focusing on emancipation of slaves in Africa and Asia, only five out of thirty-four articles differentiated the dynamics of women slaves' emancipation from men's.[72] Those five attributed obstacles to women's emancipation to their vulnerability within kinship systems. Owners often claimed falsely that their slave women were "wives," whose attempts to escape their husbands' control required foiling; colonial administrators normally accepted that argument. However, in German East Africa many women slaves, used largely for agricultural labor and thus not remotely presentable to colonial officials as "wives," tried to escape or claimed their freedom under German law.[73]

The search for slave women's agency can be distorted by the premise— what we term the seduction assumption—of the slave woman as temptress, which sexualized women's strategies for gaining personal freedom. Ennaji presented manumission for slave women as a general result of bearing children to the master or owner under Qur'anic provisions.[74] Hünefeldt stated that Peruvian women slaves in nineteenth-century Lima used liaisons with masters as a way to gain manumission, but her examples suggest that this strategy often failed to free themselves, although it could succeed in freeing their children by their owner.[75] Even in New Orleans, the most racially open U.S. context, the exchange of sexual services for freedom for one's children did not often succeed, since slave women's children took the status of their mother, and free fathers routinely denied their paternity due to its potential for disrupting the legitimate household.[76] The premise of the slave woman as seductress must also be used with care lest it distract attention in some systems from the routine sexual abuse of women by blaming the victim. Landers recounts the story of Juana, which has all the emotive power of Toni Morrison's novel *Beloved*. Juana killed her two children when her cruel owner sold her away from them and then survived her trial for murder by using mechanisms available within Spanish law.[77]

The life histories that women slaves themselves recounted show their struggles, resistance, ambitions, and interiority as, by writing, they declared their status as active subjects, not just passive objects.[78] Many of the best studies of women and slavery focus on these narratives, which demonstrate strong desires for freedom.[79] Freedom is a central theme in the narratives of East and Central African women slaves analyzed by Marcia Wright. Wright's account of Bwanikwa, for instance, illustrates the importance of manumission in Bwanikwa's life due to her recognition that full assimilation depended on free status. She experienced none of the assimilation of women slaves emphasized elsewhere in the literature on slavery in Africa.[80]

Scholars of slavery who, like Orlando Patterson, have defined slavery as entailing a loss of honor for slaves, omit consideration of women. Free women in systems that valued male honor were usually bearers of male honor, effectively possessed by men but not themselves possessors of it. Slave women were merely symbols of male honor, which entailed male enforcement of female virginity or virtue for free wives but for slave women meant vulnerability to rape. Ramón Gutiérrez pointed to the oppositional construction of honor in the Hispanic Southwest. "The [Spanish] aristocracy found in a slave's infamy the meaning of their own honor." He went on to note that "the maintenance of virtue among aristocratic females was possible only because Indian and *genizaro* [slave] women could be forced or persuaded to offer sexual service . . . women were pawns in the honor system."[81]

Cultural influences, intersections, interstices, and diffusion are the foci of a growing scholarly literature on the Atlantic diaspora, stressing identity issues in terms of self-claimed cultures—that is, Africans' adaptations of their backgrounds in new environments of enslavement in the Americas—rather than in terms of race; the latter is arguably a white-imposed construct. However, this literature has paid scant attention to women's particular, gendered roles in the process of transmitting cultures from Africa. Within feminist thinking one strand emphasizes women's distinctive qualities and accomplishments as sources of female identity. Thus, some have emphasized the notion of a pan-female culture including all women, slaves as well as free, that is complementary or opposed to men's and to some degree sex segregated. Carol Eastman explored what she called the "gender-based dual nature" of Kenyan Swahili culture, in which "the fusion of African and Arab cultural influences . . . represents the differential and dichotomous influence[s] of men and women." Women in this case belonged to a distinct African "female sub-culture" descended from slave women from the interior, while men inherited Arabized influences from their fathers. Assimilation there, contrary to Margaret Strobel's observations in the same region, meant the cultural influence of slave women on free persons, both male and female, rather than vice versa.[82]

Discussion of slave and free women in coastal West Africa, daughters of European trader-fathers and African women with local kin connections, has focused on their agency as mediators between interior cultures and those of the Atlantic and Europe.[83] Mulatto women slaves in the Americas, often sexually used or abused by whites, occupied similarly liminal spaces and negotiated their liminality in various ways. For instance, in the francophone Caribbean such women slaves had considerable flexibility to negotiate advantages from sexual liaisons with their owners, though anglophones were more inflexibly racist and tolerated fewer opportunities for negotiation from the margins.[84] Brooks stressed the many mediating functions performed by enslaved women across cultural divides in the eighteenth and nineteenth centuries in the Southwest, which created a single regionally integrated culture rather than dual ethnically divided ones.[85]

Intersectionality is an influential black feminist concept pertaining to identity among oppressed groups, so that to live as black, female, and lesbian, for instance, in the United States is to inhabit an intersection of statuses that do not merely add the disadvantages of each but rather multiply them.[86] Jennifer Morgan in *Laboring Women* utilized the complex manifestations and connections of intersectionality in focusing on slave women's biological reproductive functions and centering "the lives of enslaved women in the colonial period . . . not simply [as] an exercise of inclusion but [as] a foundational methodology." In doing so Morgan analyzed how slavery changed the meaning and experiences of reproduction for slave women.[87] Hünefeldt also considered "how conceptions of integration and identity may or may not appear" along gradations of servitude.[88]

Within the framework we propose here, the status and identity axes of slavery intersect in kinship, since kinship links establish identity categories as well as rights. When slave women were assimilated into lineages, as in some African societies, their situation blurred the boundary between free and slave women, often to the detriment of freeborn women, by emphasizing uncertainties linked to kin status in aspects of women's identities. Brooks did not see the Southwestern slave trade as disastrous for its female victims but rather as an opportunity for captives who had "the ability to embrace the complex politics and social networks of which it [the trade] was composed."[89] At the other end of the slavery continuum, women snatched into the slave trade from among the Mang'anja of Central Africa experienced catastrophic losses of security and identity, as documented by Elias Mandala in *Work and Control in a Peasant Economy*. Onaiwu Ogbomo in *When Men and Women Mattered* examined gender relations within a society subjected to slave raids, the Owan of Nigeria.[90]

Pamela Scully pointed out that slaves, slave owners, and English abolitionists at the Cape in South Africa all conceptualized the meanings of slavery and freedom partly through the language of family and gender relations, and that this language in turn shaped access to freedom during and after slavery. These different groups connected gender to discourses of race and class to define the postemancipation era as a struggle over the meanings of femininity and masculinity. Therefore, slave emancipation was as much a "story of culture and identity [as] of the emergence of free wage labor."[91] Thomas Holt emphasized the construction of freedom in Jamaica as entailing "gendered spheres of activity and authority," hardworking republican citizenship for men and housewifery for women, while Frederick Cooper pointed out that African emancipation also "posed a problem of power and gender relations."[92]

For women in slavery, then, studies from the Americas and Africa have shown that agency was closely tied to notions of identity, which in turn has linkages to ideas about ethnicity, race, work, gender, and sexuality.

All these played into notions of citizenship. We need more work exploring these issues in all contexts, including other regions, religion, and
male sexuality, in particular.

Research on slavery can be strengthened by more systematic attention to
women and gender, especially outside the Americas, as well as to class,
race, sexuality, and other fundamental factors influencing slavery. Jennifer Morgan put it very well: "When we invoke race and gender as
critical analytic categories, we set in motion radical changes. The way
we understand the configuration of power, the individual and collective
meaning attached to events, the construction of communities, the
rhythms of cultural encounter and transformation, the very terms of
change, are all transformed . . . if one dismantles the assumptions about
antecedents."[93] Our theoretical historiography of gender, women, and
slavery here has unpacked a number of problematic assumptions regarding three aspects of slavery as it concerns women. In dealing with the
first axis of slavery regarding rights and status of women slaves, we found
that analyses have suffered from the normalization of the male slave and
the omission of women slaves. Similarly, the tendency to universalize
definitions of slavery that focus on rights and status sometimes perpe-
trated distortions along gendered lines. Some definitions helped mask
the history of pervasive "domestic" slavery for women, but its recovery,
however difficult, is all the more urgent since slavery helps to explain
many contemporary forms of unfree labor. In addition, gendered studies
have supported Kopytoff and Miers's idea of a continuum of statuses and
rights across slavery systems, especially as regards women, for whom slavery and freedom were or are related and relative notions, always subject
to renegotiation in a myriad of ways.

Regarding the work axis there have been strong tendencies to under-
value slave and free women's labor and to conflate that work with slave
women's presumed status as concubines, which we have termed the
harem assumption. Both tendencies make women's work invisible, while
not counting sex work as work. If women now often complain of a double day doing both their employers' and their own household work,
women slaves often suffered superexploitation that included a quadruple
workload. Under U.S. chattel slavery women did: fieldwork from sunup
to sundown; spinning in the evenings to meet quotas; sex work; cooking,
gardening, laundry, and childcare for their owners; and domestic labor
for their families.[94] Work therefore was and is at least as defining an element in slavery for women as it was and is for men, an aspect of slavery

not confined to the Americas. It also greatly affected emancipation of slave women, which often came more slowly for women than men because of their differential assimilation into the workforce and into families.

Lastly, gendering the analysis of citizenship, agency, and identity is vital in order to understand the implications of slavery for free, freed, and slave women. "Universal" categories that exclude women have also done a great disservice in this area. Gendered analysis, for instance, yields new perspectives on enslaved women's narratives but could be applied also to men's narratives. The impact of dominant discourses regarding appropriate behavior for men seems to be that we have relatively little that speaks to their sexuality. Homosexual rape, for instance, is a taboo subject both for scholars and in narratives, which may mandate strategic but careful attention to their silences. What if, instead of assuming the nature of the psychological impact of castration on slave eunuchs, we explored it instead? In addition, if harems were theoretically about compulsory heterosexuality, we might also want to look at them in terms of male and female homosociality.

How identity and citizenship are constructed and gendered is a topic with recognized contemporary salience but has largely been ignored with regard to women in slavery. Women, slave and free, have often been assumed to be universal victims and lack agency, that vital part of identity, while they have been excluded not only from having the rights of citizens but also from notions of ideal citizenship.

This re-modeling of women and slavery is intended to be neither essentializing nor definitive but rather to open up new ways of discussing both. If there is a consistent aspect of slavery in various societies it was that it constantly changed its forms and functions, obligations and rights, slaves' productive and reproductive work, and processes of identity formation, sexuality, agency, and the construction of ideals of citizenship. Even within any one slave's life her experiences of slavery could change, since, as Kopytoff and Miers posited, slavery is a process rather than a fixed status.[95]

In the end it is clear that only a holistic gendered analysis of slavery can help us understand the past and improve the future, both to illuminate slavery historically and eliminate slavery as a multifaceted contemporary phenomenon. Joan Scott noted that historians need "analysis not only of the relationship between male and female experience in the past but also of the connection between past history and current historical practice."[96] Slavery is a contemporary issue; trafficking in women takes place from the Philippines through the United States to eastern Europe,

from India to China, and from Mauretania to Sudan. Some forms of slavery apply only or mostly to women or endure because mostly women are
victimized by them.[97] The world capitalist economy has revised slavery to
meet its demands for profits. We can understand the persistence of the
traffic in women and children only if we re-model our history, as elo-
quently urged by Chatterjee: "What is needed is not so much a history from
below, but a history from within, a history of exile from natalities and the
recovery of belonging, a history in which nothing was too ephemeral and
no grain of sand—the annas and pice of a slave-girl's peculium [small
savings], or the petty fines paid by a slave-concubine—too tiny to make
up the bedrock of a colonial empire."[98] We can do better in both our
analyses and practices, which should not obscure but elucidate that which
is still vital within the world community. Incorporating women's and
gender history into our analyses of servitude is both a scholarly and an
ethical necessity.

NOTES

1. Patricia van der Spuy, "Gender and Slavery: Towards a Feminist Revision,"
South Africa Historical Journal 25 (1991): 184–95; Bridget Brereton, "Searching for
the Invisible Woman," *Slavery and Abolition* 13, no. 2 (1992): 86–96. Jennifer L.
Morgan, *Laboring Women Reproduction and Gender in New World Slavery* (Philadelphia: University of Pennsylvania Press, 2004), 5, notes that after the 1980s there
were only four monographs on women and New World slavery.

2. Hilary Beckles, *Natural Rebels: A Social History of Enslaved Black Women in
Barbados* (London: Zed, 1989), 5.

3. Monique Deveaux, "Feminism and Empowerment: A Critical Reading of Foucault," in *Feminist Approaches to Theory and Methodology*, ed. Sharlene Hesse-Biber,
Christina Gilmartin, and Robin Lydenberg (New York: Oxford University Press,
1999), 247.

4. Joan Wallach Scott, *Gender and the Politics of History* (New York: Columbia
University Press, 1988), 25.

5. David Brion Davis, "Looking at Slavery from Broader Perspectives," *American
Historical Review* 105, no. 2 (2000): 452–66.

6. Gerda Lerner, "Women and Slavery," *Slavery and Abolition* 4, 3 (1983): 174–77.

7. Joseph C. Miller and Daniel H. Borus, "Slavery: A Supplementary Teaching Bibliography," *Slavery and Abolition* 1, no. 1 (1980): 65–110; Joseph C. Miller and
Thomas E. Ridenhour, "Annual Bibliographical Supplement (2001)," *Slavery and
Abolition* 23, no. 3 (2002): 167–317. Works deemed to be focused on women and/or
gender either had titles with those terms in them or concerned topics that by necessity focused on women or girls (family did not qualify as such a category since it is
possible to analyze families without prioritizing women or girls).

8. Van der Spuy, "Gender and Slavery"; Brereton, "Invisible Woman."

9. Mary Helen Washington, "Meditations on History: The Slave Woman's Voice," in *Invented Lives: Narratives of Black Women, 1860–1960*, ed. Washington (New York: Doubleday, 1987), 3–5.

10. Well over half the bibliographical entries for 2001 in *Slavery and Abolition* concern chattel slavery in the Americas. A review of the numbers arguments can be found in David Northrup, ed., *The Atlantic Slave Trade*, rev. ed. (Lexington, MA: D. C. Heath, 2000), whose first edition not only omits female authors but also fails to mention any sources on women and slavery in its recommendations for further reading. Gender analysis is also largely absent from a five-hundred-page recent reader on slavery edited by Stanley Engerman, Seymour Drescher, and Robert Paquette, *Slavery* (New York: Oxford University Press, 2001).

11. Alan Gallay in *The Indian Slave Trade: The Rise of the English Empire in the American South, 1670–1717* (New Haven: Yale University Press, 2002), waits until pages 311–12 to say that the trade overwhelmingly included women and children. See also Margaret Newell, "The Changing Nature of Indian Slavery in New England, 1670–1720," paper presented at Ohio State University Early Modern History Seminar (November 2001), and James F. Brooks, *Captives and Cousins: Slavery, Kinship and Community in the Southwest Borderlands* (Chapel Hill: University of North Carolina Press, 2002).

12. G. Ugo Nwokeji, "African Conceptions of Gender and the Slave Traffic," *William and Mary Quarterly* 58, no. 1 (2001): http://www.historycooperative.org/journals/wm/58.1/nwokeji.html.

13. Indrani Chatterjee, *Gender, Slavery and Law in Colonial India* (New Delhi: Oxford University Press, 1999), 1–2; Ibrahim M. Jumare, "The Late Treatment of Slavery in Sokoto: Background and Consequences of the 1936 Proclamation," *International Journal of African Historical Studies* 27, no. 2 (1994): 303–22; Elizabeth Thompson, *Colonial Citizens Republican Rights, Paternal Privilege, and Gender in French Syria and Lebanon* (New York: Columbia University Press, 1999).

14. H. J. Nieboer, *Slavery as an Industrial System* (The Hague: Martinus Nijhoff, 1900), 3–4; Moses I. Finley, *Economy and Society in Ancient Greece* (New York: Penguin, 1981), 97–98; Orlando Patterson, *Slavery and Social Death* (Cambridge: Harvard University Press, 1982), 38.

15. Igor Kopytoff and Suzanne Miers, introduction to *Slavery in Africa: Historical and Anthropological Perspectives*, ed. Miers and Kopytoff (Madison: University of Wisconsin Press, 1977); James L. Watson, "Transactions in People: The Chinese Market in Slaves, Servants and Heirs," in *Asian and African Systems of Slavery*, ed. Watson (Oxford: Basil Blackwell, 1980), 223–50.

16. Lerner, "Women and Slavery," 174–77.

17. Angela Y. Davis, *Women, Race and Class* (New York: Vintage, 1983), 2–29.

18. Deborah Gray White, *Ar'n't I a Woman? Female Slaves in the Plantation South* (New York: Norton, 1985); Jacqueline Jones, *Labor of Love, Labor of Sorrow: Black Women, Work, and the Family from Slavery to the Present* (New York: Basic Books, 1985).

19. Patterson is referring to the efforts of upper-class free Roman women to establish their legal autonomy. By extension, this argument would root mid-nineteenth-century U.S. slave women's notions of freedom in the simultaneous dominantly

white women's rights movement, whereas just the opposite was true. The women's rights movement came out of the abolition movement, which supports Patterson's thesis. Orlando Patterson, *Freedom in the Making of Western Culture* (New York: Basic Books, 1991), xiii–xiv, 250–55.

20. Robin Blackburn, *The Making of New World Slavery: From the Baroque to the Modern, 1492–1800* (London: Verso, 1997), 4–5; David Brion Davis, *Slavery and Human Progress* (New York: Oxford University Press, 1984), 14, ch. 5.

21. Linda Martin Alcoff, "Feminist Theory and Social Science: New Knowledges, New Epistemologies," in *BodySpace: Destabilizing Geographies of Gender and Sexuality*, ed. Nancy Duncan (London: Routledge, 1996), 13–27.

22. Claire C. Robertson and Martin A. Klein, "Women's Importance in African Slave Systems," in *Women and Slavery in Africa*, ed. Robertson and Klein (Madison: University of Wisconsin Press, 1983), 6, 15; Brooks, *Captives and Cousins*, 268.

23. Ira Berlin, *Many Thousands Gone: The First Two Centuries of Slavery in North America* (Cambridge, MA: Harvard University Press, Belknap Press, 1988), 136–37, 157; Robert Olwell, "'Loose, Idle and Disorderly': Slave Women in the Eighteenth-Century Charleston Marketplace," in *More than Chattel: Black Women and Slavery in the Americas*, ed. D. Barry Gaspar and Darlene Clark Hine (Bloomington: Indiana University Press, 1996), 97–110.

24. Christine Hünefeldt, *Paying the Price of Freedom: Family and Labor among Lima's Slaves, 1800–1854* (Berkeley: University of California Press, 1994), 5, 32–45, 80–81, 95–96, 205–6.

25. Sandra Lauderdale Graham, *House and Street: The Domestic World of Servants and Masters in Nineteenth-Century Rio de Janeiro* (Cambridge: Cambridge University Press, 1988), 4, 11, 62, 21, 80–82, 104–5, 109, 141n7. For women's status in North American Spanish law, see Quintard Taylor, *In Search of the Racial Frontier: African Americans in the American West, 1528–1990* (New York: Norton, 1998); Q. Taylor and Shirley Ann Moore, eds., *African American Women Confront the West, 1600–2000* (Norman: University of Oklahoma Press, 2003).

26. Jane Landers, *Black Society in Spanish Florida* (Urbana: University of Illinois Press, 1999), ch. 6; Larry E. Rivers, *Slavery in Florida: Territorial Days to Emancipation* (Gainesville: University Press of Florida, 2000).

27. Brooks, *Captives and Cousins*, 5–6, 30–31, 34n54, 180; Ramón A. Gutiérrez, *When Jesus Came, the Corn Mothers Went Away: Marriage, Sexuality, and Power in New Mexico, 1500–1846* (Stanford: Stanford University Press, 1991), 181–83.

28. Jumare, "Late Treatment."

29. Ehud Toledano, "Slave Dealers, Women, Pregnancy and Abortion: The Story of a Circassian Slave-Girl in Mid-Nineteenth Century Cairo," *Slavery and Abolition* 2, no. 1 (1981): 53–68; Judith Tucker, "Gender and Islamic History," in *Islamic and European Expansion: The Forging of a Global Order*, ed. Michael Adas (Philadelphia: Temple University Press, 1993), 48.

30. K. R. Bradley, *Slaves and Masters in the Roman Empire: A Study in Social Control*, Latonium Revue d'Etudes Latines, vol. 185 (Brussels: Latomus, 1984); Bradley, *Slavery and Society at Rome* (New York: Cambridge University Press, 1994). Sarah B. Pomeroy, *Goddesses, Whores, Wives, and Slaves* (New York: Schocken, 1975). See

also Pomeroy, *Women in Hellenistic Egypt: From Alexander to Cleopatra* (Detroit: Wayne State University Press, 1990); Pomeroy, *Spartan Women* (New York: Oxford University Press, 2002). With the notable exception of David Wiles, the classicist contributors to *Slavery and Other Forms of Unfree Labour*, ed. Leonie Archer (New York: Routledge, 1988) ignored women and gender.

31. S. R. Joshel and S. Murnaghan, *Women and Slaves in Greco-Roman Culture: Differential Equations* (London: Routledge, 1998), 1–21. Walter Scheidel makes a thoughtful effort to uncover the hidden history of rural working-class women in ancient Greece and Rome. Scheidel, "The Most Silent Women of Greece and Rome: Rural Labour and Women's Life in the Ancient World," *Greece and Rome* 52, no. 2 (1995): 202–17; *Greece and Rome* 53, no. 1 (1996): 1–10. See also Barbara McManus, *Classics and Feminism Gendering the Classics* (New York: Twayne, 1997), 18–19, 58–59.

32. Nell Irvin Painter, "Slavery and Soul Murder," in *Black on White: Black Writers on What It Means to Be White*, ed. David R. Roediger (New York: Schocken, 1992), 328–30.

33. Kevin Bales, *Disposable People: New Slavery in the Global Economy* (Berkeley: University of California Press, 1999).

34. Elaine Pearson, "Trapped in the Traffic," *New Internationalist* 337 (2001): 25, 28–29. *National Geographic*'s special issue on contemporary slavery (September 2003) relied primarily on Bales. Similarly, the fact that most of the crimes that are the subject of late-night reality TV shows are against women goes unquestioned and unanalyzed.

35. Walter Rodney, "African Slavery and Other Forms of Social Oppression on the Upper Guinea Coast in the Context of the Atlantic Slave Trade," *Journal of African History* 7, no. 3 (1966): 431–43; Eric Williams, *Capitalism and Slavery* (Chapel Hill: University of North Carolina Press, 1944); Williams, *History of the People of Trinidad and Tobago* (New York: Praeger, 1964), 83–85.

36. Robert Miles, *Capitalism and Unfree Labour: Anomaly or Necessity?* (London: Tavistock, 1987), 178, 222.

37. Claire Robertson and Iris Berger, introduction to *Women and Class in Africa*, ed. Robertson and Berger (New York: Africana, 1986); Rosemary Hennessy and Chrys Ingraham, eds., *Materialist Feminism: A Reader in Class, Difference, and Women's Lives* (New York: Routledge, 1997).

38. Bales, *Disposable People*.

39. Patterson, *Slavery*; John Blassingame, *The Slave Community: Plantation Life in the Antebellum South* (New York: Oxford University Press, 1979).

40. Susan Mosher Stuard, "Ancillary Evidence for the Decline of Medieval Slavery," *Past and Present* 149 (1995): 3–48.

41. J. Morgan, *Laboring Women*, 146ff.

42. A. Davis, *Women, Race*, 11.

43. Claude Meillassoux, introduction to *The Development of Indigenous Trade and Markets in West Africa*, ed. Meillassoux, studies presented and discussed at the Tenth International African Seminar at Fourah Bay College, Freetown, Sierra Leone, 1969 (London: Oxford University Press, 1971), 3–48; English translation, 49–86; Meillas-

soux, ed., *L'esclavage en Afrique précoloniale* (Paris: Maspéro, 1975); "Rôle de l'esclavage dans l'histoire de l'Afrique occidentale," *Anthropologie et sociétés* 2, no. 1 (1978): 117–48, translated as "The Role of Slavery in the Economic and Social History of Sahelo-Sudanic Africa," in *Forced Migration: The Impact of the Export Slave Trade on African Societies*, ed. Joseph E. Inikori (London: Hutchinson, 1981), 74–99.

44. Robertson and Klein, "Women's Importance."

45. Ibid., 3–25, sec. 4.

46. Joseph C. Miller, *Way of Death: Merchant Capitalism and the Angolan Slave Trade, 1730–1830* (Madison: University of Wisconsin Press, 1988), 101–2, 135–36. Elsewhere Miller demonstrates further thinking about the issues involved in analyzing women and slavery. For slave fertility rates in similar contexts, see John Thornton, "Sexual Demography: The Impact of the Slave Trade on Family Structure"; Robert Harms, "Sustaining the System: Trading Towns along the Middle Zaire"; Marcia Wright, "Bwanikwa: Consciousness and Protest among Slave Women in Central Africa, 1886–1911," all in Robertson and Klein, *Women and Slavery*, 48, 95–110, 246–67.

47. Leslie Peirce, *The Imperial Harem: Women and Sovereignty in the Ottoman Empire* (New York: Oxford University Press, 1993); Fatema Mernissi, *Dreams of Trespass: Tales of a Harem Girlhood* (Reading, MA: Addison-Wesley, 1994). Using concubinage as an exclusive explanation for contemporary slavery for women, Jan Hogendorn illustrates the concubine assumption in "Abolition and Anti-Slavery," in *A Historical Guide to World Slavery*, ed. Seymour Drescher and Stanley L. Engerman (New York: Oxford University Press, 1998), 5. See also Varsha Joshi, *Polygamy and Purdah: Women and Society among Rajputs* (Jaipur: Rawat, 1995).

48. Paul Lovejoy, *Transformations in African Slavery: A History of Slavery in Africa* (Cambridge: Cambridge University Press, 1983), 6, 9, 12, 126, 133. See also Lovejoy, "Concubinage and the Status of Women Slaves in Early Colonial Northern Nigeria," *Journal of African History* 29, no. 2 (1988): 245–66. Lovejoy has recently paid more attention to the situation of slave women in the Americas.

49. Patrick Manning, *Slavery and African Life: Occidental, Oriental, and African Slave Trades* (Cambridge: Cambridge University Press, 1990), 116; Edna G. Bay, *Wives of the Leopard: Gender, Politics, and Culture in the Kingdom of Dahomey* (Charlottesville: University of Virginia Press, 1998).

50. Mohammed Ennaji, *Serving the Master: Slavery and Society in Nineteenth-Century Morocco*, trans. Seth Graebner (New York: St. Martin's, 1999), 11–13, 28.

51. Paul Baepler, *White Slaves, African Masters: An Anthology of American Barbary Captivity Narratives* (Chicago: University of Chicago Press, 1999), 11; Brooks, *Captives and Cousins*, 290.

52. Graham, *House and Street*, 30ff.

53. Judith Carney, "Rice Milling, Gender and Slave Labour in Colonial South Carolina," *Past and Present* 153 (1996): 108–34.

54. Edna G. Bay, "Servitude and Worldly Success in the Palace of Dahomey," in Robertson and Klein, *Women and Slavery*; Bay, *Wives*, 340–67. See also Robertson and Klein, "Women's Importance," 9–10. An earlier effort that broached some of these issues was Boniface Obichere, "Women and Slavery in the Kingdom of Dahomey," *Revue d'histoire d'outre-mer* 66 (1978): 5–20.

55. Harriet Jacobs, *Incidents in the Life of a Slave Girl*, ed. Jean F. Yellin (1861; reprint, Cambridge, MA: Harvard University Press, 1987); Henry Louis Gates Jr., ed., *Classic Slave Narratives* (New York: Oxford University Press, 1988); William R. Andrews, ed., *Six Women's Slave Narratives* (New York: Oxford University Press, 1988); Hannah Crafts, *The Bondwoman's Narrative*, ed. Gates (New York: Warner, 2002); Thelma Jennings, "'Us Colored Women Had to Go through a Plenty': Sexual Exploitation of African-American Slave Women," *Journal of Women's History* 1, no. 3 (1990): 15–74; Steven E. Brown, "Sexuality and the Slave Community," *Phylon* 42 (1984): 1–10; Diana E. Axelsen, "Women as Victims of Medical Experimentation: J. Marion Sims' Surgery on Slave Women, 1845–1850," *Sage* 2, no. 2 (1985): 10–13.

56. For North American sexuality related to slavery, see Catherine Clinton and Michele Gillespie, *The Devil's Lane: Sex and Race in the Early South* (New York: Oxford University Press, 1997); Anthony Parent and Susan Brown Wallace, "Childhood and Sexual Identity under Slavery," *Journal of the History of Sexuality* 3 (1992–93): 363–401; Maria Diedrich, "'My Love Is Black as Yours Is Fair': Premarital Love and Sexuality in the Antebellum Slave Narrative," *Phylon* 47, no. 3 (1986): 238–47.

57. Sandra E. Greene, *Gender, Ethnicity, and Social Change on the Upper Slave Coast: A History of the Anlo-Ewe* (Portsmouth, NH: Heinemann, 1996).

58. Claire Robertson, "Claiming Freedom: Abolition and Identity in St. Lucian History," *Journal of Caribbean History* 34, no. 1–2 (2000): 89–129.

59. Hegel, as interpreted by Alcoff, "Feminist Theory," 24.

60. Ira Berlin and Philip Morgan, introduction to *Cultivation and Culture: Labor and the Shaping of Slave Life in the Americas*, ed. Berlin and Morgan (Charlottesville: University Press of Virginia, 1993), 1.

61. Patterson, *Slavery*; Blassingame, *Slave Community*.

62. "Slave and Freed Women, Work and Identity," Slave Routes: The Long Memory Conference, UNESCO/Institute of African-American Affairs/Smithsonian/Schomburg Library Conference, New York University, October, 1999; Robertson, "Femmes esclaves et femmes libres: travail et identité de l'Afrique à l'Amérique," *Cahiers des Anneaux de la Mémoire* 5 (2003): 123–46.

63. Scott, *Gender*, 18–20.

64. The common reference to "women in slavery," as opposed to "women *and* slavery," considers women as victims of slave systems rather than as participants at all levels, with varying statuses and degrees of agency.

65. Claude Lévi-Strauss, *The Raw and the Cooked* (New York: Penguin, 1966).

66. Catherine Clinton, *The Plantation Mistress: Woman's World in the Old South* (New York: Pantheon, 1982) pioneered this literature, notably furthered by Elizabeth Fox-Genovese, *Within the Plantation Household: Black and White Women of the Old South* (Chapel Hill: University of North Carolina Press, 1988); Marli F. Weiner, *Plantation Women in South Carolina* (Urbana: University of Illinois Press, 1997).

67. Margaret Strobel, "Slavery and Reproductive Labor in Mombasa," in Robertson and Klein, *Women and Slavery*, 111–29; see also Strobel, *Muslim Women in Mombasa* (New Haven: Yale University Press, 1979).

68. Peter Haenger, *Slaves and Slave Holders on the Gold Coast: Towards an Understanding of Social Bondage in West Africa*, ed. J. J. Shaffer and Paul Lovejoy, trans. Christina Handford (Basel: P. Schlettwein, 2000).

69. Rosalind Pollack Petcheskey, "The Body as Property: A Feminist Re-vision," in *Conceiving the New World Order: The Global Politics of Reproduction*, ed. Faye Ginsburg and Rayna Rapp (Berkeley: University of California Press, 1995), 397.

70. Lucille Mathurin Mair, *The Rebel Woman in the British West Indies during Slavery* (Kingston: Institute of Jamaica, 1975); Hilary Beckles, *Natural Rebels*; Bernard Moitt, *Women and Slavery in the French Antilles, 1635–1848* (Bloomington: Indiana University Press, 2001).

71. Hilary Beckles, "Caribbean Anti-Slavery: The Self-Liberation Ethos of Enslaved Blacks," *Journal of Caribbean History* 22 (1988): 1–19.

72. Suzanne Miers and Richard Roberts, eds., *The End of Slavery in Africa* (Madison: University of Wisconsin Press, 1988); Martin A. Klein, ed., *Breaking the Chains: Slavery, Bondage, and Emancipation in Modern Africa and Asia* (Madison: University of Wisconsin Press, 1993); Suzanne Miers and Martin Klein, eds., *Slavery and Colonial Rule in Africa* (London: Frank Cass, 1999). The authors in Miers and Klein's and Miers and Roberts's collections were specifically requested to include women in the analyses. Suzanne Miers, pers. comm., 3 December 2003. Because Kwabena Opare-Akurang ignored gender, he could not explain the failure to enforce the 1874 Gold Coast ordinance abolishing slavery. Opare-Akurang, in Miers and Klein, *Slavery and Colonial Rule*, 149–66. For a corrective, see Claire C. Robertson, "Post-Proclamation Slavery," in Robertson and Klein, *Women and Slavery*, 220–45.

73. Jan-Georg Deutsch, "The 'Freeing' of Slaves in German East Africa: The Statistical Record, 1890–1914," in *Slavery and Colonial Rule in Africa*, ed. Miers and Klein, 109–32.

74. Ennaji, *Serving the Master*, 35.

75. Hünefeldt, *Paying the Price*, 130–40.

76. Judith Schafer, "Open and Notorious Concubinage: The Emancipation of Slave Mistresses by Will and the Supreme Court in Antebellum Louisiana," *Louisiana History* 28 (1987): 165–82.

77. Toni Morrison, *Beloved: A Novel* (New York: Plume, 1998); Landers, *Black Society*, 187.

78. Jacobs, *Incidents*; Mary Prince, "History" in *Classic Slave Narratives*; Hannah Crafts, *Bondwoman's Narrative*.

79. Maria Jaschok, "Chinese 'Slave' Girls in Yunnan-Fu: Saving (Chinese) Womanhood and (Western) Souls, 1930–1991" and other articles in *Women and Chinese Patriarchy: Submission, Servitude, and Escape*, ed. Maria Jaschok and Suzanne Miers (London: Zed, 1994); Toledano, "Slave Dealers."

80. Marcia Wright, "Bwanikwa"; Wright, *Strategies of Slaves and Women: Life-Stories from East/Central Africa* (New York: Lilian Barber, 1993).

81. Gutiérrez, *When Jesus Came*, 153, 190, 208–10, 214–15, 221.

82. Carol M. Eastman, "Women, Slaves and Foreigners: African Cultural Influences and Group Processes in the Formation of Northern Swahili Coastal Society," *International Journal of African Historical Studies* 21, no. 1 (1988): 1–2, 20; Eastman,

"Waungwana na Wanawake: Muslim Ethnicity and Sexual Segregation in Coastal Kenya," *Journal of Multilingual and Multicultural Development* 5, no. 2 (1984): 97–112; Strobel, *Muslim Women*.

83. George E. Brooks, "A Nhara of the Guinea-Birsau Region"; Bruce L. Mouser, "Women Slavers of Guinea-Conakry"; and Carol P. MacCormack, "Slaves, Slave Owners, and Slave Dealers," in Robertson and Klein, *Women and Slavery*, 271–339. See also Hilary Jones, "History and Memory: Unraveling the Past in Saint Louis, Senegal," paper presented at Seventh Midwest African Studies Conference, Ann Arbor, March 2002.

84. Moitt, *Women and Slavery*, 9, 59, 176; C. L. R. James, *The Black Jacobins: Toussaint L'Ouverture and the San Domingo Revolution* (New York: Vintage, 1963), 37–44. Both works, however, are tinged with the harem assumption. Literary criticism also addresses identity issues; see A. James Arnold, "From the Problematic Maroon to a Woman-Centered Creole Project in the Literature of the French West Indies," in *Slavery in the Caribbean Francophone World: Distant Voices, Forgotten Acts, Forged Identities*, ed. Doris Y. Kadish (Athens: University of Georgia Press, 2000), 164–75.

85. Brooks, *Captives and Cousins*, 101–3.

86. Paul Gilroy, *The Black Atlantic: Modernity and Double Consciousness* (Cambridge, MA: Harvard University Press, 1995); Michael Gomez, *Exchanging Our Country Marks: The Transformation of African Identities in the Colonial and Antebellum South* (Chapel Hill: University of North Carolina Press, 1998); Alex Bontemps, *The Punished Self: Surviving Slavery in the Colonial South* (Ithaca: Cornell University Press, 2001); Philip D. Morgan, *Slave Counterpoint: Black Culture in the Eighteenth-Century Chesapeake and Lowcountry* (Chapel Hill: University of North Carolina Press, 1998); Kristin Mann and Edna G. Bay, ed., *Rethinking the African Diaspora: The Making of a Black Atlantic World in the Bight of Benin and Brazil* (London: Frank Cass, 2001). For a classic explanation of intersectionality see Kimberle Crenshaw, "Demarginalizing the Intersection of Race and Sex: A Black Feminist Critique of Antidiscrimination Doctrine, Feminist Theory, and Antiracist Politics," in *Feminist Legal Theory*, ed. Katherine T. Bartlett and Rosanne Kennedy (Boulder: Westview, 1991), 57–80.

87. J. Morgan, *Laboring Women*, 10–11.

88. Hünefeldt, *Paying the Price*, 213–14.

89. Brooks, *Captives and Cousins*, 103.

90. Elias Mandala, *Work and Control in a Peasant Economy* (Madison: University of Wisconsin Press, 1990), ch. 2; Onaiwu Ogbomo, *When Men and Women Mattered: A History of Gender Relations among the Owan of Nigeria* (Rochester, NY: University of Rochester Press, 1997).

91. Pamela Scully, *Liberating the Family? Gender and British Slave Emancipation in the Rural Western Cape, South Africa* (New York: Heinemann, 1997), 15, 176.

92. Thomas C. Holt, "The Essence of the Contract The Articulation of Race, Gender and Political Economy in British Emancipation Policy, 1838–1866," in *Beyond Slavery: Explorations of Race, Labor, and Citizenship in Postemancipation Societies*, ed. Frederick Cooper, Thomas C. Holt, and Rebecca J. Scott (Chapel Hill: University of North Carolina Press, 2000), 45–46; Frederick Cooper, "Conditions Analo-

gous to Slavery Imperialism and Free Labor Ideology in Africa" in Cooper, Holt, and Scott, *Beyond Slavery*, 127.

93. J. Morgan, *Laboring Women*, 196.

94. Claire C. Robertson, "Africa into the Americas? Slavery and Women, the Family, and the Gender Division of Labor," in Gaspar and Hine, *More than Chattel*, 22–24.

95. Miers and Kopytoff, *Slavery*; Chatterjee, *Gender, Slavery*, 26.

96. Scott, *Gender*, 31.

97. Shrine slavery in Ghana and slave prostitution, for instance. Brian S. Woods, "The Slave Girls of Ghana," *New York Law School Journal of Human Rights* 17, no. 2 (2001): 875–81.

98. Chatterjee, *Gender, Slavery*, 239.

12

DOMICILED AND DOMINATED

Slaving as a History of Women

JOSEPH C. MILLER

Women in recent years are becoming a principal and long overdue focus of slave studies, as the field has grown beyond its original focus on enslaved men in the modern Americas and the ancient Mediterranean. Other parts of the world, previously little known or entirely misapprehended, are beginning to reveal starkly novel, in fact apparently quite anomalous, qualities. Not least among them is that before the development of plantation economies in the Americas, with their familiar modern stereotype of slaves as males toiling in mines and plantation fields, slaving had primarily involved females.

The majorities of African men taken across the Atlantic and concentrated in large disciplined protoindustrial workforces in the Americas undermined the viability earlier and elsewhere of what had been a strategy of recruiting girls and women, isolating them as outsiders dispersed within many, sometimes large, private households. There they were valued, as slaves, not as productive labor in a commercial sense but rather for their sheer presence and in some cases also for their progeny. The anomalous male majorities in the modern Americas gave slavery a new, public, institutionalized quality that left the women among the enslaved with an anomalous, often notoriously prurient significance as sexual objects as restrictive mores and politicized gender emerged in the wake of European Enlightenment humanism and the development of modern civic societies.

Associating women with early practices of slaving is not a new idea, of course. Greek phalanxes and Roman legions razing cities, raping women,

and killing enemy warriors are a cliché so trite that the human consequences for, and of, the women seized are all but reduced to caricature.
This exaggerated image in turn conveys overtones of "manly men" (in
fact usually boys) just doing the wild things that boys will do, particularly
when they are unleashed in uniformed armed gangs far from home, hyped
by the exhilaration of violence and victory, if not also by more substantive stimulants. These Hollywood visions have thus not often led to serious consideration of alternative means of enslaving or the consequences
of capture for the women and children of the vanquished males, as the
slaves they became, or for their masters. Gerda Lerner locates the origins
of patriarchy throughout the world's history in habits of mind formed out
of male warriors' unrestrained abuses of the foreign women they seized
and enslaved.[1] Her argument is a loosely associational one, basically noting the parallel degrees of male power and control attributed to both
slavery and patriarchy and documenting mostly ancient Mediterranean
body counts calculated in terms of the numbers of women and children
seized. She does not attempt to delineate a coherent historical sequence
from raping to slaving or to establish the causation that she implies.

Orlando Patterson takes Lerner's point a step in this direction in his
meticulous account of the invention of freedom as an ideal of individual
autonomy, or escape from domination, in multiple contexts—internal/
mental/emotional, interpersonal, and abstractly civic.[2] He reads the
dramatic, philosophical, and literary texts of ancient Greece and Rome
to ascribe the origins of the concept, beyond Lerner's pragmatics, to the
women held in slavery at the dawn of a "Western civilization" built
around it. Patterson then follows the path of this liberating ideal, rather
than lingering on women and slavery elsewhere in the world, or for
that matter in Europe, through the only world culture to raise the yearn-
ing he attributes to ancient enslaved females to a universal human ideal
through its philosophical and spiritualized formulations in Rome and
early Christianity toward its resurrection as a practical civic ideal during
the European Enlightenment. As for civic freedom, it was not until the
twentieth century that civic participation was implemented for women,
even in the world's most politically inclusive nations. Effective protection of women from personal abuse remains a challenge even in the
twenty-first century.

This chapter reverses Lerner's focus on men capturing the women of
other men defeated on the fields of male conflict to attempt a historical
sketch of slaving throughout the world, more comprehensively than implicitly male public levels of Western civilization, with accents on the

utility of women for private purposes that I will term domestic. In this broader history of slaving throughout the world, literally from the beginning of history until recently, and in some places currently, the capture and retention of women, not the slaughter of their men, was the point of slaving. The slavers were generally parties marginal to the politics of the worlds in which they lived, who captured women in calculated and very effective strategies of recruiting outsiders essentially for the political, if also incidentally economic, struggles inherent in all human communities, particularly before the modern triumph of material accumulation.

SLAVERY, GENDER, AND HISTORY

The axiomatically male "slave" who prevails in studies of slavery throughout the world, in spite of efforts of many historians now extending over more than a quarter of a century, derives from an implicit modern abolitionist paradigm. Masters dominate; slaves, women as well as men, resist in one way or another. This emphasis on domination—in exactly Patterson's terms—tends to make gender equivalent to slavery and thus merely inserts women into the prevailing male paradigm of exploitation, shame, and consequently resistance as the only strategy available, or of any conceivable interest, to the enslaved.[3] But gender and slavery parallel one another only on this single, abstracted logical axis of power. Once created, thus, as Lerner puts it with "origins" against some presumably less unpleasant (but unexamined) background, neither form of domination—slavery or gender—seems to have changed significantly.

In fact, both gender and enslavement have resonantly dynamic histories as strategic responses to the particular circumstances of specific times and places. Like all historical processes, they have changed through incremental steps, motivated by infinitely varying, complex, and differentiated contexts. Further, in terms of historical processes thus conceived, gender contrasts radically with enslavement. Gender is a relationship of power internal to a community (or society or culture, depending on one's preferred analytical lens). To disable insiders otherwise sharing a vital cultural and societal presence (social vitality, one might say, to coin a phrase complementing Patterson's "social death"),[4] one must attribute to them an inherent—but false—inferiority. Biophysical—undeniable and immutable, at least to the modern eye—deviations from an arbitrary (or politically negotiated) and narrowly defined norm are defined as defects. Sexual difference possesses these characteristics in an almost ideal form, since it bears an intuitive, highly emotional, even instinctual intensity, at least for males, and particularly for men who fancy themselves as real, primarily in their correspondingly physical virility. Highly sexualized bodily characteristics thus trump any other imaginable personal abilities, individual achievements, family connections, or—in modern civic regimes—legal standing. Since women are profoundly necessary in the most elemental reproductive sense, they cannot be physically segregated. Instead they are excluded ideologically from every sociological field of power, which are thereby gendered exclusively and irrefutably male.

Gender, in excluding people already present, is thus much closer to modern racism than to slaving, which by definition brings new people, outsiders, onto a local scene. Gender's entirely artificial displacement of socially significant difference onto the physical body contrasts with the real, but circumstantial and temporary, cultural (or political, or even social) alienness of people acquired and assimilated (or, if one prefers, for the moment, dominated) as slaves. On a global scale, in spite of modern efforts to impose permanence and heritability on slavery, enslavement is inherently ephemeral as a societal standing. As a temporary state it is as accessibly manipulable for women as the (male) master's dependence on their services, sexual and otherwise, and possible willingness to manumit them or marry them, or both.

The other leading embodiments of inferiority, parallel to gender in their genetic inevitability, are ancient naturalist ideologies of animality or even bestiality (in all senses), or the inherent qualities attributed in Africa to ethnicity or in India to caste, or the politicized "race" (as distinct from incidental and socially insignificant variations in individual physiognomies) introduced in modern times to replace slavery in the Americas as generations of native-born slaves and their freed descendants of (very selectively attributed!) "African" descent grew up there. Thus neither gender nor race "add" cumulatively to enslavement among the modern political woes of women; instead, they succeed slavery historically, both for individuals as new women slaves integrated themselves in the contexts they entered, and also collectively over time as modern gender replaced slaving and other disabling strategies as means of dominating females of local birth and connections.

A historicized narrative of strategies of slaving by specifiable interests contextualized earlier in time or located elsewhere, can contextualize the lingering masculinist focus on the historically unique and very modern institutionalized slavery of the Americas as male. The key aspect of slaving was moving individuals, violently or not, into new surroundings where they found themselves alone, disabled culturally, and hence in positions of overwhelming vulnerability. They remained in such helpless straits only temporarily, and their degrees of isolation varied, depending on the contexts, primarily cultural and social, that they entered. One thus cannot interpret the often-scattered evidence of slaving earlier and elsewhere by (always deficient) comparison to the modern Americas.

Such a historicized narrative proceeds on an exceedingly broad scale— notionally the last forty thousand years or so, and so no more than the bare logic of the argument appears here,[5] supported by references to only the most (I hope aptly) selected examples to illustrate the basic point: that slaving should 'be understood on global scales as a recurrent strategy of moving people, mostly and centrally girls and women. They were not necessarily outsiders in our modern sense of national identities, or even always culturally alien. Overt force was at most a secondary factor in dominating them; anyone placed in vulnerable isolation tends to cower, if only to survive. The purposes of acquiring women and their children were not to exclude them but rather to include them in families, lineages, palace retinues, temple communities, and other domiciliary collectivities—notionally households—that made up what I will call societies or polities that were composite in character.[6] That is, what counted were local face-to-face communities that reproduced people, and people built them up significantly by recruiting females as slaves.

Societal exclusion at the level of the large anonymous collectivities of the modern world (nations, abstracted societies, and so on) was a secondary consequence of these primary motivations, and it was not a motivating consideration for the slavers. In fact, for women integration and vitality within households tended to be related inversely to their public visibility. The multiplicity of such intimate communities and the intensity of belonging within them thus contrast with the premise of a single homogeneous mass of otherwise unattached individuals that underlies all modern political theory, whether monarchical (in which all are subject, similarly, to a singular monarch) or national (in which the subjects are absolutely sovereign, and therefore necessarily equally so), and hence all the modern theories of politicized slavery derived from it.

Under the actual historical circumstances of composite, or compound, political environments that prevailed earlier and elsewhere, it was not necessary to proclaim or enforce a subordinated public status for the women and children taken into households and moved around among them. The circumstances of removal themselves and the prevailing societal norms of private household patriarchy (in senses involving age as well as masculinity) made public regulation of their status—religious monotheisms or secular—not only irrelevant but also potentially intrusive on the autonomous domains of *familiae* in Rome, or the Greek *oikos*, or—in Africa—the lineage, or the Islamic or other households including harems of women, or any other face-to-face primary domiciliary community. As history, that is: as incremental, processual change (as distinct from the radically contrasting typological abstractions accented by structural and institutional modeling), slaving (not institutionalized slavery) worked because it extended and amplified prevailing practices of transferring dependent females among these households. It thus intensified existing contexts and did not contrast with them, and certainly not abominably so as modern (ideological) abstractions rightly reassessed its individually disabling consequences in a new world of personal autonomy rather than the former worlds of responsible patronage, or—as masters under assault from abolitionists defended themselves in the nineteenth-century United States—paternalism.[7]

This historicized argument from strategies shifts the focus from Patterson's emphasis on civic or social exclusion to domestic inclusion, the complementing face of the double-sided coin of slavery, replaces perpetual domination with temporary vulnerability, and contextualizes its dynamic from a presumed solitary master oriented obsessively toward his socially isolated slave to include other compelling concerns of both with the large and complex communities, public as well as private, in which both in fact lived. The slaves were not the problems, except personally and incidentally, perhaps aggravatingly, but historically inconsequentially; slaving, bringing in outsiders as a strategy of marginal masters to get ahead of more established political rivals, was.

HISTORICAL PATTERNS OF SLAVING

Domestic Communities

Starting at the beginning (~40,000 BP), Orlando Patterson has called attention to the psychological and hence sociological efficacy of internalizing social bonds by immolating captured enemies—males—in gruesome collective torture and sometimes intensely ritualized consumption of their physical remains.[8] Tens of millennia ago, at the ancient transition from late hominids to early humans, even momentarily functional senses of community would not have been presumed. Late hominids, or their early human descendents, lived in small numbers in open environments where lands were plentiful, people in short supply, and group identification mostly opportunistic. Anyone then could find a place in any of many other small, only incipiently communal groupings, all of them persistently short of numbers.

In these unstructured circumstances, groups tortured male enemy warriors whom they captured in occasional conflicts and took women and children they captured directly into statuses that modern observers have attempted to understand by analogy to adoption, marriage, and other modern sorts of relationships. This accent on assimilation stresses the apparent contrast with the residual disabilities of "outsider origins" in more structured social aggregates that are preserved through reproduction. However, people then would have understood grouping as essentially contingent, with participants (more than "members") understood as hailing from the most varied personal backgrounds. Everyone came from somewhere else, and so the issue was not so much rank inherited within the group but rather recency of arrival and whether participants in them retained options to move on again or had invested in local relationships in order to remain. Women captured and removed from groups presumed enemies had few choices, since slaughter of their menfolk normally destroyed any social options they might otherwise have had. One appreciates the effect of the ritual immolation of captured enemy males more fully if one takes account of the likelihood that the witnesses to their slaughter included their widows and sisters.

In agricultural economies based on hoe techniques—in Africa, the Americas, the southeast Asian archipelago, and Oceania—men were the superfluous sex. There women routinely worked the fields, and men tended to focus on intermittent and seasonal activities like hunting, on the high-intensity phases of ongoing highly irregular cycles of cultivation and harvesting, and on technical specializations involving mobility—fishing, herding livestock, metallurgy, and so on. The intermittence of such responsibilities left them available for other unpredictable and irregular—but often profitable—projects involving strength or speed, or both, such as raiding (though less so home defense), commercial travel, and—revealingly—dispensability in mining and other lethally dangerous undertakings supportive of war and commerce. Men captured in wars would then have been disposed of rather than kept, no longer immolated by nascent collectivities but rather killed (and their sexual parts often claimed as trophies for individual warriors aiming to advance by demonstrating valor and contributions to the politics of groups integrated around a strongly communal ethos).

Women are thus males' means to accumulation of progeny. As historical agents, men are demographically inert; women create, but men de-

stroy and are destroyed. Women and reproduction were therefore determinants of historical change elsewhere in the world, particularly where
hoes remained the primary implements of agricultural production. There
labor—mostly female—was the scarce factor of production to wield these
much less efficient implements of cultivation to feed families. Women
and children, not lands to produce the food surpluses enabled by the
plow, were in demand. Collectivities—classically, groups organizing
themselves around complementary differentiation by sex and seniority—
described themselves through metaphors of reproductive relationships
among kin. Groups defined in terms of women bearing children calculated their successes in terms of their ability to increase their numbers
and thus to multiply and deepen their connections with their neighbors
via carefully arranged marriages of their young women. Sex was a plea-
surable incident between individual males and females; but marriage
was a reproductive responsibility that men and women assumed on behalf of their respective communities of kin. Marriage and reproduction
were thus political. As efforts at in increasing populations succeeded,
pressures on these domestic groups grew apace, intensifying political
competition among communities of kin also intimately dependent on one
another. The men in charge of these groups favored slaving as a strategy
of recruiting additional women to preserve their own communities beyond the women from neighboring communities whom they married
legitimately.

A historical perspective on the processes through which people create
novelty out of whatever preceded emphasizes that they can do so only by
lengthy series of incremental steps. Applying this processual perspective
to what happened next in the broad history of slaving, we should expect
a further adaptation, and an increasingly anomalous distortion, of these
primordial practices of incorporating females and juveniles. One may
thus (schematically) infer the next stage of strategic incorporation of
women and children when population densities had grown, for reasons
possibly including tendencies to increase the available laboring capacity
of populations by acquiring nubile girls and women through slaving. In
drought-prone subtropical regions, scarcities of food forced foraging families into increasing and laborious dependence on crops, exposing the
people who thus became cultivators, no longer able to move around in
pursuit of fresh terrain, to periodic famine. When the historical process
of forming human communities reached the threshold of dependence on
plow agriculture in river valleys around the subtropical world—let's say
ten thousand years ago—basic demographic pressures would have tended

to make female children relatively—or at least occasionally—surplus to their communities' primary needs for males for field labor and for defense. One Malthusian implication of more productive agricultural technologies in the hands of males—plows, oxen, wheeled transport for surpluses—seems to be that female fecundity, however necessary, could also become a liability.

Farming communities facing such recurrent scarcities of food, particularly the poorer among them, quite realistically disposed of surplus female reproductive potential that promised only to increase the number of bellies that had to be filled.[9] In more recent circumstances of dearth, the evidence of such disposal of girls is ubiquitous: new mothers, or more likely their male relatives, exposed girl infants they could not support or abandoned them to families in need of domestic services to support privileged ways of living that also made them better able to feed additional hungry mouths. In elemental demographic terms, such disposal of girls transferred human reproductive potential to wealthier populations able to support it, and even to capitalize on it, with the rich living better and the poor staving off total collapse only barely. Such transfers of girls would have accelerated where urban centers of wealth and ostentation developed, but these concentrated populations also created mountains of refuse, and the accumulated filth supported diseases that also made cities demographic sinkholes, eventually tending to encourage further inflows of the females surplus to family needs in the countryside.

The extent to which such girls qualified as slaves would have depended then, as it continues to do in modern recurrences of this truly ancient tendency, on the degree to which they arrived in disoriented isolation. None of the parties involved recognized the dichotomy between slave and free created by modern ideologies of homogenous and mutually exclusive civic categories, in which one either belongs individually and fully to a nation or society, or one doesn't. Identities instead were relational, situational, and thus flexible, even multiple depending on one's momentary circumstances. To the extent that the desperate rural families who abandoned their girl children gave up any further responsibility for them, or to the (very likely extensive) extent that families forced to forsake them had also lost any ability to protect their own interests, and to the likely considerable extent that the urban households that took them in also took advantage of their relative independence of despised rural clients, these girls were alone, abandoned, vulnerable, and—as children—surely disoriented and utterly dependent. To the contrasting degree that rural client families managed to send girls to live with urban patrons interested in preserving the relationship, they might become wards, or even pawns pledged—in theory only temporarily—against credit extended in cash or grain or in other life-sustaining forms.[10]

Focusing on *slaving*, as this chapter does, rather than on slavery, emphasizes the processes of foreclosure, betrayal of trust, management of family crises—urban as well as rural—and ordinary human greed at the expense of the least indispensable or most vulnerable girls in them. These inevitabilities of human life can readily be appreciated for their potential to leave girls and women—as Patterson puts it—"natally alienated" by stages and in varying degrees that culminated in the abject, if frequently relatively brief, initial isolated vulnerability characteristic of enslavement.[11] From the points of view of the slavers, what we see as slavery they could well have seen as unfortunate and abusive extensions of efforts to minimize unavoidable hardships, hence sacrifices and trade-offs, the inevitable losses of life. Eighteenth- and nineteenth-century African and Asian authorities protested against the abolitionist ambitions of European colonial authorities in exactly these terms. Abolitionists scorned their claims as hypocritical; historians need not indulge in comparably arrogant (and political) dismissals.

In the long run, general tendencies emerged in much of Asia from infinitely numerous and various, if specifically unrecorded, incidents like these. The implication of such probabilities for slaving and women is to emphasize the collective distress threatened by the specifically female capacity to reproduce. Under these circumstances the tendency on the part of the men responsible for large families to dispose selectively, in one way or another, of girl children, was arguably conscientious. However saddening such disposals might be to the mothers and girls they thus separated from one another, girls were unfortunate but unavoidable accompaniments of fathers' quests for sons to do the work and carry on the name that would preserve the family for "posterity." Hence the contribution of distinctively female fertility to thinking of slaving as primarily, normatively, involving women and girls. One need not invoke the much more occasional circumstances of war, rape, and seizure of defeated enemies' women to account for this premise. Contrary to Lerner, history suggests that slaving in ancient times was as often volitional as it was imposed by violence and must also have rested on prior (not subsequent) patriarchy, as senior male heads of poor households disposed of the girl children of the young mothers in them.

Military Polities

The inherent multiplicity and inclusiveness of polities composed of many recognized domestic domains" of kinship differed radically from modern civic political environments premised on homogeneity, a singular standard of equality that led to the exclusionary category of institutionalized slavery. Elsewhere, and earlier, historians cannot productively focus on the public aspects of abstract societies—that is, the civic, government-recognized, direct political presence of autonomous individuals, with active participation (or accessibility or protection) for everyone resident in political communities thus defined. The nineteenth-century idea of quasi-racialized nationality is the eventual purest, and also most reductive, expression of modern notions of community as homogeneity, rather than complementary diversity. Recognizing the modernity of the premise of equality—very intensely embraced for the opportunity it promises to individuals (however seldom it may deliver)—in political participation (or participatory polities) is fundamental to distinguishing institutionalized slavery (and also gender) from earlier slaving (and sexually defined social complementarities). It is that unhistoricized premise of modern civic uniformity that defines the slave's "death" as social, meaning excluded from national or civic aspects of lives that are in fact lived in much more multiplistic dimensions. Or—as it is then easy to phrase the point—the only aspect of slaves' lives presumed to matter in the conventional understanding of slavery is that they are "denied civil rights" or "lack a moral [i.e., civic] personality" or simply are outsiders to this single civic component of human existence in multiple dimensions.[12]

Nearly everywhere else in world history this political level of life, which essentially regulated occasional interactions among strangers, or encounters (not relationships) beyond the communities in which everyone lived nearly all the time, left ongoing intimate relations to the latter. "States" could not be said to exist there in any familiar sense; the overarching polity was secondary, external, and even alien to the familiae basic to Roman society, the oikos in ancient Greece, or the lineages in Africa. In places like these, males were anomalous as slaves, and they were decidedly uncommon in most historical contexts anywhere in the world before the northern Atlantic in the late seventeenth century. Men, particularly young able-bodied ones, were potential competitors for women and heirs, unless as eunuchs rendered impotent by castration.

From the perspective of the local communities composing these polities—including the imperial extension of the highly composite republic of large aristocratic and military familiae—the imperial court at Rome was conceptually a larger, very powerful household. It thus became the central focus of these groups' networks of alliances or external patrons— the single great patron to whom everyone else was in perpetual debt. The imperial court, as power personified, and as essentially military, carried strong overtones of maleness. Unlike the domestic households compos- ing the polity, contrastingly and complementarily gendered female and seeking women to reproduce them, the imperial household (though not the imperial or royal lineage seeking to control it) inherently reproduced itself by slaving rather than through female fecundity. Only thus could it achieve the (contrastive) autonomy that would-be rulers sought from the people around them whom they purported to rule, but on whose repro- duction they were otherwise profoundly dependent. The realities of human life are always reciprocal; individual independence is, of course, an illusion, or an ideology. Military power, particularly when aided by cavalry techniques developed in Asia in the third and second millennia BCE, put warriors within overpowering reach of vulnerable distant and therefore alien communities, producing captives of both sexes in un- precedented numbers. Men, as the classical sources from this era cited by Lerner show, were dispensable, and women and children captured effec- tively paid the troops whom imperial regimes could not otherwise afford for their efforts and for the dangers they surmounted.

Mercantile

Merchants mounted the inevitable historical challenge to the power of these militarized composite polities. Wherever commercialization of the domestic communities composing them remained incidental, and mer- chants remained dependent on provisioning the armies and distributing the spoils of military expansion, enslaving local girls and women tended to support the urbanizing consequences of managing success. But mer- chants in the eastern Mediterranean invested currencies and commercial credit they had developed to negotiate exchanges among themselves in domestic communities otherwise claimed by the warlords as sources of taxes and tribute. Using cash or extending credit, classically food in times of looming starvation, they indebted members of these communi- ties directly to themselves. The resulting persistent rural commercial debt, payable in cash or equivalents, was distinct from the balanced reci- procities that peasant collectivities maintained among themselves. The rural cultivators' primary means of paying what they owed, whether as labor to produce salable surpluses or as collateral implicitly backing these obligations, was their wealth in people, in dependent women and children within domestic communities headed by senior males legally competent to contract debt on behalf of the group. The women and children were thus vulnerable to concession to external creditors.

Merchants in effect thus inserted themselves into the older tendency of famine-stricken families to abandon female infants or send girls to wealthy patrons by lending them money or grain to stave off starvation in the short term. Against these critical needs they might well have appeared as potential saviors, but in the long run they sustained overpopulation and forced further, future involuntary concessions of nubile young women, consigning them to something not unlike the (thus perhaps aptly named) world's oldest profession. In highly commercialized modern contexts, only nominally more voluntaristic, this prostitution of female children, now including boys as well as girls, continues as one growing form of "contemporary slavery."[13]

By claiming women in satisfaction of debts, merchants also inserted themselves between warlords and the populations they taxed. But enslaving females did not surface as a concern in the essentially male public spheres of commerce or politics during earlier stages of this process of mercantile intrusion on domestic households. The practice was, after all, a private matter among commercial patrons and their indebted clients. But further intensification of mercantile slaving through indebting agricultural families extended to extracting males, as the legally responsible heads of households, or forced them to pledge sons or other male dependents against deepening indebtedness.[14] Merchants evidently reached such pervasive degrees of wealth in the eastern Mediterranean during the first half of the last millennium before the current era. Judaic "jubilee" laws of that era freed subjects of kings enslaved for debt at intervals sufficiently regular to disable overly ambitious creditors without destroying more responsible businessmen. We hear of the same triumph of Solon (596–594 BCE), who recruited the populace of Athens, or saved it for the owners of the lands they cultivated, by eliminating peasants' debts to merchants.

In such regions, as merchants encroached on the male domain of public affairs, commercialized strategies of slaving thus became matters of urgent political concern. By extracting local men as slaves, they threatened to erode the availability of the male participants in the polities of the era, targets of such immediate and compelling interests to the state as payers of taxes and availability for military conscription, not to mention occasional recruitment for monumental construction projects. Slavery, or in fact not slavery itself but rather the *slaving* that transferred people out of nascently inclusive political domains or merely locally among the communities constituting them, then became visible by the public standards of conventional modern scholarship. Rulers, attempting to create more inclusive monarchical states out of compound domains, codified written public laws—as distinct from previous personal dicta and ad hoc fiats—to further their ambitions to rule directly.

Heads of composite military regimes thus tried to advance their strategies of governing by protecting the people, formerly secluded within domestic domains, whom they thus transformed into subjects by protecting them against merchants threatening to foreclose on the communal components of their domains. The enslaving of local men, to which unrestrained commercial accumulation eventually led, thus threatened to overwhelm the delicate balances of composite polities. Only in Africa in the eighteenth century did the warlords, and later merchants, consolidate their power by encouraging—not repressing—commercialized slaving; in so doing, they abandoned or threatened local supports and left themselves dependent on Atlantic commercial credit.

But in Judea and Greece and then Rome kings and emperors managed to forestall what amounted to an impending ancient bourgeois revolution mounted by merchants enslaving local debtors. The resulting Roman law of slavery was in fact a compendium of laws regulating manumission, defining degrees of civic standing for the manumitted, or citizenship and availability to the imperial state, with residual rights retained by the manumitters. The interest of Roman jurisprudence in slaves as such was secondary, since these people attained recognition by the Roman state only as freedmen. Slaves appeared in law primarily within a subset of general commercial regulations, which reflected not slavery but rather *slaving*, the transactional moments in the lives of the people thus moved. To treat the legal status of transactions involving people these laws invoked the standard legal principle of reasoning by analogy with other more conventional sorts of commercial transactions—hence the later-definitive invocation of the analogy (in Rome, for these very limited purposes of transferring particular interest) of *res* (thing), the notion of living chattel (personal, rather than collective, or "real," property), exemplified (as legal principle, not personal characterization) by domestic livestock, for instance, cattle.

These commercial aspects of slaving—that is: acquisition of personnel through purchase—were not gendered but implicitly referred primarily to the men eligible to enter the public sphere through manumission.

They left the women slaves relatively invisible, except when they occasionally passed through public markets. However, the majority of transfers of women and children undoubtedly continued as off-market private
transactions among related households, as infant girl foundlings retrieved from alleyways, and other very ancient private ways of taking
females in as slaves.[15]

With commercial prosperity growing in the wake of military conquests
and brutally efficient plundering and needs for provisioning all around
the Mediterranean, merchants used their money and credit to challenge
both the military rulers of the composite polities and the great urban
households and peasant collectivities that constituted them. Generally
in Asia and around the Mediterranean, the contenders of these three
types settled into uneasy standoffs that continued into the recent past.
The best-known examples of this pattern arose, of course, from the tense
compromise in the Islamic ecumene at the center of this vast region after
the eighth century or so. There the parties to this tripartite struggle took
the familiar form of clerical, literate, and learned, legal heirs to the religious charismatic communalism of the Prophet Muhammad, military conquerors who competed to claim secular authority in his name as caliphs
and emirs, and communities of merchants who, in practical terms, integrated the geographically vast and varied but politically divided world,
supporting its local and regional military powers. Rather than reading
slaving in Muslim Asia and northern Africa during the twelve centuries
from about 700 AD to about 1900 as a single, static, culturally homogeneous Islamic type, with the usual Orientalist bias toward considering
it as primarily involving sexually enticing (to males) females kept in
harems,[16] historians must instead recognize deep processes of change
under way within the recurring tensions of slaving and the primacy of
gendered strategies —of men for military purposes as well as of women for
the households of the wealthy—in sustaining them.[17]

Males and Modernity in the Americas

Christian counterparts of these domestic premises of enslaving women—
though not of men—extended to the European shores of the Mediterranean. Italian merchants carried the ancient model of enslaving women
into the Atlantic in the sixteenth century but then shifted their emphasis to males as the Americas developed as an arena of profound commercialization. The ensuing trade in male slaves from Africa led to significant majorities of male slaves in the New World. It was there that men
became the political economic backbone of the specie-producing mines

and commodity-producing plantations that made the Americas so commercially valuable. That is, with African men European slavers converted historic strategies of enslaving females for household and community reproduction to dedicated and driven production of nonconsumable commodities by enslaved males. The unprecedented masculinity and commercialization of slaveries in the Americas in turn made men the hallmarks of the presentist conventional literature on slavery everywhere around the globe.

As Portuguese merchants and Spanish military aristocrats started to realize deep-seated European lusting for a tropical cornucopia of precious metals—African lands of gold, and mountains of gold and silver in the Americas—Europeans began by delivering relatively costly skilled and acculturated Africans across the Atlantic for urban domestic services in the style familiar in Renaissance Mediterranean cities—Christian as well as Muslim. Early on (1542–43), the New Laws of the Hapsburg monarchy then struggling to create a united Iberian Spain, eliminated the threat to these political ambitions that slaving by a generation of rampaging (and surely raping) conquistadores posed in far-off America. By the 1520s and 1530s, these conquerors of the Aztecs, Inca, and Maya were already busy turning themselves into an independent military aristocracy in unchallenged control of native populations whom they effectively proposed to enslave on vast domains well beyond the effective reach of the crown.

The New Laws consigned the welfare of the natives to the church, in close alliance with the monarchy, and interposed royal law between the conquerors and the conquered. Later monarchs in Spain then effectively excluded domestic merchants, growing wealthy on the vast wealth in silver that developed in the later sixteenth century, by consigning deliveries of enslaved Africans to foreigners through the famous *asiento* contracts of the seventeenth century. This commercial policy also limited deliveries of Africans to replace the Native Americans as slaves to the needs of politically benign urban households in the cities of Spain's colonies and confined their transport to harmlessly foreign merchants. These restrictions that the crown thus placed on its potential military rivals and—particularly—on merchants demonstrated the same wariness of domestic domains inflated by slaving that had first appeared in the ancient centers of commercialization around the Mediterranean. In all cases, slaving was rendered all the more politically sensitive in monarchical regimes by the substantial numbers of men among the conquered natives and the male majorities among the Africans imported.

Other Europeans brought unprecedentedly large numbers of male Africans in the seventeenth century to toil in sugarcane plantations in tropical American lowlands depopulated by disease and by the slaving and other brutalities of the conquerors. The resulting hordes of angry men lived segregated in barracks and worked in large gangs, and they also died in great numbers and were replaced with still more recently imported successors. Such large aggregates of males clearly held the potential both to overwhelm and also to embolden the tiny minorities of European owners and officials in the Americas. The grandiosely self-styled (but still in fact struggling) Baroque "absolute monarchies" in Europe had to assert themselves legally or lose control.[18] The Portuguese crown attempted feebly to decree limits on commercial slaving's evident risks for its monarchical sponsors but in practice was far less absolute than in its lofty Christian pretensions. In the ultimately fabulously wealthy captaincies of Brazil it utterly failed to intrude on the privacy of sugar slavery—an industrialized and masculinized extension of the Renaissance Iberian domestic privacy of female slaving. Hence, weak monarchs in Lisbon created little subsequent legal history—with its emphasis on men—of slavery in Portugal's American possessions, until modern (and mostly foreign) pressures toward abolition in the nineteenth century made the issue a public one in late-imperial and republican Brazil.

Rather, in the cities of Portugal's huge American domain the domestic aspects of slaving (and relatively routine private manumissions) predominated, with greater emphasis on the women and the familial relations they created, and exploited, than among the majorities of males recently arrived and sent to sugar plantations, the notoriously all-but-private domains of the *senhores de engenho,* or sugar barons. The historically inverse ratio of the viability of privately enslaving women to their public visibility in Brazil had expanded to obscure also the men in slavery there. Male slaves within an acknowledged community are apparently anomalies so anxiety-inducing that they are difficult to acknowledge, and all the more so as the alleged masters know, but cannot admit, their ultimate dependence on them. Parallel tendencies toward denial appear in gender, of course, with men's sheer reproductive dependency evident, but obsessively obscured, in terms of the physical generative capacities that women possess but that they do not.

Elsewhere in the Americas thoroughly commercialized plantation enterprises, epitomized by Caribbean plantation production of sugar, drew the attentions of the stronger monarchs of northern Europe. The French and the British, in particular, concentrated great numbers of enslaved

African males on tiny islands. They found themselves constrained to accept women from merchants seldom able to buy males in Africa in the numbers they demanded and drove them into the canebrakes to produce commodities. In Martinique and Guadeloupe, where the French developed their first American plantations, Louis XIV, the most absolute of the Europe's Baroque generation of monarchs in the second half of the seventeenth century, faced the classic monarchical dilemma of converting distant American conquests into sources of wealth for himself without dangerously enabling the merchants whom he needed to do so. Trying to consolidate royal power at home and simultaneously concerned to convert private private plantations abroad to colonies in the modern sense of government-controlled dependencies, the Sun King asserted monarchical authority through another characteristic codification of law. In the famed Code Noir of 1684–85 his ministers synthesized the premises of female domestic slaving that all of Europe had inherited from ancient Rome with the male commercial initiatives in the New World.

This second New World monarchical legal intrusion on the historic privacy of female slaving, rephrased in the commercially oriented laws of the early-modern Atlantic as a matter of personal property, arose explicitly from fears of the unprecedented risks of managing so many African men in spaces so distant and confined, and thus as vulnerable, as these small islands in the Antilles. But in terms of the historic European and Asian tensions between monarchical power and male slaving, it attempted to reconcile political conflicts between domestic autonomy and public accountability as old as politics itself. The French code, following Portuguese and Spanish Catholic precedent, enlisted the church's sacramental authority over marriages and births among the enslaved—essentially over their reproduction—in the service of modulating the planters' otherwise absolute claims to the privacy of their property in human beings. But the planters in Martinique and Guadeloupe, and later in the much larger French colony of Saint Domingue on the western end of the formerly Spanish island of Hispaniola, were more commercially dynamic than continental France, or at least sufficiently integrated into the Dutch and then the English West Indian commercial networks that they could afford to ignore the crude forms of administrative control over deliveries of new Africans extended by Louis' successors in Paris.

Planters triumphed over both the Code Noir's moral exhortations to care responsibly for the people they enslaved (mostly the women, one suspects) and its effort to define public, royal authority in the islands—that is, to quell unrest among the African men then giving fits to planters.

The huge majorities of men taken to Saint Domingue, the most brutal and profitable production regime in the Caribbean, eventually demonstrated the anticipated danger in 1791 by taking advantage of planters' momentary distraction from policing and security in the wake of revolution in France. In the resulting "Haitian revolution" men, many of them former slaves, created an independent nation led by blacks. However epochal Haiti may seem, looking backward from the present, historians might better contemplate it as an expectable outcome of the highly risky dynamics of merchants assembling too many males beyond the range of effective military constraint. The exuberant commercial prosperity of eighteenth-century merchants bringing males to Saint Domingue culminated in disaster for the planters burdened with attempting to control them.

Finally, fewer laws decreed from London encumbered merchants and planters in the English and then British Caribbean and North America in their attempts to grapple with the anomalies of attempting to control African men assembled in large and volatile aggregates through public commercial strategies of slaving. In the sugar islands of the West Indies, where these men, as well as smaller numbers of women, outnumbered English settlers and estate managers everywhere by as much as ten to one, the problems of policing were enormous. The tiny cohort of planters—who were the islands' closest, though still faint, approximation to a political public—dealt with them with exemplary brutality.[19] The enslaved men conspired, if we are to believe the anxious rumors that circulated, and actually revolted with genuinely threatening frequency, not to mention the ominous presence of renegade maroons left in acknowledged control of some of the mountainous regions of the largest of the sugar islands, Jamaica.

Historians have noted, though only in passing, the frequency with which women reported on these plots among their menfolk. But the categorical and racialized accents on solidarity among people defined only as ungendered slaves and blacks, prevailing in the literature, have distracted attention from this tendency of the women in slavery to betray the plotters among their male counterparts. Attention to explaining these women's motivations suggests at least the possibility of sexual politics among the enslaved. A residual, faint echo of Old World domestic female slavery, often of "colored," or métis, women born in the islands and their children by white fathers, reverberated in even these most extreme examples of commercialized modern enslavement of males. The male violence of discipline and revolt desexualized other women as members of the work gangs in the islands' canebrakes, their reproductive capacities suppressed by the physically depleting work demanded of them. With integration of women and men in these unisex, or unsexed and ungendered, gangs, tensions between the sexes nonetheless surely emerged within them, complicated, of course, by white male masters' sexual exploitation of the women they owned as slaves. The occasional favoritism and even personal fondness that drew a few of these women into the less conflictive ambiance of planters'—or more often overseers'—households thus could have prompted their reported collaboration with masters pressuring less privileged men to the point of desperate rebellion.

The survival strategies of women in the protoindustrial slavery of Caribbean sugar plantations generally emphasized manipulating the men attracted by their sexuality, as distinct from femininity, all but destroyed for those consigned to work in the fields but reclaimed—where possible—by raising children, including those of their masters. By the usual (politicized, but not gendered) views of slavery, this proposition may appear highly politically incorrect, if not also improbable or even impossible. However, on global scales, these uniquely—and not unrealistic—female strategies of surviving enslavement, even exploiting its available intimacies, would have resurrected Old World strategies of females in slavery. It would have made sense for them to capitalize on their physical capacities as women, otherwise helpless but reproductive and sexually desirable to men whom they could not control.

In socially multiplistic and differentiated cultures in Africa,[20] women were celebrated for their fecundity; hence femaleness remained ungendered in the modern sense of being politically disabling, and physical females could function as "men." But in the Americas the individuating and leveling effects of commercialization universalized the competitiveness among males limited in composite polities elsewhere to public places. For enslaved women, the likely strategy was closer to the African communal ethos of belonging—that is, trying to avoid the further separation of being uprooted yet again, thus suffering anew the vulnerability of isolation, or—equally if not more distressing—losing children they had borne.[21] To the ends of remaining, of belonging, they used the personal and emotive strategies effective within the intimacy of the domestic households in the Old World, where nearly all their predecessors had lived. All the more so as commercialized slaving in the Atlantic radically intensified the prospect of being forced to start over, again and yet again. The unpredictably changing economic conditions of remote and abstract markets invited, even forced, owners to survive by selling the people whom they owned as slaves. An intimate relationship might lessen this risk.

The large scales of laboring forces on American plantations and other productive enterprises—in the tropics, approaching numbers in the hundreds—severely reduced opportunities to form the personal ties that would have added ties of patronage and even some sense of moral responsibility for (if not to) their dependent families. Older (or, one might emphasize, more) ethical systems throughout Africa and Asia from ancient Greek philosophy to early (and some later) Christianity to Islam and beyond all had emphasized household heads' responsibilities for everyone present in their domestic domains, including the enslaved. Slaving previously had worked, in significant part, because it took advantage of the already weak (socially and politically)—that is, women and children—and dispersed them in such households, embedded in bonds of personal intimacies more than in legal bondage. The massed and masculinized modern slavery of the Americas was, at least to this extent, a contradiction in terms, or at the very least so expensive to pursue and to police that it would ultimately topple of its own ungainly weight.

Problematic Paradoxes in North America

And so it did, though not, of course, without a mighty struggle. The end of the story of slaving as a history of women, and the ultimate manifestation of the historical contradiction of attempting to enslave males in significant numbers, began in the English colonies in North America. Slavery elsewhere in the Americas thrived in significant part because high death rates among the enslaved there ensured sufficiently high proportions of newly imported replacements to limit the ability of the enslaved, mostly males, to form reproducing communities of their own. In contrast, slightly larger proportions of women among the slaves arriving on the North American mainland seem to have been enough to set the survivors on a path of reproducing themselves, thus shifting the effective character of enslavement toward a native-born community, often of generations depth.

The rice and tobacco planters of the mainland were economically marginal to the England's eighteenth-century Atlantic empire and could not compete seriously with their much wealthier planter counterparts in the sugar-rich islands in the West Indies for the majorities of new males. The relative modesty of mainland slaving thus condemned them to accept African women unwanted by planters in the Caribbean. Always short of hands, these North American masters encouraged their reproduction, or perhaps initially tolerated it out of sheer inability to prevent it, though taking care to specify that all children born to enslaved women would inherit their mothers' status as slaves. Thus, in a generation or two, enslaved women on the estates of the Chesapeake tidewater and Carolina Lowcountry were creating plantation communities of a peasantlike multigenerational quality.[22] However despised and excluded by their masters, among themselves they were no longer alone.

As African women and then their African American daughters in the Lowcountry and in the Chesapeake created these very unslavelike families, albeit all also owned by their masters, they thus produced a variant of slavery very "peculiar" in the context of global historical patterns of slaving, one even more radically contradictory than other attempts to work male slaves in large numbers elsewhere in the Americas. Elsewhere the cutting edge of viability for slaving was its continuing flow of isolated, disoriented new arrivals; in North America children born locally to enslaved women found at least limited acceptance in the households of their birth, their knowledge, and connections greatly lessening the disabilities under which they would otherwise have suffered.

Elsewhere, women had been more valuable as potential contributors to, and even as members of, families and households than they had been for the cash they might generate through sale. But to North American planters, always exposed to indebtedness, their children were assets, even collateral for the credit enabling commercial expansion. The ability of the women enslaved to create families—however compelled some also were by masters no less given to sexual exploitation of vulnerable females than were their counterparts elsewhere—gradually freed their owners from the necessity of continued costly imports. By thus relieving their owners of the need to borrow to buy replacements, they also obviated slaving's basic premise: maintaining proportions of isolated newcomers among the enslaved sufficient to disable subversive collaboration. They also managed to construct significant—if also always precarious—slave households on the estates where most of them lived in the early and mid-eighteenth century.[23] These women thus set the parameters of a growing population of native-born slaves within which the rest of the history of North America would develop, including the audacity of the rebel planters and merchants in the colonies in 1776. Key players in this "American revolution"—in some arguable part, at least—dared to take this step toward independence because of debts deriving from the slaving required to acquire more men and also because these female slaves' children (often also their own) had released them from any need to buy and pay for more.

The less prosperous slave-owning gentry of the Middle Atlantic and Southern colonies also added a distinguishing populist element to politics on the mainland, beyond the overwhelmingly commercial tone of British slaving and absentee planting in the Caribbean. They turned to the poor (free) farmers and townsmen of the colonies to muster local political support, particularly in the 1760s, after the government of George III in London began to raises taxes on consumption in its already indebted North American colonial dependencies. They extended their distinctive heritage of English "liberties" from monarchical grants of privilege to a claim to civic public initiative then unmatched anywhere in the world. In the new United States, numerous settlers of modest means but accorded full civic standing under the constitution of the new republic—farmers, artisans, traders, sailors—closed off prospects for slaves to compete with them by purchasing comparable freedom on their own or, if freed gratuitously by their owners, to support themselves.

Additionally, the high proportion of European women present as wives—more or less voluntarily in the colonies and then in the nascent United States—produced children with "legitimate" interests in the estates that their menfolk had exposed them to all the risks of life in the early Americas to build. In the commercial circumstances of the Americas, where wealth inhered in assets rather than in offspring, they excluded the slave children of their husbands—masters of their households as well as of the women enslaved—from any claim to these inheritances, even to paternity itself. These legitimate wives, as reproducers and increasingly gendered as dependent as the nineteenth-century politics of populism made a practical and populist reality of the Bill of Rights, thus again—as elsewhere in the world—exploited other women in slavery as the only available people politically weaker than themselves. The modern gendered solidarity of females as yet flickered only faintly.

Hence the distinguishing inflexibility of North Americans' application of the general European rule of matrilineal descent for slaves, or rather limiting civic identity to one inherited exclusively through legitimate mothers. Hence also the eventual distinctively rigid racialization in the United States of an otherwise general axiom of slavery, which had once secured the children of slave women in the interests of the households that had harbored them. In the United States matrilineal status as slaves instead became the means of excluding individuals from an emerging modern civic society. Later, race condemned anyone bearing any detectable taint of African ancestry as black, thus making slave men, freedpeople, and eventually their emancipated children all invisible in an

America defined reassuringly as exclusively white.[24] To this unique North American "public," anxious about their political liberties since colonial times under the developing intensity of monarchy in England and dependency in the Americas, awareness of these enslaved men, never in fact far below surface of the anxious imaginations of many, at times became a public preoccupation verging on panic.

This very particular North American outcome of holding women in slavery nonetheless became the instance that subsequently defined the modern paradigm of slavery as a public institution, seemingly male. The commercialized slaveries of the Americas were predominantly male; domestic slaving elsewhere had been—and also remained in varying degrees—as a history of women. But in North America—decidedly unlike the British Caribbean, the French Antilles, Brazil, or Cuba—the female majority of those in slavery was determinative in leaving families of native-born, English-speaking, Christian descendants, certainly the case by the paradigm-forming years of the antebellum generation in the 1840s and 1850s, and particularly by counting both the women and their uniquely female extensions, their children. The highly commercial indebtedness of their owners, increasingly marginalized by the financial growth of the growing industrial and banking sectors of the Atlantic economy, forced them to retain families in relentless highly institutionalized slavery.

SLAVERY, WOMEN, AND GENDER

Over the forty or fifty thousand years of human history, slaving had recurred as an endlessly viable strategy of recruiting, from external sources, the vital personnel who enabled household heads to compete from positions of growing marginality within more and more structured political contexts. Girls and women constituted the isolated individuals extracted from their families of origin and included in new households through this profoundly contradictory, tragic, and thus all-too-human tendency to seek short-run survival of communities at the expense of indefinitely extending the problems that threatened them. Slaving was private, or domestic, and concerned primarily with the prosperity—or reproduction—of whatever reproducing collectivities were recognized, all of them ultimately dependent on women for the progeny who might preserve them, for the food and laborious preparation of it that would sustain them, and for all the other essential tasks not diminished in significance in the least (in fact, quite the contrary) by terming them domestic.

Cash exchanges were not the primary means of sustaining individual autonomy that they have become in modern times; rather, everyone needed places to belong.

Households were primary units of production, and enslaved women in them worked, but work was the daily lot of nearly everyone, of either sex or any age. The women brought into households as slaves added distinctive value primarily in their ability to contribute children uncontested by maternal relatives, who were thus promising future bearers of the prospects of the collectivities that claimed them. Dispersed in the secluded courtyards or walled compounds of private families, their social vulnerabilities, which remained long after they had survived the personal disoriented vulnerability of their initial displacement, surely contributed to the undisputed power of the male heads of the households where they lived. In this very precise sense their presence enabled the patriarchal inclinations of their masters, husbands, and fathers. Unlike males, they presented relatively manageable problems to discipline at home, and beyond its confines they constituted no significant threat to a long sequence of aspiring, recurrently more public political authorities.

Commercial environments were another matter. In the sixteenth- and seventeenth-century Atlantic, merchants enslaved men for productive labor on unprecedentedly large scales, far beyond what metropolitan monarchical law or royal armies were prepared to manage. The increasing and eventually overwhelming numbers of enslaved African men then became dark specters looming in the increasingly racialized imaginations of their self-styled masters, from "rebellion to revolution."[25] By buying African men they converted slavery in the Americas from a strategy focused on females, which over tens of thousands of years had sustained the domestic components of every culture created anywhere in the world, to a self-contradiction.

Earlier and elsewhere, militarized monarchies had repeatedly recognized the intolerable threats posed by large gangs of armed slave mercenaries under the command of aristocratic rivals or mercantile intrusions on indebted peasant communities. The resulting ancient public laws of slavery thus dealt not with the ubiquitous but politically unproblematic enslavement of women and girls but rather only with the males enslaved, or rather the males not deliberately worked directly to death in such dangerous and debilitating occupations as reclaiming salt marshes or rowing galleys or diving for pearls or mining in the ancient Mediterranean as well as in the modern Americas. Rapid demise or effective quarantine of enslaved men generally worked well enough to preserve viable majorities of women among the enslaved. Where mortality failed, first and with distinctive political effect in North America, the exception proved the rule that slaving and men did not mix well, for masters or for monarchs and even less—in the United States—for popular majorities.

But because the men they enslaved to cultivate sugar and other commodities in the Americas nonetheless added significant impetus to the growth of commercialization in Europe and the Americas and, second, because of the accompanying growth in public consciousness on the part of the English participants at the forefront of this process, enslaved African males demanded public political attention. In these ways they almost at once became preoccupations of political economists, the theorizers of public economy, then the concern of leaders and members of small participatory and populist religious sects, and eventually of monarchical, and particularly of national, governments themselves. The many men enslaved in the Americas thus almost immediately raised to intolerable intensities the problematic politics that elsewhere and previously had kept strategies of slaving focused on women. Their sheer presence, increasingly seen as an abomination in a modern civic polity premised on human equality before categorical law, as well as their direct actions, thus ended slavery there in less than two centuries.

But abolition, in effect a populist political strategy of the capitalist interests consolidating their control over emergent national governments in the nineteenth century, focused only on the politically problematic among the enslaved—the males, the "men, and brothers."[26] Abolition in the Atlantic thus represented the fully modern extension of the imagined—but more than obviously unattained—homogenizing ideals of European commercial interests that had emerged in the preceding century. Subsequent, and not only coincidentally virulent, racism then resurrected ancient tropes of rampaging black rapists. European men struggling under the repressive sexual mores of the Victorian era—themselves gendered expressions of the fearful implications of the unrestrained individual autonomy at the heart of modernity—projected impulses declared base onto the black men freed. The women, white and black, no longer displaced, were isolated and dominated in the domiciliary domesticity of the modern nuclear family—or at least those whose respectable husbands and masters could afford to keep them there. Households had shrunk from their historic significance as robust, female-populated units of production and reproduction to hollow shells of material consumption. The political weakness of women was reimagined as physical in origin, and women in modern nations were walled off, once again, from public political spaces; and they were also newly deprived of the appreciated positions that household economies had once provided them. It would take another century of feminism—turned outward on the male public sphere by the absence of new, vulnerable enslaved women and girls who gave other women degrees of female authority within the compounds, great houses, and courtyards of the world of old—to begin to emancipate all women, "free" as well as the formerly enslaved. Race today constitutes the remaining challenge

NOTES

1. Gerda Lerner, "Women and Slavery," *Slavery and Abolition* 4, no. 3 (1983): 173–98; See also Lerner, *The Creation of Patriarchy* (New York: Oxford University Press, 1986).

2. Orlando Patterson, *Freedom in the Making of Western Culture* (New York: Basic Books, 1991).

3. Essentially the argument of Claire Robertson and Marsha Robinson, "Remodeling Slavery as If Women Mattered," in this volume, and in the tone set by Lerner, *Creation of Patriarchy.*

4. Orlando Patterson, *Slavery and Social Death: A Comparative Study* (Cambridge, MA: Harvard University Press, 1982).

5. This chapter develops one aspect of a more complex and longer argument being developed in Miller, *Slaving and History* (New York: Cambridge University Press, forthcoming). Epistemological aspects of the argument will be elaborated further in Miller, *The Problem of Slavery as History* (New Haven: Yale University Press, forthcoming), developed from the inaugural David Brion Davis Lectures given at the Gilder-Lehrman Center for the Study of Slavery and Resistance, Yale University, 7–9 February 2005. As the central historical argument has few correlates (known to me) in the essentially structural (sociological and economic) literature on slavery, I will make no attempt to list even the most excellent and basic works, except for occasional references to parallels in specific concepts.

6. For this idea as it is beginning to emerge in Africa, see the notion that Roderick J. McIntosh elaborates in terms of power as "heterarchy" in *The Peoples of the Middle Niger: The Island of Gold* (Oxford: Blackwell, 1998); McIntosh, *Ancient Middle Niger: Urbanism and the Self-Organizing Landscape* (New York: Cambridge University Press, 2005). For another elegant phrasing, see Kassim Kone, review of *In Quest of Sunjata: The Mande Epic as History, Literature, and Performance,* ed. Ralph A. Austen, *African Studies Review* 44 (2001): 156–58.

7. This is essentially the contrast between the characterizations of slavery in Africa in *Slavery in Africa: Historical and Anthropological Perspectives,* ed. Suzanne Miers and Igor Kopytoff (Madison: University of Wisconsin Press, 1977); Claude Meillassoux, *Anthropologie de l'esclavage: Le ventre de fer et d'argent* (Paris: Presses Universitaires de France, 1986), trans. Alide Dasnois as *The Anthropology of Slavery: The Womb of Iron and Gold,* foreword by Paul E. Lovejoy (Chicago: University of

Chicago Press, 1991). Miers and Kopytoff accent domestic practice while Meillassoux emphasizes broader theoretical and structural issues.

8. Patterson, *Making of Western Culture*, ch. 1.

9. Also see the alternative economic phrasing of the same population dynamics in Gwyn Campbell, "Female Bondage in Imperial Madagascar, 1820–95," in the companion volume to this one.

10. On pawnship in relatively modern African contexts, see Paul E. Lovejoy and Toyin Falola, eds., *Pawnship, Slavery, and Colonialism in Africa*, expanded ed. (New Brunswick, NJ: Africa World, 2003).

11. See Patterson's famous multicomponent definition in *Slavery and Social Death*, 12.

12. Along these lines, for the United States, see Laura F. Edwards, "Enslaved Women and the Law: Paradoxes of Subordination in the Postrevolutionary Carolinas," in this volume. The phrases quoted come, of course, from classic sociologically inspired definitions of slavery: Frank Tannenbaum, *Slave and Citizen: The Negro in the Americas* (New York: Knopf, 1947); Moses I. Finley, "Slavery," *International Encyclopedia of the Social Sciences*, ed. David L. Sills, 19 vols. (New York: Macmillan/Free Press, 1968), 14:307–13; and culminating in Patterson, *Slavery and Social Death*. Meillassoux, in spite of a heavy theoretical emphasis on materialism, in fact defines slavery essentially in terms of female fertility, or lack thereof, as a population exploited below its own subsistence, that is unable to reproduce itself. Meillassoux, *Anthropology of Slavery*.

13. Kevin Bales, *Disposable People: New Slavery in the Global Economy* (Berkeley: University of California Press, 1999).

14. An unnoticed regularity of kidnappings of young men by intimates and associates of their older male relatives is evident in the few accounts of boys who survived the Atlantic Middle Passage in the eighteenth century. Jerome S. Handler, "Survivors of the Middle Passage: Life Histories of Enslaved Africans in British America," *Slavery and Abolition* 23, no. 1 (2002): 23–56. Children could hardly have been expected to understand possible financial circumstances behind what they experienced as unaccountable betrayals.

15. With the promising exception of Francesca Reduzzi Merola and Alfredina Storchi Marino, eds., *Femmes-esclaves: Modèles d'interprétation anthropologique, économique, juridique* (Rome: Jovene Editore, 1999).

16. Martin A. Klein, "Sex, Power, and Family Life in the Harem: A Comparative Study," in the companion volume in this set, *Women and Slavery*, vol. 1, *Africa, the Indian Ocean World, and the Medieval North Atlantic*, ed. Gwyn Campbell, Suzanne Miers, and Joseph C. Miller (Athens: Ohio University Press, 2007).

17. Limitations of space unfortunately preclude providing details; the standard literature gives primarily the generalizing cultural and static tone. The works of Ehud Toledano are most historically sensitive. Toledano, *Slavery and Abolition in the Ottoman Middle East* (Seattle: University of Washington Press, 1997); Toledano, "The Concept of Slavery in Ottoman and Other Muslim Societies: Dichotomy or Continuum," in *Slave Elites in the Middle East and Africa*, ed. Miura Toru and John Edward Philips (London: Kegan Paul International, 2000), 159–75; and the excellent

Toledano, *As If Silent and Absent: Bonds of Enslavement in the Islamic Middle East* (New Haven: Yale University Press, 2007).

18. Lauren Benton, *Law and Colonial Cultures: Legal Regimes in World History, 1400–1900* (New York: Cambridge University Press, 2002); Benton, "Legal Spaces of Empire: Piracy and the Origins of Ocean Regionalism," *Comparative Studies in Society and History* 47, no. 4 (2005): 700–724.

19. Vincent Brown, *Specter in the Canes: Death and Power in the World of Atlantic Slavery* (in preparation). See also Brown, "Spiritual Terror and Sacred Authority in Jamaican Slave Society," *Slavery and Abolition* 24, no. 1 (2003): 24–53.

20. Again, parallel to what McIntosh has elaborated as "heterarchical."

21. Jennifer L. Morgan, *Laboring Women: Reproduction and Gender in New World Slavery* (Philadelphia: University of Pennsylvania Press, 2004).

22. The elegantly documented exemplary study is Lorena S. Walsh, *From Calabar to Carter's Grove: The History of a Virginia Slave Community* (Charlottesville: University Press of Virginia, 1997).

23. My approach to the dynamics of slaving in North America refers to, but does not rely on, a range of literature masterfully integrated in historical terms, for the first time, by Ira Berlin, *Many Thousands Gone: The First Two Centuries of Slavery in North America* (Cambridge, MA: Harvard University Press, Belknap Press, 1988), and artfully extended and consolidated by accenting the unique reproductive success of these women in Berlin, *Generations of Captivity: A History of African-American Slaves* (Cambridge, MA: Belknap Press, 2003).

24. A deliberate reference to Ralph Ellison, *Invisible Man* (New York: Random House, 1952).

25. In the paradigmatic phrasing of Eugene Genovese, *From Rebellion to Revolution: Afro-American Slave Revolts in the Making of the Modern World* (Baton Rouge: Louisiana State University Press, 1979).

26. For precisely this point, further, within the parallel "republican" context of the French Antilles, see Myriam Cottias, "Gender and Republican Citizenship in the French West Indies, 1848–1945," *Slavery and Abolition* 26, no. 2 (2005): 233–45; reprinted in this volume. Similarly, Bernard Moitt, "Freedom from Bondage at a Price: Women and Redemption from Slavery in the French Caribbean in the Nineteenth Century," *Slavery and Abolition* 26, no. 2 (2005): 247–56; also in this volume.

CONTRIBUTORS

Henrice Altink is a lecturer in modern history at the University of York (U.K.). She has published extensively on representations of Jamaican slave women and the workings of the Apprenticeship System in Jamaica and is currently working on the construction of womanhood in the African Jamaican community, 1865–1938. Her publications include *Representations of Slave Women in Discourses on Slavery and Abolition, 1780–1838* (2007); "'To wed or not to wed?': The Struggle to Define Afro-Jamaican Relationships, 1834–1838," *Journal of Social History* (Fall (2004); and "Imagining Womanhood in Early Twentieth-Century Rural Afro-Jamaica," *Journal of Caribbean History* 40, no. 1 (2006). She may be reached at ha501@york.ac.uk.

Laurence Brown is Lecturer in Migration History at the University of Manchester. He has published articles on migrant networks in postemancipation Martinique and Barbados in the *Journal of Caribbean History* (2002) and the *New West Indian Guide* (2005). In the edited collection *Imperial Careering: Colonial Lives across the British Empire* (2006) he examined how indentured Asian migration was reshaped by global interactions between the Atlantic, Pacific, and Indian oceans during the nineteenth century. He is currently completing a monograph on the history of migration in the Caribbean.

Gwyn Campbell holds a Canada Research Chair and is the director of the Indian Ocean World Centre in the Department of History, McGill University (gwyn.campbell@mcgill.ca). Born in Madagascar and raised in Wales (where he worked as a BBC radio producer in English and Welsh), he holds degrees in economic history from the universities of Birmingham and Wales. He has taught in India, Madagascar, Britain, South Africa, Belgium, France, and Canada and served as an academic consultant to the South African government in the lead-up to the 1997 formation of an Indian Ocean regional association. He has organized a series of international conferences on slavery following the "Avignon format" (after the place where they were inaugurated), the latest—"Sex, Power, and Slavery" at McGill University in 2007—to mark the bicentenary of the British Anti-Slave Trade Act. As author, editor, or coeditor, he has more than one hundred publications, a significant proportion of which are on the theme of unfree labor and slavery.

MYRIAM COTTIAS, colonial historian, is a researcher at the Centre National de la Recherche Scientifique (CNRS; CRPLC, Université des Antilles et de la Guyane) and directs the Centre International de Recherches sur les Esclavages, sponsored by the CNRS. She has edited *Esclavage et dépendances serviles: Histoire comparée* with Alessandro Stella and Bernard Vincent (2006) and *D'une abolition, l'autre: Anthologie raisonnée de textes consacrés à la seconde abolition de l'esclavage dans les colonies françaises* (1999). Her recent publications include *De la nécessité d'adopter l'esclavage en France: Texte anonyme de 1797* (2007), coedited with Arlette Farge, and *La question noire: Histoire d'une construction coloniale* (2007).

LAURA F. EDWARDS is a professor in the History Department at Duke University. She is the author of *Gendered Strife and Confusion: The Political Culture of Reconstruction* (1997) and *Scarlett Doesn't Live Here Anymore: Southern Women in the Civil War Era* (2000). She is currently working on *The People and Their Peace: The Re-Constitution of Governance in the Post-Revolutionary South*. Contact: ledwards@duke.edu.

RICHARD FOLLETT is Reader in American History at the University of Sussex, Brighton, England. He is author of *The Sugar Masters: Planters and Slaves in Louisiana's Cane World, 1820–1860* (2005) and multiple articles on slavery and emancipation in the American South. He was founding editor of the periodical *Atlantic Studies* and now works on race and labor in the late nineteenth-century U.S. South and on the psychology of American slavery. Contact: r.follett@sussex.ac.uk.

TARA INNISS (Innisst@aol.com) is a recent PhD graduate from the University of the West Indies, Cave Hill Campus, in Barbados. Her research focuses on children's health during slavery and the apprenticeship period in the English-speaking Caribbean. She also recently completed the Master of Social Development program at the University of New South Wales in Sydney, Australia. She now works as a development consultant in the Caribbean.

BARBARA KRAUTHAMER is an assistant professor of history at New York University. She has published articles and completed a forthcoming book manuscript on African American slavery and emancipation in the Choctaw and Chickasaw nations. She is currently a fellow-in-residence at the Schomburg Center for Research in Black Culture, where she is working on a book about runaway slave women in eighteenth-century South Carolina and Georgia. She can be reached at bk39@nyu.edu.

SUZANNE MIERS is a professor emerita of history at Ohio University. She is the author of *Slavery in the Twentieth Century* and coeditor of *The End of Slavery* and other books. For further biographical details, see "A Tribute to Suzanne Miers" in this volume.

JOSEPH C. MILLER is the T. Cary Johnson Professor of History at the University of Virginia, where he has taught since 1972. He is a historian of early Africa with training at the University of Wisconsin–Madison under Jan Vansina and Philip D. Curtin. His early research on oral traditions in Angola led to Atlantic-scaled interests in the Angola-Brazil trade in slaves and a 1988 monograph, *Way of Death: Merchant Capitalism and the Angolan Slave Trade, 1730–1830*; to a comprehensive bibliography of slavery and slaving throughout the world about to appear (sponsored by the Virginia Center for Digital History) in searchable online format; and to a long-term effort to historicize the study of slavery on a global scale, developed significantly through his participation in the series of Avignon conferences that have led to the current, and other, volumes of papers. Further details are available at www.virginia.edu/history/faculty/miller.html.

BERNARD MOITT is associate professor and chair of history at Virginia Commonwealth University in Richmond. He has published several articles and chapters in anthologies on francophone African and Caribbean history, with particular emphasis on gender and slavery. The author of *Women and Slavery in the French Antilles, 1635–1848* (2001), he is also editor of *Sugar, Slavery and Society: Perspectives on the Caribbean, India, the Mascarenes, and the United States* (2004). Contact: bmoitt@vcu.edu.

KENNETH MORGAN is Professor of History and Deputy Director of the Centre for American, Transatlantic and Caribbean History (CATCH) at Brunel University, London. His publications concentrate on the social and economic history of Britain and her colonies and on music history.

He is the general editor of British Records relating to America in Micro-form (BRRAM) and is a Fellow of the Royal Historical Society. His books include *Bristol and the Atlantic Trade in the Eighteenth Century* (1993); *Slavery, Atlantic Trade, and the British Economy, 1660–1800* (2000); and *Slavery and the British Empire: From Africa to America* (2007). Contact: kenneth.morgan@brunel.ac.uk.

CLAIRE ROBERTSON is a professor of history and women's studies at The Ohio State University. She has conducted fieldwork in Ghana, Kenya, and Saint Lucia and published six books, including *Sharing the Same Bowl*, which won the African Studies Association's Herskovits Award in 1985, and more recently *Genital Cutting and Transnational Sisterhood*, which won the Peggy Koppelman Award from the Popular Culture Association and American Culture Association in 2003. She has also published a number of articles on the subjects of African women, slavery, education, trade, feminist theory, and other topics. She may be reached at Robertson.8@osu.edu.

MARSHA ROBINSON is an assistant professor of African Diaspora history at Otterbein College in Westerville, Ohio, where she lectures on the history of Africa, African Americans, and Western civilization. She is revising a monograph on the legacy of ancient Saharan feminism as it affects Islamic, Spanish, and American legal and political history. Her publications and conference papers cover topics ranging from women's rights in Islam to the significance of genetic anthropology in researching African Berber contributions to Spanish history. Contact MRRobinson @otterbein.edu.

FELIPE SMITH (felipes@tulane.edu) is an associate professor in English at Tulane University, where he teaches American and African American literature. He has published *American Body Politics: Race, Gender, and Black Literary Renaissance* (1998) and is currently working on his second book, *The Dark Side of the Modern: Race and the Jazz Age*. He has also published essays on Toni Morrison, Alice Walker, F. Scott Fitzgerald, and Claude McKay.

MARIZA DE CARVALHO SOARES is an associate professor in the department of history at Universidade Federal Fluminense-UFF, Brazil. She is the Director of Núcleo de Estudos Brasil-África-NEAF at UFF. Her best-known book, *Devotos da Cor: Identidade étnica, religiosidade e escravidão no*

Rio de Janeiro, século XVIII, which came out in Brazil in 2000, is currently under contract with Duke University Press to be translated into English. Contact: marizacsoares@ig.com.br.

INDEX

WOMEN AND SLAVERY

VOLUME ONE

Africa, the Indian Ocean World, and the Medieval North Atlantic

CONTENTS